A Primer on American Labor Law

Other books by William B. Gould IV

Black Workers in White Unions: Job Discrimination in the United States. Cornell University Press, 1977.

Japan's Reshaping of American Labor Law. MIT Press, 1984.

Strikes, Dispute Procedures, and Arbitration: Essays on Labor Law. Greenwood Press, 1985.

Labor Relations in Professional Sports (with Robert C. Berry and Paul D. Staudohar). Auburn House, 1986.

Agenda for Reform: The Future of Employment Relationships and the Law. MIT Press, 1993.

A Primer on American Labor Law
third edition

William B. Gould IV

The MIT Press, Cambridge, Massachusetts, and London, England

This book was set in Baskerville by .eps Electronic Publishing
Services and was printed and bound in the United States of
America.

Library of Congress Cataloging-in-Publication Data

Gould, William B.
  A primer on American labor law / William B. Gould IV.—3rd ed.
    p. cm.
  Includes bibliographical references and index.
  ISBN 0-262-07149-5 (hc).—ISBN 0-262-57099-8 (pbk.)
  1. Labor laws and legislation—United States. I. Title.
KF3369.G68 1993
344.73′01—dc20
[347.3041]   93-19038
                                                            CIP

Contents

Preface to Third Edition

There have been numerous developments since the second edition of this book appeared seven years ago. Inevitably there is a seemingly endless train of litigation before the National Labor Relations Board. The Board now appears to be less ideological and more balanced than at the time of the second edition and thus its decisions and conduct as of the end of 1992 are less controversial than was the case throughout most of the 1980s. Though some of the decisions are significant and thus worthy of attention in this third edition, the shrinking percentage of employees represented by unions in the United States—it is now approximately 15% of the work force—has reduced the Board's impact and influence and that of the American labor arbitration system as well.

Deregulation in transportation has produced nonunion competition for the organized sector, and that in turn appears to be primarily responsible for more litigation in the organized sector of those industries. One of the consequences of deregulation is thus the emergence of new precedent under the Railway Labor Act, which covers both railroads and airlines.

Nature abhors a vacuum and individual rights—both of the statutory and common law variety—have continued to expand for unorganized employees who constitute the vast majority of the work force in the United States. Wrongful discharge litigation is even more important in this arena than it was at the time of the second edition. Although there have been important state supreme court decisions in jurisdictions like California and Michigan which have limited employee rights and remedies, a new line of authority—again, emphasizing the relationship between the unorganized and organized sectors—has sanctioned the filing of wrongful discharge actions under certain circumstances by employees who are represented by unions and covered by collective bargaining agreements containing clauses that provide for the invocation of arbitration procedures. The complete impact of these decisions has yet to be felt.

Moreover, intertwined with many of the wrongful discharge common law actions are drug and alcohol testing issues involving dismissals or sometimes simply the institution of new policies that might lead to dismissals. (Unions have been active in protecting such individual rights both under the National Labor Relations Act and the Railway Labor Act as well as in arbitration). Although Montana has enacted a wrongful discharge statute discussed in this new edition, no state thus far has fashioned a comprehensive statute in this arena notwithstanding proposals by a California state bar committee in 1984 (the author was co-chairman of this committee) as well as more recent ones of a similar nature emanating from the Uniform Law Commissioners. But Congress and the state legislatures have enacted a series of statutes affecting employment relationships—two of the more prominent being the Workers' Adjustment and Retraining Notification Act of 1988 and the Employee Polygraph Protection Act of 1988. The former law modestly emulates legislation and case law already in existence in western Europe and Japan which provides employees with notice, consultation, and other rights in connection with layoffs triggered by economic considerations.

But two of the most important legislative ventures have provided for new forms of protection against discrimination. The Americans With Disabilities Act of 1990 provides far reaching protection against discrimination in employment for both the physically and mentally handicapped. In October of 1991, after two years of bitter dispute, a Democratic Congress and President George Bush agreed upon amendments to title VII of the Civil Rights Act of 1964 in a new law, the Civil Rights Act of 1991 (sometimes referred to as the Danforth-Kennedy Act). This Act was triggered by a series of Supreme Court decisions in 1989 and 1991 which interpreted civil rights legislation in a narrow fashion and the new legislation was a manifestation of Congress' disagreement with the Court in this arena.

The Civil Rights Act of 1991, however, went beyond reversal of Supreme Court decisions. It allowed for applicants and employees to obtain punitive and compensatory damages already available in racial discrimination and wrongful discharge actions in sex, religious, and disability discrimination cases. Many believe that the debate about the new law increased the attention given to sexual harassment in the workplace and the Senate Judiciary Committee hearings involving the confirmation of Justice Clarence Thomas to the United States Supreme Court—Justice Thomas was alleged by Professor Anita Hill to have sexually harassed her when she was employed by the Equal Employment Opportunity Commission—triggered the statute's enactment with its newly established remedies for sexual harassment as well as other forms of discrimination.

Although federal legislation and most state laws do not address the issue, more focus is now being provided to discrimination on the basis of sexual orientation against men and women who are homosexuals. In California, where the issue has been particularly prominent, Governor George Deukmejian and Governor Pete Wilson have vetoed legislation that would have prohibited this kind of discrimination in the workplace. (However, in 1992 Governor Wilson signed into law more legislation that is slightly more limited than that which he had previously vetoed.) This, like the kind of discrimination addressed by the 1990 and 1991 federal statutes, will continue to receive attention throughout this decade.

The Family and Medical Leave Act of 1993, signed into law by President Clinton on February 5, addresses issues that possess some relationship to antidiscrimination law. It provides that employers with fifty or more workers are obliged to allow employees to have up to twelve weeks of unpaid, job-protected leave to take care of a newborn or newly adopted child, to take care of a sick child or parent, or because of an employee's own serious health problem. Under fair employment practices legislation, frequently such leaves could be obtained only if it could be shown that the policy was sexually discriminatory.

A particularly interesting development is a consent decree entered into between the United States Department of Justice and the International Brotherhood of Teamsters which provided for highly detailed governmental supervision of union elections as well as substitution of the secret ballot box direct election procedure for the indirect election of national leaders at a convention. Of course many other labor organizations provide for indirect election of leaders. But the teamsters' consent decree should not only enable reform inside that union and deal with problems of corruption, but it also may have implications for the labor movement and encourage secret ballot box internal union procedures.

While the labor movement has had more than its share of difficulties in the United States in the past couple of decades, one small but highly visible segment has gone from success to success. It consists of the unions that represent professional athletes, particularly the Major League Baseball Players Association[1] and the National Basketball Players Association. These unions have negotiated collective bargaining agreements that have facilitated average compensation in the million dollar range. Even the football players, without a union since their 1987 strike,[2] have been able to improve their position by virtue of antitrust litigation[3] and a new collective bargaining agreement negotiated early in 1993.

Finally, one of the most important issues in the 1990s and the early part of the next century is likely to be whether the

American industrial relations system can become more co-operative rather than adversarial. The Board's 1992 *Electro-mation, Inc.*[4] decision is but the first of a number of decisions dealing with the unlawfulness of employer-assisted or in-spired employee committees that operate in a nonunion environment and sometimes where a union can exist as exclusive bargaining representative. This will be an issue that will be discussed both in the courts and in the Congress.

I am indebted to Sheila Cohen, Barry Deonarine, Timo-thy S. Gould, and Henry Y. Dinsdale for research conducted in connection with the third edition, as well as Kathleen Schneider who has not only typed the manuscript but played a major role in the technical problems as well as legal research involved in organizing a newer edition such as this one. Mr. Dinsdale—a distinguished Canadian labor lawyer in his own right and a JSD candidate at Stanford—has been especially helpful in providing me with a number of memos that have served both to update information previously pre-sented in the first and second editions and to address issues covered for the first time in this one.

Preface to Second Edition

There have been a number of significant developments in labor law since 1982, when the first edition of this book was published. In industries confronted with deregulation or with foreign competition, the advent of concession bargaining (coupled, in some instances, with new limitations on management's prerogatives) has changed the labor-management landscape. Numerous decisions—many too inconsequential to be mentioned in a book such as this—have been issued by the National Labor Relations Board (whose composition and outlook changed dramatically before the end of President Reagan's first term) and the Supreme Court. Indeed, the labor movement's disillusionment with the NLRB prompted AFL-CIO President Lane Kirkland to opine about the desirability of repealing the National Labor Relations Act.

The decline of the labor movement to approximately 19 percent of the work force has led to unprecedented soul-searching on the part of labor.

An interesting by-product of the decline of organized labor has been the growth in the importance of the rights of individual employees outside the union environment. Wrongful-discharge litigation initiated by nonunion employees has become the most discussed issue in the field of labor law.

As I have reflected on the changes for this second edition, I have found the comments and criticisms of Reinhold Fahlbeck, Professor of Law at the University of Lund and the Stockholm School of Economics and Visiting Fellow at the Stanford Law School, particularly insightful. Professor Fahlbeck, a Swedish labor lawyer with expertise in American Labor Law, has been both generous and unrelenting, and I am most grateful to him.

I am also grateful to Joseph Costello and Elizabeth Smith of the Stanford Law School for providing material for the notes, and to Mary Ann Loughram and Maxine Emery for their skillful typing.

Preface

The idea of this book grew out of lectures that I gave in the early 1970s at the AFL-CIO Labor Studies Center in Washington, DC, and at the University of Illinois Institute of Industrial Relations in Champaign, Illinois. The audiences were trade unionists (mostly local officers and shop stewards), and the subject was labor law and labor arbitration. The discussions were lively and the questions stimulating. I became aware that many people had an institutional incentive to learn about labor law, and I quickly realized that the existing literature was not reaching them; in fact there really was no book aimed specifically at such an audience. This impression was confirmed by a series of talks that I gave to similar audiences at the Institute for Industrial Relations at the University of California at Berkeley. My contact with corporate representatives at some of the institute's functions made it clear that both sides of the bargaining table were interested in obtaining a basic outline of the labor-law system, one that would not be so encyclopedic as to be intimidating.

In the mid-1970s I began to lecture on American labor law to labor academics, American-studies specialists, trade unionists, employers, and government officials in various countries in Europe, Asia, Africa, and Latin America. In most of these countries I was asked to recommend a book that provided foreigners with an outline of American labor law. My inability to recommend such a book finally induced me to write *A Primer on American Labor Law*. Structured seminars sponsored by the U.S. Department of State and the U.S. International Communications Agency in such countries as India and Brazil and lectures given under the auspices of the Kyoto American Studies Seminar helped organize my thinking for this book, as did some of my lectures to my Labor Law I classes at the Stanford Law School.

There are other books on American labor law that are more detailed and involved than this one. Readers who wish to go farther should consult the lengthier volumes aimed at university students, such as *Labor and the Law* by Charles O. Gregory and Harold A. Katz (third edition), or those written for American academics and lawyers, such as *Basic Text on Labor Law* by Robert A. Gorman and *The Developing Labor Law*, edited by Charles Morris. Those who desire to explore employment-discrimination problems further may wish to consult my *Black Workers in White Unions: Job Discrimination in the United States*. The most encyclopedic text in this area is *Employment Discrimination Law* by Barbara Schlei and Paul Grossman. The best case book aimed at American law students as of this writing is *Employment Discrimination Law: Cases and Materials* by Arthur B. Smith.

A Primer on American Labor Law is more descriptive than analytic. It is intended for those who would not otherwise be exposed to the American labor law system: labor and management representatives, foreigners, neutral parties involved in labor dispute resolution and having a special interest in the United States or industrial relations, general-practice lawyers who occasionally represent a union or a company but are not specialists in the field, students of labor relations and labor law, and even practicing labor-law specialists who have some interest in a brief comparison with foreign systems.

Many people have helped make this book a reality. My audiences and classes made me think and rethink my material and its presentation. William Keogh of the Stanford Law

School, Robert Flanagan of the Stanford Business School, and the late Norman Amundsen of the University of California's Institute of Industrial Relations read and commented on my drafts. I am grateful to the Stanford Law School students who provided valuable research and note material: Debra Roth, Todd Brower, Alan Reeves, and Karen Snell. I am particularly appreciative of the work done by Mr. Reeves, who suggested some textual changes and shouldered the major burden of the notes. And it would have been impossible to produce this work without the extremely valuable and skillful typing and organizational work of Clarie Kuball and Mary Enright.

The research for this book was supported by the Stanford Legal Research Fund, which was made possible by a bequest from the estate of Ira S. Lillick and by gifts from Roderick E. and Carla A. Hills and other friends of the Stanford Law School.

Finally, I could not have completed the book without the patience of my wife, Hilda, and my three sons, Bill, Tim, and Ed, during my long absences abroad and in my office at the Stanford Law School.

1

An Overview

American labor law and the American industrial relations system have a symbiotic relationship, and neither can be understood without reference to the other. This should come as no surprise; after all law, lawyers, and litigation play a major role in our society. Our collective bargaining system has been devised predominantly by labor and management, however, not by the government and the courts. In fact we often forget—and foreign observers fail to grasp—that our most important tool in the resolution of labor disputes is our private arbitration system, which operates outside the formal legal system of courts and administrative agencies. Before examining the history and substance of American labor law, then, let us begin with their impetus in the American industrial relations system: organized labor.

As a result of the evolution of the industrial relations system in the United States, the unions have a remarkably different attitude toward law than, for instance, those in Britain. This is not to say that American trade unions do not have a healthy and often well-founded distrust of lawyers; one can see this attitude manifested in countless ways. But the unions are not against the law here. And this is because the American unions—especially the industrial unions that emerged during the Great Depression of the 1930s—obtained political power before industrial power. American unions were willing and eager to look to the law as a useful adjunct to their growth and the achievement of recognition and bargaining relationships with employers.

Trade unionism came late to the United States. There were stirrings among American workers toward the end of the nineteenth century (particularly in the 1880s), first under the banner of the Knights of Labor which attempted to organize unskilled as well as skilled workers (a venture doomed to failure). The second major effort was by the American Federation of Labor (AFL), initially led by Samuel Gompers, who espoused an approach to trade unionism that focused on what labor could achieve at the bargaining table. The AFL, a central federation to which various unions were attached, strove to avoid becoming formally affiliated with a political party as the European unions had. Gompers's refrain, "We shall reward labor's friends and punish its enemies," reflected a philosophy that involved labor in the political process with political parties but did not provide for formal affiliation. To this day, however, the AFL-CIO, the umbrella organization for national unions, plays an active political role; except in 1972, the AFL-CIO has supported every Democratic party presidential candidate since Adlai Stevenson.

At the turn of the century, the power and prestige of Gompers and of the AFL were being used on the behalf of skilled craftsmen organized on an occupational basis. The masses of workers, who had often been shunned by the craft unions as unorganizable, were not affiliated with major industrial unions (or with unions of any kind) until the 1930s. At that juncture new unions, such as the United Auto Workers, the United Steelworkers, and the United Rubber Workers, came forward. They sought to organize and represent production workers and skilled tradesmen under the umbrella of a new federation, the Congress of Industrial Organizations (CIO), and they grew with the law. To some extent their structure was shaped by the law as the National Labor Relations Board, operating under the National Labor Relations Act, fashioned units or categories of job classifications, for the purpose of bargaining on an industrial basis, that permitted the inclusion of semiskilled and unskilled workers in the same bargaining unit with tradesmen.[1]

All of this is in contrast with the history of organized labor in Britain, where great general unions that organized workers without regard to job classification or industry reached out to organize the semiskilled and the unskilled through the "new unionism" of the 1880s. In Britain the unions had industrial power before political power, and so they used their position and strength to fend the law off and to keep it out of their affairs. This was a central thrust of labor legislation in the first Asquith liberal government, in which the trade unions had some influence. The Trades Disputes Act of 1906 was designed to create immunity in the courts for trade-union activities.[2] In the United States a similar policy of laissez-faire was adopted at the time of the Norris-LaGuardia Act[3] but was quickly abandoned in 1935 with the passage of the National Labor Relations Act, which provided for the right to engage in collective bargaining. For better or for worse, to this day the American trade unions continue to look to the law, and to the National Labor Relations Board in particular, for sustenance.

Another important feature of the American industrial relations system is that it is (again, by European standards) a decentralized bargaining structure. In Europe, particularly on the continent, the pattern is multiemployer or industry-wide bargaining. In Germany the primary function of the unions since World War II has been to bargain regional tariffs or agreements establishing a minimum rate for a geographical area of the country. In Sweden wage bargaining takes place on a centralized basis—initially between the Central Labor Federation (LO) and the Swedish Employers Federation—and along industrywide lines with the involvement of the major industrial unions.[4] Industrywide bargaining is also the rule in Britain, although to a lesser extent. In all of these countries there is a local organization to represent employees, but the local entity usually does not possess nearly as strong a presence or as much contact with the national trade union as in the United States. In Britain, shop stewards bargain for pay rates and sometimes for other conditions of employment, often in committees that are independent of the national trade-union structure. In Germany *Betriebsrate* (shop committees, or works councils) are involved by statute in a wide variety of employment decisions and sometimes have veto power over employers' decisions.[5] In recent years German unions, particularly in the metals industry, have come to play a more substantial role in the plant and to be more integrated with the system of works councils as a matter of law. In Sweden there are local clubs (roughly equivalent to American local unions) that operate on a plant basis, but many plants are too small to have one.

In the United States the percentage of eligible workers who are organized into trade unions is lower than the percentages in Europe and Japan.[6] Where organization exists, though, it is clear that a plant-level presence tied to the national union structure is much stronger in the United States than in any of the other industrialized countries. The local union, which has a formal affiliation in its dues-sharing structure with the national or international union, is often organized at the plant level. Depending on the number of members and the amount of dues, some of the officials of the local, such as the president and the secretary treasurer, may be employed full-time by the local and paid out of the workers' dues. However, in many locals all of the officials are full-time employees of a company; when they are involved in negotiations or grievance handling, their wages may be paid either by the company (the collective bargaining agreement often provides for this) or from the local union's treasury.

Most collective bargaining agreements in the United States are negotiated at the plant level, with the involvement of the local union. The agreements are relatively detailed and comprehensive. One of the most important functions of locals relates to the processing of grievances over an agreement's interpretation. Locals are sometimes involved in the final step of the procedure, arbitration. The local usually pays the union's share of the costs of arbitration, and if the local and the employer are particularly disputatious, this can be a considerable drain on the local's treasury. However, because most disputes are resolved at the lower steps of the process, the local is quite dependent on members of grievance committees, which are composed of full-time employees. Similarly the local depends for grievance processing on the shop stewards, who are also full-time employees involved in a vital function on behalf of the union.[7]

Another structural variation arises from the union's basis of organization and its organizing rationale. So far we have only considered locals that are organized on a single-plant basis. Locals may also be organized on a multiplant or a multicompany basis ("amalgamated locals"). More broadly, they may be affiliated with a national craft, industrial, or general union. General unions are somewhat exceptional in the United States; the best example is the International Brotherhood of Teamsters, the largest American union (which does, however, have a base in one industry: transportation). Officials of national unions may be involved in the bargaining of the agreement, but most of the negotiating staff will be local officials.

Today most unions are affiliated with the merged AFL-CIO, which was formed in 1955. This federation has a no-raiding agreement that is binding on its affiliates. The craft unions play a dominant role in its leadership and policy. The Teamsters are not affiliated with the AFL-CIO; they were expelled in 1957 because of a controversy relating to corruption in their unions. The United Mine Workers and the International Longshoremen and Warehousemen (the West Coast dockers) are also unaffiliated. In 1968 the United Auto Workers withdrew because of dissatisfaction with the AFL-CIO's policy and leaders, but in 1981 they returned to the fold.[8]

Another important aspect of the American system is the wage consciousness of the trade unions.[9] Historically American trade unionism has been hard-hitting in its economic demands. In part this is thought to be attributable to the lack of class solidarity among many American workers. Because a labor organization cannot appeal to workers on a class basis, the appeal must be based on wages and fringe benefits. This has helped produce what some have called "business unionism" or "bread-and-butter unionism."

Many of the matters handled by labor and management at the bargaining table in the United States are dealt with legislatively in Europe. This is particularly true of fringe benefits, such as vacations and vacation pay, holidays, unemployment compensation, medical insurance, and hospitalization benefits.

Traditionally, protection against dismissal without cause, and compensation of workers laid off or dismissed because of plant closure or the contracting out of work, have been addressed by collective bargaining in the United States. In Europe "unfair dismissals," whether for economic reasons or on disciplinary grounds, are dealt with through legislation. But recently a number of state courts, following the lead of the Supreme Court of California,[10] have held that employers cannot dismiss employees without just cause, arbitrarily, or in bad faith.[11] (Chapter 11 contains a more thorough discussion of this development.) Some states have enacted legislation regulating plant closures and layoffs attributable to them.[12] In Japan, in contrast to both America and Europe, lifetime employment for "permanent" workers in large companies is guaranteed under a system that is promulgated unilaterally by the companies, outside the collective bargaining system.[13]

Thus the number of subjects to be discussed and resolved through collective bargaining is considerably greater in the United States than in Europe and Japan. Without a welfare state system like those in Europe, and without paternalism like that in Japan, American unions must (or should) be active in their negotiations with management. The appeals that the unions make to recruit workers cover many items. The American system encourages unions to push for more at the bargaining table. It encourages management to install laborsaving devices to increase productivity (a phenomenon that seems to have declined in recent years). The decentralized system of bargaining and the wage-conscious behavior of unions also encourage American employers to resist union organizational activities. Accordingly there are many more organizational and recognition disputes than in other industrialized countries. Anticipated labor costs and potential competition problems promote such resistance, which is in part responsible for the heavy caseload of the National Labor Relations Board (NLRB). Most of the more than 40,000 unfair labor practice charges per year[14] that have been processed by the NLRB involve allegations of discriminatory discipline and discharge of workers, frequently during organizational campaigns. The NLRB is engaged in more litigation than any other federal agency.

In Germany or Scandinavia a dispute can be resolved on an industrywide basis, and the parties are bound to the solution. But in the United States essentially the same kind of dispute can come before the NLRB again and again because different employers and workers see their situation as slightly different from that considered in an earlier decision, and they are not bound by any adjudication or decision on an association or industrywide basis. Moreover because most of the cases involve discipline or dismissal, they are essentially questions of fact, and no general rule can dispose of most of them.

The American industrial relations system has myriad characteristics. Which of those touched on here are primary, secondary, and so on, has been debated extensively, but few would debate that our body of labor law rests firmly on the system's fundamental characteristics. How has that come to be?

2

Industrial Relations and Labor Law before Modern Legislation

In the United States and in Europe the Industrial Revolution brought competition between employers for distant markets. This created an environment in which labor was increasingly treated as a raw material or a commodity, and it is therefore hardly surprising that a profound sense of discord was generated between workers and their employers. This historical development cannot be divorced from any consideration of industrial relations and labor law in the United States today.

American and European workers sought to band together and to protect themselves against the attempts of business combinations, trusts, and monopolies to reduce labor costs. The courts in the United States and the parliament in England, through their "anticombination" statutes, sought to brand such worker combinations as unlawful conspiracies in restraint of trade—a restraint that might diminish free competition between employers. In the United States the law of conspiracy was criminal law, and indictments were obtained against combinations of workers trying to raise wages. The leading case in which the criminal conspiracy doctrine was applied was the Philadelphia *Cordwainers* case of 1806.[1]

Certain issues raised in the *Cordwainers* case remain with us today:

- How could individuals who had no "permanent stake" in the business become substantially involved in making decisions relating to it? As the prosecution said in *Cordwainers*, "Will you permit men to destroy it [business] who have no permanent stake in the city; men who can pack up their all in a knapsack or carry them in their pockets to New York or Baltimore?"

- What is to be the proper and appropriate sphere of interest for workers? What could be regarded as a management prerogative with which employees could not interfere? Very much involved in any consideration of this question was the Tory idea—promoted by America's first secretary of the treasury, Alexander Hamilton—that private organizations such as unions interfered with the rapid increase in manufacturing and therefore with national prosperity.

- How could prices of products be set safely if the workers were to wait until order books were swelled to capacity—when the time would be propitious—to put pressure on employers for higher wages? How could commercial contracts be negotiated in distant markets under such circumstances?

- What was to be done about the emergence of these new combinations of private societies and their pressure on individuals to comply with the combination's notion of the collective interest? As Job Harrison testified in the *Cordwainers* case, "If I did not join the body, no man would sit upon the seat where I worked . . . nor board or lodge in the same house, nor would they work at all for the same employer."

These were but some of the issues raised in *Cordwainers*. The case did not decide definitively whether the combination itself was an unlawful conspiracy or whether it was necessary to prove that its object was the improvement of wages and working conditions, but it served as a legal weapon for employers and thus stultified union growth.

Numerous judicial decisions in the nineteenth century made efforts by workers to improve their wages and working conditions through combinations an unlawful criminal conspiracy. In 1842 a landmark decision heralded a new judicial approach to the control of union activity. The Supreme Judicial Court of Massachusetts, in *Commonwealth v. Hunt*,[2] enunciated a test that was to figure in the debate about the role of the judiciary in labor disputes during the twentieth century. It rested upon an assessment of tactics, motive, and intent. In *Hunt* the court approved the closed shop, which requires a worker to join the union prior to employment, as a lawful objective. Said the Court:

The manifest intent of the association is to induce all those engaged in the same occupation to become members of it. Such a purpose is not unlawful. It would give them a power which might be exerted for useful and honorable purposes, or for dangerous and pernicious ones. If the latter were the real and actual object, and susceptible of proof, it should have been specially charged. Such an association might be used to afford each other assistance in times of poverty, sickness, and distress; or to raise their intellectual, moral, and social conditions; or to make improvement in their art; or for other proper purposes. Or the association might be designed for purposes of oppression and injustice . . . . An association may be formed, the declared objects of which are innocent and laudable, and yet they may have secret articles, or an agreement communicated only to the members, by which they are banded together for purposes injurious to the peace of society or to the rights of its members. Such would undoubtedly be a criminal conspiracy, on proof of the fact, however meritorious and praiseworthy the declared objects might be.[3]

Although the *Hunt* decision was a break from reliance upon the criminal-conspiracy doctrine a vehicle to thwart union growth, and although it did not abolish the doctrine, the court refused to assure that the objectives of workers were improper. The criminal-conspiracy doctrine began to fall into disuse. But other legal theories were wed against the unions.

The rule followed by the courts in the civil arena was the "prima facie tort" doctrine: that the intentional infliction of economic harm upon another party is a tort, and thus unlawful, unless justified by a legitimate purpose. This meant that a labor union was liable on the face of it in damages for losses sustained by virtue of a private wrong done to another party (economic pressure through strikes and picketing by the union aimed at an employer).

But was the self-interest of the workers a legitimate purpose, or was a judicial balancing of competing economic interests (workers, employers, and the public) required? All too often the courts opted for the latter standard. With no defined guidelines to be followed, the courts were able and willing to use their own social and economic predilections to determine what constituted "legitimate purpose." As Cox, Bok, and Gorman have said, "On the civil side . . . the volume of labor litigation sharply increased, and although it is impossible to reconstruct the legal atmosphere of the post–Civil War period, it seems fair to say that when the labor disputes engendered by the conflict over union organization were taken to the courts, the judges were substantially free, despite the scattered precedents, to create new law appropriate to the new occasion, guided only by the vague 'principles' which emerged from rulings upon more familiar situations."[4]

In 1896 the Supreme Judicial Court of Massachusetts granted an injunction against picketing or "patrolling" because such conduct had the effect of interfering with freedom of contract and the right to employ an individual at a price agreeable to the parties.[5] Such interference with business, in the court's view, was a "private nuisance" and, accordingly, enjoinable. This meant that the judiciary prohibited the unions from patrolling, and that disobedient individuals could be fined or imprisoned. Justice Oliver Wendell Holmes, dissenting from the decision, argued that patrolling did not necessarily carry with it the threat of unlawful activity or bodily harm:

There was no proof of any threat or danger of a patrol exceeding two men, and as of course an injunction is not granted except with reference to what there is reason to expect in its absence, the question on that point is whether a patrol of two men should be enjoined. Again, the defendants are enjoined by the final decree from intimidating by threats, expressed or implied, of physical harm to body or property, any person who may be desirous of entering into the employment of the plaintiff, so far as to prevent him from entering the same. In order to test the correctness of the refusal to go further, it must be assumed that the defendants obey the express prohibition of the decree.[6]

Moreover Holmes argued against the "justifiable conduct" test (that only economic pressure or picketing whose object is justifiable in the court's judgment is protected from an injunction): "The true grounds of decision are considerations of policy and of social advantage, and it is vain to suppose that solutions can be obtained merely by logic and general propositions of law which nobody disputes."[7]

Holmes continued to dissent against the *"prima facie* tort" doctrine, simultaneously expressing skepticism about the ability of trade unions to obtain a larger share of wealth through collective pressure (except at the expense of the less organized workers).[8] This matter continues to generate considerable controversy,[9] but Holmes's basic theme was simply that the courts ought not to devise their own policies in the absence of instructions from elected legislatures.

Meanwhile, as the American Federation of Labor emerged beyond embryonic form, a new judicial weapon against the growth of trade unions was developed. Its statutory basis was to be found in the Sherman Antitrust Act of 1890.[10] The Sherman Act, a reaction to the abuses of trusts that had achieved prominence and strength in the wake of the Industrial Revolution and the westward migration, had as its rationale the prohibition of conduct suppressing competition between businesses. Soon after its enactment, some employers argued that unions and their economic pressure achieved the same objectives and therefore violated the statute. Restraint of trade had been attacked by the courts before the Sherman Act, but the approach taken was a judicial refusal to enforce contracts that, for instance, provided for the boycott of an employer departing from an industry practice or agreement on allocation of markets or prices. The statutory scheme of the Sherman Act provided that unlawful conspiracies could be attacked in the courts.

During the debate about the Sherman Antitrust Act, Congress had not really addressed the statute's applicability to labor. At common law the phrase "restraint of trade" had meant aggregations, pools, or combinations whose object was to control the supply and price of products in order to suppress competition among companies shipping goods across state lines and thereby establish a monopolistic position in the industry. At common law, proving restraint of trade required evidence of motivation to harm or restrain others in the pursuit of their occupations.

The first test of the applicability of antitrust legislation to labor came before the Supreme Court in 1908 in the case of *Loewe v. Lawlor*,[11] or *Danbury Hatters* as it became more popularly known. This case involved a secondary boycott engaged in by the United Hatters of North America, which had called a strike against the D.E. Loewe Company for the purpose of unionizing the company. The union attempted to get consumers to boycott the company's hats in various states across the country. The union and its allies, the American Federation of Labor and other affiliates, attempted to boycott not only the company but any person who patronized the company. Because the union's efforts were aimed at parties other than the employer with which the union had a dispute, the tactics were referred to as "secondary" activities. The Supreme Court concluded that the antitrust laws applied to labor. Said Chief Justice Melville Fuller, speaking for the Court: "The records of Congress show that several efforts were made to exempt, by legislation, organizations of farmers and laborers from the operation of the act and that all of these efforts failed, so that the act remained as we have it before us."[12]

The impact of *Danbury Hatters* was devastating for organized labor. The unions, and many others, felt that the statute had been interpreted improperly, inasmuch as organized labor was not the focal point of congressional debate that took place prior to the enactment of antitrust legislation. Moreover, because the Sherman Antitrust Act provides for treble damages rather than the actual amount of the losses incurred (as well as criminal sanctions), the final judgment after fourteen years of litigation in *Danbury Hatters* awarded a substantial amount of money ($250,000). What was particularly troublesome about the judgment was that the members of the union were individually and personally liable. Though the case was settled in 1917 for slightly over $234,000 and the AFL was able to obtain $216,000 in voluntary contributions from union members, the fact that labor had to "pass the hat" to avoid the foreclosure of members' homes made the case unforgettable.

Immediately after the Supreme Court's decision in *Danbury Hatters* in 1908, the labor movement began a campaign to reverse the decision and the applicability of the Sherman Antitrust Act to trade unions. In 1908 the Democratic Party promised to amend antitrust legislation so as to reverse the Court's decision, and in 1912 it did so again in the following language: ". . . labor organizations and members should not be regarded as illegal organizations in the restraint of trade."[13] After Woodrow Wilson was elected president in 1912, these efforts culminated in the Clayton Antitrust Act of 1914, which Samuel Gompers immediately characterized as labor's Magna Carta and Bill of Rights and the most important legislation since the abolition of slavery. The two key provisions of the Clayton Act were found in sections 6 and 20.

Section 6 stated that "the labor of a human being is not a commodity or article of commerce. Nothing contained in the antitrust laws shall be construed to forbid the existence and operation of labor . . . organizations, instituted for the purposes of mutual help . . . or to forbid or restrain individual members of such organizations from lawfully carrying out the legitimate objects thereof; nor shall such organizations, or the members thereof, be held or construed to be illegal combinations or conspiracies in restraint of trade, under the antitrust laws."[14] Gompers said that section 6 constituted "sledgehammer blows to the wrongs and injustices so long inflicted upon the workers," and that "this declaration is the industrial Magna Carta upon which the working people will rear their structure of industrial freedom."[15] But what did section 6 mean? Only one theme emerged clearly: Antitrust laws were not to be deemed to forbid the existence and operation of labor organizations, and therefore, although such organizations are by definition anticompetitive in that they seek to suppress competition between workers in the same plants, companies, wider geographical areas, and ultimately throughout the nation, they were not to be regarded as illegal.

Supplementing this approach was section 20 of the Clayton Act, which Gompers had characterized as the "Bill of Rights" portion. Section 20 stated that no restraining order or injunction should be granted by any U.S. court in "any case between an employer and employees, or between employers and employees, or between employees, or between persons employed and persons seeking employment, involving, or growing out of, a dispute concerning terms or conditions of employment" unless a showing of irreparable injury was made, and there was therefore no adequate remedy at law. A restraining order or an injunction is designed to force a person or entity to do something. Injunctions often had been—and still are—designed to force a union to stop striking, picketing, or engaging in other forms of economic pressure against the employer. Section 20 also prohibited injunctions where workers struck, or peacefully picketed, or urged individuals to cease patronizing "any party to such dispute." The language was broad, yet section 20 did not explicitly address the question of what kinds of union economic pressure were to be appropriate. Because the statute did not limit restraining orders to disputes between an employer and its employees, one might assume that secondary boycotts were not to be regarded as unlawful. But when the Court did confront this issue, in *Duplex Printing Press Co. v. Deering*,[16] organized labor and Samuel Gompers received a rude surprise indeed.

The Supreme Court's decision in *Duplex* destroyed most of the hopes and expectations of organized labor about the Clayton Antitrust Act. *Duplex* arose out of a suit for injunctive relief to restrain a secondary boycott against a printing-press manufacturer in Battle Creek, Michigan, employing about 200 machinists in the factory in addition to some office employees and others. The company followed an "open shop" policy, purportedly refusing to discriminate against either union or nonunion men. The union, which had as its goals a closed shop in which only union members could be employed, the eight-hour day, and the union scale of wages, called a strike at the factory. When only a few of the workers joined in the union's efforts, the union attempted to boycott the company's products by warning customers that it would be better for them not to purchase from the company, threatening customers with sympathetic strikes, and inciting the employees of customers to strike against their employers. It also notified repair shops not to do repair work on Duplex presses and threatened union men with the loss of their union cards if they assisted in the installation of Duplex presses. The Duplex company brought an antitrust action against the union for unlawful restraint of trade.

The Court stated that a distinction between a primary and a secondary boycott was material to the question of whether union conduct was immunized by virtue of the Clayton Act. The Court first examined section 6 and stated the following:

> The section assumes the normal objects of a labor organization to be legitimate, and declares that nothing in the antitrust laws shall be construed to forbid the existence and operation of such organizations, or to forbid their members from lawfully carrying out their legitimate objects; and that such an organization shall not be held in itself—merely because of its existence and operation—to be an illegal combination or conspiracy in restraint of trade. But there is nothing in the section to exempt such an organization or its members from accountability where it or they depart from its normal and legitimate objects and engage in an actual combination of conspiracy in restraint of trade.[17]

The Court then focused on section 20 of the Clayton Act, noting that the provision specifically forbade the issuance of restraining orders or injunctions in U.S. courts where there was a labor dispute between an "employer and employees" and that the first paragraph's prohibition of orders in such circumstances "unless necessary to prevent irreparable injury to property, or to a property right" where there was no adequate remedy of law (that is to say, where the wronged party could not be adequately compensated through damages) was merely "declaratory of the law as it stood before."[18] Said the Court: "The first paragraph merely puts into statutory form familiar restrictions upon the granting of injunctions already established and of general application in the equity practice of the courts of the United States."[19] The Court noted that the second paragraph referred to cases where the parties were "standing in proximate relation to a controversy" of the kind designated in the first paragraph. Noting that the majority of the circuit courts of appeals had previously concluded that the words "employers and employees" should be treated as referring to "the business class or clan to which the parties litigant respectively belong," the Court nevertheless concluded that any construction of the statute that would preclude employer relief where union secondary activity was involved against employers "wholly unconnected" with the Battle Creek factory was a statutory construction "altogether inadmissible."[20] With a somewhat selective glance at legislative history, the Court rejected the "views and motives of individual members" of Congress and relied on committee reports that it recognized were not "explicitly" addressed to the question of whether secondary as well as primary boycotts were to be permitted. Significantly, the Court made clear its condemnation of the damage done to "many innocent people"—secondary employees and employees who were "far remote" from the "original" dispute.[21]

Justice Louis Brandeis, in a strong dissent in which he was joined by two other justices (including Holmes), stated that the contest between the Machinists' Union and the company involved "vitally the interest of every person whose cooperation is sought." Said Brandeis: "May not all with a common interest join in refusing to expend their labor upon articles whose very production constitutes an attack upon their standard of living and the institution which they are convinced supports it? Applying common-law principles the answer should, in my opinion, be: 'Yes, if as a matter of fact those who so cooperate have a common interest.'"[22] Brandeis noted that "centralization in the control of business brought its corresponding centralization in the organization of workingmen," and that a single employer might threaten the "standing" of the entire labor organization and its members. When it did so, said the dissent, "the union, in order to protect itself, would naturally refuse to work on his materials wherever found."[23] Addressing the antitrust-law question, Brandeis noted that the Clayton Act was the "fruit of unceasing agitation, which extended over more than twenty years and was designed to equalize before the law the position of workingman and employer as industrial combatants."[24] The dissenting opinion noted that use of the "malicious combination" doctrine, which had made actionable trade union activity that judges had deemed harmful and therefore unlawful.

The ideas of the proponents of new legislation had been "fairly crystallized" by 1914, said Justice Brandeis, and the principal theme that had emerged was a desire to remove the judiciary from involvement in labor disputes and consequent determinations based on their own social and economic viewpoints. Part and parcel of this view was that workers had suffered as a result of judicial involvement and that considerable confusion about the demarcation line between lawful and unlawful union conduct had ensued. Brandeis then noted that the Clayton Act had not referred to employers and employees in the employ of the same employer, and that under strict technical construction the statute could have no application to disputes between employers of labor and workingmen, "since the very acts to which it applies sever the continuity of the legal relationship."[25] That is, if a work stoppage was commenced, the striker was no longer in the employ of the company and could be replaced. Thus, under a technical statutory interpretation, primary strikers who had a dispute with no one other than their own employers could be excluded from the act's protection.

In conclusion, Justice Brandeis noted that although his view of the law was that each party could conduct an industrial struggle in its own self-interest, no "constitutional or moral sanction [should be ready to attach] to that right."[26] The overriding theme of the dissent was that the intent of Congress had been to remove the judges from defining what constituted "self-interest" and therefore appropriate action.

Organized labor's hopes were once again dashed by the majority opinion in *Duplex*. Indeed, the implications of *Duplex* were even more devastating than those of *Danbury Hatters*. In the first place, the Clayton amendments now provided employers as well as the U.S. government with the authority to sue for injunctive relief against unlawful labor disputes. This posed a considerable problem toward the end of the 1920s. Second, *Duplex* and its progeny represented the apogee of the "unlawful objectives" test. Justice Brandeis's concerns that judicial involvement meant that the judicially imposed social and economic predilections of a proentrepreneur judiciary were soon to be realized. And the result of *Duplex* clearly was that the language of section 20 of Clayton was mere surplusage at best.

The difficulties of applying the "unlawful objectives" test articulated in *Duplex,* the opportunity for judicial bias, and the artificial nature of judicially fashioned boundary lines became apparent in *Coronado Coal Company v. United Mine Workers.*[27] The opinion was written by Chief Justice Taft. Evidence established that a strike had been prompted by the "keen competition" between nonunion employers and employers that had bargaining relationships with the union, and the Court concluded that this demonstrated an unlawful attempt to prevent the manufacture and production of goods and to restrain control of their supply entering into interstate commerce. Consequently the Court held that where a union was engaged in a primary or local strike against an employer, unlawful intent within the meaning of antitrust laws could be demonstrated through specific evidence because the restraints on trade were "indirect." However, where the union activity was secondary inasmuch as employers whose employees were not directly involved in the dispute itself were the subject of pressure, the restraint was direct and unlawful intent could be inferred from the economic tactic.

The road was thus open to the very kind of judicial meddling and abuses that had created "unceasing agitation" of the kind described by Justice Brandeis. Particularly ominous in this regard was the above-noted availability of injunctive relief to employers (as well as the government) by virtue of the 1914 Clayton statute. Employers used this tool with increasing frequency in the 1920s, encouraged by the sympathetic response of the judiciary. Frankfurter and Greene have chronicled the many abuses that came to be associated with this aspect of the judicial process in their classic book *The Labor Injunction.* What follows here is a brief summary of their study and the comments of other scholars.

Employers filed motions for injunctive relief, or orders requiring organizations and industries to do certain things whenever strikes or picketing occurred at plant premises. (Generally the economic pressure was for the purpose of securing organization or some collective bargaining relationship.) The basis for obtaining such relief was not testimony and exhibits in a formal proceeding where witnesses could be subjected to cross-examination as well as examination but generalized affidavits that were simply altered in minor respects to suit the details of the case. Moreover injunctive relief was usually sought and obtained on an *ex parte* basis; the union's attorney was generally not present.

Generalized orders fashioned by the courts prohibited any individual from striking and picketing on the grounds that irreparable harm (harm that could not be compensated through a damage award) would be caused to his or her employer. In this connection, the courts often formulated a doctrine of vicarious responsibility under which the union could be held liable for the acts of any individual without regard to any showing of relationship between the union and the individual's conduct. Moreover, since most motions for injunctive relief were aimed at enjoining union efforts that were effective in the sense that they were likely to inflict immediate harm upon the employer, the motions were obtained expeditiously. The injunction would be in the form of a temporary restraining order. A temporary restraining order, which can be dissolved after a period of time or converted into a permanent injunction restraining the strike, was rarely if ever reversed at the time that the permanent injunction was sought. But the significant element of restraint was not only the failure to reverse but the granting of the injunction without thorough fact-finding. As Felix Frankfurter and Nathan Greene said:

The injunction cannot preserve the so-called *status quo*; the situation does not remain in equilibrium awaiting judgment upon full knowledge. The suspension of activities affects only the strikers; the employer resumes his efforts to defeat the strike, and resumes them free from the interdicted interferences. Moreover, the suspension of strike activities, even temporarily, may defeat the strike for practical purposes and foredoom its resumption, even if the injunction is later lifted. Choice is not between irreparable damage to one side and compensable damage to the other. The law's conundrum is which side should bear the risk of *unavoidable* irreparable damage. Improvident denial of the injunction may be irreparable to the complainant; improvident issue of the injunction may be irreparable to the defendant. For this situation the ordinary mechanics of the provisional injunction proceedings are plainly inadequate. Judicial error is too costly to either side of a labor dispute to permit perfunctory determination of the crucial issues; even in the first instance, it must be searching. The necessity of finding the facts quickly from sources vague, embittered and partisan, colored at the start by the passionate intensities of a labor controversy, calls at best for rare judicial qualities. It becomes an impossible assignment when judges rely upon the complaint and the affidavits of interested or professional witnesses, untested by the safeguards of common law trials—personal appearance of witnesses, confrontation and cross-examination.[28]

Beyond these problems was the fact that judges, without the presence of juries, often imposed contempt penalties in the same cases in which they had issued the injunction initially. (Contempt penalties—sometimes fines, sometimes imprisonment—are imposed by the courts on parties who disobey or are contemptuous of the court's orders.) Contempt problems arose regularly, sometimes because of liability that was imputed to the union by conduct of other parties through the "vicarious responsibility" doctrine.

All of this created an environment in which respect for the law and the judiciary, a critical prerequisite for a functioning modern democracy, was increasingly undermined. The concerns expressed by Justices Brandeis and Holmes in previous opinions became increasingly vexatious after the *Duplex* decision and the increased popularity of the labor injunction. Again, partly because of the efforts of Frankfurter and Greene, Congress was lobbied to reform the law. Again, the proponents of reform were successful in obtaining legislation. But this time the legislative package was different.

In the Norris-LaGuardia Act of 1932, Congress attempted to learn from the past and to speak more unambiguously, and to protect the statute against a *Duplex*-type interpretation. This objective was to be accomplished in a number of ways, foremost among them the broad declaration that jurisdiction was to be denied to the federal courts in certain kinds of labor disputes. Section 1 stated that no federal court would have "jurisdiction to issue any restraining order or temporary or permanent injunction in a case involving or growing out of a labor dispute, except in a strict conformity with the provisions of this Act."[29] Section 13 went on to attempt to reverse the impact of *Duplex's* narrow definition of "labor dispute." The new provision referred to nearly every kind of labor dispute,[30] and quite clearly secondary stoppages were included within the definition. Section 4, operating with the definitions provided by section 13, stated that in any case growing out of the labor dispute the federal courts were precluded from issuing any injunctions except where violence or fraud was involved. Even where violence or fraud was involved, an order restraining such a stoppage was to be available only after a hearing had been conducted and a finding of facts set forth—and the hearing was to be conducted with examination and cross-examination rather than with the kinds of affidavits to which the federal courts had become accustomed prior to 1932. Although temporary *ex parte* orders could still be allowed, they were made permissible for a period of time not to exceed five days and on showing of "substantial and irreparable injury" to the employer's property as well as the posting of a bond. The right to trial by jury was provided in connection with contempt cases, and the prohibitions contained in the injunction were required to be specific in defining the conduct forbidden as well as the parties who were affected by the order, thus presumably diminishing the number of cases that might go into such contempt proceedings.

Additionally the Norris-LaGuardia Act addressed an issue that had been a matter of controversy for some time in the

United States. The "yellow dog" contract, through which employers required workers to stay out of unions as a condition of employment, was declared to be contrary to the public policy of the United States and thus unenforceable in any federal court. The Norris-LaGuardia approach to the "yellow dog" contract reflects the statute's general philosophy. Though the law promoted the doctrine of freedom of association for all workers as a matter of public policy, it contained no machinery for implementing this freedom. Norris-LaGuardia was a laissez-faire approach to industrial relations, a strongly worded series of instructions to the federal courts to keep their hands off labor disputes because they had made a mess of things by intervening in the past. Their handling of labor disputes had been inexpert and insensitive to the concerns and expectations of workers in an industrialized society. The act represented a strong warning to the courts not to engage in dubious statutory interpretation so as to avoid what appeared to be the intent of Congress—a tactic in which many thought the Court had engaged in *Duplex*. The theme of this statutory approach, denial of jurisdiction to the courts, was consistent with laissez-faire.

One major problem was left unresolved by Norris-LaGuardia, and another was soon to appear. The first involved the question of what impact, if any, Norris-LaGuardia had upon criminal prosecutions and damage actions pursued by employers or the government under antitrust legislation. The remedies, as well as injunctions, were available under the antitrust statues, but Norris-LaGuardia explicitly addressed the issue of injunctive relief alone. The second question related to the basic inequality between capital and labor in the United States in the early 1930s. Was it enough to simply reverse *Duplex* and deny the federal courts jurisdiction in labor disputes? Would it not be necessary to provide protection for organized labor, which had been confronted with company-dominated and company-assisted unions, company spies, the blacklisting of union members, surveillance, and other forms of harassment as well as the dismissal of union organizers who were employees?

The Supreme Court dealt with the first of these two problems in *United States v. Hutcheson*, which dealt with a government criminal prosecution against a union that had been engaged in a jurisdictional dispute over work assignments with another union. Justice Frankfurter, speaking for the Court, concluded that the Norris-LaGuardia prohibitions had broader scope than the denial of jurisdiction to federal courts in connection with injunctions. Said the Court:

The Norris-LaGuardia Act removed the fetters upon trade union activities, which according to judicial construction [section] 20 of the Clayton Act had left untouched, by still further narrowing the circumstances under which the federal courts could grant injunctions in labor disputes. More especially, the Act explicitly formulated the "public policy of the United States" in regard to the industrial conflict, and by its light established that the allowable area of union activity was not to be restricted, as it had been in the *Duplex* case, to an immediate employer-employee relation. Therefore, whether trade union conduct constitutes a violation of the Sherman Law is to be determined only by reading the Sherman Law and [section] 20 of the Clayton Act and the Norris-LaGuardia act as a harmonizing text of outlawry of labor conduct.[31]

The Court further stated that the relationship between Norris-LaGuardia and Clayton had to be understood in its historical context and not read as a "tightly drawn amendment to a technically phrased tax provision."[32] Accordingly, the statutes were to be regarded as "interlacing" and part of one body of federal labor law. Therefore, where the courts were denied jurisdiction in labor disputes for the purpose of injunctive relief, they were also restricted in connection with criminal prosecutions and damage actions designed to suppress the kinds of union activity at which Norris-LaGuardia was aimed.

What then was the range of activity that would be immune from antitrust law? The test, said the Court, was one of self-interest. In vivid contrast to the position taken in *Duplex* and some of its antecedents, the Court was at pains to state that what was to be regarded as "licit and the illicit" had no relationship to the "wisdom or unwisdom, the rightness or wrongness, the selfishness or unselfishness of the end of which the particular union activities are the means."[33] The

Court stated that so long as the union acted in self-interest and did not combine with nonlabor groups, union activity could not be prohibited. The problem of antitrust liability for unions that combine with nonlabor groups for certain objectives remains a major issue in American labor law, but *Hutcheson* is significant because of the freedom it provides to trade unions to engage in strikes, picketing, and boycotts.

The second major break with the past took place three years after the passage of Norris-LaGuardia. The enactment of the National Labor Relations Act, which created a national administrative agency to conduct representation elections to determine whether a union could represent employees as exclusive bargaining representative and to determine whether certain unfair labor practice violations had been engaged in, was an event of vast significance for American industrial relations. This marked the end of a brief interlude of laissez-faire toward labor relations as reflected in the Norris-LaGuardia Act.

3

The National Labor Relations Act

The National Labor Relations Act of 1935 forms the basis of legal regulation of collective bargaining in the private sector. Other statutes, such as the Fair Labor Standards Act of 1938, provide substantive guarantees for individual employees who work for employers engaged in interstate commerce and a "floor" below which workers should not fall.[1] In the case of the FLSA, minimum wages and maximum hours are provided. The minimum wage became $4.25 per hour in 1991.[2] The Walsh-Healy Act[3] and the Davis-Bacon Act[4] provide minimum conditions for employees of government contractors. During the 1970s other federal legislation (referred to in chapter 11) was enacted. State legislatures have enacted their own laws in this area, and sometimes their minimum wage is in excess of federal requirements.[5] In contrast to regulation in the wage arena, the United States has very little law relating to vacations. Thirty-nine of the 50 states have no statutory vacation law whatsoever,[6] and there is none at the federal level.

Prior to the National Labor Relations Act, Congress had already provided for collective bargaining in the railroad industry through the Railway Labor Act of 1926.[7] Furthermore the National Labor Board (under the auspices of the National Industry Recovery Act,[8] the pre-NLRA National Labor Relations Board, and an executive order of the president) had been conducting elections, albeit under statutory machinery that was unenforceable before the Supreme Court's holding that the NIRA was unconstitutional.[9]

The constitutional basis for the National Labor Relations Act is the commerce clause of the U.S. Constitution: article I, section 8. This provision allows Congress to enact legislation when it regulates commerce between the various states of the union. The constitutional theory upon which the statute is predicated is that statutory regulation of labor and management is necessary to diminish industrial strife that could disrupt interstate commerce. The Supreme Court, at the time of the NLRA, had struck down a number of the Roosevelt administration's laws providing social and economic reform. But by a 5–4 vote, in *NLRB v. Jones & Laughlin Steel Corp.,*[10] it upheld the constitutionality of the act. This came at a time when the Roosevelt administration was attempting to expand the Court in order to change the drift of its decisions. Chief Justice Hughes joined the majority of the Court in *Jones & Laughlin* in declaring the statute constitutional. His previous involvement on the other side of similar issues prompted wags to say "A switch in time saves nine."

Whatever Hughes's motivation, the Court accepted the constitutional theory that Congress could regulate labor relations so as to avoid interference with the shipment of goods across state lines. Ironically, as so often happens in connection with great social movements, when expectations are on the rise, once the statute was passed the amount of industrial strife increased significantly.[11] Yet it is fair to say that, over more than fifty-eight years, the Board's work has contributed substantially to the promotion of industrial peace in the United States.

The particular significance of the NLRA (which in 1935 was called the Wagner Act after its principal author, Senator Robert Wagner of New York) was that it provided for regulation of some labor disputes by an expert agency—the National Labor Relations Board—whose principal headquarters were and are in Washington, DC. Congress had departed from the laissez-faire philosophy of Norris-

LaGuardia, but it could not be said to be reviving traditional outside involvement and the potential for abuses associated with antitrust laws and the labor injunction—although the courts now had appellate jurisdiction over the Board.

The NLRB was one of a number of administrative agencies established under New Deal legislation promoted by the Roosevelt administration. The Wagner Act provided that employees were to be protected in their free choice to protest working conditions they deemed unfair, to organize into unions and select representatives, and to oblige management to bargain in good faith with the union that represented a majority of the workers in an appropriate group or unit. As noted earlier, these rights were to be enforced through representational elections in which the majority would vote on which (if any) labor organization would represent them and through unfair labor practice machinery through which the NLRB interprets the statute to determine whether management or labor has engaged in unfair practices. (Labor unions' unfair labor practices were added to the law through the Taft-Hartley amendments in 1947.) In contrast with the administrative agencies that preceded it, the focus of the new board was on the development of a body of case law that would govern large portions of the relationship between labor and management.

Orders issued by the NLRB (often referred to as the "Labor Board" or just the "Board") are not self-enforcing. Enforcement of the Board's orders is obtained through the circuit courts of appeals. There are twelve such tribunals in the United States, and they are just below the Supreme Court in the judicial pyramid. In the event that labor or management does not comply with an order enforced in the court, contempt proceedings (which can result in civil and criminal penalties, although the latter are rarely invoked) take place before the circuit court and not the Board.

Just as the Great Depression promoted the idea of self-organization among workers, both as a balance against big business[12] and as a form of industrial democracy, so also the outbreak of strikes at the end of World War II—when the pent-up demands of labor manifested themselves in indus-

trial warfare that disrupted a number of key industries—
helped create an environment conducive to limitations on
the rights of unions. Changes in the National Labor Relations Act were enacted through the Taft-Hartley amendments. In addition to the rules relating to appropriate units,
the organization of the National Labor Relations Board and
the unfair labor practice provisions were altered.

The National Labor Relations Board

The Board, which had been one entity, was split into two
separate sections by the Taft-Hartley amendments. On one
side, there is a five-member board with its principal offices
in Washington, DC (the "judicial" side of the Board). On
the other side, also with its principal offices in Washington,
is the "prosecutorial" side of the Board, which is headed by
the General Counsel. (It cannot be regarded as prosecutorial in the strict sense of the word because it cannot seek
criminal penalties or sanctions.) The two offices were sepa-
rated because it was thought to be unfair and inconsistent
with due process to have the same party investigate and
adjudicate. Quite obviously, when one party has already completed its investigation and made a decision to proceed with
an unfair labor practice proceeding, that party may be less
than completely objective in subsequent adjudication of the
case.

The members of the Board and the General Counsel are
appointed by the president with the advice and consent of
the Senate. Officials on both sides—prosecutorial and judicial—work together in connection with the Board's functions relating to representational matters, including the
establishment of appropriate units and the conduct of
elections.

The Taft-Hartley amendments, which imposed a variety of
legal obligations upon unions, created a split between the
General Counsel and the Board for unfair labor practice
cases because the authors felt that employers had been
denied due process by a pro-union Board acting as prosecutor, judge, and jury. If the hearing is held before the prosecutor who investigated and who has a stake in obtaining the

conviction, fairness has been denied the accused. This sense that the pendulum had swung too far toward labor in the period between 1935 and 1947 pervades other amendments that were made to the statute in 1947 and 1959.

Preemption and Primary Jurisdiction for the NLRB

In the Wagner Act and the Taft-Hartley amendments, Congress intended to define carefully the role of the courts and the NLRB in labor relations. The amendments make it clear that collective bargaining agreements are contracts enforceable in court but that most allegations of unfair labor practices may be heard only by the Board and ultimately by the federal courts.

Unions and employers can pursue allegations of breach of contract in state or federal courts. Before the enactment of the Taft-Hartley amendments, it was difficult for employers to sue unions in state courts for breach of contract because in many states the collective bargaining agreement was regarded as a "gentlemen's agreement" and not a court-enforceable contract, and because often the court insisted that unions, as voluntary unincorporated associations, be sued in the name of each individual member, which was difficult in practice. Ironically, although the statutory provision that made collective bargaining agreements enforceable in the federal courts was prompted by Congress's concern that unions were acting irresponsibly and often in violation of their collectively negotiated contract provisions, the fact is that the unions have made considerable use of this provision of the law by insisting successfully that recalcitrant or unwilling employers proceed to arbitration where there is a dispute over the meaning of the collective bargaining agreement.[13] Most of the actions relating to the enforcement of agreements have been brought by the unions —principally because they are actions to compel arbitration or to enforce an arbitrator's award.[14]

The peculiar federalist system of the United States is the wellspring of the doctrines of preemption and primary jurisdiction, which are applied in the National Labor Relations Act's unfair labor practice provisions. Congress's intention to create an expert agency for labor matters is apparent in the NLRB General Counsel's broad discretion over whether to issue an unfair labor practice complaint[15] (and thus whether a hearing on the issue will be held) and in the exclusion of the courts as a forum for initiating unfair labor practice cases.

Where Congress has the constitutional authority to legislate, the federal law may be supreme—and state jurisdiction may be ousted completely—where Congress chooses. The supremacy of federal law springs from article VI of the U.S. Constitution. The courts have fashioned a doctrine of preemption that is based on the Supremacy Clause and the Commerce Clause.[16] Whenever Congress has legislated in detail, the courts consider whether Congress intended to deprive the states of jurisdiction in the particular field (as the courts put it, whether Congress intended to "occupy the field").[17] The reason for the doctrines of preemption and occupation of the field is that conflicting interpretations of a law by state courts may frustrate the objective of the national legislation. That is, even if the state courts interpret the very same National Labor Relations Act that Congress enacted, they may interpret it in a different way than the Board would.

Accordingly the Supreme Court has held that whenever the subject matter involved in a labor controversy is "arguably" protected by section 7 of the NLRA or prohibited by the unfair-labor-practice provision applicable to both unions and employers in section 8, federal and state courts are deprived of jurisdiction.[18] In applying the doctrine of preemption of the NLRA, the Supreme Court has stated that usually the Board has primary jurisdiction to determine the question of whether the subject matter involved in a labor controversy is protected or prohibited by the NLRA before the courts intervene.[19] This is because the Board is the expert agency entrusted with special responsibility to interpret the statute, and if the courts were to step in without the benefit of the Board's interpretation, their exercise of jurisdiction and interpretation of the statute and national labor policy could cause mischief for the uniform federal scheme Congress intended to apply in labor-management relations.

To be sure, there are exceptions to the preemption doctrine. For instance, where a suit is brought for breach of collective bargaining agreement, the state retains jurisdiction even where the subject matter also involves an unfair labor practice. Cases involving the duty of fair representation are another exception to the rule. Moreover a series of Supreme Court decisions[20] have permitted the states to assume jurisdiction where actions are brought alleging libel[21] or harm suffered under statutes designed to protect an individual's emotional injury,[22] or trespass by union organizers seeking to impart their message to employees or to the public on private premises,[23] or violence or a threat to peaceful order. The Court has also inferred congressional intent to confer regulatory authority upon the states when federal statutes provide some room for state action on the subject matter in question.[24]

Recent decisions have cast some doubt on the continued viability of the strong pro-preemption posture taken by the Supreme Court in labor cases.[25] This trend is manifested in a 1993 unanimous Supreme Court ruling that a state authority, when acting as the owner of a construction project, may enforce a private collective bargaining agreement negotiated by private parties.[26] However, one can still safely say that the states have been limited in dealing with labor controversies involving the portion of the private sector that is covered by the NLRA and the portion of those cases over which the Board has chosen to assume jurisdiction under its authority to regulate employers and unions involved in interstate commerce.[27] As a result of the 1959 amendments to the NLRA, the Board cannot decline jurisdiction over any cases over which it would have assumed jurisdiction under the standards as of August 1, 1959.[28]

Although the Board's jurisdiction over commerce is broad,[29] it does not extend to foreign crews employed by foreign ships operating under flags of convenience,[30] inasmuch as there must be an affirmative intention by Congress to regulate such employers given the delicate consideration of international relations involved. However, the Supreme Court has approved the NLRB's assertion of jurisdiction over foreign flag vessels where the dispute between labor and management focused upon wages paid to American residents who did not serve as members of the crew but rather performed casual longshore work.[31] Similarly, where the International Longshoremen's Association refused to load or unload cargo destined for or originating in the Soviet Union, in protest against that country's invasion of Afghanistan, the dispute was held to be in "commerce" and within the NLRB's jurisdiction.[32]

The significance of the two doctrines of preemption and primary jurisdiction for the Board in connection with the General Counsel's authority is enormous. The doctrines make it difficult for a substantial number of cases to be heard on their merits in an open hearing. In part, the disinclination of a substantial number of Americans to protest this state of affairs is attributable to the preference by labor and management representatives (especially the former) for the supposed expertise of the Board and the unease many Americans have about judicial competence in labor matters, given the historical experience.[33] The irony here is that the preemption doctrine has expanded because the Taft-Hartley amendments broadened the Board's jurisdiction. Thus statutory provisions aimed at restricting labor have deprived what was in many instances a more hostile state judiciary of jurisdiction over labor—jurisdiction that could be devoted to restraining strikes, picketing, and other actions through damages and criminal prosecution.

Who Is Covered by the NLRA?

The coverage provided by the National Labor Relations Act is narrow.[34] Public employees at the federal, state, and local levels are excluded, as are agricultural workers, domestic servants, and supervisory employees. Sometimes the enterprises of the Indian Tribes have been found to be excluded from the coverage of the Act on the ground that the assertion of jurisdiction would interfere with the tribe's powers of internal sovereignty.[35]

This exclusion does not mean that it is illegal for such workers to engage in collective bargaining. Indeed collective bargaining for public employees and legislation at the federal, state, and local levels protecting the right of the workers to join unions has become part of the American labor landscape. For example, although most states do not protect the right of farm workers to engage in collective bargaining, California has a comprehensive statute that is in many respects superior to the NLRA in the protection it affords to workers.[36]

There is no logical basis for the exclusion of the workers referred to above. Essentially their exclusion from the NLRA's protection relates simply to the fact that they had little political clout when the legislation was enacted. American labor law has traditionally excluded large groups of workers from its coverage.[37]

Additionally certain workers besides those mentioned above are excluded from the definition of "employee" within the meaning of the Act; for example, independent contractors are specifically excluded by section 2(3).[38] Because the First Amendment to the Constitution provides for a separation of church and state, the Supreme Court has held that lay teachers of religious and secular subjects are not covered by the NLRA in the absence of an explicit indication by Congress that it intended to give the NLRB jurisdiction over such individuals.[39] Although the statute does not provide explicit exclusionary language, the Supreme Court, in *NLRB v. Bell Aerospace Company*,[40] has held that managerial employees who formulate and implement company policy are also excluded from the bargaining unit. Such employees of course are not eligible to vote in NLRB-conducted elections.

In 1980 the Supreme Court held that at least under certain circumstances, faculty members in universities are properly excluded from the definition of "employee" because they are managerial employees.[41] The Court's reasoning, expressed by Justice Powell's majority opinion, is based on a presumed identity of interest between the faculty and the administration. The decision, like *Bell Aerospace,* was by a vote of 5–4. One of the majority opinion's deficiencies is that it overlooks the frequent clashes of interests between faculties and administrations. Another problem is the failure to recognize that labor can be involved in both confrontation and cooperation, as the UAW's recent interest in having workers on auto manufacturers' boards vividly demonstrates. This inability of the Court to perceive the need of a union or any society to have a collective bargaining model that promotes cooperation is disturbing indeed.

Access to the Law's Protection

What benefits are provided by the National Labor Relations Act for workers who are covered by it? In the first place workers, as well as labor organizations and employers, may file a petition with the NLRB requesting an election to determine whether a particular labor organization represents the majority of workers within an appropriate group of employees. Such an election is conducted by secret vote, and ballots are generally cast at the plant where the workers are employed. More than half of the workers who vote in the Board-conducted election must vote for the union if the employer is to be required to bargain with it.[42]

Although in some countries organizations seeking to represent workers must register and be screened, no such situation exists in the United States. However, in order for a labor union to file a petition requesting representation and to impose bargaining obligations upon management, it must be a "labor organization" as defined in the NLRA: an organization "of any kind, or any agency or employee representation committee or plan, in which employees participate and which exists for the purpose, in whole or in part, of dealing with employers concerning grievances, labor disputes, wages, rates of pay, hours of employment, or conditions of work."[43] So as to provide the greatest scope for freedom of association under the statute, this provision has been interpreted liberally to permit a wide variety of organizations to obtain the benefits of the statute. There is no requirement of involvement in any particular industry or company, and the collective bargaining experience of another (perhaps larger) labor organization does not freeze out an organization that may seek to represent workers in the same industry.[44]

But the statutory scheme is designed to confer exclusivity on a labor organization. That is, once an organization receives majority support in an appropriate unit, the employer is under a statutory obligation to bargain with no other organization for the workers in that unit. All workers covered by or included in the unit, whether they are members of the union or not, have their wages, hours, and working conditions regulated by the collective bargaining agreement between the union and employer unless the contract between labor and management states otherwise. In professional sports, where contracts allow for bargaining between employers and individual players, there are good examples of such special contracts between labor and management. Stars, such as the now retired Fred Lynn, the Red Sox erstwhile centerfielder who pioneered new contracts with the California Angels, and Baltimore Orioles, the Detroit Tigers, and San Diego Padres, are now dwarfed financially by multimillionaires like fastball pitcher Roger Clemens, outfielders Barry Bonds and Bobby Bonilla, and secondbaseman Ryne Sandberg—the leaders among many now able to command handsome salaries on the basis of individual bargaining.[45]

The collective bargain itself will, in many circumstances, provide for a wide range of benefits to be negotiated in an individual contract of employment; the wage or salary is one such benefit. But the situation in professional sports is not representative of most collective bargaining in which wages as well as other benefits and conditions are shaped by unions and employers on an almost totally bilateral basis. And even in sports it is the collective agreement that sets minimum salaries and addresses the question of when players become free agents so that they may bargain with other teams. Indeed the union representing soccer players in North America has the authority under its collective agreement to veto individual contracts. The National Football League Players' Association has proposed (without success) collective negotiation of maximum as well as minimum salaries. But the National Basketball Players' Association has agreed to a salary "cap" or limit that each club cannot exceed. Also players' unions have become concerned about, and sought to regulate, some of the practices of agents who represent athletes.

Appropriate Unit

What is an appropriate unit of workers? An appropriate unit is to be established by the NLRB among a group of workers who have a "community of interest" with one another. The principal forum for collective bargaining in the United States is an appropriate unit of workers established at the plant. But the statute and numerous decisions of the Board and the courts make it clear that an appropriate unit can be established at the company level and sometimes—where there is consent on both sides—on a multiemployer or industrywide basis.

The principal considerations that the Board and the courts use in determining what constitutes an appropriate unit are the following:

- whether the employees are under common supervision,
- whether the employer's bookkeeping relating to employee concerns, payment of wages, and other benefits is organized on a plant, a multiplant, or a multicompany basis,
- on what basis the employees have communicated or bargained in the past,
- whether the employees have contact with one another at the workplace and whether, for instance, they clock in and clock out at the same location,
- if there is a dispute relating to whether the unit is appropriately multiplant in scope, the extent to which employees are transferred between plants (temporarily or otherwise),
- similarity in the type of work performed,
- similarities in wages, hours, and working conditions, and
- the desires of the employees.

Though the last point can be considered along with the others, the Taft-Hartley amendments make it clear that the NLRB cannot declare an appropriate unit by considering the workers' wishes alone.[46]

Often the question of what constitutes an appropriate unit is a difficult one. Very often the union will want a small unit. For instance, if a chain has five restaurants in the same city, the union will undoubtedly try to establish a unit in one or two of them because it can channel a great deal of effort into organizing a small group of employees (which can then serve as a "building block" for organizing others). Another reason for the union's desire to establish a smaller unit is its reliance upon secrecy to ward off a counterattack by the employer. Secrecy is less likely to be realized if the union tries to organize all of the chain's facilities in the city simultaneously. In such circumstances the employer generally wants the broader unit because of his or her interest in uniformity of practices and conditions of employment in all the facilities. Not only does this make administration easier, but also it tends to minimize the potential for discord and discontent among employees who might complain about differences in benefits and conditions which they perceive as putting them in an inferior position. Also the employer generally favors a broader unit for the very same reasons that the union favors a small unit: The union will have more difficulty trying to reach a larger number of employees, and the employer's campaign to undercut the union is more likely to succeed under such circumstances. The sooner the employer finds out about the campaign, the better he or she is able to thwart the union's organizing efforts. As the Supreme Court has said, "virtually every Board decision concerning an appropriate bargaining unit—e.g., the proper size of the unit—favors one side or the other."[47]

Before the Taft-Hartley amendments, where the factors were roughly equal and where the union desired the smaller unit, the Board would accede to the union's wishes on the ground that if a broader unit than that petitioned for was to be established as the appropriate unit, collective bargaining would probably not exist for the employees at all. This would be so not only because the union would be unlikely to win an election among employees in all of an employer's facilities but also because it would be unlikely that an election would ever be held. Under the administrative rules of the NLRB, for an election to take place, 30 percent of the employees within the appropriate unit must indicate that they want an election held to determine whether collective bargaining will exist. This is called the "showing of interest." If (to take our example) the appropriate unit is one or two of the chain's restaurants, it is likely that an election will be held because the union's organizational efforts will have reached a substantial number of the employees and will have persuaded a number of them to sign petitions or authorization cards indicating their interest in the union or in a Board-conducted election. If the unit is a larger one, it will be unlikely that an election will be held at all because less than 30 percent of the workers will support an election. Today the NLRA precludes the Board from fashioning an appropriate unit on the grounds that the union has organized the employees in that particular area. The statute says that "the extent that the employees have organized shall not be controlling." However, the extent of organization may still be taken into account along with the other factors mentioned.[48]

Although the Board has relied upon the extent of organization in conjunction with other factors to establish a unit at one location in a multilocation industry as presumptively appropriate,[49] recently it has established large units in universities[50] and hospitals.[51] The larger the unit, the more difficult a union organizational effort is likely to be.

One unit issue that has been litigated relates to whether "on-air programmers" who appear before the microphone in the broadcast industry—announcers and disc jockeys—constitute a separate unit for the purpose of bargaining. The Board has held that such employees should be within a separate unit because they "constitute a homogeneous, readily identifiable cohesive group" by virtue of their talent, which separates them from other employees—that is, "voice, diction and personality."[52] But in a case involving a northern California radio station featuring modern jazz, *KJAZ Broadcasting Company*,[53] the Board held that there is no "recognized distinction" where "on the air programmers do not share a substantial community of interest separate and apart from other employees of the Employer." Said the Board: "In its commitment to the jazz idiom, the Employer has historically hired only employees with an in-depth knowledge of jazz, a 'talent' shared by all its employees."[54]

Ever since the passage of the National Labor Relations Act there have been conflicts between craft and industrial unions about the unit for representation. (In the early days of the Act, such disputes arose out of the fact that management often favored craft unions because they were regarded as more conservative.) The problem is particularly troublesome in the United States because there are large numbers of both craft and industrial unions. In contrast, Britain and Australia are plagued with jurisdictional stoppages caused by proliferation of craft unions, and in Germany and Scandinavia industrial unions are dominant.

In the United States craft unions are able to survive where the appropriate unit is fashioned on an occupational basis. Conversely, a broader unit is more to the liking of the big industrial unions. Where the question of craft or industrial unit is extremely close, the desires of the employees are to govern according to the rarely used "globe election process," which pools votes into two units when the smaller or craft group provides a majority vote for the union seeking two units.[55] If those pooled votes give that union a majority of the voters, it is certified; if there is no majority, the Board orders a runoff election between the highest vote getters.

Another issue that arises quite frequently relates to "craft severance," the extent to which a class of skilled workers may opt out of an appropriate unit that includes semiskilled and unskilled workers. Prior to 1947 in most such cases the NLRB did not permit workers to separate themselves from the broad group. The Taft-Hartley amendments reversed this position, and the Board cannot now regard a craft as inappropriate for bargaining on the grounds that a different unit had been established previously. Today the Board determines whether craftsmen will be granted a separate unit on the basis of the following factors:

- whether the proposed unit consists of a "distinct and homogeneous group of skilled journeymen craftsmen" who are "performing the functions of their craft on a nonrepetitive basis" or are located in a functionally distinct department "where a tradition of separate representation exists";
- the history of collective bargaining and the potential for collective bargaining if the history is continued;
- the extent to which the employees who wish to opt out have maintained a separate identity for themselves;
- the pattern of collective bargaining in the industry generally;
- the degree of integration of the employer's production processes; and
- the extent to which the union seeking to represent the skilled workers has experience in representing the particular craft involved.

The criteria above provide some notion of the kinds of problems that are involved in determining what constitutes an appropriate unit. They should also provide a bit of an appreciation of the changes that took place through the Taft-Hartley amendments, which were designed to protect employees against unions that sometimes run afoul of these interests. Particularly the Taft-Hartley amendments were concerned with protecting the interests of skilled trades against industrial unions that (at least in the tradesmen's view) did not always adequately take their interests into account.

Though the Act provides that an appropriate unit is to be established "in each case," the Supreme Court has approved of the exercise of broad rule-making authority by the Labor Board in connection with its establishment of eight bargaining units in acute care hospitals.[56] Said Justice Stevens for a unanimous Court: "The requirement that the Board exercise its discretion in every disputed case [involving an appropriate unit] cannot fairly or logically be read to command the Board to exercise standardless discretion in each case."[57] The practical effect of the Court's holding is to expedite the administrative process at a very critical stage of representative selection by workers to avoid delay which can dissipate interest in collective bargaining. Generalized rule making allows for avoidance of detailed ad hoc appropriate unit determination which produces delays.

Holding an Election

After the appropriate unit has been found, if there is a 30 percent showing of interest the regional director in the NLRB field office orders an election. At a prehearing conference the regional director attempts to resolve the unit issue and the question of who is eligible to vote without a full hearing. If he or she is successful, a consent agreement is signed by all parties.

There are two kinds of consent agreements. One provides that the regional director's decision on all challenges to ballots and to the conduct of the election is final and binding; the other permits the parties to appeal on such matters to the Board in Washington. Sometimes all employees eligible to vote are named in the agreement.

If there is no agreement, a hearing will be held on the unit and eligibility issues. Theoretically this is not supposed to be an adversary or court-style proceeding, but sometimes the participating lawyers (as well as lay people) make it that way. Sometimes a second or third labor organization (besides the one that filed the petition) will be present and will file a motion to intervene. Any union that can show that it has signed up one employee as a supporter may be on the ballot at the election. If the second or third union (any number of unions may intervene) has a 10 percent showing of interest, it may participate fully in the hearing. If no union or the "No" vote has a majority, a runoff is held with the two highest votegetters on the ballot.

Within seven days of the regional director's decision to order an election or approve the consent agreement for the election, the employer must file with the NLRB three copies of a list of the names and addresses of all employees in the unit.[58] One copy is sent to the union so that it may communicate with employees during the campaign.

Elections are generally held on the employer's premises. If the union objects, the election is held elsewhere. A representative of the NLRB supervises the conduct of the election,[59] and all parties are entitled to have observers. Objections to the conduct of the election by the unions or the employer or disputes about the eligibility of voters that might affect the election's outcome must be filed with the regional director within five days of the election. The regional director will investigate but need not hold a hearing to determine the validity of the objections unless a party challenging the election shows through specific evidence relating to specific individuals material issues of fact sufficient to support a prima facie showing of objectionable conduct.[60] If the objections are found to be valid, the election will be set aside and another will be held.

Objections are the preferred method for resolving disputes about election conduct. The filing of an unfair labor practice charge "blocks" resolution of the representation issue, delaying the election and the above-described procedures until the unfair labor practice issue is resolved.[61] The theory is that absent resolution of the unfair labor practice issues, the potential for interference with employees' freedom of choice exists.

The central theme of these procedures is the employees' freedom of choice. Employees must exercise that choice free of workplace pressures from the union or the employer. It is hoped that the choice will be an informed one. The goal is to realize majority rule in an expeditious and informal manner. Accordingly, except where the NLRB directly contradicts the language of the NLRA,[62] its decisions on representation issues are not reviewable in the federal courts. But, as a practical matter, an employer (but not a labor organization) may obtain review of the NLRB's representation decision by refusing to bargain with a union that has been certified, thus triggering an unfair labor practice proceeding.[63]

4

Unfair Labor Practices

As we saw in chapter 3, neither the members of the National Labor Relations Board, nor the judicial side of the Board, nor the courts can adjudicate unfair labor practices unless the NLRB General Counsel determines that a complaint should be issued. But labor law decisions are made almost every working day of the year in unfair labor practice proceedings (and, to a lesser extent, in representation elections). Some of these decisions are very important and precedent setting.

What are "unfair labor practices?" As noted earlier, both employers and labor organizations may engage in such practices. Employers' unfair labor practices were written into the law in 1935 and have remained unchanged. An employer is prohibited from interfering with, restraining, or coercing employees in any way in connection with their right to engage in concerted activities, to protest working conditions, and to join labor organizations for the purpose of collective bargaining (or to refrain from any of these things). The union may not restrain or coerce workers in the exercise of their rights protected under the statute (the language here is slightly less ambitious than that applied to employers). Surveillance of union activities, use of union "spies," interrogation of employees about union activities, threatening employees for being involved in the union, and promising benefits if employees desist from union activity are among the prohibited employer actions.[1] Indeed in 1980 the NLRB held that an employer may not lawfully "initiate questioning about employees' union sentiments even where the employees are open and known union supporters and the inquiries are unaccompanied by threats or promises."[2] However, in 1984 the Board, characterizing its earlier position as a per se condemnation of interrogation inconsistent with Board precedent,[3] held that such an approach "ignored the reality of the workplace" and that interrogations could be viewed as unlawful only with reference to "all of the circumstances."[4]

The rules relating to employer conduct regarding inquiries about union support applied to relationships between employers and incumbent unions, as well as the unorganized workplace. In a 5–4 decision authored by Justice Thurgood Marshall,[5] the Court has held that the Board's position, which does not presume lack of union support because the strikebreakers have taken the jobs of the strikers, is an appropriate reading of the Act. This decision was joined in by Chief Justice William Rehnquist who expressed the view that an employer should be allowed to poll employees with regard to their support for the union.[6] The Board's view as expressed in *Texas Petrochemicals Corp.*[7] is that employers can only legitimately poll workers about their continued support for an incumbent union if they have "reasonable doubt" about the union's majority status. The Board noted that in determining whether an employer may petition the Board for the decertification of an incumbent union or whether it may withdraw recognition from a union altogether,[8] it will apply the same standards applicable to a poll.[9] Appropriate notice of the poll must be given to the employees because of the potential for a ". . . blitzkrieg effort [through which] an employer could rid itself of a low profile, majority union."[10]

Although the Supreme Court has yet to resolve the interrogation issue that is enmeshed with the case law on polling, it has held in *NLRB v. Exchange Parts Co.*[11] that the bestowal of benefits during a union organizational campaign is unlawful. Said the Court: "The danger inherent in well-timed increases in benefits is the suggestion of a fist inside the velvet glove. Employees are not likely to miss the inference that the source of benefits now conferred is also the source from which future benefits must flow and which may dry up if it is not obliged."[12] Similarly an NLRB election may be set aside and a new election ordered where a union waives its initiation fees for those who sign up with the union before the election.[13]

At the same time employers have both a constitutional and a statutory right of free speech, although they may not use it to coerce employees or to dissuade them from union affiliation through the promise of benefits. But it is frequently impossible for the NLRB to determine whether an employer's statement—such as "if the union wins the election, its demands will require me to close the plant"—is coercive or merely an economic prophecy about which the workers should be informed before making an intelligent decision. What is an economic prophecy to a tough truck driver in Detroit may be coercive to a textile mill worker in South Carolina.[14]

Neither may an employer provide financial assistance to a labor organization.[15] If the NLRB finds that an employer has done so, it must issue an order to cease and desist.[16]

Yet these provisions, enacted at the time that the Wagner Act regarded a labor-management system as naturally adversarial rather than cooperative, have posed considerable problems in recent years. In *Electromation, Inc.,*[17] the Board held that it was unlawful for an employer to constitute a so-called action committee. The Board held that if the employee committee, in this case the action committee, (1) provided for employee participation, (2) had a purpose to deal with employers, (3) concerned itself with conditions of employment that were the statutory subjects, and (4) involved a committee or plan that was in some way representative of the employees, then the Board would be called upon to determine whether unlawful domination or assistance existed. In this case the Board found unlawful "domination" because it was the employer's idea to create the action committee, the employer drafted the goals of the committee and the employer provided financial assistance for it. But the decision left open the question of whether other committees that focus open "quality" or "efficiency" might be lawful. Moreover it did not address the question of so-called cooperative efforts where a union is already on the scene as exclusive bargaining representative.[18]

Here, as with other unfair labor practices, the NLRB also orders the party that has acted unlawfully to post notices at its premises in conspicuous places so that the matter will be brought to the attention of the employees.[19] The notices are posted almost automatically in the United States, but in Japan this is done much less often (although that country has unfair labor practices provisions in its law by virtue of the 1945 American occupation). In Japan the posting of a notice seems to be more unacceptable or harmful to an employer's reputation.

An American employer may not assist in the creation of a labor organization or in its attempt to gain recognition. If the NLRB finds that an employer has done so, it may order that the employer withdraw recognition from the organization, or even that the organization be "disestablished" (completely eliminated).[20]

An employer may not discriminate in connection with working conditions against workers because of their union membership or lack thereof. However, a union may negotiate with an employer a collective bargaining agreement that includes a "union security clause" requiring that workers pay periodic dues and initiation fees as a condition of employment. If a worker refuses the union's request to pay, he or she may be dismissed from employment (unless the worker's objection is religious). This form of union security agreement is frequently referred to as a "union shop" or "agency shop"—as distinguished from a "closed shop," which requires that a worker become a union member prior to being hired. The closed shop was outlawed by the Taft-Hartley amendments.[21] States may prohibit the negotiation of any such union security agreements, and twenty-one of them have enacted "right-to-work" legislation accomplishing this objective.[22] (Some regard "right-to-work" as a misnomer; the legislation does not provide for any right to work, but it does protect workers who do not wish to pay union dues from dismissal.)

In no situation is a union security agreement imposed by law. Where there is no right-to-work legislation, labor and management are free to enter voluntarily into such agreements. The unions have argued, with a good deal of persuasiveness, that such agreements are necessary inasmuch as the union has a duty of fair representation to bargain for all employees in the bargaining unit regardless of their union affiliation or lack thereof. Workers who do not have to pay dues receive the same benefits as those who do, and therefore have a financial advantage over dues-paying workers. The unions refer to such workers as "free riders."

Other countries have grappled with this problem. In Britain the Trade Union and Labor Relations Act of 1976 provided that an employee could be dismissed pursuant to a closed-shop agreement unless the worker had religious objections. However, the Employment Act of 1980 broadened the grounds for objection to conscience or deeply held personal conviction. (In the United States a 1980 amendment to the NLRA also provides for religious objections, and it seems possible that the law may be interpreted to protect personally held "religious or moral convictions.")[23] An employee could also refuse to join if he or she held a job classification prior to the closed shop and refused to join thereafter. Finally, 80 percent of the workers had to approve a closed shop entered into after August 15, 1980. (In the United States a majority of workers may vote to "deauthorize" a union security agreement and thus prohibit its negotiation by the union.) The Employment Act of 1982 provided that where ballots were conducted for the first time on August 15, 1980, or thereafter, the dismissal of a worker under a closed-shop agreement would be unfair where support for the agreement of 80 percent of employees entitled to vote or 85 percent of those voting had not been evidenced within the past five years. The 1982 statute also protected employees who have been "unreasonably" excluded or expelled from membership against dismissal under a closed shop agreement. But the Employment Acts of 1988 and 1990 have made it unlawful to either refuse to hire an applicant or dismiss a worker because of union membership, thus outlawing the closed and union shops in Britain altogether.

The closed shop is unlawful in Germany and France—in the former country this is due to constitutional guarantees of liberty. In Sweden, although it is lawful, most unions and employers do not appear to require membership as a condition of employment.

In the United States other unfair labor practice provisions prohibit the employer from retaliating against a worker who has cooperated with the NLRB or testified in an NLRB hearing. And, finally, the employer is obliged to bargain in good faith with a union that has been designated by a majority of the employees in an appropriate unit as their exclusive bargaining agent. The difficult concept of good faith is described in more detail below.

The Taft-Hartley amendments have imposed unfair labor practice restrictions on unions as well as employers. As noted earlier, the union may not "restrain and coerce" employees. Therefore a union may not lawfully engage in violence, disorder, or mass picketing that interferes with the movement of employees or the public into and out of the employer's property or premises. Of course the states and localities may prosecute criminal conduct, and to a limited extent, the federal government is the prosecutor (e.g., in cases of violence committed in connection with extortion[24] and other criminal acts).[25]

A union may not cause an employer to discriminate against a worker merely because he or she is not a union member. (Outside of the union security context, this situation generally arises in connection with a union's encouraging an employer to discriminate against workers of another rival union.)

A union is obliged to bargain with an employer in good faith. The proponents of the Taft-Hartley amendments were concerned that certain strong unions had adopted a "take it or leave it" attitude in their dealings with employers. A number of unions would simply come to the bargaining table and present the area contract (the contract negotiated with most employers in the area). Where the employer was small and without economic power, the union expected no discussion or negotiation. Sometimes a union would simply throw a proposed contract on the table and tell the employer to sign it. The obligation of unions as well as employers to bargain was intended to cure this problem.

Unions are also obliged not to engage in "secondary boycotting." A secondary boycott (frequently accompanied by picketing) is intended to force a second or secondary employer to refrain from doing business with a primary employer with whom the union has a dispute over, for instance, recognition, wages, or conditions of employment. Like the union-shop–closed-shop issue, the issue of secondary boycotts is deeply divisive. Free societies want to protect both solidarity and innocent third parties. In Britain the Employment Act of 1980 made union officials and members liable to damage suits where employees engage in picketing at establishments or locations where they are not employed. The 1982 act made unions themselves liable for injunctive relief or damages where the conduct was authorized or endorsed by a responsible person. But the Employment Act of 1990 has amended the 1982 statute so as to make trade unions liable in damage actions for acts of all of their officials, including shop stewards and committees, unless the union effectively repudiates them.

Secondary economic pressure of any kind can create liability unless it is targeted at supplies going to or from the business with the dispute, or unless the struck work is transferred to a second employer. In the United States, when secondary boycott charges are filed, the NLRB is obliged to give them investigative priority. If the regional office finds cause to believe that the statute's secondary boycott provisions are being violated, it must immediately petition the federal district court for a temporary injunction against the violation. Additionally a party may file suit for damages caused by a secondary boycott. In essence, then, three proceedings can take place: an administrative proceeding of the kind described above that would normally take place in an unfair labor practice matter, a petition for injunctive relief in federal district court, or a suit for damages.

The 1959 Landrum-Griffin amendments[26] to the National Labor Relations Act prohibit the negotiation of "hot cargo" clauses in labor contracts, which allow workers to refuse to handle goods that are "hot" (produced by an employer with whom the union has a dispute). Again the idea is that the union ought not to involve an innocent or neutral employer in a dispute with which that employer has nothing to do. Subcontracting clauses in labor contracts that preclude an employer from contracting out work to nonunion employees are made illegal by this provision. However, labor and management may negotiate contract clauses that forbid subcontracting to employers who provide inferior conditions of employment to their employees if the object of the contractual provision is to preserve work for the bargaining unit's members,[27] and there are provisos in the statute that give the unions more strength in the clothing and construction industries because of the economic peculiarities of those industries.[28] In this situation no provision is made for damage suits as in secondary boycott cases. Similarly there is no provision for temporary injunctive relief, since what is involved is not a work stoppage or picketing but only the existence of an unlawful contract clause.

Another major unfair labor practice protection under the Landrum-Griffin amendments outlaws organizational or reorganizational picketing to secure recognition for the union without the preferred method of selection through a secret ballot vote—or, more specifically, without the support of a majority of workers in the appropriate unit. This procedure was enacted in reaction to the use of "blackmail" picketing to pressure an employer to recognize a union without any consultation with the workers. Congress found that some unions (particularly the International Brotherhood of Teamsters) would often picket a firm (particularly one whose work force was composed of racial minorities), force the employer's recognition, and negotiate an agreement without the workers' interests at heart. The objective was simply to get workers to authorize payroll deductions for union dues.[29] The workers would never hear from the union, and the working conditions (usually substandard) would not change.

Work stoppages arising out of jurisdictional disputes between unions over the same work are unlawful. If labor and management have not negotiated procedures to resolve such a conflict,[30] the NLRB is empowered to do so.[31] As is the case with secondary boycotts, the employer may sue the union in court without utilizing the NLRB's administrative procedures.

The Statute of Limitations

Section 10(b) of the National Labor Relations Act states that the NLRB cannot issue a complaint if the alleged unfair labor practice occurred more than six months before the filing of a charge with the Board.[32] This provision also is part of the Taft-Hartley amendments, and in 1960 the Supreme Court held that maintenance of an agreement containing a union security clause bargained by a minority union[33] was barred by the Act's statute of limitations where the agreement had been executed more than six months in advance of the charge.[34] The decision has not ended litigation on this subject. In 1984 the Board held that it will "henceforth focus on the date of the alleged unlawful act, rather than on the date its consequences become effective, in deciding whether the period for filing a charge under Section 10(b) has expired." Furthermore "[w]here a final adverse employment decision is made and communicated to an employee—whether the decision is nonrenewal of an employment contract, termination, or other alleged discrimination—the employee is in a position to file an unfair labor practice charge and must do so within 6 months of that time rather than wait until the consequences of the act become most painful."[35] Similarly section 10(b) bars a charge where a party has "notice of a clear and unequivocal contract repudiation . . . ." At that point, the moment of repudiation, the

unfair refusal to bargain occurs and the legality of the refusal ". . . depends on the evidence that the parties muster
as to the repudiator's right to take that action at that time."[36]

Filing and Prosecution with the NLRB

Any person can file a charge alleging that a union, or an
employer, or one of its agents has engaged in an unfair labor
practice within the meaning of the National Labor Relations
Act. The NLRB, through its representatives of the General
Counsel at regional offices throughout the United States,
will generally provide such a party with a form in which to
set forth the allegation of a violation of the law. A worker
may fill out the form in the regional office, often with the
assistance of Board officials.

Once the charge is filed, the regional director, acting
under the authority of the General Counsel, will investigate
to determine whether there is cause to believe that the law
has been violated. If there is found to be cause, a complaint
will be issued at the local level;[37] otherwise, the charge will
be dismissed (although generally an attempt will be made
to induce the charging employee to withdraw the charge or
to resolve it through some form of informal settlement).
Between 80 and 90 percent of the charges filed with the
NLRB are resolved through some form of settlement or
withdrawal[38]—most often at the stage when the investigation
has been completed but before anything has taken place
subsequent to the decision to issue a complaint. Indeed, in
1984, 94.6 percent of all cases viewed by the Board as meritorious were settled or withdrawn. If the charge is dismissed,
the charging party may appeal the decision to the General
Counsel in Washington. However, it is rare for a charging
party to prevail in Washington—and quite frequently Washington officials had been directly involved in the initial
decision to dismiss the charge. If the charge is dismissed,
normally that is the end of the matter unless the charge
raises some issue on which the individual can file an action
in court, such as an allegation that the union breached its
duty to represent all its employees within the bargaining unit
fairly, or that the employer violated the collective bargaining

agreement. Such allegations frequently raise issues that are separate and apart from the question of whether a party has committed an unfair labor practice under the National Labor Relations Act.

Theoretically, if there is a conflict in testimony or a question of credibility, the General Counsel should not resolve the factual issue administratively and dismiss the charge. This kind of issue should be resolved in an open hearing subsequent to the issuance of a complaint by the General Counsel. However, in many cases private parties (particularly unions) allege that the General Counsel resolves conflicts of fact administratively and makes it impossible for the matter to be considered in a full hearing, where the examination and cross-examination of witnesses might reveal the truth more effectively.

The General Counsel, as can be seen, has broad discretion. Indeed the courts have thus far held that the General Counsel has plenary authority to determine whether an unfair labor practice complaint should be issued[39]—that is to say, even arbitrary conduct by the General Counsel cannot be reversed by the courts. The Supreme Court has yet to consider this issue.

The issuance of a complaint triggers a hearing before an administrative law judge (they were previously called "trial examiners" but insisted on a more exalted title). These judges, with offices in Washington, San Francisco, New York, and Atlanta, are representatives of the judicial side of the NLRB. They are independent, although they are supposed to follow the precedent and authorities that are decided by the five-person Board.

A hearing is held before the administrative law judge at which the General Counsel's lawyers represent the charging party, and the employer or union charged with the violation appears as a "respondent." Sometimes the charging party will be represented by his or her own lawyer, and it is now established that the charging party is a party to the litigation with the same rights and privileges possessed by the General Counsel and the respondent.[40] The hearing generally takes place in one of the regional NLRB offices. Although the rules of evidence used in the federal district courts apply, the hearing is often more informal than the normal courtroom proceeding. The administrative law judges, like the Board members, are not really judges in the sense that they possess self-enforcing authority and do not wear robes. Although lawyers always represent the Board and usually represent the respondent as well, there is no requirement that one be a lawyer to appear and argue before the administrative law judge or the Board. Very often a union that is the charging party represented by the General Counsel will send a local official or a shop steward to represent its interests, and quite frequently the union's interests are represented more than adequately by such individuals.

The hearing generally takes place on consecutive days without interruption. Generally the notice of hearing states that the hearing is to take place on a designated date, and on each day thereafter until the matter is completed. After the matter is completed, the parties submit briefs to the administrative law judge, and he or she then renders a decision (which is in fact a recommended order). If there are no exceptions or appeals to be taken from the decision of the administrative law judge within twenty days of its issuance, the decision is adopted by the five-member Board in Washington. If exceptions are filed, the transcript, briefs, and other relevant documents are sent to the Board in Washington for consideration and decision. Only about 4 percent of all unfair labor practice charges reach the Board in Washington for a decision.

Although oral argument by the lawyers and other representatives is permitted (in addition to the presentation of evidence through witnesses and exhibits), the five-member Board in Washington rarely hears oral argument. Most of its decisions are based solely on the papers submitted to it subsequent to the decision of the administrative law judge.

Most of the cases involve factual issues relating to alleged discriminatory discharges and dismissals of workers. There is no way that the Board can evaluate these matters more effectively, from a transcript and briefs, than the administrative law judge who actually saw the witnesses, observed their demeanor, and made resolutions relating to credibility. In the vast majority of cases, the administrative law judge's decisions are approved by the Board in their entirety or with only slight modification. The problem here is that a considerable amount of time is consumed by the Board at this stage.

Most cases are decided by three of the Board's five members. The record of the case is filed in the executive secretary's office, and the case is then assigned on a rotation basis. One member is assigned the case. Three members are simultaneously designated to serve on the panel considering the case, and a legal assistant is assigned. Ultimately the Board member and his or her Chief Counsel will become involved in the drafting of the decision, but generally the three representatives of the Board meet first. At this meeting a decision will be made as to whether the Administrative Law Judge's decision should be affirmed, affirmed in part, or reversed. If an opinion must be drafted, it will then be put together in the office of the Board member to whom the case was assigned initially. (Often, when the Board affirms the administrative law judge's decision, the opinion will simply state that fact; this is called a "short form" opinion.)

If any Board member thinks a case is important, it will be discussed and considered at a weekly meeting of the members. A vote is taken and an opinion (sometimes a dissenting opinion as well) is written and circulated. In recent years the language used by various Board members where there has been a disagreement on important cases has been rather biting and sharp—at least when one compares it with the language used by the courts.

The Appellate Procedure

Because the NLRB is an administrative agency and not a court, its orders are not self-enforcing. Generally the Board issues an order that the respondent cease and desist from engaging in unlawful conduct. When workers have been discriminatorially discharged, back pay will be awarded. Sometimes respondents will be required to remedy their violations.

Once a decision by the Board has been rendered, one of two things happens. If the Board determines that the respondent is unwilling to comply with the decision, it must file a petition in the court of appeals for the district where the case arose.[41] This court is the appellate level immediately below the Supreme Court. Because of the increasing caseload, there are often delays at this stage of the process as well. It is often months before the Board is able to file a petition for enforcement, and in many circuits a considerable period of time will elapse before the court has an opportunity to hear the case. The respondent or the charging party, if it wishes, may file a petition for a review or an appeal. Subsequent to the decision of the court of appeals, a petition for a writ of *certiorari* or review may be filed with the United States Supreme Court. An overwhelming number of these petitions are not granted. One can readily understand why this is so; approximately 5,000 petitions are filed each year, and the Supreme Court has the time to hear only around 150 of these cases.[42]

Summary

We now have most of the general framework of the National Labor Relations Act, as amended in 1947, and we have also touched on some court rulings and later legislative amendments. Among the subjects covered have been the constitutional basis of the NLRA; the organization of the NLRB and the roles of the Board, the General Counsel, and the regional offices; the jurisdictions of the courts and the NLRB; the extent of the NLRA's coverage; the definition of "labor organization" and the concept of exclusivity; the definition of "appropriate bargaining unit"; the election procedure; the definition of "unfair labor practice" for employer and union activities; and the handling of unfair labor practice charges. As we turn to the establishing of the collective bargaining relationship and to the law's application in that process and in the life of the established relationship, we will be fleshing out the skeleton. The one piece of the structure that we have not yet touched on—remedies—will be better understood afterward.

5

Establishing the Collective Bargaining Relationship: Organization and Recognition

This chapter addresses the problems that arise when a union attempts to establish itself as the exclusive bargaining agent for an appropriate unit of workers.[1] It deals with the tactics labor uses and the restraints the law places upon it. (Of course no precise line can be drawn between the legal tactics that are available to labor and management in the organizational context and those that may be used once the collective bargaining relationship has been established. Accordingly the reader should keep the basic concepts and principles discussed here in mind when reading the succeeding chapters.)

Recruitment and Organization

In an organizational campaign, unions and employers are concerned with union attempts to surmount obstacles to communication with workers, union efforts to protect union adherents in the workplace, the tactics that may be employed, and the circumstances under which recognition can be compelled. Unions recruiting workers will generally make contact with a small group of potential union adherents. At the early stages of a union effort this contact may be made secretly, to make it less likely that the employer will counterattack with antiunion communications or unlawful reprisals.

The names, addresses, and telephone numbers of employees in the unit are important to the union for this purpose, but the NLRB requires the employer to make them available only at a much later stage, after the regional director has ordered an election.[2] Often this is too late. The union needs the information early in the campaign, when secrecy is desirable—long before it seeks access to company property or files a petition. The competing interest is the privacy of the employee who does not want to be bothered by solicitation, letters, and telephone calls.

Sophisticated full-time organizers are often used,[3] and literature on other union-negotiated contracts is sometimes distributed. Sometimes the union will send the employer a list of workers who have signed cards authorizing the union to represent them or indicating the worker's support for an NLRB election. (This will be done where the union believes that management will be less likely to retaliate against union supporters if it is unable to plead ignorance of their identities.) Where union adherents at a small plant are vocal and management imposes disciplinary sanctions upon them, the NLRB will sometimes infer management's knowledge of individual workers' support for the union even though such knowledge cannot be proved. Under this "small plant" doctrine, unlawful motive can be inferred.[4]

Exclusivity and the Obligation to Bargain

Fundamental to an understanding of the rules relating to organizational disputes (and of American labor law generally) are the principles that underlie the doctrine of exclusivity as it has been defined by the Supreme Court. The essential concern of the courts has been that the collective interest should govern over individual advantages once the majority of workers in an appropriate unit have designated the union as their bargaining representative. In large part this rule exists because individual contracts could serve as an obstacle to organization and permit employers to "divide and conquer." Accordingly, the Court held, in *J.I. Case Co. v. NLRB*,[5] that individual contracts of employment cannot be utilized by an employer as a basis for precluding negotiations with the union on the same subject matter. The Court held that an individual hiring contract was "subsidiary" to the terms of a collective bargaining agreement, and that therefore such a contract cannot waive any of the agreement's benefits "any more than a shipper can contract away the benefit of filed tariffs, the insurer the benefit of standard provisions, or the utility customer the benefit of legally established rates."[6] Wherever there was no obligation to bargain with a union, an individual contract could be entered into or relied upon. But, said the Court:

Individual contracts, no matter what the circumstances that justify their execution or what their terms, may not be availed of to defeat or delay the procedures prescribed by the National Labor Relations Act looking to collective bargaining, nor to exclude the contracting employee from a duly ascertained bargaining unit; nor may they be used to forestall bargaining or to limit or condition the terms of the collective agreement. . . .

We are not called upon to say that under no circumstances can an individual enforce an agreement more advantageous than a collective agreement, but we find the mere possibility that such agreements might be made no ground for holding generally that individual contracts may survive or surmount collective ones. The practice and philosophy of collective bargaining looks with suspicion on such advantages. Of course, where there is great variation in circumstances of employment or capacity of employees, it is possible for the collective bargain to prescribe only minimum rates or maximum hours or expressly to leave certain areas open to individual bargaining. But except as so provided, advantages to individuals may prove as disruptive of industrial peace as disadvantages. They are a fruitful way of interfering with organization and choice of representatives; increased compensation, if individually deserved, is often earned at the cost of breaking down some other standard thought to be for the welfare of the group, and always creates the suspicion of being paid at the long range expense of the group as a whole. Such discriminations not infrequently amount to unfair labor practices. The workman is free, if he values his own bargaining position more than that of the group, to vote against representation; but the majority rules, and if it collectivizes the employment bargain, individual advantages or favors will generally in practice go in as a contribution to the collective result.[7]

Of course there are special groups of employees, such as entertainers, professional athletes, and even university professors, who do not fit into the mold of the normal collective bargaining process.

Discriminatory Discipline and Dismissal

The very first problem a union confronts in an organizational campaign is how to protect employees who are dismissed or disciplined. The obvious approach for a union organizer faced with this problem is to file an unfair labor practice charge with the NLRB. But how does a union or an employee prove that the employer has discriminated against the worker because of union activity or other protected activity? The Supreme Court has never squarely addressed or resolved the question of what kind of evidence must be adduced in order to make out discriminatory intent.

The classic case arose in the Court of Appeals for the Third Circuit and involved the problems of one Walter Weigand. As the court said, the case of Walter Weigand was "extraordinary":

If ever a workman deserved summary discharge, it was he. He was under the influence of liquor while on duty. He came to work when he chose and he left the plant and his shift as he pleased. In fact, a foreman on one occasion was agreeably surprised to find Weigand at work and commented upon it. . . . He brought a woman (apparently generally known as the "Duchess") to the rear of the plant yard and introduced some of the employees to her. He took another employee to visit her and when this man got too drunk to be able to go home, punched his time card for him and put him on the table in the representatives' meeting room in the plant in order to sleep off his intoxication. Weigand's immediate superiors demanded again and again that he be discharged, but each time higher officials intervened on Weigand's behalf because as was naively stated he was a "representative" (in an organization that was unlawfully "dominated"). . . .[8]

When Weigand joined the CIO-affiliated union, he was discharged. The NLRB and the court found that the discharge was due to union activity, despite the employer's contention that it was based on accumulated offenses. Thus Weigand was ordered reinstated. (Some courts have awarded back pay to such individuals but refused to reinstate them[9]—and the Board and the courts have taken the view that where postdischarge conduct is indefensible, the Act's remedial protection is not available for the purpose of reinstatement.)[10]

The Supreme Court has addressed the troublesome issue of mixed motives (i.e., when the employer has both valid and unlawful reasons for dismissal) in both free-speech and NLRA cases. The Court has held than an employer, once confronted with a showing that constitutionally protected conduct in the form of free speech played a "substantial" role in the decision not to rehire, could still show by a preponderance of evidence that it would have reached the same decision in the absence of the exercise of protected conduct.[11] The test is whether the employer would have dismissed or not hired "but for" the speech, where the speech was the "primary reason for the dismissal or refusal to rehire."[12] I have criticized this decision as unduly restrictive in the context of First Amendment litigation, and my judgment is that the same is true in connection with any attempt to apply it to NLRA cases.[13] Quite frequently the employer has more than one reason for a dismissal. The Court's recent rulings make it difficult for an employee with a less than unblemished record to succeed in such cases.

Nonetheless, the NLRB adopted the Supreme Court's test in First Amendment cases for purposes of the NLRA in *Wright Line*.[14] " . . . we shall require that the General Counsel make a *prima facie* showing sufficient to support the inference that protected conduct was a 'motivating factor' in the employer's decision. Once this is established, the burden will shift to the employer to demonstrate that the same action would have taken place even in the absence of the protected conduct."[15] The NLRB stressed that the General Counsel still has the burden of producing the preponderance of evidence to establish a violation—the burden that the General Counsel assumes in any unfair labor practice proceeding before the Board. As a practical matter, however, the slight burden that is thrust upon the General Counsel as part of the *prima facie* case and the explicit burden on the company to come forward with reasons for the action may give the General Counsel access to important information at an early point in the hearing and thus a competitive advantage that he or she would not otherwise enjoy.

The Supreme Court unanimously affirmed the Board's position in *NLRB v. Transportation Management Corp.*[16] Justice Byron White, the author of the Court's opinion, specifically approved of the Board's burden-shifting rules relating to the employer's obligation to produce evidence subsequent to a showing that illegal conduct was a substantial or motivating factor in the treatment of the worker. Said the Court:

> The employer is a wrongdoer; he has acted out of a motive that is declared illegitimate by the statute. It is fair that he bear the risk that the influence of legal and illegal motives cannot be separated, because he knowingly created the risk and because the risk was created not by innocent activity but by his own wrongdoing.[17]

The Court stated that the proviso in section 10(c) of the Taft-Hartley Act that seems to separate (and thus put out of the law's reach) discharges "for cause" from those interdicted by the statute has no applicability to mixed-motive cases. Said the Court:

> The "for cause" proviso was not meant to apply to cases in which both legitimate and illegitimate causes contributed to the discharge. . . . The amendment was sparked by a concern over the Board's perceived practice of inferring from the fact that someone was active in a union that he was fired because of antiunion animus even though the worker had been guilty of gross misconduct.[18]

Where employer conduct is "inherently destructive" of employees' self-organization rights, no proof of an antiunion discriminatory intent is necessary to establish that the law has been violated.[19] In some circumstances the focus will be on the impact of the employer's conduct on the employee.[20]

Union Access to Company Property

One of the major problems a union is confronted with in an organizational campaign is how to communicate with the employees it seeks to organize. The leading case in this regard is *Republic Aviation Corp. v. NLRB,*[21] in which the employer had prohibited all solicitation in the factory or offices on company property. An employee who had been warned of the rule solicited union membership in the plant by passing out application cards to employees during his own free time on the lunch break. He was dismissed. Three other employees were dismissed for wearing UAW-CIO caps and union steward buttons in the plant after being requested to remove them. The NLRB found that the dismissal of the workers, and also the rule itself, constituted unfair labor practices, and that therefore the employer's conduct had improperly interfered with the employees right to "organize mutual aid without employer interference."[22] The special problem posed in this case was that there was no evidence that the plant's location made solicitation away from company property ineffective in reaching prospective union members. Thus the employer contended that the union could communicate elsewhere without interfering with the company's property rights. However, the Supreme Court approved the NLRB's conclusion that the employer had no business justification for precluding the activity outside of work hours and that such a rule could therefore be presumed to be an "unreasonable impediment to self-organization" and unnecessary in connection with the maintenance of production or discipline.[23]

A number of basic issues involving employee activity and the promulgation of rules by the employer have plagued the Board for years. The Board had concluded that employer promulgated rules prohibiting solicitation and distribution of literature during "working time"—even when promulgated in conjunction with prohibition against activity during "working hours"—were presumptively invalid because of their ambiguity;[24] that is, the worker would not know of his or her right to engage in union activity during paid lunch breaks and rest periods. In 1984 the Board, with Member Don Zimmerman dissenting, overruled this decision and held that rules couched in terms of "working time" are lawful.[25] The Board's view was that the meaning of "working time" and "working hours" within the context of no-solicitation rules had "attained substantial understanding," and that "many unions and employers had fashioned their instructions, policies and rules" so as to make clear the availability of paid rest periods for union activity.[26] A majority of the Board has also held that no-solicitation rules that make an exception for charitable solicitation are not per se invalid.[27] Disparate enforcement of such a rule, in contrast to a "small number of isolated beneficent acts"[28] or "an employer's toleration of isolated beneficent solicitation,"[29] can run afoul of the law.

A few years after *Republic Aviation,* when the Supreme Court considered the access of nonemployee union organizers to company property, it looked at the matter quite differently—even though the employees' right to communicate, albeit with more expert outside assistance, was involved. In this context the Court did consider the availability of alternate avenues of communication to be relevant.[30] In this case the NLRB had noted that other means of communication (the mail, telephones, etc.), as well as the homes of the workers, were open to the union. The Court, which found that the situation did not involve workers who were isolated from communication attempts or who lived on company property,[31] stated:

. . . when the inaccessibility of employees makes ineffective the reasonable attempts by nonemployees to communicate with them through the usual channels, the right to exclude from property has been required to yield to the extent needed to permit communication of information on the right to organize.
. . . no . . . obligation [similar to that owed to the employees in connection with their right to solicit during nonworking hours on company property] is owed nonemployee organizers. Their access to company property is governed by a different consideration. The right of self-organization depends in some measure on the ability of employees to learn the advantages of self-organization from others. Consequently, if the location of a plant and the living quarters of the employees place the employees beyond the reach of reasonable union efforts to communicate with them, the employer must allow the union to approach his employees on his property. No such conditions are shown in these records.[32]

However, as the Supreme Court noted in another context, "The place of work is a place uniquely appropriate for dissemination of views concerning the bargaining representative and the various options open to the employees."[33]

In 1978 the Supreme Court concluded that the right of workers to distribute literature on nonworking portions of the employer's property extends to disputes that involve neither organizational nor bargaining disputes.[34] The Court held that the distribution of the union newsletter expressing opposition to a state's right-to-work law and to a presidential veto of an increase in the minimum wage fell within the "right to engage in other concerted activities for the purpose of . . . mutual aid or protection" protected by section 7 of the NLRA. On the other hand, "purely political tracts" are unprotected, even though the election of political candidates, for instance, can have an effect on employment conditions.[35]

Another group of cases involving union access to company property has to do with "quasi-public" property or facilities (those generally open to customers or the public). In *Central Hardware Co. v. NLRB*[36] the Supreme Court was confronted with a rule prohibiting nonemployees from soliciting in the parking lots of retail establishments. The NLRB held that this prohibition was overly broad and violated the NLRA. In this case the Board relied on a Court decision that a shopping center was the functional equivalent of a business district, in which First Amendment rights can normally be asserted. But the Court, in an opinion written by Justice Lewis Powell, ruled that this decision had no applicability to the NLRA.[37] The Court characterized the principle involved in the issue of the access of nonemployee union organizers to employers' property as follows:

This principle requires a "yielding" of property rights only in the context of an organization campaign. Moreover, the allowed intrusion on property rights is limited to that necessary to facilitate the exercise of employees' [section] 7 rights. After the requisite need for access to the employer's property has been shown, the access is limited to (i) union organizers; (ii) prescribed nonworking areas of the employer's premises and (iii) the duration of organization activity. In short, the principle of accommodation . . . is limited to labor organization campaigns, and the yielding of property rights it may require is both temporary and minimal.[38]

The Court stated that precedent relative to "large" shopping centers was not applicable to every private property open to the public. Said the Court: "Such an argument could be made with respect to almost every retail and service establishment in the country, regardless of size and location."[39] Accordingly Powell concluded that the Board and appellate court had erred in relying on the shopping-center precedent to establish protection for union access.

The next important case was *Hudgens v. NLRB*,[40] which concerned a group of union members who, while engaged in peaceful primary picketing within a privately owned shopping center, had been threatened with arrest for criminal trespass. Preliminarily Justice Potter Stewart, speaking for the Court, noted that the rights and liabilities of the parties in this case were "dependent exclusively" upon the National Labor Relations Act and not upon the First Amendment. This arbitrary determination eliminated any potential for confusion arising out of inconsistency between constitutional and statutory standards. The Court noted that early decisions involving access to company property had involved a determination of what the "proper accommodation" would be in a given case.

The Court stated that there were differences among some of the earlier decisions that involved organizational activity carried on by nonemployees on the employers' property. The Court pointed to three such differences and remanded the case to the NLRB. Said the Court: "The context of the [section] 7 activity in the present case was different in several respects which may or may not be relevant in striking the proper balance. First, it involves the lawful economic strike activity rather than organizational activity. . . . Second, the [section] 7 activity here was carried on by Butler's employees (albeit not employees of its shopping center store), not by outsiders. . . . Third, the property interests impinged upon in this case were not those of the employer against whom the [section] 7 activity was directed, but of another."[41]

Upon remand the NLRB took the position that economic activity of the kind involved in *Hudgens* warranted "at least equal deference" as organizational picketing. The Board further took the position that the pickets were entitled to at least as much protection as nonemployee organizers in some of the cases that had appeared before the Court previously. But the Board noted that the messages of organizational campaigns and economic strikes were aimed at different audiences. In *Hudgens* the pickets were attempting to communicate with the public that would do business with the employer as well as with the employees who had not joined the strike. Said the Board:

> One difference between organizational campaigns as opposed to economic strike situations is that in the former the section 7 rights being protected are those of the intended audience (the employees sought to be organized), and in the latter the section 7 rights are those of the persons attempting to communicate with their intended audience, the public as well as the employees. A further distinction between organizational and economic strike activity becomes apparent when the focus shifts to the characteristics of the audience at which the section 7 activity in question is directed. In an organizational campaign, the group of employees whose support the union seeks is specific and often is accessible by means of communication other than direct entry of the union organizers onto the employer's property, such as meeting employees on the street, home visits, letters, and telephone calls.[42]

The NLRB noted that the general public was the "more important component of the audience" and that often the mass media were not "reasonable" means for publicizing a labor dispute. With regard to the Court's statement that the property rights impinged upon were not those of the employer against whom the picketing was aimed, the Board noted that the property, although privately owned, was open to the public and was the equivalent of sidewalks, which are normally public property. In this regard the Board, which since *Hudgens* had extended those principles to property such as the interiors of private banks, seems to have been reviving a First Amendment approach that the Supreme Court had used in connection with picketing on private property in shopping centers.[43] Moreover the Court may have given union activity on employer property more protection by concluding that the states may expand the right to distribute literature (and presumably to picket) at a shopping center, despite the owner's constitutional interest in his property, under circumstances where access would be denied under federal law.[44]

Hudgens has spawned litigation about union access that has come back to the Supreme Court and may do so yet again. The NLRB, with the approval of the Ninth Circuit Court, has held that a union's picketing of the forty-sixth floor of a bank (in an economic dispute) with protected by the NLRA;[45] communication there was regarded as more effective by both the Board and the Ninth Circuit Court. But in another case, one involving organizational solicitation and the employer's refusal to supply employees' names and addresses, the Fourth Circuit Court reversed the Board's holding that the union had no other effective alternative. The court characterized the union's efforts as "lackadaisical."[46]

The Board has attempted to fashion rules relating to nonemployee organizer access to private property,[47] the most recent effort being the *Jean Country*[48] decision. In this case the Board held that the availability of reasonable alternative means of access to private property is a factor that must be considered in each access case. This does not mean that in each case the evidence must establish that the union actually attempted to use reasonable alternatives but rather that objectively the evidence must establish that "reasonably effective alternative means [access to private property] were unavailable in the circumstances."[49] The Board stated that it would be the "exceptional case where the use of newspapers, radio and television will be feasible alternatives to direct contact."[50] Section 7 rights, which are "central" in the spectrum established in *Hudgens,* are the right to organize and to protest unfair labor practices. In addition to the nature of the right ". . . the identity of the employer to which the right is directly related (e.g., the employer with whom a union has a primary dispute), the relationship of the employer or other target to the property to which access is sought, the identity of the audience to which communications concerning the Section 7 right are directed, and the manner in which the activity related to that right is carried out." Factors to be taken into account in assessing property rights are ". . . the use to which the property is put, the restrictions, if any, that are imposed on public access to the property, and the property's relative size and openness." The Board stated that quasi-public traits tend to lessen the private nature of the property because it is apparent that the public is extended a broad invitation to come on the property, and not necessarily with the specific purpose of purchasing a particular product or service."[51] Relevant factors on alternative means of communication include ". . . the desirability of avoiding the enmeshment of neutrals in labor disputes, the safety of attempting communications at alternative public sites, the burden and expense of nontrespassory communication alternatives, and, most significantly, the extent to which the exclusive use of the nontrespassory alternatives would dilute the effectiveness of the message."[52]

However, in a far-reaching opinion, the Supreme Court in *Lechmere v. NLRB,* by 6–3 vote, has reversed the *Jean Country* rule and its balanced protection for nonemployee organizers.[53] Stated Justice Thomas for the majority: "By its plain terms . . . the NLRA confers rights only on *employees,* not on unions or their nonemployee organizers."[54] The Court's view in *Lechmere* was that only where access to employees outside an employer's property was "infeasible" did it become necessary to balance employee and employer's rights—and that infeasibility could be established only as a narrow exception to the general rule, namely where employees were located in isolated facilities such as logging camps, mining camps, and mountain resort hotels. There, said the Court, employees might be ". . . isolated from ordinary flow of information that characterizes our society."[55] Particularly instructive was the Court's view of what could constitute alternative means of communication. Said Justice Thomas, ". . . signs (displayed for example from the public grassy strip adjoining . . . [the employers] parking lot) would have informed the employees about the union's organizational efforts."[56] The Court was of the view that a contrary rule would be aimed at providing success for the unions, not access to employees.

In the wake of *Jean Country*, secondary handbilling which is aimed at following the struck product to a secondary situs has had been held to be protected.[57] But the Court of Appeals for the Ninth Circuit has held that because the exception applying to nonemployee organizers who are attempting to reach employees is a narrow one, no access to private property may be provided where union organizers are trying to advertise their dispute to customers.[58] However, it would appear that the reasoning of *Lechmere* is applicable to the ways in which nonemployee organizers would reach employees and not customers and that therefore the Board's pre-*Lechmere* rules might remain valid as they applied to the public or customers. Nonetheless, the Court's hostility to union access on private property supports the Ninth Circuit's view in *Sparks Nugget*.

Aside from isolated facilities such as those described by Justice Clarence Thomas, the only circumstances in which nonemployee organizer appear now to have access to private property are where the property is governmental or of a governmental nature,[59] or where the employer has allowed other organizations—other than the employer itself[60]—to have access.[61]

Despite the doctrine of preemption, unions may encounter still other obstacles to access from state criminal-trespass statutes. Thus the role of the states is double-edged, for the Supreme Court has held (in a divided vote) that criminal-trespass statutes may be used by owners against union organizers. Generally the American doctrine of preemption, because of the supremacy of federal law, deprives the states of authority to act in areas such as labor-management relations where Congress has legislated extensively.[62] But in cases of trespass the owner may call on the police or other law-enforcement authorities for assistance—possibly even if the NLRB were to rule that union organizers have the right to be on the property in question.[63] Since the Board's administrative process generally moves less quickly than state courts, the employer may prevail regardless of how firmly the union activities are protected by the National

Labor Relations Act unless the Board enjoins the state court proceedings.

In 1991 the Board held that once the General Counsel issues a complaint[64] on a *Jean Country* theory, a state court proceeding is preempted by federal law[65] and thus may be enjoined. These decisions remain intact under *Lechmere* notwithstanding its repudiation of the former decision.[66] The impact of course is far more limited than it was prior to 1992.

Even though most of the prominent litigation on organizers' access involves nonemployees, there remain a considerable number of areas for dispute involving solicitation of employees by employees and the right of employees to distribute literature. As we have seen, there is a presumption of illegality when an employer bans solicitation by employees outside of their working hours. However, this presumption does not apply in the case of retail department stores. There the employer may prohibit all solicitation in the selling area during working and nonworking hours.[67] Similar broad nonsolicitation rules are permitted in restaurants and fast-food outlets.[68] After the NLRA was amended to include nonprofit health-care institutions,[69] the full NLRB ruled unanimously that a broad nonsolicitation rule was presumptively invalid "in areas other than immediate patient care areas such as lounges and cafeterias."[70] The Supreme Court approved of solicitation in hospital cafeterias and coffee shops;[71] it was not persuaded by the argument that, since the public and patients were admitted to the cafeteria of the hospital, the rule for restaurants should apply. The main function of a hospital is patient care and therapy, not the serving of cafeteria food, and the cafeteria is a natural gathering place for employees and can be used for solicitation with little interference with patient care. Thus the balancing of employees' rights to organize and employers' rights to maintain discipline here favors allowing a presumption that a ban on solicitation in the cafeteria is illegal. However, in a later case the Supreme Court refused to extend this principle to sitting rooms and corridors, and expressed serious doubts that the presumption of illegality applied with respect to those areas.[72]

Although it appears that employees do not possess a statutory right to post union notices on bulletin boards,[73] an employer may not deny employees the right to post union notices while permitting other noncompany information to appear.[74] This practice constitutes unlawful discrimination.

Finally, it is important to note that the NLRB has held that nonemployee organizers may have access to company property to respond to an employer's speech made to a "captive audience" of workers during work hours where the employer has a legitimate but very broad nonsolicitation rule.[75] In these circumstances the Board found a glaring imbalance in opportunities for organizational communication and an interference with the right to organize.

Organizational Picketing

For the union, burdens as well as benefits attend organizational picketing. In the 1960 *Curtis Bros.* decision[76] the Supreme Court, speaking through Justice William Brennan, held that an attempt by a trade union representing a minority of the workers to impose a bargaining obligation on an employer through picketing was not an unfair labor practice within the meaning of the Taft-Hartley amendments. The argument of the employer and the NLRB before the Court was that the picketing inevitably violated the free choice of employees to join or refrain from union activity, which is protected by the NLRA. The Court, referring to some of the constitutional cases that have protected picketing, noted that "in the sensitive area of peaceful picketing Congress has dealt explicitly with isolated evils which experience has established flow from such picketing."[77] Accordingly the Court was unwilling to find a basis for statutory violation in the absence of the "clearest indication in the legislative history" of the statute.[78]

Amendments passed by Congress in 1959 purported to regulate organizational picketing in certain key respects. The idea was to permit the NLRB to enjoin picketing aimed at subverting a valid collective bargaining relationship already entered into with another union and organizational picketing aimed at reversing a union's defeat at the ballot box within twelve months of the election. The most complicated of these picketing regulations in this respect is section 8(b)(7)(C),[79] which limits picketing aimed at obtaining recognition to a "reasonable period of time" not to exceed thirty days. Informational picketing is exempted from the statutory prohibition unless it has the effect of interfering with deliveries. An expeditious election is held without the usual showing of interest prerequisite and without an administrative hearing about an appropriate unit because of the need for prompt relief. Picketing and strikes can cause irreparable harm to an employer.

The NLRB and the courts have taken the position that area-wage-standard picketing (picketing protesting wages and working conditions that are inferior to those offered by comparable employers in the geographic labor market) is not prohibited by the NLRA, and recent Board decisions have affirmatively protected employees who engage in such picketing from discipline and discharge under the *Jean Country* doctrine.[80] Picketing, although it may not be engaged in for an unreasonable period of time with a view toward obtaining recognition through economic pressure rather than the ballot box, may be engaged in if it is informational in nature. Where picketing, despite unlawful recognitional intent, is simply an attempt to advertise a dispute to the public, the Board cannot find an unfair labor practice unless there is more than isolated interference with deliveries. This rule has meant that a union, with competent counsel, can easily escape the organizational-picketing provisions of the NLRA unless the picketing proves disruptive.

There are two particular difficulties with the restrictions on organizational picketing. On the one hand, Congress was deeply concerned with prohibiting "blackmail" picketing, which was often engaged in by labor. On the other hand, organizational picketing occurs in a significant number of legitimate situations, particularly in the South and in rural areas where the union has a genuine concern with the plight of workers who need protection. Employers' counterattacks against organizational drives, sometimes involving unlawful tactics, frequently make it difficult for a union to demonstrate majority support through the ballot box. Under such circumstances picketing to dissuade employees from working and others from doing business with the employer may be a legitimate weapon.

Moreover the Supreme Court has attempted to establish a demarcation line between different kinds of picketing that occur in organizational efforts. The Court has seen "publicity" picketing as the kind of expression of thought that is protected by the First Amendment.[81] However, "signal" picketing, which is not only aimed at employees but also designed to produce an immediate response on the part of union members who are subject to union disciplinary sanctions, is deemed to be conduct that can be controlled and regulated by Congress and sometimes the states.[82] Specifically the "informational picketing" proviso is meant to protect "publicity" picketing against government prohibition, even though it might be part of a union effort to secure recognition without an NLRB-approved election. The thinking of Congress was that an unduly broad prohibition against organizational picketing might not only be bad policy (because of the legitimate situation referred to above) but might also be constitutionally deficient.

Secondary Picketing

Secondary picketing is another tactic that has created legal difficulties for the trade-union movement. If the union is successful, the primary target of the boycott is more likely to settle on the union's terms or to recognize the union if the dispute has a recognitional objective. Such disputes can arise both where a union has recognitional objectives and where there is an established relationship with the primary employer and the dispute is about wages, hours, and working conditions.

As noted above, the Norris-LaGuardia Act reversed the common-law view of secondary boycotts and their illegality that had been accepted by the Supreme Court. But Congress, through the 1947 Taft-Hartley amendments, revived the secondary-boycott prohibitions both for the purposes of NLRB administrative hearings and for the purposes of damage suits in federal and state courts, though it did not do so in connection with disputes arising under the Railway Labor Act.[83] The Board, as with organizational picketing, is obligated to give investigative priority to unfair labor practice charges involving secondary picketing and is mandated to proceed directly in a federal district court to obtain an injunction if the regional attorney in the NLRB field office has reasonable cause to believe that a violation is being committed. Additionally secondary economic pressure undertaken by virtue of a so-called most-favored-nation agreement obligating the union to get the same or better from the secondary target than have been obtained from the primary target, can still constitute a conspiracy in violation of antitrust law.[84]

The NLRA then is designed to protect third parties who are innocent or wholly unconcerned with the dispute in question. But who is an innocent party? Who is wholly unconcerned? In a sense even the general public has an interest if it will pay less for an employer's goods if the union loses a strike. On the other hand, many employers who have commercial relationships with the primary target of a strike have absolutely nothing to do with the dispute, and therefore it would seem unfair to involve them.

As written, the NLRA purports to prohibit economic pressure—or the threat thereof[85]—aimed at bringing about a cessation of business between the primary employer and other employers. Literally this might mean that a union-established picket line at the primary employer's premises that was intended to dissuade the importation of strikebreakers by another company to perform the striking workers' jobs would be unlawful because the object would be to obtain a cessation of business between the primary employer and the company importing the strikebreakers. However, the Supreme Court has not read the statute that way.[86] The first exception to the literal language of the statute is based on the "ally" doctrine, which has permitted workers to picket a secondary employer when the union is pursuing work that would have been performed by the primary employer's workers before the strike but has been farmed out to the secondary employer.[87]

Organizational disputes can affect more than one employer and thus create secondary problems in other contexts. The 1959 amendments make unlawful collective bargaining agreements containing "hot cargo" clauses (which, as mentioned above, permit employees to refuse to handle goods produced by an employer with whom the union has a dispute—e.g., one whose products do not carry a union label) or subcontracting clauses (which preclude contracting out work to a nonunion employer).[88] The reason is that such contractual provisions have a secondary objective: to influence the labor relations policies by organizing workers through a third innocent party, the employer who has signed the contract. On the other hand, subcontracting clauses that preserve the bargaining unit's work (e.g., agreements that prohibit subcontracting work to employers who provide substandard working conditions) are lawful.[89]

However, the Supreme Court held in the landmark case of *NLRB v. Denver Building Trades*[90] that, where an object of picketing is to interfere with the secondary employer and its employees and their relationship with the primary employer, a violation of the statute can be made out. This case arose in the context of "common situs" picketing and multiemployer construction facilities, where a picket line at the primary employer's facilities would necessarily affect the secondary employees by attempting to persuade all employees to refuse to work. This would place great pressure on the primary employer to accede to union demands and would stand a good chance of success—particularly because employee response in the construction industry is likely to be automatic and triggered by a "signal."[91] The difficulty in reconciling *Denver Building Trades* with the ally doctrine and the Court's subsequent holding that common situs picketing at an industrial establishment where the employer maintains separate gates for outside contractors does not violate the statute[92] has created an anomaly that is inequitable for building-trades workers. On an number of occasions (most recently in 1977)[93] this has led the AFL-CIO Building Trades Department to press for legislation that would reverse *Denver Building Trades* and permit common situs picketing. The concern of the building trades in this regard has increased in recent years as nonunion construction work has spread, but every effort on their part has been unsuccessful. Even when both houses of Congress passed a common situs bill, President Gerald Ford vetoed it.[94] The prevailing view has accepted the employer's position that if *Denver Building Trades* were to be reversed, unions would have considerable power to organize an entire building site by involving employers (other subcontractors) who have no interest in the dispute.

It would appear as though the construction unions have another advantage not possessed by other labor organizations: Congress exempted the construction industry, along with the clothing industry, from the secondary-boycott prohibitions contained in the statute's treatment of "hot cargo" clauses. However, the Supreme Court seems to have said that the construction industry proviso does not immunize from the secondary-boycott prohibitions all union picketing intended to obtain an agreement under which the general contractor could subcontract work to employers who had signed contracts with the picketing union.[95] In *Woelke & Romero Framing, Inc. v. NLRB*,[96] the Court indicated that some kind of collective bargaining relationship between the picketing union and the contractor was a prerequisite to the protection of the construction industry proviso, and it left open for future resolution the question of whether the union could seek a clause limiting the subcontracting of work to unionized subcontractors to one particular job site or to a geographic area, such as a county, within the union's jurisdiction. The Court unanimously held that a construction union may lawfully seek and negotiate such a clause for a geographic area.[97] The Court held that where there is a collective bargaining relationship between a union and a contractor, demonstrating the union's interest in organizing that employer's employees, a subcontracting clause is lawful under the construction industry proviso—even though such a clause induces "top-down organizing" (organizing by pressure from other employers rather than through union recruitment), which Congress regarded as an evil when it enacted the secondary-boycott prohibitions.

The Court stated that the proviso was intended not only to avoid jobsite friction between union and nonunion workers but also to mitigate the impact of *Denver Building Trades*. Said Justice Marshall, speaking for the Court:

. . . we believe that Congress endorsed subcontracting agreements obtained in the context of a collective-bargaining relationship—and decided to accept whatever top-down pressure such clauses might entail. Congress concluded that the community of interests on the construction jobsite justified the top-down organizational consequences that might attend the protection of legitimate collective bargaining objectives.[98]

Another part of the secondary-boycott issue relates to secondary consumer picketing (picketing to dissuade the public from patronizing retail establishments rather than to dissuade employees from working). The Supreme Court has construed the statute to permit peaceful secondary picketing that addresses the primary dispute. However, as is the case with so many secondary-picketing problems, the proposition is more easily stated in the abstract than applied to concrete situations. In the *Tree Fruits* case[99] the union had called a strike against fruit packers and warehousemen who were doing business in Yakima, Washington. The struck firms sold their apples to the Safeway chain of retail stores in and about Seattle. The union instituted a consumer boycott of the apples and placed pickets in front of a number of the stores in that city. The pickets distributed handbills and wore placards that said "To the Consumer: Non-union Washington State apples are being sold at this store. Please do not purchase such apples. Thank you. Teamsters Local 760, Yakima, Washington."[100] The Supreme Court held that not all secondary consumer picketing was prohibited by the statute, and that Congress had legislated against "isolated evils." Conceding that the public might not read picket signs and handbills aimed explicitly at the primary employer, the Court held that where the union's appeal was "closely

confined to the primary dispute" the secondary-boycott prohibitions were not violated.[101]

This Supreme Court ruling on secondary consumer picketing is difficult to apply to economically dependent or
captive secondary employers who purchase only from the
primary employer. Examples of this are gasoline stations and
exclusive franchise dealers of major automobile companies.
It is impossible for the union to confine its appeal to the
primary employer in a way that will not be aimed at the
entire structure of the secondary employer in this situation.
At Safeway it was different because the Yakima apples were
only one of many products the company was handling. A
divided Court held that where the picketed secondary employer is economically dependent upon the primary employer, the union violates the statute's secondary-boycott
prohibitions by engaging in consumer picketing because the
secondary employer cannot shift to another product (a possibility that was open to Safeway).[102] The Court theorized
that the only possible response by the secondary employer
is to shut down, even though some such employers might
be able to obtain new products or business relationships.
Thus the picketing would necessarily bring a neutral party
into a dispute in which it is not involved—the very abuse at
which the secondary-boycott prohibitions are aimed.

The Court rejected the contention that First Amendment
protection was invaded by Congress inasmuch as the statute
is aimed at unlawful objectives, namely spreading "labor
discord by coercing a neutral party to join the fray."[103] Justice
Stevens, in a concurring opinion, characterized the activity
at issue as signal picketing: "The statutory ban in this case
affects only that aspect of the union's effort to communicate
its views that calls for an automatic response to a signal
rather than a reasoned response to an idea."[104] Subsequently
a unanimous Supreme Court spoke approvingly of Justice
Stevens's characterization of consumer picketing as signal
picketing.[105] The Court's simultaneous bestowal of First
Amendment protection on a civil-rights boycott is puzzling
and troublesome.[106]

Meanwhile, a unanimous Court, speaking through Justice White, has held that peaceful handbilling without picketing or patrolling protesting the existence of substandard wages is not a violation of the Act.[107] To rule otherwise, said the Court, would pose "serious questions of the validity of [the secondary-boycott prohibitions in the statute] under the First Amendment."[108] The Court drew a sharp distinction between picketing and leafletting. Said the Court with regard to the latter activity:

That a labor union is the leafletter and that a labor dispute was involved does not foreclose this analysis. We do not suggest that communications by labor unions are never of the commercial speech variety and thereby entitled to a lesser degree of Constitutional protection. The handbills involved here, however, do not appear to be typical commercial speech such as advertising the price of a product or arguing its merits, *for they pressed the benefits of unionism to the community and the dangers of inadequate wages to the economy and the standard of living of the populace.* Of course, commercial speech itself is protected by the First Amendment . . .[109]

Compulsory Recognition of a Union

In a number of relationships, the union establishes majority status and recognition without certification by presenting to the employer authorization cards indicating that a majority of the employees in an appropriate unit desire to be represented by the union. Prior to the 1947 amendments, the NLRB permitted unions to be certified for the purpose of representing employees on the basis of authorization cards and petitions as well as electoral victories. (Certification by the Board obligates the employer to bargain for specific job classifications for a unit and protects the union from challenge by rivals.) The 1947 amendments eliminated certification through any method other than an election conducted by the Board. (Unions, employees, and the employer— where a demand is made upon it—may petition the board for an election.) But can a union obtain legally binding recognition from the employer without a Board election and certification on the basis of authorization cards or petitions? This was the issue presented to the Supreme Court in *NLRB v. Gissel.*[110] The Court found that legislative history relating to the Taft-Hartley amendments did not preclude union recognition on the basis of authorization cards without certification. Although the Court noted that the election process possessed an "acknowledged superiority," it held that authorization cards were not "inherently unreliable."[111] Indeed the Court stated that cards "may be the most effective—perhaps the only—way of assuring employee choice" where unfair labor practices had made it impossible to test employees' free choice through the ballot box.[112]

But the Court left open a number of questions in *Gissel*. Does an employer have an obligation to recognize the union on the basis of authorization cards where it has not committed independent unfair labor practices that would taint the electoral process? Must the employer, if it wishes to protect itself, petition the NLRB (as it is permitted to do by the Taft-Hartley amendments)[113] for an election? In 1974 the Court held by a 5–4 vote that even where the union presents authorization cards indicating that a majority of the employees support the union and where that support is also manifested through a refusal to cross a union picket line, the employer is not acting in "bad faith" by refusing to recognize the union.[114] It is the union that has the burden of taking the next step and invoking the electoral process.

Another unresolved issue is related to the question of when recognition may be thrust upon an employer that has engaged in extensive or egregious unfair labor practices. Under such circumstances *Gissel* makes it clear that the union could obtain recognition on the basis of authorization cards where it has a majority. But suppose the unfair labor practices make it impossible for the union to collect a majority and (more specifically) that the union alleges that but for the employer's unfair labor practices it would have obtained a majority of the cards, or that there is a reasonable likelihood that the union would have obtained majority status. The employer in this situation would profit from its wrongdoing by engaging in more effective illegality—by nipping the union organizational drive in the bud before it is able to establish itself. Two courts of appeals have held that recognition may be imposed upon an employer under such circumstances.[115] The issue has not yet come to the Supreme Court. In one of the two aforementioned cases, *United Dairy Farmers' Cooperative Association*,[116] the Board split in three different directions on this issue. None of the Board members who participated in *United Dairy Farmers' Cooperative Association* are serving on the Board today.

Member Penello took the position that a nonmajority union could not obtain a bargaining order under *Gissel* under the NLRA.[117] Members John Truesdale and Betty Murphy held that the statute contemplated such an order, but only when there was no "reasonable likelihood of ever holding a [fair] election."[118] Chairman John Fanning and Member Howard Jenkins took the position that a majority bargaining order could be imposed where the Board had initially attempted to determine majority status through an election and where there was "very good probability that, had employee sentiment been allowed to emerge, it should have favored the union."

It was in this posture that the Third Circuit Court of Appeals heard the matter late in 1980 and held that the Board does have remedial authority to impose a nonmajority bargaining order where "outrageous" and "pervasive" unfair labor practices have been committed.[119] Judge A. Leon Higginbotham, writing for a unanimous panel,[120] noted that the court has not squarely answered this question in *Gissel*. But careful restrictions on the employer's behavior during Board-conducted elections, said the court, were necessary, "since the employer has disproportionate economic power."[121] Said the Third Circuit Court:

The rationale for selecting bargaining representatives by certification election evaporates . . . when the employer has committed such serious unfair labor practices that the laboratory conditions of the past election, as well as any election in the immediate future, are destroyed. In these circumstances, because of the employer's attempt to undermine employee free choice, the goal of a free uninhibited certification election simply cannot be attained regardless of the reparative actions which may be attempted by the Board. Other means to protect employees must be pursued.[122]

Judge Higginbotham properly noted that *Gissel* was a remedy case and that, although both an election and evidence of majority support through authorization cards would have been preferable to the imposition of a bargaining order where no majority order had been evident, the failure to recognize remedial authority for the Board under the circumstances would have undermined the statutory goal of majority choice. Said Judge Higginbotham: "Unions which would have attained a majority in a free and uncoerced election if the employer had not committed unfair labor practices would be deprived of recognition merely because of the employer's illegal conduct. . . . The absence of such authority might create incentives for employers to engage in illegal prophylactic action with the purpose of preventing the attainment of a card majority."[123] Accordingly the court held that the Board had the remedial authority to issue a bargaining order where the practices were so outrageous and pervasive that there was "no reasonable possibility that a free and uncoerced election could be held."[124] The court specifically avoided the question of whether the Board had the authority where there was no reasonable possibility that the union would have obtained a majority but for the action of the employer, stating that a "reasonable possibility" existed in *United Dairy* because, although the employer had committed "numerous flagrant and serious violations," the union had lost by only two votes.[125] Quite clearly the closeness of the vote will be an important factor to take into account.

Subsequently the Board squarely accepted the propriety of minority bargaining orders and the views of Chairman Fanning and Member Jenkins.[126] The Board recited a number of circumstances that prompted the fashioning of such an order: the "extreme gravity" of the violation; "mass communication" to all employees from all levels of the corporate hierarchy; and repetition and timing of unlawful conduct, which exacerbated their long-term coercive impact." The Board also noted that 46 percent of the employees in the unit has signed authorization cards.

However, a divided Court of Appeals for the District of Columbia, with Judge Patricia Wald dissenting, refused enforcement of the Board's order[127] on the ground that Congress had not intended minority bargaining orders to be within the Board's discretion and that, where Congress had intended to sanction minority bargaining, as in the construction industry, it had done so explicitly. Meanwhile the Board reversed itself in 1984 in *Gourmet Food, Inc.*[128] In reaching a conclusion opposite to the one reached two years before, the Board provided this rationale:

We seriously question . . . whether a nonmajority bargaining order, in practice, is an effective remedy. The bargaining environment established at the Board's instigation alone does not replicate that which arises from employees' impetus. What is lacking is the leverage normally possessed by exclusive bargaining representatives that derives from unions' and employers' knowledge that a majority of employees at one time, in some form, united in their support for a union and may do so again in support of bargaining demands. To gain that leverage, employees may be called on to demonstrate active support for a representative in a far more open way than a secret-ballot election. Accordingly, in imposing a representative on employees, the Board may be changing only the sphere of employees' choice. And yet the Board can be no more certain that, in this new sphere of employee choice, employees can more freely exercise their choice without regard to any lingering effects of massive unfair labor practices than it can be if a new election is directed after the Board has applied traditional as well as appropriate extraordinary remedies. The Board can be certain, however, of the possibility that it is forcing a majority of employees who do not have an interest in participating in the collective-bargaining process into that process and, potentially and consequently, into desired terms and conditions of employment negotiated by an unchosen representative. Given these policy considerations we do not believe we would ever be justified in granting a nonmajority bargaining order remedy.[129]

Different rules apply in the building and construction industry by virtue of amendments to the Landrum-Griffin Act of 1959. These amendments make lawful pre-hire agreements not based upon majority support as well as union security provisions in them that require a membership as a condition of employment subsequent to seven days of the employees initial hire date.[130] The reason for this provision relates to the fact that the construction industry provides so much work that is temporary in nature, thus posing difficulties in establishing majority status at a particular worksite. In *John Deklewa & Sons, Inc.,*[131] the Board held that an employer may not unilaterally repudiate an agreement negotiated with a minority building and construction union possessing only minority support. Said the Board:

> When parties enter into an 8(f) [construction industry] agreement, they will be required . . . to comply with that agreement unless the employees vote, in a Board-conducted election, to reject (decertify) or change their bargaining representative. Neither employers nor unions who are parties to [such] . . . agreements will be free unilaterally to repudiate such agreements. During its term, [construction industry agreements will not act as a bar to a representation petition filed under the Act] . . . single employer units will normally be appropriate.[132]

Suppose a union obtains recognition on the basis of certification through an election or authorization cards, but the majority of the workers change their mind and the employer relies on this to refuse to recognize the union. The courts have held that an employer has an obligation to continue to recognize the union for a "reasonable period of time" and that where the union has been certified that reasonable period of time is for the period of the certification (one year).[133] Where the union has been recognized on the basis of authorization cards, petitions, or whatever, the employer also has an obligation to continue recognition for a reasonable period of time—but sometimes the Board has held that this period can elapse before the passage of one year.[134]

If a union negotiates a collective bargaining agreement with an employer after recognition, another union cannot step in and attempt to obtain recognition for itself. In the first place, if both unions are affiliated with the AFL-CIO, the union that raids the other may be held by the federation's "umpire" to have violated the AFL-CIO's No Raiding Pact.[135] In any event a contract negotiated between the parties is a bar to such recognition, and thus, where a union files a petition for representation with the Board and a valid collective bargaining agreement has been negotiated, the Board will dismiss the petition on the grounds that the contract bars it. The contract is a bar where it is signed by all parties—even if it is not embodied in a formal document.[136] Prior notification is required where the contract itself requires it.[137] The contract must cover workers in an appropriate unit.[138] Where there is a significant change in the identity of a contracting party, the contract is not a bar.[139] The contract bar has a duration of three years or the period of the collective bargaining agreement, whichever is shorter.[140] Between ninety and sixty days prior to the expiration of the contract, a petition may be filed challenging the incumbent union's position as exclusive representative; such a petition will be regarded as timely. If it is not filed by sixty days prior to the expiration of the agreement, it will not be regarded as timely. The purpose is to permit the parties to resolve their differences through collective bargaining without any distractions. This is why a petition cannot be filed at this time. During this sixty-day period, and independent of contract obligations, neither the union nor the employer may engage in strikes, lockouts, or any other form of economic pressure. Likewise the statute, independent of any contract obligations that the parties assume, requires labor and management to give notice of their intent to modify or terminate the agreement to the mediation agencies at the beginning of the sixty-day period.

Conclusion

The law promotes the right of workers to organize, but it tempers that concern with recognition of other principles that sometimes collide with it: free choice for employees (generally expressed through the ballot box), the circumvention of such choice through economic pressure on employers, and employers' property rights.

6

Economic Pressure and Bargaining Tactics in the Established Relationship

The National Labor Relations Act has a dual purpose, and its dual concerns are often at odds with one another. On the one hand, the statute is concerned with protecting trade unions and their members against antiunion discrimination. Quite frequently the NLRB and the courts will presume antiunion discrimination, even though there is no proof that the employer was motivated in its conduct by antiunion considerations. The underlying concern is that certain tactics may have the effect of destroying the union entirely and thus destroying the collective bargaining process. Accordingly one concern is to prop up trade unions and, by so doing, to save the collective bargaining process when it is imperiled. But simultaneously the NLRA attempts to promote the collective bargaining process as a wide-open, robust relationship in which the parties should have the widest latitude in bargaining tactics, pressure, and economic weaponry. The underlying concern is that if the NLRB and the courts try to regulate bargaining tactics, they will be regulating the substance of the collective bargaining process and ultimately the substance of the collective bargaining agreement itself. Nowhere is this concern—which is often at odds with the need to preserve free trade unions and the collective bargaining process—more clearly seen than in the landmark *Insurance Agents* decision,[1] which involved a work slow-down by the union.

In *Insurance Agents* the employer argued that the slowdown was itself an unfair labor practice—specifically an unlawful refusal to bargain, inasmuch as the tactic tends to preclude discussion—and that the union ought to be prohibited from engaging in it. The Supreme Court rejected this argument and took the position that economic pressure that might serve as an irritant rather than as a promoter of dialogue was an essential ingredient in the collective bargaining process. Said the Court:

It must be realized that collective bargaining, under a system where the government does not attempt to control the results of nego-tiations, cannot be equated with an academic collective search for truth—or even with what might be thought to be the ideal of one. The parties—even granting the modification of views that may come from a realization of economic interdependence—still pro-ceed from contrary, and to an extent antagonistic, viewpoints and concepts of self-interest. The system has not reached the ideal of the philosophic notion that perfect understanding among people would lead to perfect agreement among them on values. The presence of economic weapons in reserve and their actual exercise on occasion by the parties, is part and parcel of the system that the Wagner and Taft-Hartley Acts have recognized. Abstract logical analysis might find inconsistency between the command of the statute to negotiate toward an agreement in good faith and the legitimacy of the use of economic weapons, frequently having the most serious effect upon individual workers and productive enter-prises, to induce one party to come to the terms desired by the other. But the truth of the matter is that at the present statutory stage of our national labor relations policy, the two factors—neces-sity for good-faith bargaining between parties, and the availability of economic pressure devices to each to make the other party incline to agree on one's terms—exist side by side.[2]

Accordingly, within limits, the success and strength of one party ought not to matter in determining whether a statu-tory violation has been committed.

Protected and Unprotected Activities
Section 7 of the NLRA affirmatively protects a wide variety of employee pressures and protests aimed at the employer.

Insurance Agents simply dealt with the question of whether particularly irritating slowdowns constituted a refusal to bargain. It did not address the question of whether the activity engaged in was "protected activity" within the meaning of the Act.

If an activity is protected, employees are immunized from discipline or discharge for engaging in the activity. If it is prohibited, the NLRB may obtain a cease-and-desist order through its own administrative process against the conduct, and may eventually enforce it through a petition to the circuit court of appeals. Activity that is neither protected nor prohibited is in a "no-man's land"; employees may be dismissed or disciplined for engaging in it.

For an activity to be protected, it must be "concerted." Though it seems clear that employees' protests must be aimed at group concerns, the courts and the NLRB are divided on the question of whether one employee can engage in such conduct.[3] The Court of Appeals for the Sixth Circuit approved the Board's rule that an employee's presentation of job-related grievances aimed at getting the employer to comply with laws or regulations is protected concerted activity.[4] But the Board has reversed itself, concluding that "it will no longer be sufficient for the General Counsel to set out the subject matter that is of alleged concern to a theoretical group and expect to establish concert of action thereby."[5]

Meanwhile, in *NLRB v. City Disposal System,*[6] the Supreme Court has held that a single employee—in this case one refusing to drive an allegedly unsafe truck—is engaged in concerted activity when the worker invokes a right contained in a collective bargaining agreement. Said Justice Brennan, writing for a 5–4 majority: ". . . an honest and reasonable invocation of a collectively bargained right constitutes concerted activity, regardless of whether the employee turns out to have been correct in his belief that his right was violated."[7] Undoubtedly the tension between *City Disposal* and the Board's most recent position on concerted activities will come to the Court for adjudication soon.[8]

The Supreme Court held in the *Weingarten* case that an employee who calls on a union representative to assist in a disciplinary interview is engaged in concerted activity.[9] But this does not mean that an employer is precluded from repeating questions to employees, as might be the case in a more adversarial form.[10] Moreover the Board has held that reinstatement and back pay are not appropriate remedies for such statutory violations.[11] Initially the Board extended *Weingarten* to nonunionized establishments.[12] But the courts divided on the issue,[13] and the Board subsequently reversed itself.[14]

The NLRB has relied on First Amendment cases protecting free speech against libel actions[15] as a basis for protecting employees' complaints against employers, even though such complaints may promote "discord" and "strife."[16] This is because labor-management controversy, even when it occurs within the context of an established relationship and involves collective bargaining and grievance processing,[17] may be just as "bitter and extreme" as it is in an organizational setting where union recognition is at issue.[18] The Board has invalidated employers' rules prohibiting the distribution of "scurrilous" literature[19] and has held that employees' complaints that are protected are not rendered unprotected because they involve "animal exuberance" or "impulsive behavior."[20] They are not even unprotected when the employee accuses the boss of having an affair with someone.[21]

These cases involve a balancing process. Perhaps the most controversial cases in which employee or union conduct has been found unprotected are the "disloyalty" cases. The leading one is *NLRB v. Local Union No. 1229, IBEW*,[22] in which the Supreme Court, over the sharp dissent of Justices Felix Frankfurter, William Douglas, and Hugo Black, held that the distribution of handbills that contained a "vitriolic attack on the quality of the company's television broadcasts" by non-striking employees, but did not refer to the labor-management controversy, was unprotected. The Board subsequently extended this rule to conclude that disparagement of a company's product was unprotected even when the employees were on strike.[23] However, though the Court of Appeals for the District of Columbia has concluded that participation in a boycott of an employer is inconsistent with the "duty of loyalty,"[24] boycott signs in or on employees' cars on company property have been held to be protected.[25] On the other hand, employees who use "vulgar shop talk" more than others when engaged in concerted protest (especially in discussions with management officials) were held to be engaged in unprotected conduct.[26]

The Court of Appeals for the Eighth Circuit has held that employees' questions and statements that interrupted a captive-audience meeting because they were a "challenge and deliberate defiance, repeatedly asserted before assembled employees"[27] were unprotected. The Board has also held that it was lawful for Michigan Bell Telephone Company to require employees—in the midst of collective bargaining—to remove sweatshirts containing the slogan "Ma Bell is a Cheap Mother."[28] That slogan is unprotected when it is displayed on company property because it is considered obscene. In the same vein, the Court of Appeals for the Fifth Circuit has held, in *NLRB v. Mini-togs*,[29] that an employee who referred to the distributors of an anti-union flyer as "f−−−−−g whores" was engaged in unprotected activity but, because of her profanity as well as the fact that the statement was not part of concerted conduct, engaged in with other employees. But when a radical trade unionist employed by the Inland Steel Company was fired for protesting company conduct while wearing a shirt emblazoned with "Inland Sucks," the Board held that his dismissal was not lawful inasmuch as the employer had not relied on the shirt as a basis for his termination.[30]

One other area of contention involves the extent to which the conduct of supervisors, who are excluded from the NLRA's coverage, can be characterized as protected activity. The Court of Appeals for the Ninth Circuit, in reversing an NLRB order protecting supervisory activity, noted that supervisory conduct has been held protected when a supervisor is dismissed or disciplined for refusing to commit an unfair labor practice, when a supervisor is dismissed or disciplined for testifying before the NLRB, and when a supervisor is dismissed or disciplined as a pretext for dismissing pro-union employees working under him.[31] The court refused to accept the Board's position that supervisors should be reinstated with back pay when the employer's policy might have a coercive impact on the rank and file in the bargaining unit. The court reasoned that remedies for the employees are enough. On the other hand, however, the Court of Appeals for the Third Circuit has held that the Board may order reinstatement of a supervisor who was fired in retaliation for her relatives' participation in a union organization campaign.[32]

Faced with a case in which supervisors and employees had been dismissed because of a letter sent to the company president criticizing a manager, the Court of Appeals for the First Circuit held, in an opinion written by Judge Stephen Breyer, that the activity had to involve employees and their conditions of work to be protected.[33] In these cases involving the question of whether supervisors' conduct is protected, the Board's position had been that the activity must be part of the concern and needs of employees in order for the Board and the courts to respond affirmatively and to conclude that the employer has violated the statute. However, the Board has now narrowed the scope of protection afforded supervisors. In *Parker-Robb Chevrolet*[34] it said:

. . . although we recognize that the discharge of a supervisor for engaging in union or concerted activity almost invariably has a secondary or incidental effect on employees, we believe that, when a supervisor is discharged either because he or she engaged in union or concerted activity or because the discharge is contemporaneous with the unlawful discharge of statutory employees, or both, this incidental or secondary effect on the employees is insufficient to warrant an exception to the general statutory provision excluding supervisors from the protection of the Act. Thus, it is irrelevant that an employer may have hoped or even expected, that its decision to terminate a supervisor for his union or concerted activity would cause employees to reconsider, and perhaps abandon, their own concerted or union activity. No matter what the employer's subjective hope or expectation that circumstance cannot change the character of its otherwise lawful conduct.

. . . The discharge of supervisors is unlawful when it interferes with the right of employees to exercise their rights under Section

7 of the Act, as when they give testimony adverse to their employers' interest or when they refuse to commit unfair labor practices. The discharge of supervisors as a result of their participation in union or concerted activity—either by themselves or when allied with rank-and-file employees—is not unlawful for the simple reason that employees, but not supervisors, have rights protected by the Act.[35]

Of course the mere fact that the employer has the right to dismiss workers for unprotected activity (in the case of economic pressure, for instance) does not mean that it will happen. Dismissal or discipline might be counterproductive in the sense of producing more industrial warfare and not less.

What is protected economic pressure within the meaning of the NLRA? The Supreme Court has held that walkouts, with or without the presence of the union, are protected activity regardless of the judges' view about the wisdom of the action.[36] However, strikes in breach of grievance-arbitration and no-strike clauses negotiated by labor and management are unprotected.[37] But a no-strike obligational clause does not apply to a strike undertaken when a reopener in the contract between the parties allows them to bargain as they would when the contract expires—unless the parties themselves specifically prohibit strikes in such an instance.[38]

Slowdowns are unprotected because, in the view of the courts, such action is an attempt to require the employer to accept the employees on their own terms of employment.[39] However, the concerted refusal to work overtime is protected activity unless employees ". . . repeatedly refuse to perform mandatory overtime . . . because that conduct constitutes a recurring or intermittent strike, which amounts to employees unilaterally determining conditions of work."[40] Violent strikes and the kinds of sit-ins or plant occupations that took place in the 1930s are similarly unprotected.[41]

The Strike

Striking in itself is protected activity, although unauthorized or wildcat stoppages are unprotected because they derogate the status of the exclusive bargaining agent, who is supposed to speak on behalf of all employees within the appropriate unit. This includes dissident groups as well as those who are in accord with the union's policy.[42] Strikes in accord with union policy have been defined as authorized or ratified, and thus they are protected within the meaning of the NLRA where the Board and the courts determine that the objective of the strikers is in accord with the policy of the union.[43]

Section 13 specifically states that nothing in the NLRA is intended to interfere with the right to strike. However, there are a number of limitations on the right, and one of them is set out in the Taft-Hartley amendments' prohibition of strikes during emergencies affecting the nation's safety and health.[44] In such a situation the amendments authorize the appointment of a board of inquiry by the president to investigate the dispute but not to make recommendations. (Taft believed that the pressure to accept the recommendation would be so great that the parties would be compelled to accept it, and that this would amount to compulsory arbitration, which has traditionally been anathema to both labor and management in the United States.)[45] Subsequent to the board of inquiry's submission of a report to the president, the attorney general is authorized to seek an eighty-day injunction in federal district court, and fifteen days prior to the expiration of the eighty-day period the workers vote on the employer's last offer.

At the time of the Taft-Hartley amendments, the theory was that workers would accept offers that their militant and unreasonable union leaders were unable or unwilling to accept.[46] That theory has proved remarkably incorrect, inasmuch as every single last offer has been voted down (essentially because it is more likely to be the rank-and-file workers who are pushing the union leaders to be more aggressive and the union leaders who are urging restraint). Also any vote conducted by an outside agency (in this case, the NLRB) is likely to become a confrontation between the union and the employer and a vote over whether the workers support their union. Invariably in these situations they do. Finally, workers know very well that there is really no such thing as a last offer—especially when it is given to the workers in public. Accordingly this portion of the emergency strike provisions has not worked out very well. During the 1978 coal strike, when the president invoked Taft-Hartley's procedures, the district judge assigned to hear the case refused to make the injunction permanent because it had been disobeyed and because the government seemed less than enthusiastic about monitoring its enforcement. At the same time, it must be acknowledged that there are few situations where a dispute has not been resolved, when Taft-Hartley was invoked, without resort to other legislation or procedures.

Given that section 13 speaks of a right to strike that is not to be impaired by anything in the NLRA, the layman might think that the right to strike is somehow constitutional. A limited constitutional right to strike exists in France and Sweden, and some contend that the constitution of Japan, which protects the "right of workers to organize and to bargain and act collectively," accomplishes the same objective. In the United States, however, the Supreme Court has refused to hold that a right to strike can be inferred from the Constitution.[47] The difficulty with the protection afforded by statute is that ever since its 1938 decision in *NLRB v. Mackay Radio & Telegraph Company*[48] the Supreme Court has held that, although striking is protected conduct, employers may permanently replace striking employees with strikebreakers. In other words, even though an employer may not discharge or discipline workers for engaging in a strike, the employer, in order to keep production going and the plant open, has a business justification for permanently ousting strikers through the recruitment of strikebreakers, and thus may just as effectively deprive employees of their job security as would be the case if they were dismissed or disciplined for striking. (The House of Representatives voted to reverse *Mackay* in 1991, but the Senate filibustered the bill to death in 1992. During the 1992 campaign, President Bill Clinton supported this legislation, and it has been reintroduced in 1993.)

One particularly pernicious consequence of *Mackay* is that it provides employers with an opportunity to rid themselves not only of workers and pension obligations but also of the union itself. The employer, it must be remembered, is entitled by the Taft-Hartley amendments to file a petition for an NLRB election when there is a question about whether there should be union representation. When a number of workers are replaced, the employer's petition is filed on the ground that the workers involved in the decision to select the union are no longer in the work force. But the Supreme Court, by 5–4 vote, has held that an employer is not legally entitled to claim that it has a reasonable basis for doubting a union's majority support on the ground that strike replacements can be presumed to oppose the union.[49]

For twelve years after the Taft-Hartley amendments the Board refused to permit permanently replaced economic strikers to vote in the election, but the 1959 amendments to the statute permit such strikers to vote until twelve months after the commencement of the strike.[50] To a limited extent, this has mitigated some effects of the harsh *Mackay* doctrine.

In fairness it must be said that a growing number of limitations have been imposed upon the *Mackay* doctrine. Where the strike is caused in part by an employer's unfair labor practices, the employees are entitled to reinstatement. If after the commission of the unfair labor practices and the strike the employees offer unconditionally to return to work, they may be entitled to back pay as well.[51] And even in an economic strike, such as that which occurred in *Mackay*, the Supreme Court has held (in a decision that is difficult to reconcile with *Mackay*) that an employer may not offer extra seniority to strikebreakers—even if the employer can show that such an offer was necessary to keep production going.[52]

The Court's conclusion is based on the fact that the use of such "superseniority" as a vehicle to counterattack against the strike would greatly diminish, if not destroy, the strike weapon itself. Though the Court refused to reassess its *Mackay* decision that replacements may be hired, it was hard put to distinguish the two cases. Nevertheless, it did so on the following grounds: that superseniority affects the tenure of all strikers, whereas replacements only affect those workers who are actually replaced; that superseniority necessarily operates to the detriment of those who engage in the strike as opposed to nonstrikers; that superseniority is an offer of an individual benefit to induce employees to abandon the strike, and promises of benefits by employers are generally viewed as unlawful; that the use of new replacements with superseniority would deal a crippling blow to the strike effort; and that future bargaining would become difficult for the union because of the built-in tension between those employees who had superseniority and those who did not.

Though the Supreme Court has frequently used the National Labor Relations Act as a basis for interpreting the Railway Labor Act,[53] the 1985 United Airlines strike, in which the company bestowed superseniority on strikebreaking pilots, highlights the fact that the statutes have been interpreted differently.[54] However, the Court of Appeals for the Seventh and Eleventh Circuits seem to have outlawed such conduct under the Railway Labor Act.[55] Meanwhile, the Supreme Court, in *Trans World Airlines Inc. v. Independent Federation of Flight Attendants*,[56] applied the *Mackay* rule to an RLA dispute where the employer refused to lay off junior replacements in order to reinstate more senior full-time strikers at the conclusion of the strike. Deregulation seems to have promoted the growth of unfair labor practice litigation in the airline industry.

Further limitations were placed on the *Mackay* doctrine by the Supreme Court's subsequent holding that an employer is required to offer reemployment to strikers who have been replaced when new jobs are made available by expansion or turnover.[57] The Court has noted that section 2(3) of the NLRA provides that an individual whose work has ceased as a consequence of a labor dispute continues to be an employee within the meaning of the Act until he or she has obtained regular and substantially equivalent employment.[58] The strikers who have been replaced have preferential access to jobs when their replacements depart,[59] and the NLRB has held that no time limit may be placed on the obligation of the employer to reinstate such workers[60]—although the

Court of Appeals for the Seventh Circuit held that strikers may not displace replacements who have been laid off.[61]

A new dimension has been added to the issue of strikes by the institution of wrongful discharge actions—predicated upon breach of contract or misrepresentation—by replacements who have been dismissed to make way for employees returning from strikes. In *Belknap, Inc. v. Hale,*[62] the Court held by a 6–3 vote that such damage actions may be maintained in state court where an NLRB settlement necessitated termination of replacements because of its provision for the reinstatement of strikers. Justice White, speaking for five members of the Court,[63] rejected the argument that such actions are preempted because they interfere with the "free play of economic forces"[64] on the settlement of labor disputes that is promoted by federal labor policy. Justice Brennan, dissenting with Justice Marshall and Justice Powell, was of the view that the employer's right to replace, fashioned in *Mackay,* was "burdened" by such actions, and that the Court, by stating that strikers could be permanently replaced by replacements given "conditional" offers of employment, was shaping the balance of power between labor and management—a matter left to federal labor law.[65] The decision would seem to make the resolution of strikes over alleged unfair labor practices far more difficult.

The Lockout

What of the employer's rights? What may the employer do to utilize its own economic weaponry and protect its bargaining position? In *American Ship Building Company v. NLRB*[66] the Supreme Court held that under certain circumstances lockouts by employers are lawful under the NLRA. Until the *American Ship Building* decision it had been generally assumed that a lockout was unlawful unless an employer, confronted with a stoppage at a time when it would have perishable goods and thus would suffer irreparable harm, used the lockout at an earlier period so as to shift the economic burden to the strikers and make it less likely that a cessation of work would occur at a time that would be disastrous to the employer[67] or unless a company that was part of an employer association locked out its employees in response to an attempt by the union to divide and conquer the association by striking against one employer at a time (called "whipsawing").

In a way *American Ship Building* is consistent with the same general theme. The employer was confronted with a bargaining history in which the union had struck on a number of occasions in the past and appeared to be deliberately delaying negotiations during a slack period so that it could bring economic pressure to bear at a time when the employer needed to deliver goods and was thus weak and vulnerable. Said the Court:

Although the unions had given assurances that there would be no strike, past bargaining history was thought to justify continuing apprehension that the unions would fail to make good their assurances. It was further found that the employer's primary purpose in locking out its employees was to avert peculiarly harmful economic consequences which would be imposed upon it and its customers if a strike were called either while a ship was in the yard during the shipping season or later when the yard was fully occupied.[68]

Accordingly the Court took the position that the lockout may be utilized by management to protect its collective bargaining position. In *American Ship Building* there was no evidence that the employer was hostile to the employees' interest in organizing for the purpose of collective bargaining or that the lockout was used to "discipline" them for engaging in the bargaining process. Thus the Court noted that it could not be said that the employer's intention was to "destroy or frustrate the process of collective bargaining" or that there was no indication that the union would be diminished in its capacity to represent the employees in the unit.

The Court, in *American Ship Building*, spoke of the lockout and the strike as "correlative" in terms of statutory usage. But it seems questionable whether *American Ship Building* and the right of employers to lock out can apply where the bargaining relationship is not so well established as it was in that case—particularly in a first-contract situation where the parties are dealing with one another for the first time and the relationship is not as mature as the one in *American Ship Building*. Moreover the employer had a legitimate apprehension based on the union's previous behavior. It would have been placed in a very difficult position if it had been confronted with a strike during its boom period. In effect it was transferring the economic burden of the dispute to the employees. As in *Insurance Agents* the Court took what might be characterized as a "freedom of contract" position, permitting the collective bargaining process to operate in a robust and open-ended fashion and allowing both parties to use economic pressure to resolve their differences.

But how far can the scales be tipped in favor of the employer? May the employer buttress its right to lock out through the use of temporary or permanent replacements? Where a group of employers in a multiemployer association are "whipsawed" by one union, all employers not struck have the right to lock out, for some of the same considerations present in *American Ship Building*. They have the right to shift the economic burden to the strikers at a time propitious to the employers.[69] Rather than permit the union to establish a pattern through a minimal economic burden imposed upon its own members who continue to work in most of the plants and to pick the employers off by pressuring them one by one, a substantial burden is thrust upon the resources of the union and the employees because of employer unity. The Court has held that, in the multiemployer lockout situation, temporary replacements may be utilized to keep production going.[70]

Until the past few years the appellate courts had not been sympathetic to the view that temporary replacements could be utilized in the *American Ship Building* context where the union has not officially struck any employer,[71] but the Board, with circuit court approval, has held that the use of temporary replacements is lawful "in light of *American Ship Building*, [because] there no longer exists any meaningful distinction as to effects between lawful 'offensive' and lawful 'defensive' economic weaponry."[72] Apparently the theory of the earlier cases is that there is no substantial and legitimate business justification. But it is difficult to distinguish this sort of case—and indeed even that of permanent replacements in a lockout context—from the basic theme of *American Ship Building* and *Insurance Agents*. The idea in those cases was that the collective bargaining process can be used by both sides so long as it is not used in a manner that appears to be intended to or to have the effect of destroying the process. The test in all of these cases should be whether the union in the collective bargaining process continues to function despite the employer's tactics. This carries a certain risk, and it is difficult to articulate with precision the parameters of union and employer economic pressure under such a test. But, given the Court's concern with minimum interference with bargaining tactics on the theory that therein lies the road to regulation of the substance of the collective bargaining agreement, there is little choice. Accordingly it would seem appropriate in all of these cases involving strikes and lockouts to see whether the union is able to function as a collective bargaining representative in the wake of employer tactics: Does it collect dues? Is it able to negotiate a union security agreement requiring collection of dues as a condition of employment, and thereby to establish a relatively secure position for itself? Does it continue to process grievances? Is it able to exert economic pressure subsequent to the lockout or the replacement of strikers? All of these factors would appear to be valid for the Court and the Board to look to in future litigation.[73] But the case law is so confused that it becomes impossible to determine how far the balance may be tipped or how extreme the economic tactic may be before the statute can be said to have been violated.

The Duty to Bargain in Good Faith

Thus far we have dealt with the economic weaponry each party may bring to bear during the collective bargaining process. Labor and management employ such tactics on behalf of their demands. But what demands may be made by each side, and under what circumstances? All of this goes to the question of whether the union or the employer is lawfully bargaining in "good faith" as the statute requires.

What is good-faith bargaining? When the Wagner Act was being debated in 1935, Senator Walsh, the chairman of the Senate Labor Committee, stated that the question of how a party (at the time of the Wagner Act only an employer) would discharge its obligations to bargain under the statute was a relatively simple one. The Board would take the parties by the hand to the conference room in which negotiations were to take place. It would see that the parties were properly seated and would close the door so that negotiations could commence.[74] The difficulty is that this relatively simple picture painted by Senator Walsh in 1935 has become far more complicated. The Board has increasingly found itself pushing open the door and becoming involved in the discussions and the tactics of the parties while the process moves forward. Although the Board has been careful to state that a proposal by one side does not necessitate a counterproposal by the other, some response is required as a test of good faith. Neither side may engage in discussion that is simply "surface bargaining."[75] Neither party is required to enter into a contract. Good-faith bargaining is an attempt to consummate an agreement. However, the other party may be so obstinate, or its demands may be so unacceptable, that it becomes impossible to negotiate a contract.

In *NLRB v. American National Insurance Company*[76] the Supreme Court had held that management could insist on bargaining on the basis of a "management prerogatives" clause under which the union was ousted from involvement with important conditions of employment and under which such matters as discipline and work schedules were nonarbitrable—that is, management's position with regard to these areas would always prevail. The Court stated that the Board could not "directly or indirectly compel concessions or otherwise sit in judgment upon the substantive terms of collective bargaining agreements."[77] The Court rejected the Board's position that an employer was obligated to establish ongoing bargaining during the term of the collective agreement on these subjects.

American National Insurance dramatizes the fundamental difference between the American and German systems. In

Germany involvement by the *Betriebsrat* in a whole range of employer decisions affecting employment conditions is explicitly provided for by law. The statutory approach does not contemplate the idea that such rights as the right to veto hiring and firing decisions pending Labor Court, or conciliation determinations, or the right to have worker directors will be waived. The weakest *Betriebsrat* cannot be induced or required to relinquish any statutory right that it chooses to assert. The American approach contains an antithetical assumption; the weak must fend for themselves in obtaining some little portion of the lion's share. Generally the American statute guarantees little to the weak.

Mandatory Subjects of Bargaining

The above generalization must be qualified, for there are other cases that cut in a direction opposite to the freedom-of-contract line of authority in *Insurance Agents* and *American Ship Building* (which promotes a wide-open use of economic pressure) and that involve the NLRB and the courts in extensive regulation of subject matter at the bargaining table. To repeat, the Supreme Court—within limits—has permitted the parties to "take their gloves off" and to exert whatever economic pressure is at their disposal. Yet there is a concern that either side could completely subvert the collective bargaining process through a refusal to discuss subject matter that is important to both workers and employers.

This is why the statute prohibits the termination or modification of an agreement[78] until it expires by its own terms (although the Supreme Court permitted the bankruptcy law to override this obligation for financially beleaguered employers[79]—a holding that was later modified by statute).[80]

The Supreme Court, in the landmark *Borg-Warner* case,[81] held that there are three categories of subject matter that might be raised by the representatives of the union or the employer at the bargaining table: mandatory, nonmandatory, and illegal subjects of bargaining. Until an impasse is reached, the employer may not unilaterally change conditions of employment[82] because this would preclude or limit both sides in negotiations about unresolved items, and thus it is inconsistent with the concept of good-faith bargaining. (It is the permanence of the change that precludes good-faith bargaining.) In order for the unilateral change to be unlawful, it must be "material, substantial, and significant."[83]

With regard to mandatory subjects, both sides have an obligation to bargain to the point of impasse. This does not mean that the parties must be deadlocked on all issues or items but rather that they must be deadlocked in the negotiations generally.[84] "If either negotiating party remains willing to move further toward an agreement, an impasse cannot exist: The parties' perception regarding the progress of the negotiations is of central importance to the Board's impasse inquiry."[85]

Under the NLRA the party that refuses to bargain on mandatory subjects to the point of impasse is unlawfully refusing to bargain. The significance of such an unlawful refusal, in this context and others, is not merely that the Board will issue a "cease-and-desist" order aimed at remedying the parties' bargaining behavior. Rather it lies in the possibility that a strike ensuing as a result of such bargaining behavior would be an unfair-labor-practice strike and that therefore, in contrast to economic strikers who may be replaced, the workers would be entitled to reinstatement and possibly to back pay.[86] Accordingly the *Borg-Warner* rule can alter considerably the balance of power in a strike deemed to have been caused by the employer's posture at the bargaining table.

A nonmandatory subject is "permissive." That is to say, either party may raise the subject at the bargaining table for the purpose of discussion. It is perfectly lawful to discuss such an issue. However, when a party insists upon a position in such an area to the point of impasse, an unlawful refusal takes place under the Act. The purpose of the rule—which is extremely difficult to implement—is to exclude frivolous subjects from the bargaining table and to infer bad faith on the part of the party that clogs the table with such subjects. (Illegal subjects may not be discussed at all.) The Court of

Appeals for the First Circuit has said in order for the subject to be mandatory, it must bear a "'direct, significant relationship to . . . terms or conditions of employment,' rather than a 'remote or incidental relationship.'"[87] For instance, a union's insistence upon the employer's attendance at the annual union picnic to the point of impasse might be said to have little if anything to do with conditions of employment within the meaning of the Act.

The Board has held that an employer's insistence upon a proposal that would prohibit attempts by the union to influence funding sources was permissive and nonmandatory because it attempted to

> . . . govern employee activities which might occur *outside* the workplace and *outside* the employment relationship. Furthermore, . . . [the employer was seeking to] . . . determine the Union's position on a political issue. Neither objective is directly related to the employees' terms and conditions of employment [and therefore the subject is permissive].[88]

Thus, for instance, if the employer insisted to the point of impasse that the union limit its attempts to influence funding sources or, to take the earlier examples, not hold a picnic, or that the union elect its officers in a particular way, one would assume that the subject matter was so remote from labor-management problems as to be in bad faith.

Some mandatory subjects of bargaining are layoffs and recalls, sick leave, incentive pay, paid holidays, vacation schedules, hours of work, work rules relating to shifts of work[89] and such fringe benefits as cost-of-living adjustments and profit-sharing plans. Interest arbitration providing for arbitral resolution of future contract terms is a nonmandatory subject of bargaining because it substitutes a third party for labor and management, the appropriate parties in the collective bargaining process.[90] But the issues are not always so simple. The facts of *Borg-Warner,* and other decisions in its wake, make this clear.

In *Borg-Warner* the employer had insisted upon a "ballot" clause calling for a secret prestrike vote by all union and nonunion employees within the bargaining unit on the employer's last offer. The employer also insisted upon a "recognition" clause that excluded as a party to the contract the international union, which had been certified by the Board as the employees' exclusive bargaining agent. The Supreme Court found the employer's bargaining position with regard to both matters unlawful, inasmuch as it had insisted upon what the Court characterized as nonmandatory or permissive subjects of bargaining to the point of impasse.

It might be said that the Borg-Warner Corporation was subverting one of the basic statutory procedures, and the role of the Board, in designating an exclusive bargaining agent. Accordingly the Court's holding that the recognition clause was a nonmandatory subject of bargaining is somewhat understandable.[91] But the ballot clause is a little more difficult. Suppose an employer is concerned about the extent to which production has been interrupted by a union that he or she regards as strike-happy, and believes there is some basis for assuming that employees are out of sympathy with the union's behavior. Quite clearly the employer could insist upon a clause that would preclude employees from striking altogether, at least during the term of the agreement. Why can the employer not insist upon a ballot-box clause to achieve the same purpose?

The answer is by no means clear. The Court's rationale rests upon the notion that the prestrike ballot is an attempt to interfere with the union's internal political process and, as such, substantially modifies the collective bargaining system provided for in the NLRA by weakening the independence of the representative chosen by the employees.[92] Said the Court: "It enables the employer, in effect, to deal with its employees rather than with their statutory representative."[93]

The difficulties here are enormous. First, although the Board and the courts have taken the position that the parties need not be deadlocked on all issues in order for there to be an impasse, the fact is that it is sometimes powerless to make the assessment—and, as we have already seen, the consequences for either the union or the employer can be significant.

Second, it could be argued that involvement in the determination as to what constitutes a mandatory or nonmandatory subject of bargaining within the meaning of the Act is an indirect method of regulating the substance of the collective bargaining agreement. This is contrary to the statutory philosophy. But the counterargument is that the substance of the agreement is not being regulated—only the extent to which the subject matter may be discussed or negotiated.

A third area of contention relates to the way in which collective bargaining is to be conducted. *Borg-Warner* involves the Board in establishing the details of the parties' ground rules. This is less important in the United States than in Japan, where litigation can arise out of management's insistence that it is not obligated to bargain because of provocative union conduct such as abusive name-calling, imprisonment of the boss in his own office or factory, or the wearing of armbands.[94] The closest American analogue is a refusal by management to bargain with a union because of the violent behavior of a union leader.[95] The Supreme Court has held that an employer is obliged to bargain with a lawfully recognized union that is seeking new affiliation without taking a vote among the nonunion employees as well as the union members in the bargaining unit.[96] Justice Brennan said for the Court that a contrary rule would give ". . . the employer the power to veto an independent union's decision to affiliate, thereby allowing the employer to interfere directly with union decisionmaking that Congress intended to insulate from outside interference."[97] The need for unions to merge in order to redress the imbalance between conglomerates and unions makes this an important issue in labor law. Generally the employees are entitled to select as a union representative anyone they would like to have represent them.[98] Closely related to this kind of issue is the demand by one side that a court stenographer be present at bargaining sessions. The Board and the courts have rejected this view and held that the subject is nonmandatory in that a stenographer's presence might inhibit the free flow of discussion.[99] The goal of retaining a completely accurate record, as in an adjudicative proceeding, is a subordinate one.

The fourth major problem in this area is the difficulty of defining what is mandatory and what is nonmandatory. In a case involving an employer's subcontracting of maintenance work previously performed by employees in the bargaining unit, the Supreme Court attempted to come to grips with this issue.[100] The Court identified three governing considerations in its conclusion that the subject was mandatory. The first was whether the subject matter was within the "literal definition" of "conditions of employment." Since workers' jobs were affected by the subcontracting, it was not difficult to reach the conclusion that their conditions of employment were being affected. The second consideration was whether industrial peace was likely to be promoted through the negotiation of the issue. Of course one might say that, since the party proposing a particular subject is likely to feel less aggrieved in the event that it is able to discuss it thoroughly, it is more likely that a peaceable settlement would be reached. But this would permit any party to put any subject on the table. Third, the Court stated that the practice in the industry was important. Since many unions and employers had negotiated clauses and collective bargaining agreements providing for limitations or prohibitions on subcontracting, it was thought that this factor weighed in favor of making subcontracting a mandatory subject of bargaining. But the Court was doing what it had said in some of its "freedom of contract" cases it would never do: impose upon union and employers a procrustean rule based on practices that might well have evolved in different industries under totally different circumstances. It might be said that if some unions and some employers wished to bargain seriously about subcontracting and to incorporate clauses in their collective bargaining agreement, they should be free to do so, and that those who did not wish to do so would be allowed to go their own way. The response of the Court and the Board to this idea was that whatever is dictated by the refusal-to-bargain cases, it is not a requirement to include a particular subject within the collective bargaining agreement.

There are many problems with the last of the three criteria explained in the preceding paragraph, but some of the language in the subcontracting case and in its progeny indicates how difficult the first criterion is in actual application. The Supreme Court, and Justice Stewart in a special concurring opinion, were at pains to emphasize that the Board cannot modify the free-enterprise economy through its interpretation of labor legislation in defining what constitutes a mandatory subject of bargaining. As Stewart said:

This kind of subcontracting falls short of such larger entrepreneurial questions as what shall be produced, how capital shall be invested in fixed assets, or what the basic scope of the enterprise shall be. In my view, the Court's decision in this case has nothing to do with whether any aspects of those larger issues could under any circumstances be considered subjects of compulsory collective bargaining under the present law.[101]

Justice Stewart's concurring opinion is not very clear about the demarcation line between mandatory and nonmandatory subjects of bargaining, but the Court has relied on his thinking in attempting to draw lines. Said Justice Harry Blackmun in an opinion issued in 1981:

Some management decisions, such as choice of advertising and promotion, product type and design, and financing arrangements, have only an indirect and attenuated impact on the employment relationship. See Fibreboard, 379 U.S. at 223 (Stewart, J., concurring). Other management decisions, such as the order of succession of layoffs and recalls, production quotas, and work rules, are almost exclusively "an aspect of the relationship" between employer and employee. . . . The present case concerns a third type of management decision, one that had a direct impact on employment, since jobs were inexorably eliminated by the termination, but had as its focus only the economic profitability of the contract [between a maintenance company and a nursing home] . . . a concern under these facts wholly apart from the employment relationship. This decision, involving a change in the scope and direction of the enterprise, is akin to the decision whether to be in business at all, "not in [itself] primarily about conditions of employment, though the effect of the decision may be necessarily to terminate employment." . . . At the same time, this decision touches on a matter of central and pressing concern to the union and its member employees: the possibility of continued employment and the retention of the employees' very jobs.[102]

It seems clear that any complete closing of a business is a managerial prerogative that is beyond the scope of any portion of the NLRA[103] at least where the business is not sold as a going concern. The appellate courts have generally held that partial closings were similarly outside the reach of refusal-to-bargain charges by unions.[104] However, both the Second and Third Circuit Courts of Appeals began to fashion limitations on managerial freedom in this area.[105] In an opinion authored by Judge Morris Lasker for the Second Circuit, that court stated the following:

> We believe that the determination whether to impose a duty to bargain should not depend on the relative injury to the employer and the employees, but rather on the relative merits of the arguments put forth as to those classic considerations of whether the purposes of the statute are furthered by the decision to impose a duty to bargain in a particular case.

Accordingly the presumption that the employer has an obligation to bargain over a decision partially to close the business may be rebutted by showing that the purposes of the statute will not be furthered by imposition of a duty to bargain. Without an attempt to enumerate all those instances in which the presumption may be rebutted, a few examples may be noted for purposes of illustration. The employer might overcome the presumption by demonstrating that bargaining over the decision would be futile, since the purposes of the statute would not be served by ordering the parties to bargain when it is clear that the employer's decision cannot be changed. Other relevant considerations would be that the closing was due to emergency financial circumstances, or that the custom of the industry, shown by the absence of such an obligation from typical collective bargaining agreements, is not to bargain over such decisions. The presumption might also be rebutted if it could be demonstrated that forcing the employer to bargain would endanger the vitality of the entire business, so that the purposes of the statute would not be furthered by mandating bargaining to benefit some employees to the potential detriment of the remainder. This might be a particularly significant point if the number to be laid off was small and the number of the remainder was large.[106]

The Supreme Court categorically rejected this position by a vote of 7–2. In an opinion authored by Justice Blackmun the Court, expressing concern that the Second Circuit's standards were not sufficiently precise and would unnecessarily expose employers to back-pay liability, concluded that "the harm likely to be done to an employer's need to operate freely in deciding whether to shut down part of its business purely for economic reasons outweighs the incremental benefit that might be gained through the union's participation in making the decision."[107] The Court reasoned that it was unlikely that the union could induce the employer to change its mind and that delay would harm management's interests in speed, flexibility, and secrecy. The decision to partially close therefore is not itself a mandatory subject of bargaining, but the "effects" of the decision (severance payments, relocation allowances, retraining, and the like) are.[108] The Court has left open the question of whether management decisions on plant relocations, plant sales, automation, and types of subcontracting not covered by the previous Supreme Court decision referred to above are mandatory subjects.

Initially the Board, while sometimes limiting the thrust of *First National Maintenance*,[109] generally interpreted it so as to require the union to show that labor costs are the reason for the employer's decision.[110] But in *Dubuque Packing Co., Inc.*,[111] the Board adumbrated a test for determining whether an employer's relocation decision is a mandatory subject of bargaining. The Board held that if the relocation was "unaccompanied by basic change in the nature of the employer's operation," the General Counsel establishes a prima facie violation, and the burden shifts to the employer to establish that the work performed at the new location varies "significantly" from the work performed at the former plant—or that labor costs were not a factor and that even if they were a factor, labor cost concessions could not have changed the employer's decision.[112] In connection with the last mentioned consideration, the Board said:

> . . . an employer would have no bargaining obligation if it showed that, although labor costs were a consideration in the decision to relocate unit work, it would not remain at the present plant because, for example, the costs for modernization of equipment or environmental controls were greater than any labor cost concessions the union could offer. On the other hand, an employer would have a bargaining obligation if the union could and would offer concessions that approximate, meet, or exceed the anticipated costs or benefits that prompted the relocation decision, since the decision then would be amenable to resolution through the bargaining process.[113]

However, the elaborate test articulated in *Dubuque* does not apply to contracting out of work that does not affect the scope or direction of the enterprise[114]—that is to say, a violation will be found more easily under circumstances where the scope or direction of the enterprise is at issue. Nor did the *Dubuque* test apply to the employer's obligation to bargain before, for instance, instituting a decision to lay off workers.[115]

Meanwhile in *Milwaukee Spring I*[116] the Board seemed to fashion a route by which the potential implications of *First National Maintenance* could be circumvented, holding that layoffs due to the relocation of a plant constituted a repudiation of the contract provision that sets forth the wage rates. This important decision was reversed by a new Board majority in 1984.[117]

Frequently there is litigation about the duty to bargain during the term of the contract and the employer's right to refuse to do so when it has negotiated a "zipper clause" which, in the employer's view, zips up all future obligations regarding negotiations. A party to a collective bargaining agreement may lawfully require midterm negotiation over mandatory subjects not "contained in" the agreement.[118] But when a party has acquiesced during negotiations in the exclusion of a mandatory subject by effectively "agreeing to disagree" on the issue, and the matter is not incorporated in the contract, midterm bargaining on the subject cannot be required.[119] For the zipper clause to waive a duty to bargain, it must do so clearly and unequivocally.[120] Said the Board:

In general, a zipper clause is an agreement by the parties to preclude further bargaining during the term of the contract. If the zipper clause contains clear and unmistakable language to that effect, the result will be that neither party can force the other party to bargain, during the term of the contract, about matters encompassed by the clause. That is, the zipper clause will "shield," from a refusal to bargain charge, the party to whom such a bargaining demand is made. Similarly, under such a clause, neither party can unilaterally institute, during the term of contract, a proposal concerning a matter encompassed by the clause. That is, the zipper clause cannot be used as a "sword" to accomplish a change from the status quo.[121]

Plant Closing Legislation

In 1988 Congress, notwithstanding President Reagan's opposition, enacted the Workers Adjustment Retraining and Notification Act.[122] The Act obliges employers to provide sixty-days notice to employees or their representatives in connection with plant closures and substantial layoffs. Additionally thirteen states have enacted their own plant closing legislation.[123]

Take-It-or-Leave-It Bargaining: Boulwarism

Other difficult refusal-to-bargain charges involve "Boulwarism" (a term derived from the name of General Electric's vice president for labor relations). In essence this was a policy that required the employer to announce its final position at the outset of bargaining. The employer's idea here is that a tortured process of give and take in which the employer is excoriated for its obstinacy and unreasonableness and gradually brought down to a modified position only enhances the prestige of the union and diminishes that of the employer. The position of the General Electric Company—which created and refined Boulwarism—was that it would provide a firm and fair offer to its workers, and that it would announce to the employees what was going on in the collective bargaining so that the workers would not have to rely on the union's characterization of the discussions.[124] In some respects this resembles the union conduct that prompted the Taft-Hartley Congress to impose the duty to bargain on unions. Unions, it is to be recalled, often threw the contract on the table and told small employers to "take it or leave it." Here, however, General Electric took the position that external factors, such as a change in the economy, could alter the company's position. The prevailing view is that the mere announcement of the employer's final offer at the commencement of negotiations is not per se an unfair labor practice. Good-faith bargaining does not require the parties to make proposals and counterproposals; it merely requires good-faith intent to consummate an agreement. However, the courts have said that it is appropriate to take into account other conduct of the employer which, along with tactics such as Boulwarism, may be considered as a basis for inferring bad faith under the totality of circumstances.

Unlawful surface bargaining engaged in with an intent not to consummate a collective bargaining agreement cannot be found on the basis of whether a particular proposal is "acceptable" or "unacceptable."[125] Said the Board in another case:

In determining whether a party has bargained in good faith, making a genuine effort to reach agreement, we will seldom find direct evidence of a party's intent to frustrate the bargaining process. Rather, we must look at all of its conduct, but away from the bargaining table and at the table, including the substance of the proposals on which the party has insisted. . . . Such an examination is not intended to measure the intrinsic worth of the proposals, but instead to determine whether, in combination and by the manner in which they are urged, they evince a mindset open to agreement or one that is opposed to true give-and-take.[126]

Again freedom-of-contract cases such as *Insurance Agents* and *American Ship Building*, which are consistent with the *General Electric* "totality-of-conduct" approach, provide for the use of tactics that (at least in the short run) seem to discourage genuine dialogue. On the other hand, the Supreme Court has held that employers have an obligation to open their books and disclose financial data when they plead an inability to pay in collective bargaining,[127] in the interest of genuine dialogue between parties truly concerned with reaching a settlement. This decision, which regulates conduct and tactics, is aimed at establishing collective bargaining that will concentrate on the economic conditions confronting the employer. However, it has been circumvented by managements not asserting an inability to pay, even if that is the basis for their negotiating posture. Only employers lacking competent labor counsel fail to rely upon other considerations, such as wage comparability. The inclination to rely on the totality of circumstances (in these cases, on whether management pleads poverty) shows the courts' unwillingness to regulate too much. Only employers in unusual industries, such as baseball, have difficulty with the NLRA's disclosure requirements. Because there are no comparable wage scales to be cited in baseball, it was difficult for the owners to say that their position in the 1981 negotiations was based on anything other than their view that the industry was imperiled economically.

Moreover the Board and the courts have established a arbitrary demarcation between a position based on inability to pay and that which is predicated upon competitive pressures from other employers. Judge Richard Posner has written: "a company has stated that the test is whether the company is *unable* to pay." Said the court:

> . . . a company can survive, certainly in the short run and often in the long run, even though it is paying higher wages than its competitors. The company may have some other cost advantage; its competitors may price above their costs; the market may be expanding rapidly. The company will grow less rapidly than if its costs were lower and may stagnate or decline, but it need not die. There is thus no contradiction in a company's stating, on the one hand, that it is profitable and, on the other hand, that its costs are higher than its competitors' and it wants to reduce them.[128]

On remand, the Board has stated that the test is whether an employer's position is based upon an inability to pay during the life of the contract.[129] The Court of Appeals for the District of Columbia, noting the Board's shift from its previous position,[130] has concurred.[131]

Two comments are in order here about the duty-to-bargain concept generally and the *General Electric* case in particular. The first is that again the schizoid tendencies in the National Labor Relations Act come to the forefront. On the one hand, there is a reluctance to interfere with tactics—again the concern is that this will lead to regulation of the substance of the collective bargaining agreement. At the same time it is quite obvious that the General Electric Company was attempting to denigrate the union, to make it an ineffective bargaining agent, and perhaps ultimately to eliminate it altogether as a bargaining agent. The employees would get the message that the union could not alter the employer's basic view of what constituted a fair and firm offer and would soon begin to ask themselves why they had joined the union at all. Surely this was the basic objective of GE's strategy. The law tries to ride two difficult horses: preservation of the collective bargaining process (which argues for condemnation of Boulwarism) and freedom of contract (which eschews regulation).

Another basic problem with Boulwarism is the elusiveness of the remedy. The courts, unwilling to condemn the tactic itself, elect to rely on totality of conduct. The next time around in the bargaining process, the employer simply changes one tactic and the question of whether the totality of circumstances warrants a finding of bad faith requires another round of adjudication. To put it another way, the likelihood of a contempt sanction for misconduct is extremely remote given the lack of precision involved in any order. All of this leads to the next chapter, which is concerned with remedies.

7

Remedies and the Labor Reform Bill of 1978

The principal reasons for the considerable focus on remedies and the emergence of proposals for labor-law reform in the Labor Reform Bill of 1978 are the increased caseload of the National Labor Relations Board and the strain that caseload has placed on an administrative statutory scheme that was already convoluted and tortuous. As Chairman John Fanning of the NLRB said in testimony before the House Committee on Education and Labor:

In 1957, when I was first appointed to the Board, the agency processed a total of 16,000 cases and the Board issued 353 decisions in contested unfair labor practice cases. In the current fiscal year (1972) we will receive more than 52,000 cases and we expect to issue 1,121 such decisions. In fiscal year 1978 we estimate that 57,000 cases will be filed with the agency and we expect to issue 1,242 decisions. In fiscal year 1979 the number of cases will amount to 61,000, and our published decisions will number 1,400.[1]

This has delayed the administrative process. A worker dismissed for union activity during an organizational campaign may not obtain the remedies provided by the statute until long after they are meaningful. The worker's losses in the interim can never be adequately remedied by the law. As the House Committee on Education and Labor said: "The committee heard testimony about workers who had their homes foreclosed and cars repossessed while waiting an ultimately favorable disposition of their case. Clearly, in addition to failing to deter violations of the act, remedies under existing law also fail to compensate the victims of such illegal conduct."[2]

Remedies Mean Compensation

One reason for the difficulties with the NLRA is the Supreme Court's holding that the Act is designed to perform a remedial function and that punitive sanctions may not be imposed for violations.[3] This translates into the proposition that if an employee receives more than he or she had lost, the remedy is punitive rather than remedial.[4] In line with this approach the Act provides that interim earnings or those that would have been obtained with "reasonable diligence" be deducted from any back pay the employee receives from the employer (unemployment compensation and social-welfare benefits are not deducted, for public-policy reasons).[5] This means that back-pay hearings often take place after an unfair labor practice proceeding, and in such hearings detailed testimony is taken about the kinds of work at which the worker was employed after the commission of the unfair labor practice, or whether the worker was available in the relevant labor market.[6] Often litigation over the question of what is the relevant labor market adds to the delay.

The problem here is that the worker is exasperated with the mere award of back pay and in future situations will be unlikely to engage in protected activity. A dismissed worker may not even make use of the remedies the Board provides. As one study has noted, the number of employees accepting reinstatement was found to equal only 5 percent of all persons discriminatorily discharged where reinstatement was not offered until six months after the violation.[7] As the conservative journal *Business Week* noted, when an appeal is taken to the court subsequent to an NLRB proceeding the process can stretch for so long that the "worker is financially and emotionally exhausted."[8]

The Collective Interest

Even more troublesome is the impact that all of this can have on a union's general organizational activity. Union adherents who have not been disciplined for union activity will quickly get the message. If they are found out or retaliated against for their union activity, they will suffer similar consequences and will wait a considerable period of time before obtaining a remedy even if they are able to prove unlawful employer conduct. If the remedy is reinstatement, it may simply put them back to work in an uncongenial environment. Back pay will come only after litigation about what work they actually held or (even more vexatious) what work they could have obtained with reasonable diligence. The effect of all of this will be to encourage workers to eschew union activity and to thus kill an organizational campaign. Under such circumstances the employer is perceived as merely paying a license fee for dismissing workers unlawfully, and pays out considerably less than would have been provided in wages, fringe benefits, and other improved conditions of employment by a collective bargaining agreement—benefits that might have been negotiated had a union come on the scene.

Delays

A dramatic example of the legal abuses here concerns J.P. Stevens & Co., which according to NLRB data supplied during Representative Frank Thompson's Oversight Hearings in 1975 had at that time ninety-six different unfair labor practice cases pending before the Board, in addition to having violated the NLRA on many occasions.[9] The same hearings showed similar management misbehavior in San Francisco, a union stronghold, where some corporation attorneys have attained new levels of sophistication in achieving delay.[10] A decade later the problem remained; in some respects things were worse. In 1983 the median time from the filing of an unfair labor practice charge to the issuance of a complaint by the Board was 45 days. Another 75 to 94 days were consumed from the issuance of the complaint to the close of the hearing before the administrative law judge. From the close of the hearing to the time of the administrative law judge's decision the period was 116 days. From the administrative law judge's decision to the decision by the Board the period was 194 days (versus 120 and 143 in 1976 and 1977). The interval between the filing of the charge and the Board's decision was 627 days (versus 358 and 410 in 1976 and 1977)—and this without any appeal to the courts. The problem became worse because of a shortage of administrative law judges.

These delay problems were not temporary. The administrative delays in processing unfair labor practice complaints have not decreased in the last half of the 1980s—indeed they have worsened. Although the median time for the filing of a charge to the issuance of a complaint by the Board remained at 45 days, in 1989 the median time from the issuance of the complaint to the close of the hearing before an administrative law judge increased to 133 days. Administrative law judges in 1989 were a median of 37 days slower in issuing their decisions in 1989 than 6 years earlier, taking 153 days from the close of hearing. From the administrative law judge's decision to the decision by the Board took 259 days in 1989—up 65 days from 1983. Thus the entire process took a median of 738 days in 1989 (as compared to 627 days in 1983).[11]

In 1976 and 1977 resorting to the judicial process after an NLRB decision often took even longer than the Board's own administrative process. For instance, 37 to 50 days were consumed from the date of decision until referral of the matter for enforcement in the court of appeals. Another 38 to 43 days elapsed before a petition was filed. The agency no longer keeps such statistics, but in 1976 between 317 and 350 days elapsed from the filing of the petition until the court of appeals reached a decision. In addition quite frequently a petition for *certiorari*, or review, is filed with the United States Supreme Court. Each year more than 5,000 such petitions are filed, and only approximately 150 are granted.[12] The chances of success are remote. Again more time goes by until the litigation is finished.

Another delay comes in connection with representation proceedings before the Board after the filing of an election petition. From 1980 through 1984 half of all elections took place within 50 days of the filing of a petition. Where the parties had agreed to a so-called consent election, in which case there is no litigation about such issues as the appropriate unit, the median delay in 1984 was 41 days. These delays increased only slightly by 1989.[13] But litigious parties do not generally agree to such a procedure, and there are about half as many regional director and Board consent elections as those that take place subsequent to litigation and a hearing.

Subversion of Election Outcomes by Employers

A third variation on the same basic theme are cases where a majority of employees voting have cast their ballots for the union as their exclusive representative but the employer refuses to bargain with the union on the ground that the unit is inappropriate or that ineligible employees had voted. When an employer refuses to bargain with a union that has been certified by the Board as exclusive representative, the union files an unfair labor practice charge, the General Counsel issues a complaint, and a hearing is held before an administrative law judge. The record in the representation hearing is incorporated in the unfair labor practice record. The administrative law judge, relying upon what had already been decided by the Board, finds that the employer has unlawfully refused to bargain with the union, and this is affirmed by the Board. Then the employer appeals to the circuit court of appeals and, in some instances, petitions for *certiorari* to the Supreme Court. Between three and five years later, subsequent to the certification, the employer is ordered to bargain with the union. But meanwhile the improved wages, fringe benefits, and other conditions of employment that might have been negotiated have been lost to the employees. Moreover the employees, frustrated by the lack of collective bargaining and confronted with the employer's legally defensible position[14] that it cannot bargain with the union while the representation issue is pending in the courts, have achieved nothing, while unorganized employees have forged ahead. The lesson for the employees is that a vote for the union has made life more difficult for them.

In the *Ex-Cell-O* decision[15] the NLRB held that a remedy providing the employees with benefits lost during the interim period (a "make-whole" remedy) would have been an impermissible imposition of contract terms upon the parties and thus was beyond the Board's remedial authority. The Board, however, has fashioned remedies including litigation expenses in cases where the violation was "clear and flagrant."[16]

Expediting the Administrative Process

The Labor Reform Bill of 1978 attempted to cope with many of the problems described above. Inasmuch as the principal problem was delay, it provided for "summary affirmance" of administrative law judges' decisions by the National Labor Relations Board. Since most issues are ones of fact (i.e., of whether the management representative or the employee is telling the truth about the basis for discipline or discharge), the administrative law judge is presumably in the best position to make such a decision; the Board could never assess credibility or demeanor on the basis of a dry transcript. Approximately 74 percent of all contested cases taken to the Board subsequent to the administrative law judge's decision are adopted without any modification or minor clarification—a "short form" adoption. More than 80 percent of administrative law judges' positions are affirmed by the Board. Accordingly the Labor Reform Bill would have provided that one party could petition for summary affirmance on the ground that the issue was essentially fact and not law or a novel issue of law.

The Board now has the authority to seek relief from the federal district court where a delay would produce irreparable harm to the charging party. Section 10(j) of the NLRA authorizes the Board to obtain temporary injunctive relief to preserve the status quo as it was prior to the unfair labor practice pending hearings before the agency.[17] In the case of a discharge this would require reinstatement of the worker pending appeal. However, the Board has not been particularly successful in convincing the federal courts that such relief is appropriate—indeed it has been argued, sometimes with a good deal of merit, that the Board has been excessively cautious in seeking such relief. (In fairness to the Board, it should be pointed out that delay is built into its own internal process by the statute; concurrence of the five-member Board must be sought subsequent to a decision by the General Counsel to seek such relief. This stands in sharp contrast to section 10(1) of the Act,[18] which mandates the regional attorney—without the involvement of the General Counsel in Washington or the full Board—to seek injunctive relief in connection with certain kinds of union unfair labor practices.)[19]

The Labor Reform Bill would have encouraged both the Board and the courts to seek and fashion temporary injunctive relief by providing criteria under which the courts could issue injunctions. For instance, the bill was intended to make possible injunctions against discharges where the union had not negotiated its first contract. Accordingly the desire was to promote collective bargaining when it was most vulnerable to complete undermining through unlawful management conduct. Another useful proposal here would have been to allow the Board to seek injunctive relief at the regional level so as to expedite the Board's own internal process, just as the regional office has such authority in connection with certain unfair union practices referred to above.

All of these proposals were attempts to cope with delays in the administrative process that dimmed the prospect of collective bargaining even where the union had the allegiance of a majority of the workers. But there still remained the problem of effective remedies. The Labor Reform Bill would have provided for the awarding of more than back pay to dismissed workers. The House favored double back pay and no deduction for interim earnings; the Senate, more modestly, would have provided for one and a half times the amount of back pay. Similar remedies are available in different forms in the antitrust and equal-employment-opportunity fields. (The provision in some of the reform proposals for compensation to be awarded automatically, rather than only where employer conduct had been malicious or deliberate, may have been a flaw.)

Another concern over the Labor Reform bill was that more comprehensive relief in the form of double or one-and-one-half damages would not deter wrongdoing but would simply represent a more expensive "license." Accordingly it was proposed that any party found by the Board to have willfully violated Board orders would be barred, upon authorization by the secretary of labor, from participating in federal contracts for three years. This weapon is currently available in connection with equal employment opportunity, but the record of law enforcement in that area has not been particularly good.[20] Government, which wants to have its contracts with private employers fulfilled, generally seems able to find a basis for moving ahead with the future contracts rather than canceling, debarring, or whatever.

Finally, the Labor Reform Bill would have reversed the *Ex-Cell-O* decision, in which the NLRB refused to provide "make-whole" relief for employees where employers refused to bargain with a certified union and utilized the appellate process. As noted above, the only remedy is a court order obligating the employer to bargain—years after the initial obligation. The bill provided that in cases where the employer had unlawfully refused to bargain for an initial contract, employees would be awarded compensation for the delay in bargaining. The workers would receive an amount based on the average wage settlements negotiated by workers at plants where collective bargaining had proceeded lawfully, and would receive wages and fringe benefits retroactively from the time of the unlawful refusal to bargain until bargaining was commenced.

Still a recidivist employer might well not be affected by any of these remedies where a union was attempting to obtain a first contract. In a final analysis, the only effective remedy for a union is one that puts it in a position to obtain a collective bargaining agreement. It is the inability to get a first contract that, more than anything else, has stimulated demands for reform of the present laws. In hearings before the House Subcommittee on Labor-Management Relations, Jack Crowley, president of the San Francisco Labor Council, concurred in this view: "If the union wins an election, then there should be some sanction imposed upon the employer, if the employer has delayed the case at any stage of the proceeding. Such a sanction could include the awarding by the Board of benefits to the employees represented by the union that are consistent with the contracts that the union has in the geographical area in the identical or similar industry in which the individual employer is involved."[21] One difficulty with this kind of approach is that both unions and employers are less than enthusiastic about anything that smacks of compulsory arbitration in the wage or economic area—even though some unions recognize that this is the only effective remedy in many cases. In a number of Canadian provinces—Ontario, Quebec, British Columbia, Newfoundland, and Manitoba—such objections have not been allowed to override the provinces' experiment with first-contract arbitration as a remedy for unfair labor practices.

The Labor Reform Bill was defeated in 1978. (More accurately it was not voted upon on its merits because of a filibuster in the Senate.) Of course there were considerable arguments put forward by the employers on the merits. The most formidable of these was that severe remedies would be counterproductive in that they would create fewer settlements and more numerous and longer delays. There would be more of an incentive to litigate because the cost of settlement would be greater, and thus there would be more cases, hearings, and delays.

The problem of delay and ineffective remedies remains an important one in labor-relations law. It is sure to be addressed in the years to come. In the meantime, however, the labor movement's failure to obtain reform and its frustration with the Reagan Board have prompted AFL-CIO's President Lane Kirkland to promote the idea that the National Labor Relations Act ought to be repealed.[22]

8

Dispute Resolution in the Established Relationship

Dispute-resolution machinery, whether it is devised by private parties or imposed by legislation, generally focuses on two quite different problems. The first relates to disputes that arise during the term of the collective bargaining agreement, usually involving its interpretation. These are called "rights" disputes; the question is what resolution should be made where the parties disagree as to the application or interpretation of the agreement. The second area is "interest" disputes; that is, disputes that arise over the terms of the new collective bargaining agreement (generally after the expiration of the old one). These disputes, frequently resolved under guidelines or criteria established by the parties or by legislation, generally concern wages and other economic issues that go right to the core of the bargaining relationship. The mode of dispute resolution can vary. In the United States we have generally utilized mediation, fact finding, or arbitration. Mediation involves the intervention of a third party, appointed by labor and management or by government, whose role it is to attempt to get the parties to resolve their differences amicably. The mediator has no authority to do anything—even to make recommendations to the parties as to how the matter should be resolved. Mediators often play innovative and important roles in the resolution of disputes, although sometimes they simply carry coffee from the labor side to the management side. But the third party's function is to clarify the issues, appeal to the parties' reasoning processes by using the arts of persuasion, and (when specifically authorized by the parties) to make recommendations to them. The mediator must have the parties' confidence. They must be able to entrust their secrets and confidences to the mediator, without fear that this information will be leaked to the other side. A skillful mediator is able to make use of such information in making suggestions, structuring the dialogue, or formulating proposals.

Fact-finding differs from mediation in the sense that fact-finders not only may investigate the dispute but may make public recommendations for its resolution. The theory is that pressure is placed upon the party who resists the recommendations to come to terms because the public or those interested in the dispute will exert pressure upon whichever side is more obstinate. Usually we tend to associate the use of mediation and fact-finding with interest disputes relating to the terms of a new contract, but this is not always the case. Both mediation and fact-finding can be and are used in connection with grievance or rights disputes.

When we speak of arbitration in the United States, we generally mean private, voluntary negotiations conducted with the mutual consent of the parties—a pattern that contradicts the general impression that foreigners have of the American system as written into and governed by law. (The Railway Labor Act, which covers airline and railway workers, and some state laws relating to public-sector disputes mandate arbitration, and interest disputes in the public sector have assumed great importance in recent years.) Arbitration in the United States is encouraged by the National Labor Relations Act and by Supreme Court decisions handed down since the early 1960s. However, the practice of arbitration developed prior to and in some circumstances in spite of the law, since in some jurisdictions arbitration agreements were considered void as against public policy. Jealous courts did not wish to have their jurisdictions undermined.

Arbitration began in the United States before the turn of the century, appeared in 1903 in the form of the "umpire" system of the Anthracite Coal Commission, was accepted by the hosiery and clothing industries in the form of the "impartial chairman" system in the 1920s, and was well on its way even prior to the Wagner Act of 1935. It gained greater impetus through the War Labor Board, which, operating under the emergency conditions of World War II, encouraged, nurtured, and in some instances imposed no-strike obligations and arbitration machinery. All of this was well in advance of Taft-Hartley, which merely ratified a trend the parties had evolved for themselves.

Arbitration Defined

Arbitration is quite different from mediation, which also involves third-party intervention. In the United States and in other countries it means a decision-making process, although many arbitrators rely upon mediatory skills as well. Indeed the use of mediation was a prominent characteristic of both the "impartial chairman" system and some of the permanent umpireships that existed during the 1940s. In the final analysis, however, a decision or award can be issued by the third party. This is the significance of arbitration as opposed to other modes of dispute resolution.

Interest arbitration is a relatively rare phenomenon in the United States.[1] However, as collective bargaining has extended itself into the public sector, where striking has been considered less acceptable, interest arbitration has become popular as a substitute for strikes. The Postal Reorganization Act's provision for interest arbitration in the Postal Service was utilized in 1984 when a Board of Arbitrators, chaired by Dr. Clark Kerr, rendered the first arbitration award ever rendered at the federal level.[2]

Moreover an increasing number of jurisdictions have begun to use "final-offer" arbitration, under which the arbitrator is required to select one of the two parties' last offers.[3] Some of these states make the same provision for police, and some for municipal employees or even public employees generally. Twenty-four jurisdictions have passed statutes providing for some form of binding interest arbitration.[4] Final-offer arbitration is designed to force both sides to be reasonable and thus to avoid one of the major objections to interest arbitration (particularly when it is compulsory): that it will erode the collective bargaining process and keep both sides from compromising out of fear that the arbitrator will "cut the baby in half." This fear inhibits the give and take and the flexibility that are prerequisites to collective bargaining, because those who compromised would feel that they had sacrificed their position with the arbitrator. Because of the uncertainty about whose offer will be selected, both sides are induced to be reasonable and compromise. Final-offer arbitration has been used in salary disputes in baseball. It also has been suggested as the procedure to be used in Taft-Hartley and Railway Labor Act emergency disputes.[5]

By 1976 the steel industry seemed to have adopted interest arbitration through its negotiation of the Experimental Steel Negotiating Agreement,[6] but it appears as though the parties have now discarded this approach. The theory in an industry such as steel is that the prospect of a strike prompts present and potential customers to buy from foreign producers, particularly the Germans and the Japanese. Once customers are motivated to buy elsewhere they often become permanent customers. The assurance that a dispute will be resolved through arbitration and not a strike is likely to hold customers who would otherwise be lost.

But it is grievance or rights arbitration involving disputes during the term of the agreement that is the most important aspect of the American experience. Some 95 percent of collective bargaining agreements negotiated between labor and management in the United States contain arbitration clauses, and all but 1 percent permit one of the two sides to obtain arbitration during the term of the contract without obtaining an agreement from the other side to arbitrate the particular dispute in question. To be sure, there are exceptions to this pattern. In the National Trucking Agreement there is no provision for arbitration. In the construction industry only 70 percent of the agreements contain arbitration clauses, and it appears that arbitration is used less than in manufacturing, even where it is provided for by contract.

At this point it is important to distinguish between different modes of arbitration. Most arbitration in the United States is ad hoc; that is, an arbitrator is selected to hear a particular dispute during the term of the contract. At one time it was thought that permanent umpireships, with one individual or a rotating list of individuals chosen for the term of the agreement to resolve disputes, were going to be the wave of the future. However, despite the apparent desirability of an arbitrator who is not a stranger to the industry or company and is therefore presumably more expert, only 12 percent of arbitration clauses provide for permanent umpireship today.

Where there is ad hoc arbitration, the arbitrators are often chosen from lists prepared by the Federal Mediation and Conciliation Service (an autonomous governmental mediation unit) and the American Arbitration Association (a nonprofit organization that provides arbitration services to private parties throughout the country). Sometimes state mediation agencies that are analogues or counterparts to the Federal Mediation and Conciliation Service perform the same function. No one really knows how much arbitration takes place in the United States, since most arbitrations appear to arise out of private communications between the parties and the individual arbitrators.

Most of the more experienced arbitrators are among the 600-odd members of a professional association called the National Academy of Arbitrators, who are chosen on the basis of the number of cases they have heard and the reports of the parties who have appeared before them or heard about them. Since the early 1970s there have existed programs for the recruiting and training of new arbitrators who will be acceptable to both labor and management. These programs have been promoted by universities, the American Arbitration Association, and the American Bar Association.

The Advantages of Arbitration

Why do Americans use arbitration rather than the courts to resolve their disputes? There are five principal reasons. The first is that the system, for the most part, has been a voluntary one, devised by the parties to deal with their own problems. The American system is intended to fit the parties' own peculiar needs; this is the reason for its rich diversity and the difficulty of making generalizations about it. When one understands this, some of the difficulties of determining what constitutes a mandatory subject of bargaining under the *Borg-Warner* line of cases become more apparent. The system is by no means uniform, although the parties are interested in what their counterparts are doing in other industries and often appear to emulate what is done elsewhere.

Second, in most relationships grievance-arbitration machinery resolves problems before arbitration has to be invoked as a last resort. Most contracts provide for three to five steps in which discussions take place between increasingly high-ranking labor and management representatives without outside involvement. At these steps attempts are made to resolve differences on an informal basis (in the first instance, between an employee and/or a union steward and the line manager) and to clarify what is in dispute. This aspect of the process is not always informal and free of trouble. In litigation arising under the National Labor Relations Act's unfair labor practice machinery, the Supreme Court held that an employer's denial of an employee's request that her union representative be present at an investigation interview violated the statute.[7] However, the NLRB has limited the scope of the Court's decision through its holding that there is no statutory right to union representation where the employer has already reached "a final, binding decision to impose certain discipline on the employee prior to the interview."[8] Of course the parties may handle this matter differently under the provisions in their collective bargaining agreement if they wish to do so.

A third reason for the acceptance of arbitration is its relative informality. The principle of *stare decisis*, which

American courts use to bind the court to legal doctrines established in the past, is not applicable to arbitration proceedings.[9] In other words, what another arbitrator has previously decided where the same facts are in evidence may be persuasive authority, a second arbitrator has discretion to consider the matter anew. At the same time arbitrators will often adhere to the "law of the shop" in the form of past practices, settlements, or arbitration awards in the plant in which the dispute arose. Lawyers are present in an increasing number of instances, and each party is always represented, exhibits are generally introduced, and generally there are witnesses (who need not be sworn but are in more instances, and who may be examined and cross-examined). However, arbitrators do not follow judicial rules on the admissibility of testimony and other evidence. Greater formality may be a sign of a less mature relationship, though not always. Transcription by a court stenographer generally implies formality, but it may well be worthwhile—particularly if many facts are in dispute, if many witnesses contradict one another, or if complex contract interpretations are involved.

Fourth, the principal attraction of arbitration for both sides is that it is more expeditious than litigation (although the American system has recently developed some deficiencies: delay, expense, and difficulty in coping with employment discrimination). Finally, to some extent arbitration serves as a substitute for the right to strike for a period of time. This is a major part of the legal theory that has developed in the area. Although the American system has by no means eliminated unauthorized stoppages in breach of contract, it has reduced the inclination to strike—particularly in discipline and discharge disputes, where workers know that an impartial arbitrator will determine cases on merit. Unions with negotiated peace machinery rarely make the strike weapon the mode of dispute resolution in the first resort, even when no-strike clauses permit them to strike after an exhaustion of procedures over certain subject matters.

Other Attractions of Arbitration

For the union two of the main attractions of the arbitration process are the ability to have a built-in planned dismissal machinery that protects workers against arbitrary actions by the employer and the removal of the union from the inevitable political crossfire in disputes over who should be promoted or transferred to a particular job. Since seniority is all important and promotion is at the heart of a good number of grievances, the union is removed from the political battle by defending a relatively objective standard before the employer and, if necessary, the arbitrator.

For the employer it is particularly significant that arbitration usually guarantees an uninterrupted period of industrial peace. Moreover, although employers are required in many instances to consult with the union under the duty-to-bargain provision of the National Labor Relations Act before engaging in unilateral changes in working conditions,[10] the assumption behind the arbitration process is that management decides first and that the union challenges the employer's authority through the grievance machinery.

The Arbitration Process

The hearing is usually held on the company's premises, since that is where the parties are and where most of the witnesses will be found. If the union wants neutral ground, usually that can be arranged. Quite frequently the hearing takes place in a motel or hotel of the parties' choosing. I have sometimes held hearings at the Stanford Law School and other institutions where I have taught.

The hearing usually begins with each side summarizing its position and with the formulation of a submission to indicate what issue is in dispute. Sometimes the parties can take the better part of a day or even more on this submission, and it becomes necessary to move on to the evidence in the hope that the issue will become clearer as more is learned about the case. Most arbitrators will suggest that the parties allow the arbitrator to define the dispute in the event that they are unable to define it themselves; invariably they will agree to this.

As mentioned above, there are exhibits, examinations, and cross-examinations. Often a transcript is not taken, and the arbitrator takes his or her own notes on the testimony. A stenographer makes it easier for the arbitrator; on the other hand, nothing can boost the financial cost of arbitration more quickly for the parties than the presence of a court stenographer to take down and transcribe the proceedings.

When the hearing is concluded, the parties sometimes submit briefs, and the arbitrator retires to his or her office to write an opinion and make an award. Although an opinion is not required under American law, the practice is to write one, and the parties would be deeply concerned if the arbitrator issued an award without an opinion.

On the West Coast docks, among other places, labor and management rely on bench awards (awards that must be rendered orally or in a short period of time, and are sometimes limited in length) in walkouts over safety disputes. When notified by "beeper" that a dispute is in progress, the arbitrator goes to the docks, listens to the arguments, and issues an award. Though the parties on the docks are entitled to get an opinion in writing, they generally do not ask for one. Bench awards are becoming more common beyond the West Coast docks, and their use is sometimes specified in contracts.

The arbitration process has been satisfactory to most of the parties that have used it. Although appeals may be taken to the courts, generally the parties adhere to the arbitrator's award without recourse to the judicial process. In this atmosphere it is not the least bit surprising that the arbitrator is paid by the parties. The fee and the costs are usually split equally, although sometimes the loser pays all, sometimes the company pays all (regardless of the outcome), and sometimes a different allocation is agreed upon (usually with the company paying the greater percentage). These obligations are covered by the contract.

The Subject Matter of Disputes

The kinds of disputes likely to come before arbitrators in grievance matters involve a wide variety of issues. Most prominent are dismissals, discipline, and questions relating seniority to promotions or layoffs. Disputes over job classifications, what kind of work is to be performed, and whether employers can contract out work previously performed by the bargaining unit's employees are all grist for the arbitrator's mill. Contrary to foreign belief, the process is not excessively legalistic, although it has had tendencies in that direction in recent years. Contract interpretation is usually involved, but there is much more than that. Great scope is left to the arbitrator, who must determine whether a worker has been dismissed for "just cause" within the meaning of the collective agreement. A good deal of common sense, rather than a technical knowledge of labor law, is a prerequisite for functioning as a competent arbitrator.

The Limitations of Arbitration

There are considerable problems with grievance arbitration in the United States. William J. Usery, former federal mediation and conciliation director and secretary of labor, has noted that one out of three strikes takes place during the term of an agreement[11]—although it is not clear to what extent these stoppages are in fact in defiance of arbitration and no-strike machinery or to what extent the machinery is deficient.

Moreover the arbitration process has had considerable difficulty in coping with employment discrimination.[12] This is not altogether surprising, since unions and employers— who control grievance arbitration—are often the parties accused of discrimination. The courts have not treated employment discrimination arbitration in the same manner as other types of arbitration. This is important because an increasing number of arbitrations involve allegations of race, sex, national origin, and religious discrimination.

Quite frequently the arbitrators who are identified with a position favoring fair employment practices are civil-rights activists not chosen by the parties. In addition very few arbitrators are members of minorities or are women. The National Academy of Arbitrators, whose membership is involved in important and prestigious arbitrations (but by no means a significant percentage of all the hearings that take place in this country), has a very small number of minority and women members. In important employment-discrimination arbitrations, as well as other kinds of cases that go to third-party neutrals, unions and employers may not be willing to select an arbitrator who is not a member of the Academy. Of course this statistical absence is by no means dispositive of the question of whether arbitration can cope with employment discrimination. The federal judiciary, in the early years of the Civil Rights Act of 1964,[13] was of considerable assistance in providing an expansive interpretation of the statute, which benefited minorities and women, yet until 1977 there were very few minority members or women on the federal bench. (The number is still small.)

But the problem is that arbitrators, whatever their race or sex, must necessarily be responsive to the interests of those who appoint them—labor and management—and not necessarily to those of third parties who have no direct involvement in either the selection of or word-of-mouth recommendations for future cases. Arbitrators, like other people, are not often likely to bite the hand that feeds them, and they can be counted on to respond to the parties' conscious and subconscious expectations about standards to be applied in finding contract violations and in fashioning remedies.[14] An additional problem is that arbitrators are often unaware of the requirements of employment-discrimination law, which is usually made relevant to the arbitration by virtue of the fact that the no-discrimination clause obligates the parties not to violate the law.

Finally, because unions and employers control the arbitration process, they are not generally sympathetic to third-party representation when it is demanded by minority members and women who feel that the union would not be vigorous enough in pursuing their interests. Invariably third-party representation or a representative or counsel of the employees' choosing has been rejected where it has been inconsistent with the position of labor and management.[15]

The Role of Courts

Although the law is on the periphery of some aspects of the labor arbitration process, it nevertheless is important. Except under the Railway Labor Act and in states with legislation requiring arbitration in public-sector disputes, the law becomes involved only where the parties voluntarily negotiate agreements. In the former situation arbitration is sometimes mandated, but generally it is for the parties to decide.

The landmark decisions relating to the law of arbitration are *Textile Workers Union v. Lincoln Mills*[16] and the *Steelworkers Trilogy*.[17] What is particularly ironic about the *Lincoln Mills* decision and some of the Taft-Hartley amendments, which have promoted the arbitration process (a process the unions were generally interested in achieving), is that those amendments were passed out of a concern for the disciplining of unruly and troublesome trade unions that were thought to be unfaithful to no-strike clauses they had negotiated. Because unions are voluntary unincorporated associations at common law, many state jurisdictions held that a union could be sued only in the names of its individual members—a considerable task. This was made even more difficult when a union had members outside of the state jurisdiction in which it was being sued. Traditionally the problems involved with "serving" out-of-state defendants (putting them on notice of the suit, a requirement of due process) have given rise to a good deal of litigation.[18]

Section 301 of the National Labor Relations Act was designed to change this. It made collective bargaining agreements enforceable in the federal courts. After disposing of some constitutional problems with the statute,[19] Justice Douglas, speaking for a majority of the Court in *Lincoln Mills*, concluded that arbitration clauses were enforceable in the federal courts inasmuch as they were the quid pro quo for no-strike agreements. The Norris-LaGuardia Act, which barred injunctions in labor disputes, was held to be inapplicable because arbitration did not involve problems that were "part and parcel" of the abuses that had given rise to the Norris-LaGuardia Act.[20] Congress, said the Court, had intended to promote the arbitration process, and had done so through Taft-Hartley. (Indeed the Court subsequently held that although the parties may explicitly contract for a process of economic warfare to resolve their disputes, judicial review, even where there is no arbitration clause providing for a private system of adjudication, is preferable to the use of strikes, lockouts, and other forms of economic pressure.)[21]

But *Lincoln Mills* raised more questions than it answered. What was to be the role of the judiciary with respect to arbitration; would the courts interject themselves into the arbitration process and thus usurp the role accorded to arbitrators by labor and management? Would state courts still preserve their jurisdiction in breach-of-labor cases, and thus in arbitration disputes, even though Taft-Hartley gave to the federal courts jurisdiction—that is, would the state courts be ousted by the doctrine of preemption? Would employers be able to sue for violations of collectively negotiated no-strike clauses despite the bar against injunctions in labor disputes contained in Norris-LaGuardia, or were such violations again "part and parcel" of the abuses at which Norris-LaGuardia was aimed? Could individuals maintain suits for violations of collective bargaining agreements, and to what extent could they bypass the union in so doing?

The Court answered the first of these questions in the landmark *Steelworkers Trilogy* cases. The issue confronted in those cases related to the circumstances under which the judiciary would order the parties to go to arbitration and the extent to which the courts could review the arbitrator's award. The Court, again with Justice Douglas speaking for a substantial majority, concluded that Taft-Hartley's public policy promoting arbitration[22] required that all doubts about whether the dispute was arbitrable should be resolved by the courts in favor of arbitrability. Moreover the court concluded that an arbitrators's award could not be reversed by the Court unless it manifested clear infidelity to the contract. And though most arbitrators write opinions, as the parties expect, the Court stated that an opinion is not necessary as a matter of federal labor law.

The Court's reasoning drew upon the judicial experience with arbitration—best represented by the New York Court of Appeals decision in the *Cutler-Hammer* case,[23] which had involved the judiciary in the interpretation of collective bargaining agreements (the very function the arbitrator was commissioned by the parties to perform). The Supreme Court noted that courts, under the guise of determining arbitrability issues, had become involved in interpretations of collective bargaining agreements or the merits of the underlying grievance. For instance, in the first of the *Steelworkers Trilogy* cases[24] the issue was whether the company had properly subcontracted work outside the bargaining unit under the collective bargaining agreement. But an examination of the question of whether a subcontracting dispute was arbitrable necessarily focused on a number of considerations that an arbitrator would consider in determining the merits of the underlying grievance issue of whether the company had the right to contract out work under the agreement: bargaining history, past practice between the parties, and the like. A detailed examination of the merits of the arbitrability issue would send the courts down a slippery slope at whose bottom they might become ensnared in the merits of the dispute itself; by so doing, they would deprive the parties of their bargain that the arbitrator would have jurisdiction over such matters.

The Court concluded that all doubts should be resolved in favor of arbitrability and that a detailed examination of the arbitrability issue should be avoided for the reasons stated. The Court also noted that the processing of frivolous grievances has a therapeutic effect on the relationship between labor and management and gives each employee a "day in court." Additionally Justice Douglas noted that the parties, through negotiating an arbitration clause in their contract, had bargained for the arbitrator's expertise. (Some arbitrators would hardly recognize themselves from Douglas's glowing characterization of their abilities; however, the arbitrator's expertise is an important theme in the *Steelworkers Trilogy* rationale.) As Justice Douglas wrote:

The labor arbitrator's source of law is not confined to the express provisions of the contract, as the industrial common law—the practices of the industry and the shop—is equally a part of the collective bargaining agreement although not expressed in it. The labor arbitrator is usually chosen because of the parties' confidence in his knowledge of the common law of the shop and their trust in his personal judgment to bring to bear considerations which are not expressed in the contract as criteria for judgment. The parties expect that his judgment of a particular grievance will reflect not only what the contract says but, insofar as the collective bargaining agreement permits, such factors as the effect upon productivity of a particular result, its consequence to the morale of the shop, his judgment whether tensions will be heightened or diminished. For the parties' objective in using the arbitration process is primarily to further their goal of uninterrupted production under the agreement, to make the agreement serve their specialized needs. The ablest judge cannot be expected to bring the same experience and competence to bear upon the determination of a grievance, because he cannot be similarly informed.[25]

The Court was also influenced by the argument that arbitration of labor disputes is essentially different from commercial arbitration involving business relationships and other matters. The Court stated that the collective bargaining agreement is "more than a contract"; it is a "generalized code to govern a myriad of cases which the draftsman cannot wholly anticipate."[26] The Court's view was that the mature labor agreement contained manifold ambiguities and gaps because of the nature of the agreement. In essence, since the law compels the parties to bargain with one another and imposes a relationship (if not the contract itself) upon the parties, it can be called a "shotgun marriage" dictated by economic force or law. In such a situation more than the usual number of unforeseen contingencies and ambiguities remain to plague the parties. Sometimes the parties will be aware of the problem and yet recognize that it makes more sense to submit a dispute to an effective resolution process because of the cost of disagreement at a particular time.

The Court said that collective bargaining is an effort to "erect a system of industrial self-government",[27] that the compulsion to reach agreement and the "breadth of the matters covered, as well as the need for a fairly concise and reliable instrument," produce a relatively peculiar contract for which the arbitration process is available to the parties in the event of the disagreement about interpretation. However, the Court has said that where there is no arbitration procedure and the parties are left to their own devices in the form of economic pressure such as strikes and lockouts, the availability of such weaponry does not preclude judicial enforcement.[28]

Thus all doubts about arbitrability, said the Court, should be resolved in favor of arbitration. Subsequently the Court, in a sweeping opinion authored by Justice White, concluded that unless the parties "clearly and unmistakable provide otherwise, the question of whether the parties agreed to arbitrate is to be decided by the court, not the arbitrator."[29]

Arbitration awards fashioned by arbitrators are enforceable in federal or state court in the absence of manifest infidelity to the contract itself or to some "explicit public policy," which "must be well defined and dominant, and is to be ascertained by reference to the laws and legal precedents, not from general considerations of supposed public interests."[30] In yet another arbitration opinion authored by Justice White, the Court avoided the question posed by the union that a court may only refuse to enforce an award where the award itself violates a statute, a regulation, or "other manifestation of positive law" or would compel employer violation of the law. Rather the Court stated that it not sanction broad judicial discretion to set aside awards as against public policy.[31] Said the Court:

. . . at the very least, an alleged public policy must be properly framed under the approach set out in [precedent] and the violation of such a policy must be clearly shown if an award is not to be enforced.[32]

But what of the other problems? For instance, could the employer obtain injunctive relief for violation of the no-strike clause despite the broad prohibitions of the Norris-LaGuardia Act?

The No-Strike Clause

The Supreme Court first answered the preceding question negatively in the *Sinclair* decision in 1962. Justice Black, a strong proponent of the literal use of language in the constitutional area of First Amendment litigation, noted that Norris-LaGuardia was a bar to the issuance of injunctions for employers—even though unions could obtain injunctions in the form of motions to compel arbitration clauses. Eight years later, however, the Supreme Court reversed *Sinclair* in the landmark *Boys Market* decision.[33]

In *Boys Market* a 5–2 majority concluded that injunctions against violations of no-strike clauses could be issued by the federal courts where the underlying grievance that had given rise to the controversy, over which the strike was taking place, was itself arbitrable under the collective bargaining agreement. The Court's rationale rested upon a number of considerations. The first was that state court jurisdictions still remained available to parties seeking enforcement of labor contracts and that, in states where there were no "baby Norris-LaGuardia Acts," employers were free to sue for injunctive relief in state courts. The problem insofar as injunctive relief against no-strike violations was that employers had an incentive to proceed in state courts, even though federal labor law applied there as well as in the federal courts. In other words, in the interest of uniformity it seemed undesirable to have an employer-initiated action moved from state to federal court. This created, said the Court in *Boys Market*, "an anomalous situation which, in our view, makes urgent the reconsideration of *Sinclair*."[34] With the removal from the state to the federal courts, the states were ousted from jurisdiction that they had possessed in breach-of-contract cases prior to the enactment of the Taft-Hartley amendments—even though Supreme Court authority had said that state-court jurisdiction should supplement that of the federal courts. As the Supreme Court said in *Boys Market*:

It is ironic indeed that the very provision that Congress clearly intended to provide additional remedies for breach of collective bargaining agreements has been employed to displace previously existing state remedies. We are not at liberty thus to depart from the clearly expressed congressional policy to the contrary.[35]

The Court, as it said in commenting on *Sinclair*, was confronted with a dilemma. On the one hand, the availability of state-court jurisdiction in labor injunction cases involving violations of no-strike clauses made the state judiciary the preferred forum for labor-contract interpretation where federal law was to apply. On the other hand, the availability of removal from the state court subsequent to the exercise of jurisdiction deprived the states of preexisting remedies for breach of contract by unions—even though the statute had been aimed, in particular, at union behavior that was inconsistent with its no-strike obligations.

A second reason the Court found *Sinclair* less than satisfactory was because it was inconsistent with the basic federal labor policy recognized in both *Lincoln Mills* and *Steelworkers Trilogy:* that the no-strike obligation was the quid pro quo for an undertaking by the employer to submit grievances to the process of arbitration. Said the Court:

Any incentive for employers to enter into such an arrangement is necessarily dissipated if the principal and most expeditious method by which the no-strike obligation can be enforced is eliminated. While it is of course true, as respondent contends, that other avenues of redress, such as action for damages, would remain open to an aggrieved employer, an award of damages after a dispute has been settled is no substitute for an immediate halt to an illegal strike. Furthermore, an action for damages prosecuted during or after a labor dispute would only tend to aggravate industrial strife and delay an early resolution of the difficulties between employer and union.[36]

Third, the Court rejected the argument that Norris-LaGuardia was a bar to an injunction because it and Taft-Hartley were aimed at a different problem. The Court noted that a considerable number of union strikes and picketing activities were enjoined and that a substantial number of abuses were being committed by the federal courts in this connection. But the Court noted that the labor organizations had grown in strength and "developed toward maturity" and that therefore Congress, in fashioning a national labor policy under Taft-Hartley, had shifted from "protection of the nascent labor movement to the encouragement of collective bargaining and to administrative techniques for the peaceful resolution of industrial disputes."[37] An appropriate accommodation between the competing policies of Taft-Hartley (which reflected the new approach) and Norris-LaGuardia (which barred injunctions in labor disputes) was to permit injunctions for violations of no-strike clauses where the underlying grievance was arbitrable. Said the Court: "The Norris-LaGuardia Act was responsive to a situation totally different from that which exists today."[38]

After the *Boys Market* decision, the Court concluded in a controversial opinion by Justice White that injunctive relief was not available in the context of sympathy strikes where it was claimed that such strikes violated the no-strike provision. The dubious reasoning[39] was that there was no underlying grievance that was susceptible to the arbitration process. However, the question of whether a sympathy strike itself violates the no-strike clause can under many collective bargaining agreements be resolved in the arbitration process. Accordingly the issuance of an injunction pending the outcome of this matter is, as Justice John Paul Stevens' dissent in this subsequent case makes clear, just as vital as it is in the *Boys Market* context.

Finally, as the Court noted in *Boys Market,* damages awards may be obtained against the union for a no-strike violation— even on the basis of a broad arbitration clause from which a no-strike obligation may be inferred.[40] However, damage actions in courts often are stayed pending arbitration of the issue, and employers do not consider arbitrators as sympathetic on this issue as the judiciary.[41] And the Court has held that in the case of wildcat strikes in which the contract is violated and in which the union is not involved, there is no affirmative obligation (unless the contract provides otherwise) for an international union to urge the local to comply with the agreement.[42] Moreover the Court has held that union representatives may not be sued as individuals when they have initiated or authorized a strike[43] and that individual rank-and-file employees may not be sued for violating a contract when they engage in a wildcat strike.[44] But the question of what responsibility the local union had to urge its members to return to work, as well as the question as to whether the local union can be held liable on a "mass action" theory that imputes liability to the union on the basis that the rank and file will not act spontaneously without some kind of encouragement from the leadership, has not been addressed by the Court.[45] The Supreme Court did rule (unanimously) that employers may not selectively impose harsher discipline upon union officials than upon rank-and-file employees for a violation of a no-strike clause,[46] but the Court did not rule on the question of whether selective sanctions may be imposed upon union officials where they have played a "leadership" role in the strike.[47]

The NLRB and Arbitration

The National Labor Relations Board has also facilitated the arbitration process through careful use of its own jurisdiction. For instance, it has held that in unfair labor practice proceedings it will not reverse an arbitrator's award where the arbitration proceedings were fair and regular on their face, where the issues raised before the Board were raised before the arbitrator, where the arbitrator's award was not "repugnant" to the public policy of the National Labor Relations Act, and where the unfair labor practice issue had been addressed by the arbitrator in some form.[48] The Board has held that the arbitrator will be deemed to have "adequately considered the unfair labor practice if (1) the contractual issue is factually parallel to the unfair labor practice issue, and (2) the arbitrator was presented generally with the facts relevant to resolving the unfair labor practice."[49] Said the Board:

> . . . we would not require an arbitrator's award to be totally consistent with Board precedent. Unless the award is "palpably wrong," i.e., unless the arbitrator's decision is not susceptible to an interpretation consistent with the Act, we will defer.[50]

Under certain circumstances the Board has held that it will stay its hand and refuse to process an unfair labor practice charge while it is pending before the arbitrator.[51] Numerous exceptions to the latter proposition have developed.[52] Meanwhile the Board has reverted to a policy of more pristine deferral.[53]

Successor Employers

In *Wiley v. Livingston* the Supreme Court held that "the disappearance by merger of a corporate employer which has entered into a collective bargaining agreement with a union does not automatically terminate all rights of the employees covered by the agreement, and that, in appropriate circumstances . . . the successor employer may be required to arbitrate with the union under the agreement."[54] The question of successorship is determined by a number of factors— namely whether the business of both employers is essentially the same, whether employees of the new enterprise are doing the same jobs in the same working conditions under the supervisors, and whether the new entity has the same production process, produces the same products, and has the same body of customers. Said the Court in establishing the test in *Fall River Dyeing & Finishing Corp. v. NLRB:*

[the] . . . emphasis on the employees' perspective furthers the Act's policy of industrial peace. If the employees find themselves in essentially the same jobs after the employer transition and if their legitimate expectations in continued representations by their union are thwarted, their dissatisfaction may lead to labor unrest.[55]

Accordingly, as the Court has noted:

. . . to a substantial extent the applicability of [successorship] . . . rests in the hands of the successor. If the new employer makes a conscious decision to maintain generally the same business and to hire a majority of its employees from the predecessor, then the bargaining obligation of § 8(a)(5) is activated.[56]

A mere decline in jobs and job classifications with a smaller management hierarchy will not undermine a finding of successorship.[57] However, the Court has held that although a successor employer has a duty to recognize the union of the predecessor, the NLRB cannot impose the labor contract upon the successor employer[58] because to do so would contradict the Court's instruction to the Board to eschew the imposition of contract terms upon labor and management.[59] In a third case the Court limited the thrust of *Wiley* by holding that it applies only where there is *substantial continuity* in the work force.[60]

The Individual Employee

Shortly after the *Steelworkers Trilogy* the Supreme Court held that individuals may sue in federal and state court for violations of collective bargaining agreements; however, the rule has been carefully circumscribed in a number of respects. In the first place the grievance-arbitration machinery must be exhausted prior to the initiation of a lawsuit.[61] But even more formidable are the barriers that exist by virtue of the Court's decision in *Vaca v. Sipes,*[62] a leading duty-of-fair-representation case. Since many of the issues in *Vaca* dramatize the tensions between individual and collective interests, they are more properly described in the next chapter.

But the question of union and company liability where the union declines to take the grievance to arbitration and where the employee shows—as he must if he is to prevail— that the union has violated its duty-of-fair-representation obligation and that the employer has breached the collective bargaining agreement is more appropriately addressed here.

In *Bowen v. U.S. Postal Service,*[63] a 5–4 majority of the Court held that the union is liable in damages to a discharged employee where the failure to take the grievance to arbitration has increased the employer's liability to the employee for breach of contract. Because of the considerable period of time between the potential date of reinstatement in the event of an arbitration and the court trial of a case involving duty of fair representation and breach of contract, the practical impact of *Bowen* is to impose most of the damage liability upon unions rather than employers. This is what prompted Justice White to state in his dissent that:

The union's breach, even if totally unrelated to the employer's decision to terminate the employee, now serves to insulate the employer from further backpay liability, as of the hypothetical arbitration date, even though the employer, unlike the union, can stop backpay accretion at any moment it desires, simply by reinstating the discharged employee.[64]

Arbitration and Employment Discrimination

To what extent have the rules evolved in the *Steelworkers Trilogy* litigation been applied to employment-discrimination cases? In *Alexander v. Gardner-Denver*,[65] the Supreme Court held that a final arbitration award did not preclude an individual from suing to redress employment discrimination. The Court, speaking through Justice Powell, stated that since such a lawsuit in the courts was filed under the Civil Rights Act of 1964, the individual employee was relying on independent statutory rights accorded by Congress and not on contractual rights contained in the collective bargaining agreement that would be at issue in an arbitration proceeding. The Court nevertheless stressed the importance of voluntary conciliation as well as arbitration as a means to resolve such matters—a particularly important consideration, given the substantial backlog of employment discrimination cases before administrative agencies and the courts. The Supreme Court, while rejecting a policy of deference to arbitration awards, concluded that the award could be "admitted as evidence and accorded such weight as the Court deems appropriate."[66] The Court added the following in a footnote:

> We adopt no standards as to the weight to be accorded an arbitral decision, since this must be determined in the court's discretion with regard to the facts and circumstances of each case. Relevant factors include the existence of provisions in the collective-bargaining agreement that conform substantially with Title VII, the degree of procedural fairness in the arbitral forum, adequacy of the record with respect to the issue of discrimination, and the special competence of particular arbitrators. Where an arbitral determination gives full consideration to an employee's Title VII rights, a court may accord it great weight. This is especially true where the issue is solely one of fact, specifically addressed by the parties, and decided by the arbitrator on the basis of an adequate record.[67]

This footnote has prompted some parties to negotiate special arbitration procedures addressed to particular problems of employment discrimination,[68] which are considerably different from the ordinary grievance that comes to arbitration.

Arbitration and Welfare or Minimum-Standards Legislation

In 1981 the Supreme Court, in a 7–2 opinion authored by Justice Brennan, extended the *Gardner-Denver* holding to the Fair Labor Standards Act of 1938.[69] The Court held that arbitration awards should not be deferred to where the statute in question provides minimum substantive guarantees to individual workers. The Court expressed concern that individual rights might be sacrificed by the union, which acts in the collective interest under legislation promoting collective bargaining and majority rule.

This approach has produced the same result in a case where a public employer unsuccessfully relied on an employee's defeat in an arbitration proceeding where the employee alleged that there was "no proper cause" for his discharge and that the discharge had been instituted because of his exercise of the constitutionally protected rights of freedom of speech, freedom of association, and freedom to petition the government for redress of grievances.[70] The Court's reasoning applies to statutes such as the Employee Retirement Income Security Act of 1974 and the Occupational Safety and Health Act of 1970, and it was thought to have meant that courts will not defer to arbitration awards rendered where the plaintiffs sue under those statutes—although the awards might be given "great weight," as in *Gardner-Denver.*

Application Agreements

In 1991 the Court, in *Gilmer v. Interstate/Johnson Lane Corp.,*[71] held that a dismissed employee suing under the Age Discrimination in Employment Act of 1967[72] could be subjected to compulsory arbitration pursuant to an arbitration agreement contained in a securities registration application. Although the Federal Arbitration Act of 1925, under which the suit was brought, excludes "contracts of employment," the Court stated that the issue of whether arbitration clauses contained in such agreements could be enforced was not presented because the arbitration at issue was contained in the dismissed employee's securities registration application which was a contract with the securities exchange and not the employer. The Court, speaking though Justice White in a 7–2 majority,[73] concluded that a number of aspects of arbitration which the Court has found to be deficient in *Gardner-Denver* and its progeny did not constitute barriers to enforcement of arbitration here. The Court said that there was no "inherent inconsistency" between the policies of antidiscrimination laws relating to age discrimination and arbitration of such claims. Moreover the Court rejected arguments that such arbitration would be biased in favor of employers and that discovery would be inadequate, stressing the fact that arbitrators are not bound by formal rules of evidence—a characteristic applicable to all labor arbitration proceedings. Rejecting the contention that enforcement of arbitration agreements would further inequality of bargaining power between employers and employees, the Court said: "Mere inequality in bargaining power, however, is not a sufficient reason to hold that arbitration agreements are never enforceable in the employment context."[74]

The *Gilmer* decision distinguished *Gardner-Denver* and its progeny on the ground that those cases did not involve the issue of the enforceability of an arbitration agreement over statutory claims but rather the

. . . quite different issue whether arbitration of contract-based claims precluded subsequent judicial resolution of statutory claims. Since the employees there had not agreed to arbitrate their statutory claims, and the labor arbitrators were not authorized to resolve such claims, the arbitration in those cases understandably was held not to preclude subsequent statutory actions.[75]

The second distinction drawn by the Court was that those cases involved situations where employees were represented by unions in arbitration proceedings. Thus the tension present there between collective representation and individual statutory rights was not applicable to a case involving the relationship of an individual with the employer without the involvement of the union. Finally, the Court noted that the Federal Arbitration Act, which reflects a liberal federal policy promoting arbitration grievances, was not involved in the prior cases.

These considerations, notwithstanding the Court's refusal to reach the question of whether a contract of employment can be enforced under the Arbitration Act, indicate that *Gilmer* may have substantially limited the impact of *Gardner-Denver*. In the first place, since most of the American work force is nonunion, *Gilmer* means that the Court's comments about the inadequacy of arbitration as it relates to statutory claims in *Gardner-Denver* has little or no applicability outside the organized sector of the economy. Though the Federal Arbitration Act promotes arbitration, so does the National Labor Relations Act which was involved in *Gardner-Denver*. The Court's treatment of *Gardner-Denver* suggests that its reasoning may have significant import for antidiscrimination and other statutory claims, that *Gardner-Denver* has been substantially limited and indeed reversed in the nonunion sector, and that wrongful discharge actions (referred to in chapter 11) may be effectively precluded by application form agreements if employers choose to opt for arbitration as opposed to the courts.

Arbitration in the Public Sector

Finally, there is the matter of public-sector arbitration. In the grievance-arbitration area it appears as though the *Steelworkers Trilogy* has not been followed by state courts in a number of jurisdictions.[76] But what is particularly interesting is the use of arbitration in the public sector as a means to resolve interest disputes. There has been a decline in interest on the part of some public-employee unions in the right to strike and an increased emphasis on arbitration. Most of the states with public-employee labor legislation have adopted some form of arbitration procedures for police and fire unions, and Iowa, Wisconsin, Connecticut, and the city of New York have extended arbitration to other municipal employees as well. (In Iowa all state employees are covered.)[77]

Although a number of states have passed "experimental" statutes, no jurisdiction has repealed an arbitration law and returned to another procedure such as fact-finding.

The critical question with regard to arbitration statutes is whether the procedures tend to stultify or chill the collective bargaining process and induce the parties to rely on arbitration rather than negotiations. Thomas Kochan has found that during the first decade of public-sector bargaining "a higher percentage of cases have reached impasse under both conventional arbitration and final-offer arbitration than under fact-finding procedures," that there was overdependence on arbitration "in a number of jurisdictions operating under both fact-finding and arbitration," and that in general "large jurisdictions tend to rely heavily on whatever dispute resolution is available."[78] This last observation should come as no surprise; although interest arbitration in the United States may be in its formative stage, and although there are problems with grievance arbitration, the institution, its rules, and its practice are well established.

9

The Duty of Fair Representation

The duty of fair representation, under which a union as exclusive bargaining agent has an obligation to deal fairly on behalf of all of a bargaining unit's employees (union and nonunion), has been inferred from the NLRA's grant of authority to the union to negotiate on behalf of all workers. That other nations do not have the exclusivity concept and all its consequences makes this kind of litigation peculiar to the United States.

In 1944 the Supreme Court held that the failure of a union to meet its duty of fair representation constituted a violation of federal labor law, and the NLRB subsequently held that it constituted an unfair labor practice as well.[1]

The duty of fair representation is . . . akin to the duty owed by other fiduciaries to their beneficiaries . . . some Members of the Court have analogized the duty a union owes to the employees its represents to the duty a trustee owes to trust beneficiaries . . . others have likened the relationship between union and employee to that between attorney and client . . . the fair representation duty also parallels the responsibilities of corporate officers and directors towards shareholders. Just as these fiduciaries owe their beneficiaries a duty of care as well as a duty of loyalty, a union owes employees a duty to represent them adequately as well as honestly and in good faith.[2]

In *Vaca v. Sipes*, the Court held that the federal courts as well as the Board had jurisdiction over duty-of-fair-representation cases. However, unless the collective bargaining agreement authorizes the individual to take his grievance to arbitration, the union maintains control of the grievance and may determine whether to initiate arbitration. The Court held that the individual employee has no "absolute right" to initiate arbitration and that the industrial self-government that had been created by the parties would be harmed by a contrary rule. At the same time the Court concluded that an employee could attack the union's failure to process the grievance if its actions toward an employee in the bargaining unit were "arbitrary, discriminatory, or in bad faith."[3] It is difficult to determine what the Court meant by these words. Whether a union's simple failure to process a grievance because it was lost or forgotten constitutes a failure to meet the duty of fair representation is unresolved,[4] but it certainly presents a difficulty for the employee whose grievance is meritorious. In *Vaca* the Court gave the union some discretion because a contrary rule would involve the courts in second-guessing union decisions. Just as the courts do not want to be second-guessing arbitrators, they wish to apply the same policy to the manner in which matters are dealt with at lower levels of the grievance machinery, which are even more important in industrial self-government. Moreover, because the duty applies to contract negotiations as well as administration[5] ". . . a settlement is not irrational simply because it turns out in *retrospect* to have been a bad settlement."[6]

However, the Court held by a 5–4 vote that an individual union member does not have an obligation to utilize internal union procedures and remedies prior to filing suit where the union cannot contractually reactivate the grievance in the event that it was in error in not processing it.[7] It is not entirely clear whether the individual has a right to participate in the arbitration hearing. Thus far it appears as though the union may exclude the employee without violating its duty of fair representation,[8] although recent authority casts some doubt on this.[9] Some judges appear to accept the view that a union has a duty to fairly represent the claims of junior workers competing against their more senior colleagues for the same jobs where the contract contemplates selection of employees for job vacancies on the basis of both seniority and qualifications. Unions generally support the concept of seniority as a basis for determining preference in promotions, transfers, and layoffs, and sometimes the collective bargaining agreement reflects this philosophy. In the steel industry a junior employee must be "head and shoulders" above a senior worker in qualifications in order to be selected. But more often there is a more complex interplay between seniority and qualifications set forth in the labor contract. If the view that unions have a duty to present the claims of the junior employee under such circumstances carries the day, the effect will be burdensome for the unions and revolutionary for industrial relations.

If the union has breached its duty of fair representation in handling the grievance at the arbitration, the employer may be liable to relitigation of an arbitration award despite the preference expressed in the *Steelworkers Trilogy* for the finality of arbitration awards. For instance, in dealing with an arbitration case in which employees dismissed for dishonesty had brought to the tribunal's attention evidence that the union had failed to present, the Court noted that the employer had initiated the discharges. Even though the employer was not responsible for the failure to present evidence, an award tainted by the union's failure to represent fairly was invalid.[10] Said Justice White, speaking for the Court: ". . . enforcement of the finality provision where the arbitrator has erred is conditioned upon the union's having satisfied its statutory duty fairly to represent the employee in connection with the arbitration proceedings . . . a wrongfully discharged employee would be left without a job and without a fair opportunity to secure an adequate remedy."[11]

For a while the Court's 1981 holding that a relatively short statute of limitations would apply to duty-of-fair-representation suits attacking arbitration awards[12] seemed sure to bar many otherwise valid claims. Now the statute of limitations is six months—the Court rejected a briefer period, partly because of the time it takes an employee "unsophisti-cated in collective-bargaining matters" to "evaluate the adequacy of the union's representation, to retain counsel, to investigate substantial matters that were not at issue in the arbitration proceeding, and to frame his suit."[13]

Union Security Agreements and Union Discipline

The issue of union security agreements and an employee's obligations to the union with respect to union membership has broad implications in American labor law. In *NLRB v. The General Motors Corp*[14] the Court held that except for religious objectors (who may pay an equivalent sum elsewhere by virtue of a 1980 amendment to the statute), the worker's only obligation is to pay dues and initiation fees—although many lawyers, trade unionists, corporate officials, and workers believe that more is required under the law. The obligation to pay arises thirty days after employment (seven days in the construction industry, because of the temporary nature of the work). This rule bears directly on the extent to which unions may discipline members under the National Labor Relations Act.

The leading case on this question is *NLRB v. Allis-Chalmers Mfg. Co.*[15] in which the Court held by 5–4 vote that a union may fine strikebreakers who cross picket lines by virtue of its role as exclusive bargaining agent. The Court has taken the position that "reasonable discipline" of members who violate union rules is necessary to protect the union against erosion of its status as exclusive agent. However, the Court indicated that the extent of a union's disciplinary authority could vary depending upon the extent to which workers had voluntarily assumed membership obligations beyond those requiring the payment of dues and initiation fees. The Court noted that in *Allis-Chalmers* the workers who had been fined had attended union meetings at which a secret strike vote was taken, pledged allegiance to the union's constitution, taken the oath of full membership, and fully participated in the proceedings leading to the strike. The Court indicated that if such voluntary union activity were not present, the union might well have run afoul of the law by imposing fines upon the workers. The difficulty here is that few, if any, workers know that they are not obligated to do more in a union than pay initiation fees and dues. So quite frequently collective bargaining agreements obligate them to assume membership obligations as a condition of employment, without reference to the fact that this is limited by law. The rule established in *Allis-Chalmers* seems unfair to individual employees, at least in this respect.

Subsequent to the *Allis-Chalmers* decision the Court held that a union may not fine a worker for something he or she did after resigning from the union. Although the Court initially hinted that unions might lawfully impose obligations and limitations upon the right to resign,[16] in 1985 it held by a 5-4 vote that the Board's conclusion that a union could not lawfully prohibit a member from resigning was appropriate.[17] Specifically the Court held that a union's fining employees who had resigned from the union during a strike could be regarded as an unfair labor practice and that this conclusion was a reasonable interpretation of the statute. Said the Court:

Because the closed shop was outlawed by the Taft-Hartley Act . . . it is not surprising that Congress thought it unnecessary explicitly to preserve the right to resign. . . . The Board reasonably has concluded [that the union fine] "restrains or coerces" employees . . . and is inconsistent with the congressional policy of voluntary unionism.[18]

Finally, who decides on the reasonableness of the amount of a fine levied by a union? Although for a while there was considerable debate about whether the Board had jurisdiction to invalidate "unreasonable" fines, the Supreme Court has made it clear that this question is to be resolved by the state courts and not by the NLRB.[19]

Exclusion from Union Membership and Responsibilities

There is no right under American labor law to be admitted to a union. However, exclusion from membership or activities on the basis of race, sex, color, religion, or national origin is violative of title VII of the Civil Rights Act of 1964. Although members of a union must pay dues where a union security agreement has been negotiated, they may not be compelled to pay dues that would be used for political purposes if they believe that such payment would violate their First Amendment right to free speech.[20] (This is discussed below in the section entitled "Unions and the Political Process.")

The Landrum-Griffin Bill of Rights

The Labor Management Reporting and Disclosure Act of 1959 (often referred to as the Landrum-Griffin Act) contains a bill of rights for union members,[21] largely procedural in nature, which emerged from the McClellan hearings in which considerable union corruption and other forms of abuse were exposed. Title I of the Landrum Griffin Act declared the right of every union member to equal protection, freedom of speech and assembly, reasonable and uniform dues, and freedom to sue unions and their officers.

In *United Steelworkers v. Sadlowski*,[22] which involved a hardfought campaign for the presidency of the Steelworkers, the Supreme Court, in a 5–4 decision, held that a union constitution's "outsider rule" prohibiting solicitation of or financial assistance from nonmembers for election campaigns or election-related litigation did not violate Landrum-Griffin's provisions for free speech and the right to sue. Said Justice Marshall, speaking for the majority: ". . . we do not believe that [the Landrum-Griffin Act] should be read as incorporating the entire body of First Amendment law, so that the scope of protections afforded by the statute coincides with the protections afforded by the Constitution."[23] Justice White, in a sharply worded dissent, stressed the imbalance in strength between union incumbents and challengers: ". . . leadership is not only determined to discourage opposition; it also has at its disposal all of the advantages for doing so, including the facilities of the union. Those leaders have normally appointed the union staff, the bureaucracy that makes the union run."[24] Concluding that the outsider rule was inconsistent with the Act's legislative history, the dissenters noted that "Congress intended to help the members help solve these very difficulties by guaranteeing them the right to run for office and to have free and open elections in the American tradition."[25]

The other shoe dropped in *Finnegan v. Leu,*[26] where the Court held that "rank and file union members—not union officers or employees"[27]—are protected by the Act against a retaliatory discharge by the union for the exercise of free speech. The Court's assessment of legislative history led it to the conclusion that Congress did not intend to regulate union patronage. The Court left open the question "whether a different result might obtain in a case involving nonpolicymaking and nonconfidential employees,"[28] but it seemed to ignore the difficulties for dissidents engendered by a decision that makes the bureaucracy more subordinate to the leadership.

In 1989 the Court held that the removal of an elected business agent, in retaliation for statements that he made at a union meeting in opposition to a dues increase sought by the union trustee, violated the Act.[29] The Court, in Justice Marshall's opinion, distinguished *Finnegan* on the ground that where elected officials are involved or retaliated against, union members are denied the representatives of their choice. Moreover, said the Court, ". . . the potential chilling effect on Title I free speech rights is more pronounced when elected officials are discharged. Not only is the fired official likely to be chilled in the exercise of his own free speech rights, but so are the members who voted for him."[30]

Even where a union may discipline an employee in connection with a reasonable rule in the union's constitution, procedural due process as required by section 101(a)(5) of Landrum-Griffin obligates the union to provide the member with adequate notice of charges, reasonable time to prepare a defense, and a full and fair hearing. In this connection and in others, the 1959 statute guarantees the rights only to union members, not to all employees represented by the union.

Contrary to public impression, the Landrum-Griffin Act does not guarantee members the right to ratify a union contract. However, union members have a right to equal protection, which can be modified only by reasonable rules and regulations. A union may limit eligibility to vote in contract ratifications to members in good standing.[31] Similarly "moonlighters" have been denied the right to vote because they have no "vital interest" in the outcome.[32] But in *Local 6885 v. American Postal Workers*[33] Judge Abner Mikva, speaking for the Court of Appeals for the District of Columbia, concluded that it was denial of equal protection to preclude ratification of the contract by a non-mail-processing local union when other members of mail-processing locals had been accorded such rights. One court has held that the members have the right to a "meaningful vote" in the sense that they are entitled to "adequate notice and information regarding the subject matter and nature of the vote."[34] Thus, for instance, the 1984 ratification of the Teamsters-United Parcel Agreement was deemed unlawful because emergency membership meetings had been called on short notice, members had not known that a new contract was being negotiated, and many members had been away on summer vacation.[35]

But the Court of Appeals for the Ninth Circuit, in an opinion authored by Judge Stephen Reinhardt—confronting the question of whether both the equal rights and the freedom of speech protections afforded members under Landrum-Griffin require union leaders to make a full disclosure of all the terms and provisions of the collective bargaining agreement prior to submitting the agreement to union membership before ratification—has held to the contrary.[36] Absent a contractual obligation in the union's constitutional bylaws, which would provide members with a contract or duty of fair representation action,[37] said the court, contract approval constitutes an internal union affair. Said the court in addressing the failure of union leadership to disclose:

We recognize that the conduct at issue here perpetuated, indeed exacerbated, the customary information gap between the leadership of the union and its rank-and-file members. However, unequal access to information is as inherent in the structure of the collective bargaining system, as it is in our larger democratic system. . . . Union leaders, by virtue of their status as collective bargaining representatives, necessarily possess more information about the progress and projected outcome of collective bargaining than union members. At the time of a ratification vote, the officials will inevitably know more about the final terms of the new agreement than the rank-and-file members. This would be the case even were we to require advance distribution of the entire agreement (in this case, over 140 pages). Information concerning discussions or informal understandings regarding the intended or actual meaning of ambiguous provisions is of critical importance in implementing union-management agreements. That information would not be available to rank-and-file members in any event. To attempt to ensure equal information for negotiators and members alike would be wholly unrealistic.[38]

Rejecting the argument that this decision could be characterized as supporting the principle that union democracy is "unimportant" or that federal labor law accords unions virtually unlimited power to define internal policies and procedures by fiat, the court argued that its decision was to the contrary and did not in any way interfere with federal labor policies that are designed to induce union leadership to adhere to the promises made to their members. The Ninth Circuit concluded that Congress's ". . . decision to leave the determination of whether and how contract ratification votes must be conducted to the unions reflects an understanding of the complexities of the contract negotiation process."[39]

In an opinion authored by Judge Richard Cudahy for the Court of Appeals for the Seventh Circuit, the court held that secret oral negotiations between union officials and employer representatives that modified the terms of the collective bargaining agreement that had been submitted to the membership for ratification, without any notice that it would be conditioned by additional terms, was a breach of the contract entered into between the union and its members.[40] Said the court, "To avert industrial strife, collective bargaining agreements must be more secure than garden variety contracts. Accordingly, we hold that national labor policy forbids introduction of prior or contemporaneous secret agreements to contradict fundamental terms of a ratified collective bargaining contract."[41] Judge Frank Easterbrook dissented, emphasizing the importance of "flexibility" in industrial relations. Said the dissent:

Collective bargaining agreements are relational contracts. They do not settle all important terms; rather they establish a framework within which the parties compose their differences. . . .
. . . the majority makes it clear that enforceability depends on who wins and who loses *ex post*. Negotiators need to know *while they are dickering* which agreements will be enforced and which not; people at the bargaining table in January 1983 cannot wait for a court in September 1991 to tell them which deals are sufficiently unimportant, and which turn out sufficiently favorable to the workers, to be enforced.[42]

Trusteeships

The Landrum-Griffin Act is also aimed at limiting the circumstances under which the unions may impose trusteeships, an administrative device whereby dissident local unions could be controlled and their treasuries raided by national and international union officials. Careful standards are established relating to circumstances under which the imposition of administration of trusteeships may be established, and information must be filed with the secretary of labor.[43]

Union Elections

The Landrum-Griffin Act provides that members have the right to elect their officials and guarantees the right to an election every three years.[44] Some trade unions use the ballot box and some use conventions to elect their national officials. Those unions that have relied on the direct vote seem to have had the greatest amount of internal debate and controversy—for example, there have been hard-fought elections in the United Steelworkers of America and the International Union of Electrical Radio and Machine Workers. On the other hand, the United Auto Workers, a democratic union that has established a Public Review Board to review charges by union members against officialdom, elects its national officers at a convention, and there has never been a substantial vote against the incumbents.

Much of the litigation over union elections relates to unions' eligibility requirements for candidates. The Supreme Court had struck down union bylaws limiting the right to run for major elective offices to union members who hold or previously held elective office under circumstances where the effect was to disqualify 93 percent of members for office. Similarly attendance rules requiring that a member who seeks local union office must have attended at least half of the regular meetings for three years previous to the election have been held unlawful where only 23 of 600 members would have been eligible. The Court has held that the antidemocratic effect of such rules is inconsistent with the Landrum-Griffin provision that "every member in good standing shall be eligible to be a candidate and to hold office . . . subject . . . to reasonable qualifications uniformly imposed."[45]

Although the secretary of labor is the only party who may file suit challenging an intraunion election that has already been held, the Supreme Court held in *Trbovich v. United Mine Workers*[46] that an aggrieved member may intervene in the suit. Although the secretary of labor assumes the mantle of the union member's lawyer, the Court acknowledged that the member might have "a valid complaint" about the performance of his or her lawyer and therefore ought to be able to intervene to present evidence and arguments in support of the secretary's complaint.

The Court has held that union members may not institute actions where the remedy sought is the invalidation of an election already conducted.[47] Only the secretary of labor may bring such actions. But where the relief sought is "less intrusive" the individual may bring the action without the secretary.

Not only must members have a fair opportunity to run for office as a prerequisite to an appropriate election, they must also have an opportunity to reach the members. This means that the union must honor a reasonable request to distribute campaign literature at a candidate's expense and that no monies received from dues or similar kinds of levies may be used to promote any person's candidacy. According to the

Supreme Court in *International Organization of Masters, Mates & Pilots v. Brown*,[48] a court must evaluate the reasonableness of a candidate's request. Said the Court:

A broad interpretation of the candidate's right to distribute literature commenting on the positions advocated in the union press is consistent with the statute's basic purpose.

. . . Here, in particular, a preconvention mailing would not place any burden on the Union because the candidate must assume the cost of the mailing. Moreover, in union elections, as in political elections, it is fair to assume that more, rather than less, freedom in the exchange of views will contribute to the democratic process. . . .

The concern about discrimination among individual candidates is surely satisfied by a rule that allows any candidate access to the membership before the convention as well as by a rule that denies all candidates such access. Indeed, arguably opening the channels of communication to all candidates as soon as possible better serves the interest in leveling the playing field because it offsets the inherent advantage that incumbents and their allies may possess through their control of the union press and the electoral list during the four years in which they have been in office.[49]

Employers are precluded from contributing financial support to candidates for union office. Literature, if distributed at a reduced rate for one candidate, must be distributed at a reduced rate for all. If one candidate is allowed to copy membership lists, all candidates must have the same opportunity. These privileges must be extended equally.

The 1991 Teamsters Election

Actually the most ambitious electoral reform of any labor union has been undertaken pursuant to a consent decree entered into in 1989 between the International Brotherhood of Teamsters and the U.S. Department of Justice. The decree followed an unsuccessful challenge to the 1986 election by the Teamsters for a Democratic Union (TDU), an unincorporated association comprised of Teamster members whose stated purpose was to reform and democratize the IBT.[50] Suit was commenced against the teamsters by the Justice Department under the Racketeering and Corruption Act (RICO).[51] The consent decree provided for court-appointed officers who would oversee certain Teamster operations, particularly the supervision and certification of the results of the International Brotherhood of Teamsters' 1991 elections. An administrator decides all disciplinary or trusteeship cases and has the right to veto any union expenditures, appointments, or contracts other than collective bargaining agreements.

Prior to the consent decree, all convention delegates were chosen through regular local union elections, and the convention selected the principal officers of the union: the general president, the general secretary-treasurer and sixteen vice presidents. Under the 1989 consent decree all of these offices were elected by direct rank and file secret balloting in 1991. The major dissident candidate, Ron Cary of New York, was elected President of the union with his slate on the executive board. The changes initiated and the actual results of the election appear to herald a new era of more democratically responsive leadership in the union which had been notorious for undemocratic procedures and corruption in the past. Under the consent decree an independent review board is to be established with the power to investigate and discipline corruption within the union. One member of the board is to be appointed by the attorney general, one by the union, and the third by the agreement of the first two appointees.

Unions and the Political Process

Political activity is another area of tension between unions and individual union members. One must recall Gompers' statement that labor would reward its friends and punish its enemies. Though the unions are not attached to a political party, they are very much involved in the political process. Unions have established special political arms to support those who are friendly to organized labor's position on a wide variety of issues.

It is, however, a crime for any labor organization to "make a contribution or expenditure in connection with any election at which Presidential and Vice-Presidential electors or a Senator or Representative in . . . Congress ought to be voted for" or in connection with a related primary convention. Such activity is prohibited by section 304 of the Taft-Hartley Act.

Under the Federal Election Campaign Act of 1971, as amended, unions and corporations may use their monies in connection with the election of federal candidates for the purpose of sending political messages to their own members or shareholders, for conducting nonpartisan registration and get-out-the-vote campaigns directed at such groups, and as seed money to solicit contributions to a union or corporate political action committee. Any direct contribution by labor unions to the treasuries of federal political candidates is prohibited.[52] None of the above-described prohibitions has any bearing on union contributions to state campaigns.

A nonunion member, compelled to pay dues under a union security provision in the collective bargaining agreement, may object to having his or her dues money used on behalf of certain candidates or political programs, but a union may spend dues as it wishes for purposes germane to collective bargaining. What is relevant to collective bargaining and what is relevant to the political process have been a subject of considerable debate.[53] In *Communications Workers v. Beck*[54] the Court held that these principles, initially established under the Railway Labor Act and in the public sector,[55] apply equally to employees covered by the National Labor Relations Act. In 1992 President Bush issued an executive order requiring federal contractors to notify nonunion members of their right to object to dues spent for purposes other than collective bargaining, contract administration, and grievance adjustment.[56] However, President Clinton rescinded this order soon after assuming office.[57]

Unions have been encouraged by the Supreme Court to devise their own internal rebate procedures in connection with this problem, and the United Auto Workers and the Brotherhood of Railway Clerks have done so. The UAW has provided that a dissenting member may allocate a portion of his or her dues to be used in support of "nonpartisan ideological community groups." In a unanimous opinion authored by Justice White, the Court held that a rebate procedure was legally inadequate.[58] Said the Court:

> . . . there are readily available alternatives, such as advance reduction of dues and/or interest-bearing escrow accounts, that place only the slightest additional burden, if any, on the union. Given the existence of acceptable alternatives, the union cannot be allowed to commit dissenters' funds to improper uses even temporarily. A rebate scheme reduces but does not eliminate the statutory violation.[59]

Moreover adequate information about union expenditures—not simply reference to the fact that nonmembers would not be required to pay a percentage designated by the union as nongermane—is required,[60] as well as a ". . . reasonably prompt decision by an impartial decisionmaker."[61]

In the first of these two decisions the Court established the proposition that the spending of dues money on litigation or on organizational campaigns not related to the bargaining unit was not "germane" to collective bargaining.[62] A divided Court has held that public employee union lobbying or other political activities "unrelated" to contract modification or implementation as well as efforts to secure funds for public education in the state—which might assist the negotiation of salaries for teachers—are not germane.[63]

The now rescinded Bush executive order as well as the *Beck* decision has made union involvement in the political process and the expenditure of dues for such purposes a central issue in the 1990s. Justice Frankfurter's perceptive dissenting commentary about American labor's deep historical involvement with politics and legislation seems to have been lost in the distant haze.[64]

10

The Public Sector

In recent years state and local legislation on the subjects of collective bargaining and labor in the public sector have grown considerably.[1] Forty-one of the states have some form of fairly comprehensive legislation protecting the right of public employees to organize and bargain collectively. (Some states provide that the public employer need only "meet and confer" with the union, but the practical result is often similar to that under the duty to bargain.)[2] The same trend is present at the federal level for federal employees, although federal employees still may not negotiate wages. Congress replaced an executive order originally promulgated by President John F. Kennedy with the Civil Service Reform Act of 1970.[3] The Postal Reorganization Act of 1970[4] created an independent establishment within the executive branch. Postal employees are subject to the National Labor Relations Act and the Landrum-Griffin Act, but prohibitions against federal strikes apply to them, and therefore the Postal Reorganization Act contains its own dispute-resolution procedures. Striking federal employees can be punished with felony charges and dismissal.

Public employees have a right to union membership that is protected by the right of freedom of association under the First Amendment.[5] However, the Supreme Court has balanced this right against the government's interest in regulating the speech and conduct of its employees, an interest that differs significantly from any interest in regulating the speech of all citizens.[6] The means used to advance an important governmental interest must be those least restrictive of constitutional rights.[7] The balance between the constitutional right to union membership and various important government interests is not always clear. For example, police and firefighters share in the right to join unions,[8] but whether they may be restricted in the kind of labor organization with which they may affiliate has not been definitively resolved.[9] Moreover the right of public employees to bargain collectively, let alone the right to strike,[10] is not protected by the Constitution. But a majority of the Supreme Court of California has supported the view that the right to strike enjoys some degree of constitutional protection in that state.[11]

The Supreme Court has held that a state may constitutionally prohibit union representation of workers in the processing of their grievances[12]—a less ambitious objective than that of constitutional protection for the collective bargaining process itself. Moreover exclusivity is limited. The Court has also held that teachers other than union representatives have a constitutional right to speak at open school-board meetings.[13] The Supreme Court has held that a minority union can be constitutionally denied access to teachers' mailboxes and the interschool delivery system[14] because of the Constitution's free-speech and equal-protection guarantees, despite the statutory right of minority unions or dissident employees not to be denied the right to communicate in the private sector under the NLRA.[15] Justice White, writing for a 5–4 majority, reasoned that the state has a legitimate interest in furthering the effectiveness of representation. Since the Court also noted the absence of a showing that "permission has been granted as a matter of course to all who seek to distribute material" as a basis for its decision, the Court of Appeals for the Fifth Circuit has concluded that the minority union has a right to access when the mail system is open to all employee organizations "without distinction."[16] In 1984 the Court, again deferring to the state's interest in providing the exclusive bargaining representative with communication opportunities, held that the exclusion of nonmembers from "meet and confer" sessions on employment-related matters, which are not subject to mandatory collective bargaining, was constitutional.[17]

Another line of cases involving constitutional rights for public employees arises out of wrongful discharge.[18] In 1985 the Court, speaking through Justice White, held that the Due Process Clause of the Constitution mandates that some pretermination process must be accorded public employees, who can be dismissed only for cause. The Court noted that the need for "some form of pretermination hearing" was evident from a balancing of the competing interests at stake, i.e., "the private interest in retaining employment, the governmental interests in the expeditious removal of unsatisfactory employees and the avoidance of administrative burdens, and the risk of an erroneous termination."[19] The Court has also held that not only are public employers precluded under the First Amendment from discharging employees for nonsupport of the political party in power,[20] but the principle also applies to hiring, promotion, transfer, and recall after layoff.[21]

Public-employee unionism has grown by leaps and bounds since the mid-1960s. Before that time the organization of public employees into unions lagged behind organization in the private sector for a number of reasons.

First, the legal concept of sovereignty translated itself into the idea that government was supreme and that public employees had no rights that could be asserted against their employer.

A second idea, very much related to the first, was that elected officials could not delegate their responsibility to others. Collective bargaining and arbitration therefore were considered inconsistent with the democratic process and with the idea that officials were responsible to the voters and not to trade unionists. Moreover some of the benefits associated with labor organizations in the private sector, such as grievance-arbitration machinery, were not apparent until the 1950s and 1960s, and public employees were not dissatisfied with their position. But the turmoil of the 1960s, a perceived gap between benefits in the public and private sectors, and increased attention to the public sector by a trade-union movement in search of arenas in which it could recoup its membership losses among private employees contributed to substantial changes. A surge of unionization has taken place in the public sector. Between 1966 and 1976 the American Federation of Teachers and the American Federation of State, County, and Municipal Employees increased their membership by 257 and 167 percent, respectively. (Their memberships are approximately 500,000 and 1,000,000.) The National Education Association, which like the Teamsters is not affiliated with the AFL-CIO, has a membership of 1,800,000.

Despite all this there continues to be controversy about collective bargaining in the public sector and about whether the growth of such bargaining ought to be protected by a labor law similar in content to the National Labor Relations Act. One major argument against the applicability of private sector labor law to the public sector is that the economics are different. It has been contended that the private sector is based on a market economy that has no applicability to the public sector (the Taylor report,[22] which was written in advance of New York's labor legislation, expounded this theme). Proponents of this theory have stated that the constraints in the public sector are political; as noted above, the argument is that those who make the decisions to levy taxes and raise revenues are penalized or rewarded through the democratic process. Very much related to this argument is the fact that the employment-benefit relationship or trade-off that exists in the private sector is not present in the public sector. In the private sector trade unions are restrained from making wage demands because of the discipline of the market (the loss of jobs that would be attributable to increased benefits and to the flow of work to nonunionized employers). Also, as employers are confronted with higher labor costs, they have a greater inducement to automate. Third, it is contended that public employers have less of a monopsony power than private employers because employees (particularly in cities) are able to compete effectively for employment in both public and private sectors.[23] Accordingly, proceeds this argument, public employees have more strength than their private-sector counterparts in dealing with employers. Fourth, it is argued that public employees are in a superior position because of Civil Service legislation, which traditionally has provided a much greater measure of job security than was available with unionized or nonunionized private employers. However, the security enjoyed by the public sector has been undermined recently by two factors. One is the emergence of arbitration clauses, which protect private employees against dismissal and discipline except where the employer has just cause for imposing the penalty. The second is that since the early 1970s public employers have been all too willing to respond, as most private employers do, when confronted with increased economic demands: by laying off workers to reduce the budget. To some extent this undercuts the argument that market forces do not come into play in the public sector. Moreover the tendency of many employers to contract out work previously performed by public employees resembles the behavior in the private sector. Many public employers have begun to contract out garbage collection, just as private employers have contracted out janitorial services.[24]

In the public sector those who bargain with the unions—the executive branch of the government—must rely on appropriations committees in the legislative branch to implement any arrangements that are made. (This problem does not exist at the federal level because federal public-employee unions still may not bargain about wages.) In collective bargaining it is generally desirable, if not vital, for the parties representing each side to be able to speak with authority for their constituents. Inasmuch as the public employers are fragmented, this poses practical problems in connection with collective bargaining in the public sector and makes the process more difficult.

Another difference between the public and private sectors is that the line between supervisory and other employees is more confused than it is in the private sector. One of the direct results of this confusion is that there is more of a demand for supervisory unions and sometimes for unions that include supervisory and other employees under the same umbrella.[25] This causes problems for employers relating to the loyalty of employees who in the private sector might be regarded as management or lower-level management.

The most frequently cited difference between private and public sectors is that unions in the public sector can bring pressure on their employers through the political process. It is certainly true that in recent years some unions (particularly in New York state, where 13 of 39 bills sponsored by public sector unions in 1977 were attempts by labor to gain what it has failed to obtain at the bargaining table) have frequently used legislatures to obtain, for instance, increases in pension benefits that were under negotiation at the bargaining table. The argument is that the public employer is put at a disadvantage with respect to the public employees' union in a way that does not exist in the private sector. However, it must be said that private employees' unions also may (and often try to) improve their economic benefits through legislative activity. Private-sector unions are also deeply involved in the American political process.

Many of the issues raised at the bargaining table by public employees' unions affect the public as well as the workers. A union's demand that police officers confronted with discipline or discharge be exempted from appearing before a public review board might be viewed very differently by union leaders and by black and Hispanic leaders in New York, Chicago, or San Francisco. The same is true of demands made by teachers' unions about curriculum content. This is not to suggest that such matters are inappropriate for the bargaining table. But matters such as these and whether Detroit police should be required to live in that city,[26] and whether San Jose police can wear firearms,[27] raise issues that obviously affect the public directly and therefore must be considered away from the negotiating table. At the same time, however, traditional issues such as the entitlement of federal employees to expenses incurred in negotiations under the Civil Service Reform Act have prompted the Court to note that, although "Congress unquestionably intended to strengthen the position of federal unions and to make the collective bargaining process a more effective instrument of the public interest than it had been under the Executive Order regime,"[28] the basic assumption about an adversarial relationship applies to the public sector as well as the private sector.

The most difficult public-sector issue in the United States relates to whether public employees should have the right to strike. The federal government and most of the states prohibit striking by common law or statute. However, an increasing minority of jurisdictions (Hawaii, Pennsylvania, Vermont, Alaska, and Minnesota have been the leaders) has permitted a limited right to strike to be incorporated into statute.[29] These statutes generally permit workers other than police, firefighters, and prison guards to strike, sometimes only after the utilization of impasse procedures designed to resolve disputes over new contract terms. And the Supreme Court of California has articulated the following standard: ". . . strikes by public employees are not unlawful at common law unless or until it is clearly demonstrated that such a strike creates a substantial and imminent threat to the health and safety of the public." "This standard," said the Court, "allows exceptions in certain essential areas of public employment (e.g., the prohibitions against firefighters and law enforcement personnel) and also requires the courts to determine on a case-by-case basis whether the public interest overrides the basic right to strike."[30]

The argument on behalf of public-sector striking is that it is impossible for the collective bargaining process to operate without the possibility of strikes. Unless the employer faces the prospect of inconvenience or injury, there is no inducement to compromise or negotiate seriously about wages, hours, and working conditions. Moreover it is pointed out that the line between the private and the public sector is a difficult one to draw sharply. For instance, during the 1966 transit strike in New York, public employees on one bus line were prohibited from striking by state labor legislation, but employees on another line, operating on nearby streets, were protected in their right to strike because they were employed by private operators or public utilities covered by the NLRA. It is anomalous and inequitable to impose different rules on employees performing the same tasks in connection with an issue so vital to employees and the employer.

One argument that cuts in the other direction is that the line between the industries that are essential (where strikes should be prohibited) and those that are not (where strikes should be allowed) is difficult to draw. Most observers seem to accept the view that police and firefighters should not have the right to strike, but there is little consensus about other jobs. There is considerable controversy about the propriety of strikes in public education. Does it affect the health and security of the community for teachers to strike? Most would say that a few days lost from school would not matter much, but what if a strike goes on longer? Generally the longer children are home from school, the more parents begin to perceive school services as essential, independent of the value of education. The fact that often both parents are working would seem to increase their concern about teachers' strikes.

Another problem is that where one group of workers has another process by which to resolve a dispute, such as compulsory arbitration, a generous award may have the effect of eating up all revenues available for wage increases for others. Indeed there are many instances where a generous arbitration award has encouraged strikes by workers forbidden to strike. The opponents of the right to strike for public employees often state that when one draws a line between essential and nonessential services, one is basically granting the right to strike where it would not hurt the employer and prohibiting it where it would. For example, since lawn care is a nonessential service, the gardener who mows the governor's lawn should be able to assert the right to strike.[31] But doesn't this simply give the worker the strike weapon when he or she has no muscle and therefore cannot make adequate use of it?

Opponents of the right to strike for public employees have also focused on the fact that public-sector labor relations, particularly at the municipal level, involve a number of different unions. Generally multiunion industries are "sick" industries in terms of industrial relations. Classic examples of this proposition outside the public sector are the newspaper, printing, and maritime industries. If a right to strike is granted to one union, how will other unions that are prohibited from striking react to picket lines in front of a municipal government's facilities? In the United States there is a long-standing tradition for workers to refuse to cross a picket line. Will not the right to strike for certain employees produce, at least under certain circumstances, general strikes?

The biggest argument for the right to strike in the public sector is that strikes are taking place. Hardly a month passes without a strike or another form of economic pressure in the public sector in some state. Granting the right to strike on a limited basis would bring the law into accord with reality, since the right to strike exists on a de facto basis. Under the present circumstances the imposition of fines and contempt penalties on strikers may produce a lack of respect for law and the judiciary. There is already considerable evidence of judicial reluctance to declare strikes unlawful, even where statute or common law makes them so. Even decertification, employed against the air traffic controllers as a penalty for their unlawful strike in 1981, does not always work.

The debate has shifted to substitutes for striking. Foremost among these is fact-finding. The supposed virtue of fact-finding is that a judicial type of proceeding is established that issues a formal report with recommendations. The theory is that the unreasonable party will have the weight of public pressure against it and will yield or modify its position. This is said to be especially true in the public sector, where parties are presumably more sensitive to those who pay taxes and cast votes.

A substantial number of jurisdictions provide for fact-finding, and indeed this is now one of the options made available in the federal sector.[32] But fact-finding has not always worked out as well as anticipated. Even though the resolution of public-employee disputes is the public's business and one could therefore assume that the public would be interested in the report, it is often said that little attention is given to the report by the news media. Thus the opportunity to galvanize support for the recommendations and place pressure on the resisting party is minimized. Moreover, rather than moving one of the parties to a different position, the report often hardens the parties' positions and makes it less likely that they will be able to resolve their dispute. (This seems to run contrary to the concerns that Senator Robert Taft expressed in the Taft-Hartley amendments.) Once the report has been issued, the party that perceives itself as the winning one will take no less than what the report provides for. Quite frequently the party that has lost and is excoriated by the fact-finders simply hardens its own position. As the debate becomes more public, the parties begin to posture for their respective audiences and constituencies.[33]

Finally, fact-finding does not provide for finality. A binding arbitration award does not permit a dispute to go on after the procedures have been exhausted. This, as well as other factors, has induced an increasing number of jurisdictions to adopt compulsory-arbitration provisions in the public sector.

11

Public-Interest Labor Law

Five developments since the advent of modern labor legislation that are important to workers, unions, and employers—although they do not directly involve the balance of power between unions and their members—are the Employee Retirement Income Security Act (ERISA), the Occupational Safety and Health Act of 1970, employment discrimination law (especially title VII of the Civil Rights Act of 1964), the common law of wrongful discharge in most of the fifty states of the Union, and issues relating to drug and alcohol testing and sometimes smoking as well.

The Employee Retirement Income Security Act

ERISA is the first comprehensive pension labor law enacted by Congress, although section 302(c)(5) of the National Labor Relations Act provides for the establishment of financial trust funds for the benefit of employees.[1] ERISA does not require the establishment of a pension plan, but it does require disclosure and reporting of financial and other information through the establishment of standards of "conduct, responsibility, and obligation for fiduciaries of employee benefit plans."[2] It is administered by the Department of Labor and the Internal Revenue Service. The full extent of coverage and protection under the statute is beyond the scope of this chapter, but some of its elements should be mentioned.

ERISA established mandatory vesting requirements for workers so that they receive some entitlement to pension funds before they reach retirement age. Additionally it restricts a plan's power to deprive a union member of all prior service that may be unvested. ERISA does not provide for the transferability of pensions from one company to another (often referred to as "portability"). This is a particularly important deficiency, given the mobility of the American worker. However, in the Multiemployer Pension Plan Amendment Act of 1980, amending ERISA, Congress strengthened the solvency and stability of multiemployer pension funds by circumscribing employers' withdrawals from them.[3]

ERISA provides that all "nonforfeitable" benefits must be paid. In *Nachman v. Pension Benefit Guaranty Corp.*,[4] a majority of the Supreme Court held that a plan that imposed no condition on the benefits to be paid created vested benefits in the event of a plant closure. However, the Court has held that the level of benefit offsets attributable to an employee's receipt of a worker's compensation award is "forfeitable."[5] In the same case the Court held that state law that is inconsistent with ERISA on the issue of level of benefit and offset is preempted by the federal statute. The District of Columbia Workers' Compensation Equity Amendment Act which obliged employers to provide health benefits to employees eligible for workers' compensation benefits only if the employer was already providing health benefits under a different plan was deemed to be preempted by ERISA by the Court of Appeals for the District of Columbia.[6]

The Court, in *Ingersoll-Rand Co. v. McClendon*,[7] has held that a state common law wrongful discharge action instituted to protest a dismissal that was allegedly attributable to the employer's plan to avoid contributing or paying benefits under the employee plan was preempted by ERISA.

The Occupational Safety and Health Act

The Occupational Safety and Health Act of 1970 was enacted, as the Supreme Court has said, "for the purpose of ensuring safe and healthful working conditions for every working man and woman in the nation."[8] The Supreme Court has held that the secretary of labor, in fashioning regulations dealing with particular toxic materials or harmful physical agents, must show that an exposure limit is "reasonably necessary or appropriate to provide safe and healthful employment."[9] But a major problem to be hammered out in the courts during the coming years is how significant a risk must be to warrant regulation under this act. The Court has stated that the statute does not guarantee a risk-free workplace,[10] but the Occupational Safety and Health Administration (OSHA) has not taken that position. Even though the risks are often uncertain because of lack of scientific evidence, OSHA must provide some explanation for its determination that regulation is necessary.

A critical issue involved in the interpretation of the statute is whether the Secretary of Labor is required to balance the benefits to the workers against the cost of the required charges to the employer.[11] OSHA has always taken the position that costs must be taken into account as regulations are formulated. But although OSHA has appropriately regarded the requirements of economic feasibility as a barrier to the imposition of a cost burden that would cripple or eliminate an industry, the disproportionate burden on particular plants that may be older, smaller, or less competitive cannot be equated with infeasibility. The Court of Appeals for the District of Columbia has said that "even if a few firms are forced to shut down, the standard is not necessarily economically infeasible."[12] On another occasion the same court said the following: "It would appear to be consistent with the purpose of the Act to envisage the economic demise of an employer who has lagged behind the rest of the industry in protecting the health and safety of employees and is consequently financially unable to comply with new standards as quickly as other employers."[13] And in 1981 the Supreme

Court, by a 5–3 vote, held in the "Brown lung" case[14] that a cost-benefit analysis is not contemplated by the statute. Said Justice Brennan, writing for the majority:

Congress itself defined the basic relationship between costs and benefits by placing the "benefit" of worker health above all other considerations save those making attainment of this "benefit" unachievable. Any standard based on a balancing of costs and benefits by the Secretary that strikes a different balance than that struck by Congress would be inconsistent with the command set forth [in statutory provisions]. Thus, cost-benefit analysis by OSHA is not required by the statute because feasibility analysis is.[15]

The problems of enforcing the Occupational Safety and Health Act are considerable. The secretary of labor cannot unilaterally shut down a plant when the operations are unsafe or hazardous to workers.[16] Where an employer resists on-site inspection, the Supreme Court has held that the Constitution requires the secretary of labor to obtain a warrant before an inspection;[17] this provides the opportunity for a coverup. The secretary of labor has argued unsuccessfully that a worker has the implied right to enforce the statute through a lawsuit because the government cannot cope with the large number of complaints that have been filed.[18]

Ordinarily the penalty for a violation of the statute is $1,000, but in the case of "nonserious" violations a penalty is discretionary. In the case of willful or repeated violations the penalty can go up to $10,000, but the courts are divided on the question of what number of infractions constitutes repetition and on whether a serious infraction must be both repeated and willful.[19]

What can workers do for themselves with regard to health and safety? Under the National Labor Relations Act, workers have the right to engage in walkouts aimed at protesting conditions they deem unsafe.[20] A walkout triggered by conditions that can be objectively characterized as abnormally dangerous cannot violate a union-negotiated no-strike clause in a labor contract.[21] And the Court approved interpretive regulations put forth by Secretary of Labor Ray Marshall that permit workers to refuse to work where an employee is ordered by an employer to work under conditions that the employee reasonably believes pose an imminent risk of death or serious bodily injury and where the employee has reason to believe that there is not sufficient time or opportunity either to seek effective redress from the employer or to apprise OSHA of the danger.[22] A proposal that pay be provided to employees on strike under such circumstances was rejected by Congress.[23]

In *Gade v. National Solid Waste Management Association*[24] a divided Supreme Court, in an opinion authored by Justice Sandra Day O'Connor, held that state regulation of occupational safety and health issues that have not been approved by the secretary of labor and for which a federal standard is in effect is impliedly preempted as in conflict with the Occupational Safety and Health Act. The Court came to this conclusion notwithstanding the fact that it was aimed at protecting both the workers and the public and thus had a "dual impact." Said the Court:

> . . . a state law requirement that directly, substantially and specifically regulates occupational safety and health is an occupational safety and health standard within the meaning of the Act. That such a law may also have a nonoccupational impact does not render it any less of an occupational standard for purposes of pre-emption analysis. If the State wishes to enact a dual impact law that regulates an occupational safety or health issue for which a federal standard is in effect, §18 of the Act requires that the State submit a plan for the approval of the Secretary.[25]

Employment Discrimination Law

Probably the most litigated area of "public-interest labor law" is employment discrimination. The most comprehensive legislation is title VII of the Civil Rights Act of 1964, which established the Equal Employment Opportunity Commission and which prohibits discrimination in employment on account of race, color, sex, national origin, or religion.

The EEOC, initially provided with authority to investigate and to attempt to conciliate allegations of discrimination, has since 1972 had the power to sue defendants in federal district court for alleged discrimination subsequent to resort to the administrative process.[26] It now has jurisdiction and authority over virtually every kind of discrimination in employment.[27] In 1991 the Court held that the statute does not apply extraterritorially to regulate employment practices of American employers who employ U.S. citizens abroad.[28] But Congress reversed that decision through the Civil Rights Act of 1991.[29] Although the EEOC (and the Justice Department for the public sector) has responsibility for most employment discrimination problems arising under title VII and related civil-rights legislation, private plaintiffs have carried the primary burden of law enforcement—particularly in the early days of litigation, before the EEOC had authority to sue in the courts to establish violations and provide for relief.

A series of Supreme Court decisions issued in 1989, which substantially limited the scope of title VII (discussed below),[30] prompted Congress to amend the Act through the Civil Rights Act of 1991.[31] In so doing, the circuit courts of appeal have split on the question of the retroactivity of the act to the decisions of 1989, which have been reversed or limited.[32]

Proving Discrimination

The Courts have held that statistics showing the absence or disproportionate exclusion of minority members or women from a plant or a job classification establish a prima facie case of discrimination.[33] This puts the burden on the other side to explain why there are so few of a group that alleges discrimination. Statistics may be used in class actions, in which a liability is established for large numbers of people throughout the plant or enterprise, or in individual suits, where one or a relatively small number of workers seeks to show discrimination.[34]

Probably the most important case in this field is *Griggs v. Duke Power Co.*,[35] in which a unanimous Supreme Court held that it is not necessary to show an intent to discriminate in order to prove a violation of employment discrimination law. In *Griggs* the employer's written examinations and educational requirements had the effect of making it impossible for the African-Americans in a plant to have upward mobility. A disproportionate exclusion, unless justified by a business necessity for the procedure, was found to establish a violation of law.[36] This decision, which had not been fully applied to the employment discrimination disputes in the public sector[37] (or indeed to other antidiscrimination statutes in the private sector),[38] has had enormous implications for the development of law in this area. For instance, although title VII allows employers to apply "*bona fide* occupational qualifications" in denying one sex access to a job, the Supreme Court has held height and weight qualifications that disproportionately exclude women from being prison guards invalid on the ground that this allowance was meant to be "an extremely narrow exception to" the statute's broad prohibitions against sex discrimination.[39]

In *Diaz v. Pan American World Airlines*[40] the Court of Appeals for the Fifth Circuit rejected the employers insistence upon employing only females as flight attendants, notwithstanding the claim that this served the legitimate business objective of providing psychological support for male passengers involved in the stressful experience of flight. Said the court: "[D]iscrimination based on sex is valid only when *the essence* of the business operation would be undermined by not hiring members of one sex exclusively."[41] One court has held that the employment of female registered nurses involved in the care of obstetrical patients is a bona fide occupational qualification.[42] Said the court:

Giving respect to deep-seated feeling of personal privacy involving one's own genital area is quite a different matter from catering to the desire of some male airline passenger to have . . . an attractive stewardess.[43]

The Court of Appeals for the Second Circuit has held that the privacy interest of female prison inmates does not extend to protection against being viewed while sleeping by male guards so long as suitable sleepwear was provided.[44] But a divided Seventh Circuit, in a case where privacy rights were not involved, held that the employment of female guards for female prisoners was valid because of the authorities' view that this was necessary to the rehabilitation of the female inmates, notwithstanding the absence of objective evidence or empirical studies supporting this proposition.[45]

In age discrimination cases, where the bona fide occupational qualification process is also applicable, the Court has said the following:

> The restrictive language of the statute and the consistent interpretation of the administrative agencies charged with enforcing the statute convince us that, like its Title VII counterpart, the BFOQ exception was in fact meant to be an extremely narrow exception to the general prohibition of age discrimination. . . .[46]

In 1989 the Court, in *Wards Cove Packing Co. v. Atonio*,[47] held that an employer's business necessity burden was one of establishing that the challenged practice "in a significant way [serves] . . . the legitimate employment goals of the employer."[48] The Court held that the employer's burden of proof with respect to a "legitimate business justification defense" is one of production and not persuasion.[49] Particularly troubling was the Court's view that, notwithstanding the fact that employers would have the most access to information regarding their practices, the plaintiff, in establishing its prima facie case, was required to demonstrate that a specific "or particular employment practice . . . [had] created the disparate impact under attack."[50] The Civil Rights Act of 1991 provides that this burden need not be met where the employer's decision making process is not ". . . capable of separation for analysis."[51] The employer's burden is to demonstrate that the ". . . challenged practice is job related for the position in question and consistent with business necessity."[52]

In individual cases in which allegations of intentionally disparate treatment are made, a prima facie case for discrimination is relatively easy to establish,[53] but the burden of rebuttal for the defendant is far less burdensome than for the defendant in a *Griggs* case, who must prove business necessity.[54] The Court of Appeals for the Eleventh Circuit has held that an employer rebuttal based upon subjective evidence imposed a burden more substantial than would otherwise be applicable.[55] The same holds true where the prima facie case of discrimination consists of direct evidence of discrimination, not an inference.[56] Thus in individual cases of discrimination the ultimate burden is on the plaintiff to show that the employer-defendant's conduct was a "pretext" for discrimination.

In a second of the 1989 employment discrimination Supreme Court decisions, *Price Waterhouse v. Hopkins,*[57] a divided Court[58] held that an employer that has allowed a ". . . discriminatory impulse to play a motivating part in an employment decision . . ." must prove through a preponderance of evidence that it would have made the same decision in the absence of discrimination. Again, through the Civil Rights Act of 1991, Congress reversed the Court. The statute now allows the mixed motive only to limit the remedy and not liability. Where the same action would have been taken in the absence of the impermissible motivating factor, the court may grant declaratory relief, injunctive relief, attorney's fees and costs, but not damages or an order providing for admission, reinstatement, hiring, or promotion of an employee or applicant.[59]

Bona fide Seniority Systems

Another defense against discriminatory conduct relates to the existence of bona fide seniority systems, which if negotiated by an employer and a union are not rendered violative of the antidiscrimination provisions of title VII. But what constitutes a bona fide seniority system? Initially the appellate courts (at the level immediately below the U.S. Supreme Court) held that the seniority systems that were neutral and nondiscriminatory on their face violated the statute when they carried forward the effects of past discrimination—even discrimination that antedated the effective date of the statute, July 2, 1965. That is, where blacks, Mexican-Americans, or women had been locked into low-level jobs through discriminatory hiring patterns, or through departmental seniority systems that have made it impossible for employees to bid for available high-level jobs on the basis of seniority accumulated in low-level jobs, past discrimination embodied within the present system had effectively thwarted their upward mobility.

However, in a 7–2 vote the Supreme Court held in *International Brotherhood of Teamsters v. The United States*[60] that pre–July 2, 1965, conduct could not be remedied under any circumstances and that seniority credits based on time spent in low-level jobs during that period could not be accorded to minorities or women. More significant, employees who have been frozen into low-level jobs must establish that they have been discriminated against as individuals even subsequent to a finding of liability against the employer or the labor organization for a pattern of across-the-board discrimination. Although employees who have filed applications for vacant jobs under such circumstances are presumed to have been discriminated against, and the defendant carries the burden of establishing that there was no discrimination, proceedings to determine whether individuals are entitled to seniority and back pay before either a judge or a specially appointed master can consume a considerable amount of time. Hundreds and sometimes thousands of employees or applicants may be involved.[61] As a practical matter, once liability is established in a pattern- or practice-of-discrimination case, there is a tremendous incentive for the plaintiff to settle. Plaintiffs in employment-discrimination cases do not generally have the resources (financial and otherwise) possessed by the defendants, and settlements all too often provide them with less than they would be entitled to in adjudicated proceedings.

In another 1989 decision, this one dealing with seniority, the Court, in an opinion authored by Justice Antonin Scalia, held that a seniority system that was facially nondiscriminatory but that was alleged to be rooted in a discriminatory impact attributable to intentional discrimination could not be complained of by women workers because the statutory limitations for a timely claim related to the negotiation of the agreement itself and not its subsequent application.[62] Justice Marshall with whom Justice Brennan and Justice Blackmun joined, dissented. Said the Court:

There is no doubt, of course, that a facially discriminatory seniority system (one that treats similarly situated employees differently) can be challenged at any time, and that even a facially neutral system, if it is adopted with unlawful discriminatory motive, can be challenged within the prescribed period after adoption. But allowing a facially neutral system to be challenged, and entitlements under it to be altered, many years after its adoption would disrupt those valid reliance interests [the bona fide seniority proviso] was meant to protect.[63]

But this decision was also reversed by Congress through the Civil Rights Act of 1991 which now states that whether the seniority system is facially discriminatory or not, it is the "application of the seniority system" that triggers the limitations within which a timely charge must be filed.[64]

Sex Discrimination

Although the pressure for the passage of fair-employment practices legislation emerged from the struggle for the rights of blacks, concern with sex discrimination (which almost inadvertently found its way into the language of title VII)[65] has increased considerably since the late 1970s. Except in cases involving a failure to provide equal pay for equal work—a practice prohibited by the Equal Pay Act of 1963[66]—women are exclusively reliant on title VII, on state fair-employment practices statutes (which often mirror the federal statute),[67] and on an Executive Order that not only prohibits discrimination by government contractors but explicitly requires affirmative action in recruitment and promotion without the necessity of finding discrimination.[68] Reconstruction legislation, the most prominent of which is the Civil Rights Act of 1866,[69] prohibits discrimination on the basis of race in addition to title VII. (The impact of the Civil Rights Act of 1866 was substantially limited by yet another 1989 Supreme Court ruling,[70] but this also was reversed by the Civil Rights Act of 1991.)[71] The significance of this is that women, unlike blacks, must meet some of the procedural statutory requirements contained in title VII (e.g., the finding that the employer-defendant is involved in interstate commerce, or the filing of an administrative charge within

180 days) if they do not choose to rely exclusively on an executive order or a state statute.[72]

Sex-discrimination cases present other problems not posed by racial cases. For instance, the Supreme Court was called upon to determine whether an all-inclusive disability benefits plan that failed to include pregnancy-related disabilities violated the statute. A majority of the Court answered in the negative,[73] but Congress reversed this judgment through new legislation in 1978.[74] Subsequent to the 1978 statute, the Court held that an employer's health-insurance plan that covered medical expenses of employees' spouses but limited pregnancy-related expenses of male employees' spouses discriminated against male workers, in violation of title VII.[75]

Prior to President Clinton's election to the White House in 1992, President George Bush vetoed family leave legislation twice.[76] The Family and Medical Leave Act of 1993, signed into law by President Clinton on February 5, addresses issues that possess some relationship to antidiscrimination law.[77] It provides that employers with fifty or more workers are obliged to allow employees to have up to twelve weeks of unpaid, job-protected leave to take care of a newborn or newly adopted child, to take care of a sick child or parent, or because of an employee's own serious health problem. Under fair employment practices legislation, frequently such leaves could be obtained only if it could be shown that the policy was sexually discriminatory. Protection at the state level is now prevalent, with some twenty-seven states having enacted comprehensive family leave legislation.[78]

The Court has held that requiring women to make larger pension contributions because actuarily as a group they live longer is violative of title VII. The Court conceded that women as a group may be subsidized without such a requirement,[79] but emphasized that individual women would be discriminated against. Using the same reasoning, the Court has held that retirement benefits offered employees from one of a number of insurance companies requiring sex-based differentials in contributions are unlawful when they too are based on actuarial tables.[80] However, the Court also concluded that benefits derived from contributions made prior to the date of the decision (July 6, 1983) could be calculated on the basis of the previous sex-discriminatory insurance terms. Five years later the Court held that employer liability for pension plans offering discriminatory payment options commences at the same date and employees who retired before July 6, 1983, are not entitled to a readjustment benefits payment structure.[81]

Another major issue is that raised by "sex-plus" cases (cases involving issues associated with sex). The most prominent of these is *Martin-Marietta*,[82] in which an employer had refused to employ women who had pre-school-age children but had not imposed the same condition on men. In *Martin-Marietta* the Supreme Court held that the imposition of a dual standard for men and women is discriminatory under title VII. However, disparate standards for men and women based on other considerations, such as grooming or length of hair, have generally not been viewed as unlawful.[83] The Court of Appeals for the Fifth Circuit held that an employer may properly require English-speaking Mexican-Americans not to speak Spanish in front of customers whose primary language is English, even though there is testimony that this policy reflected the societal discrimination against Mexican-Americans in this country.[84] This case is similar to the "sex-plus" cases in that it tends to make possible harm or ostracism of one group, although the policy is not based on immutable characteristics such as race, sex, and national origin.

Two developing areas in sex-discrimination law are sexual harassment and comparable worth. Sexual-harassment cases involve situations where supervisors or superiors (generally male) require sexual favors as a condition of employment or maintain a work environment in which women are made to feel ostracized for reasons having to do with sex. The Supreme Court has held that title VII prohibits discrimination based upon sex which has created a hostile or abusive work environment.[85] In an opinion authored by Chief Justice (then Justice) Rehnquist, the Court stated that the

". . . correct inquiry is whether respondent by her conduct indicated that the alleged sexual advances were unwelcome, not whether her participation in them was voluntary."[86] Said the Court:

While "voluntariness" in the sense of consent is not a defense to such a claim, it does not follow that a complainant's sexually provocative speech or dress is irrelevant as a matter of law in determining whether he or she found particular sexual advances unwelcome. To the contrary, such evidence is obviously relevant.[87]

The Court also found that employers are not "always automatically liable for sexual harassment by their supervisors," though "absence of notice to an employer does not necessarily insulate that employer from liability."[88] The Court of Appeals for the Ninth Circuit has held that in determining whether the showing with regard to the severity or seriousness of harassing conduct is sufficiently pervasive or frequent, the matter must be examined from the

. . . focus of the perspective of the victim . . . a complete understanding of the victim's view requires, among other things, an analysis of the different perspectives of men and women. Conduct that many men consider unobjectionable may offend many women . . . in order to shield employers from having to accommodate the idiosyncratic concerns of the rare hyper-sensitive employee, we hold that a female plaintiff states a *prima facie* case of hostile environment sexual harassment when she alleges conduct which a reasonable woman would consider sufficiently severe or pervasive to alter the conditions of employment and create an abusive working environment.[89]

The Ninth Circuit has also held, in an opinion authored by Judge Cynthia Hall, that while counseling may be sufficient as a first resort to remedying sexual harassment, the employer must ". . . take . . . disciplinary measures" against the offender.[90]

The Anita Hill–Clarence Thomas hearing, relating the latter's appointment to the Supreme Court in October 1991, dramatized the absence of an effective remedy for women complaining of sexual harassment who have not been dismissed or denied an employment opportunity in conjunction with such conduct.[91] The Civil Rights Act of 1991 moved to alter the situation by providing for compensatory and punitive damages in addition to back pay, interest on back pay, or other relief authorized by the 1964 statute but provided a cap for such recovery depending upon the number of employees employed.[92]

The comparable-worth cases are the sleeping giant of sex discrimination. Plaintiffs seek to impose liability on the basis of discriminatory wage differentials where the work is not equal or similar but where the wage gap between male and female employees is discriminatory. The Supreme Court, by a 5–4 vote, has taken a tentative step in this direction by interdicting intentional wage discrimination.[93] Noting that plaintiffs alleged that women were not paid in accordance with their job evaluations whereas men were, Justice Brennan, writing for the majority, stated the following:

[The suit] does not require a court to make its own subjective assessment of the value of male and female guard jobs, to attempt by statistical technique or other methods to quantify the effect of sex discrimination on the wage rates.

We do not decide in this case the precise contours of lawsuits challenging sex discrimination in compensation under title VII. It is sufficient to note that [the] claims of discriminatory undercompensation are not barred . . . merely because [the women] do not perform work equal to that of the male jail guards.[94]

Finally, the Court dealt with an issue of great consequence in *United Auto Workers v. Johnson Controls, Inc.,*[95] namely whether an employer can exclude fertile female employees from certain jobs because of its concern for the health of the fetus that the women might conceive. The Court held that the bias in the policy was "obvious" because "[f]ertile men, but not fertile women, are given a choice as to whether they wish to risk their reproductive health for a particular job."[96] The Court held that regardless of motivation, where the disparate treatment was facially explicit, the policy can only be justified if the gender-based discrimination was predicated upon a bona fide occupational qualification. The Court, in the majority opinion authored by Justice Blackmun, noted that concern for a woman's "existing or potential offspring historically has been the excuse for denying women equal employment opportunities."[97] Said the Court, expressing a disagreement with the concurring opinion's view that such policies could be lawful where there were "substantial safety risks to third parties":

It is no more appropriate for the courts than it is for individual employers to decide whether a woman's reproductive role is more important to herself and her family than her economic role. Congress has left this choice to the woman as hers to make.[98]

Sexual Orientation Discrimination

Only California, Connecticut, Hawaii, Massachusetts, Wisconsin, New Jersey, Vermont, and the District of Columbia have statutes prohibiting discrimination on the basis of sexual orientation. While legislative bills have been introduced in Illinois, the governor has vetoed them. Prior to the enactment of legislation prohibiting sexual orientation discrimination in California in 1992, both Governor George Deukmejian and Governor Pete Wilson vetoed such legislation.[99]

In *Gay Law Students Association v. Pacific Telephone and Telegraph Co.*[100] the Supreme Court of California held that homosexuality is the equivalent of political activity or affiliation within the meaning of that state's labor code which prohibits discrimination in this area. A California lower court has held that this decision has applicability to discrimination in the workplace.[101] Dismissal of a homosexual employee in California has resulted in a $5.3 million damage award.[102] The horror of AIDS during the past decade has created new discrimination problems for homosexuals and is responsible for the special regulations relating to food handling described below in connection with the Americans With Disabilities Act of 1990.

Finally, the Court of Appeals for the Ninth Circuit has held the denial of security clearance through individualized determinations that treat homosexual conduct, but not heterosexual conduct, as a negative factor is unconstitutional discrimination against gays.[103] A federal district court has held that the U.S. Department of Navy regulations that mandate the discharge of all homosexuals service members on the basis of their sexual status is unconstitutional.[104]

Accommodations of Handicaps and Religious Observances

The Court has sustained the constitutionality of title VII's exemption of religious organizations from the prohibition against the discrimination in employment on the basis of religion and held that the provision does not violate the Establishment Clause of the First Amendment in the sense that it would impermissibly entangle Church and State.[105] The Court held that Congress could appropriately minimize governmental interference in the decision-making process in religion.

Another question arising under title VII relates to religious discrimination and the extent to which employees can be required to work during a period of time when their religion forbids work. A majority of the Supreme Court has held that the imposition of more than a *de minimis* cost upon an employer under such circumstances does not make out a violation of title VII.[106] Specifically it found that the proviso in the 1972 amendments to title VII that requires an employer to accommodate employees' religious observances or practices "without undue hardship on the conduct of the employer's business" is not violated under such circumstances.

In a similar vein the Court concluded that a military prohibition against the wearing of yarmulkes by chaplains is constitutional,[107] a determination reversed by Congress. In an equally controversial decision, *Employment Division v. Smith*,[108] an opinion authored by Justice Scalia for a 6–3 majority,[109] the Court concluded that a state's denial of unemployment compensation benefits to employees discharged for ingesting peyote for sacramental purposes at a ceremony of the Native American Church did not violate the Free Exercise Clause of the First Amendment to the Constitution. Studiously avoiding the point that a state's prohibition of the drinking of alcohol might run up against Christian sacramental traditions relating to wine, the Court said:

To make an individual's obligation to obey such a law contingent upon the law's coincidence with his religious beliefs, except where the State's interest is "compelling"—permitting him, by virtue of his beliefs, "to become a law unto himself" . . . contradicts both constitutional tradition and common sense.[110]

Contrarily, the Court has held that sincerely held religious beliefs that require a worker not to work on the Sabbath pursuant to the beliefs of the Seventh Day Adventist Church,[111] or where the worker is engages in similar conduct but is not a member of an established sect or church,[112] or where the beliefs which impel the worker to refuse assignments to particular work are not held by the church itself[113] are not a basis for denying unemployment compensation benefits under the Constitution.

Similarly for two decades accommodations have been required to be made to physical and mental handicaps under the government's contract-compliance program, which is administered (as are all such efforts) by the Department of Labor's Office of Federal Contract Compliance Programs pursuant to the Rehabilitation Act of 1973.[114] More recently Congress enacted the Americans with Disabilities Act of 1990.[115]

This statute provides for both prohibitions against discrimination because of handicaps in connection with public facilities as well as in the employment relationship. With regard to the latter, the law, which became effective in 1992, prohibits employers from discriminating against a "qualified individual with a disability." An individual with a disability is defined as one who possessed a physical or mental impairment that substantially limits one or more major life activities, a record of such an impairment or one who is regarded as having such an impairment. Specifically excluded from such a definition is homosexuality, bisexuality, transvestites, transsexuals, pedophiles, exhibitionists, voyeurists, and gender identity disorders not resulting from physical impairments. Also excluded are compulsive gamblers, kleptomaniacs, pyromaniacs, and those who are currently engaged in the use of illegal drugs. Employers may hold alcoholics to the same qualifications and job performance standards as other employees, even if their unsatisfactory performance is related to alcoholism.

It is unclear whether such so-called voluntary behavior as smoking or obesity is within this statute's definition of disability. Similarly unresolved are issues relating to so-called predictive disabilities, such as lower back problems which could cause a handicap in the future. An employer must make a reasonable accommodation to the disability, although the precise standard applicable to this term remains to be determined.

The secretary of health and human services is required to publish a list of infectious and communicable diseases that can be transmitted through the handling of food and employees who have such diseases may be transferred if the danger to public health and safety cannot be eliminated by some other reasonable accommodation. The obvious focus here is AIDS, even though there is no current evidence to the effect that AIDS can be transmitted through the handling of food or beverages.

The remedial scheme for employment discrimination cases set forth in both the Civil Rights Act of 1964 and the Civil Rights Act of 1991 applies to the Americans with Disabilities Act of 1990. That is to say, punitive and compensatory damages are available as well as more traditional relief, although such damages are capped. The EEOC has jurisdiction over disability claims of discrimination.

Three years before the passage of ADA statute, the Supreme Court held that an employee with a physical impairment resulting from the contagious disease of tuberculosis may be considered to be handicapped within the meaning of the Rehabilitation Act.[116]

Age Discrimination

The Age Discrimination in Employment Act of 1967,[117] over which the EEOC also has jurisdiction now, prohibits discrimination against workers between 40 and 70 on account of age. Discrimination on the basis of years of service designed to deprive an employee of pension benefits is not age discrimination.[118] Either the EEOC or private plaintiffs may bring an action for damages suffered, and for additional monies if the violation was willful. Willful discrimination exists where ". . . the employer either knew or showed reckless disregard for the matter of whether its conduct was prohibited by the statute—applies to all disparate treatment cases under the ADEA. Once a 'willful' violation has been shown, the employee need not additionally demonstrate that the employer's conduct was outrageous, or provide direct evidence of the employer's motivation, or prove that age was the predominant rather than a determinative factor in the employment decision."[119] Except for executives in high policy positions and university faculty members (this exemption has been phased out as of 1993), retirement programs that force retirement before 70 are unlawful.[120] The Supreme Court has held that a provision of the Missouri Constitution requiring appointed state judges to retire at age 70 does not violate either the ADEA or the Equal Protection Clause of the Constitution.[121] A difficulty here is that age, like handicap, affects the ability of some people to function. But according to *Business Week*, "few [employers] complained about incompetent old workers, and only a small fraction of older people have opted to keep working anyway."[122]

In yet another 1989 ruling by the high court, it was held that although the Act allows discriminatory benefits under a bona fide employee benefits plan unless it is a substitute for age discrimination, a benefits scheme adopted prior to the Act could not be used as a subterfuge by the employer trying to avoid it.[123] Again, Congress overturned this ruling through a separate statute, the 1990 Older Workers Benefit and Protection Act, which now holds that a bona fide employee benefits plan is one where the actual payment made or cost incurred to an older worker was no less than that made for a younger worker.[124]

Remedies

As noted above, the Civil Rights Act of 1991 has amended title VII so as to provide for capped punitive and compensatory damages in connection with all discrimination prohibited by that statute. The most formidable problem in employment discrimination cases is that of remedies. The Supreme Court held in *Albemarle Paper Co. v. Moody*[125] that once liability is established by virtue of a class action or government-initiated pattern-of-practice employment discrimination case, the presumption is that back pay and other forms of equitable relief are to be awarded.[126] Prior to the Civil Rights Act of 1991, the courts held that punitive and apparently compensatory damages cannot be awarded under title VII,[127] but the Supreme Court has stated in *dicta* that punitive damages are awardable under the Civil Rights Act of 1866,[128] and a number of circuit courts have upheld this.[129] In California, the legislature, overturning a contrary Supreme Court of California ruling,[130] has held that a state agency may award both punitive and compensatory damages.[131]

The rationale for damage awards is not simply compensation but also the fact that they have a prophylactic effect on illegal conduct and wrongdoing. Employers and labor organizations[132] confronted with employment discrimination litigation began to have a very serious incentive to remedy the problem once federal courts held that class actions on this issue involving large numbers of workers could be maintained in federal courts and that back pay was to be awarded. At that point defendants became quite interested in settling litigation and obtaining waivers against future damage claims. (The latter practice has given rise to considerable litigation to determine whether the individuals solicited have knowingly and voluntarily waived their right to sue.)[133]

The federal and state governments have imposed such requirements on government contracts with judicial approval.[134] The Supreme Court's important *Bakke* decision indicated that some forms of race-conscious remedies for past discrimination are appropriate, but did not say much more.[135] The Court held in the *Weber* case[136] that voluntarily negotiated affirmative-action programs in the private sector that include quotas are compatible with civil-rights legislation.

Then in 1986, in *Wygant v. Jackson Board of Education*,[137] the Court held 5–4 that a layoff provision in a collective bargaining agreement not grounded in the finding of prior discrimination that sought to maintain racial balance in the work force was unconstitutional. Justice Powell's opinion seemed to focus upon the idea that loss of existing jobs, where based upon racial considerations, was particularly intrusive as compared to the denial of future employment opportunities.

Then, six weeks later, the Court approved race-conscious remedies in conjunction with title VII, holding that the Act does not limit courts the grant of relief only to actual victims of discrimination but rather that a defendant's history of egregious racial discrimination and its attempt to evade remedial orders warranted the establishment of numerical goals for union membership in order to increase minority membership in the union and the apprenticeship program.[138] The Court also held that a district court could enter a race-conscious consent decree embodying an agreement providing for a promotion plan that benefited minority individuals who were not actual victims of discrimination.[139] Subsequently the high tribunal approved a district court order designed to remedy unconstitutional racial discrimination that would promote one qualified black police officer for every white police officer if the work force composition was less than 25 percent black.[140]

In the third of the major employment voluntary affirmative-action cases—*Johnson v. Transportation Agency, Santa Clara County*[141]—the Court validated a plan making promotions for positions within traditionally segregated job classifications in which women had been significantly underrepresented where the agency was authorized to consider as one factor the sex of a qualified applicant. The Court, Justice Brennan writing, held that a "manifest imbalance"—the test used to validate race-conscious affirmative-action in traditionally segregated job classification in *Weber*—could trigger the basis for an appropriate sex-conscious affirmative-action plan. The Court concluded that the prima facie standard in title VII cases was not required in the cases involving statistical imbalance in affirmative action. Said the Court:

[such a standard] . . . could inappropriately create a significant disincentive for employers to adopt an affirmative action plan. . . . A corporation concerned with maximizing return on investment, for instance, is hardly likely to adopt a plan if in order to do so it must compile evidence that could be used to subject it to a colorable Title VII suit.[142]

Notwithstanding the approval given to race-conscious plans in virtually all but one of the cases noted above, in 1989 the Court held that an affirmative action program requiring prime contractors awarded city construction contracts to subcontract at least 30 percent of the dollar amount of each contract to minority contractors was unconstitutional on the ground that the city of Richmond failed to demonstrate a compelling governmental interest justifying the plan and that it was not narrowly tailored to remedy the effects of prior discrimination.[143] On the other hand, a year later a 5–4 majority concluded that minority preference policies of the Federal Communications Commission did not violate equal protection principles.[144] But the future of affirmative action is problematical, given the increasingly conservative cast of the Court. Nothing illustrates this more vividly than Justice (then Judge) Thomas' opinion in which he held an FCC policy providing extra credit to a woman on the ground of gender to be inconsistent with the constitutional right to equal protection under the law and was thus unconstitutional.[145] Chief Judge Mikva dissented vigorously on the ground that the standards established were inconsistent with *Metro Broadcasting* and inconsistent with the principles of deference to Congress.[146]

Wrongful Discharge

American common law has traditionally recognized that employment relationships are terminable at the will of either party, absent a contractual commitment to the contrary.[147] Several federal and state statutes referred to earlier have limited the applicability of this doctrine, protecting employees from discharge because of race, religion, sex, national origin, age, or union activity. Despite these protections, employers, until very recently, had considerable freedom in deciding whether or not to discharge a nonunion employee. Since the late 1970s, however, an increasing number of jurisdictions have recognized a cause of action for wrongful discharge or termination. The state courts, rather than the legislatures, are responsible for this development. Representative of the reasoning that has imposed implied contractual obligations upon employers in their dealings with individual employees is that of the New Jersey Supreme Court in 1985:

Our courts will not allow an employer to offer attractive inducements and benefits to the work force and then withdraw them when it chooses, no matter how sincere its belief that they are not enforceable. . . . Job security is the assurance that one's livelihood, one's family future will not be destroyed arbitrarily; it can be cut off only "for good cause," fairly determined. Hoffman-La Roche's commitment here was to what working men and women engaged as their most basic advance. It was a commitment that gave workers protection against arbitrary termination.[148]

A cause of action for wrongful termination does not rest only on contractual theories. It is based on any of three exceptions to the doctrine of employment at will:

- Discharges that are contrary to public policy—namely dismissals instituted because the employee refuses to act unlawfully, or because the employee performs a public obligation (e.g., serving on a jury), or in retaliation for the exercises of statutory right (e.g., free speech).[149]

- Discharges that breach implied contract of employment arising from a handbook, a policy, or some other representation.[150]

- Discharges that breach an implied covenant of good faith and fair dealing.[151]

Through mid-1992, some 43 states have adopted the public-policy exception to the doctrine of employment at will,[152] 34 have held that binding contracts of employment are implied by handbooks and other representations,[153] and 13 have recognized an implied covenant of good faith and fair dealing.[154] California courts have been the most active in applying these exceptions. In *Tameny v. Atlantic Richfield*[155] the California Supreme Court held that an employer "contravene[d] the dictates of public policy" when he discharged an employee for refusing to take part in a price-fixing conspiracy. In *Pugh v. See's Candies,*[156] an appellate court found that an employer had made an implied promise not to terminate an employee, based on the duration of the employee's employment, his promotions and commendations, assurances he received from the employer, and the employer's acknowledged personnel policies.

There are a number of developments that have emerged in the wake of the above-noted case law. The first is demonstrated by the Supreme Court of California's important 1988 decision of *Foley v. Interactive Data Corp.*[157] While the Court approved an implied contract theory such as that employed in *Pugh,* it concluded that the duty of an employee to disclose information to the employer about alleged embezzlement by his or her supervisor served only a private interest of the employer and therefore was not within the public-policy exception.[158] The Court added that a covenant of good faith and fair dealing rooted in tort rather than contract could not be found in common law apparently because it would permit juries to fashion excessive damage awards, which would lead to uncertainty in business relationships in a climate not conducive to sound commercial bargains. *Foley,* along with a subsequent decision providing that workers' compensation statutes preempt some wrongful discharge causes of action based upon the tort of intentional infliction of emotional distress,[159] has diminished the impact of the early case law.

A second area of change has been triggered by employer attempts to insert so-called at-will clauses in application form, a special application agreement, or the contract of employment with incumbent employees. These at-will clauses purport to allow employers to dismiss the worker regardless of the employer's conduct, or representations that have been made to the employee in written or oral form, implied or explicit. Sometimes the judiciary has proceeded warily in enforcing such agreements.[160] The Supreme Court of Wyoming has established fairly rigorous standards relating to the enforcement of a disclaimer that an employee handbook or manual is not a contract.[161] Employers have been emboldened and required both applicants and employees to enter into arbitration agreements to resolve the propriety of dismissals by the Supreme Court's *Gilmer*[162] decision allowing for the enforcement of such clauses in the discrimination area so as to avoid jury trials that could result in punitive and compensatory damages.

A third development in this area relates to the relationship between wrongful-discharge litigation and grievance-arbitration machinery in collective bargaining agreements. In 1988 a unanimous Supreme Court—having previously held that wrongful discharge actions were preempted where they involved an application or an interpretation of a collective bargaining agreement[163]—held that even where the same factual considerations would be addressed in a grievance under the agreement, as well as by the court considering a retaliatory wrongful discharge claim predicated upon public policy, a state court could retain jurisdiction over the discharge claim ". . . when adjudication of . . . [substantive rights a state provides to workers] does not depend upon the interpretation of such agreements."[164] This is an area of law in which there will be disputes and litigation.

Finally, there has been much discussion about legislation that would provide the employee with more access to a tribunal and, since punitive as well as compensatory damages are available in the public policy and some of the contract cases, would limit the employer's liability. Some states have enacted legislation protecting "whistle-blowers,"[165] but no states have enacted comprehensive legislation dealing with unfair dismissal.[166]

Drug and Alcohol Problems

Employee privacy is protected by the Constitutions of both Alaska[167] and California.[168] In California protection is afforded whether governmental conduct is involved or not. Additionally "[t]he common law recognizes various causes of action relating to the right to privacy. One of those is the tort of intrusion on seclusion."[169]

The U.S. Supreme Court has held that a standard of reasonableness governs public employer intrusions on constitutionally protected policy interests of government employees but, in so holding, avoided the question of whether individualized suspicion of a particular employee is an essential element of the standard of reasonableness under the Fourth Amendment's protection against unreasonable searches and seizures.[170] A balancing process has evolved in the Fourth Amendment cases similar in some respects to the employee privacy cases that have taken place in the wrongful discharge context.

The Supreme Court has held that drug testing of railway workers, so as to permit an examination of employee behavior subsequent to certain train accidents in which they were involved, constitutes a search within the meaning of the Fourth Amendment that is reasonable without the need for a warrant.[171] Said Justice Anthony Kennedy writing for the majority of the Court: "A requirement of particularized suspicion of drug or alcohol use would seriously impede an employer's ability to obtain this information, despite its obvious importance."[172]

In a more far-reaching holding, *National Treasure Employees Union v. Von Raab*,[173] the Court held that the Fourth Amendment was not violated by the U.S. Customs Service where it required a urinalysis test from employees who sought transfer or promotion to certain positions. Accordingly these cases have established the proposition that drug testing performed by private employers under compulsion of governmental regulation subjects such conduct to the Fourth Amendment's scrutiny. Second, the collection and testing of urine constitutes an intrusion upon privacy that may be balanced against governmental needs that under certain circumstances do not require a warrant.

In light of *Von Raab*—which did not involve random testing that ". . . may increase employee anxiety and the invasion of subjective expectations of privacy"[174]—where there was no showing of a drug problem among the employees affected by testing, the Court of Appeals for the Ninth

Circuit has had no difficulty sustaining random unannounced drug testing of airline employees, where ". . . a number of pilots and other airline crew members have received treatment for cocaine overdoses or addictions"[175] and there were drug problems in connection with other employees as well as drugs present in the bodies of pilots in two airplane crashes. The same court has applied this test and upheld random testing involving commercial truck drivers in light of the ". . . concern for safety and deterrence [which exceeds] the governmental interests found compelling in . . . earlier cases."[176] A divided Court of Appeals for the Seventh Circuit has held that an Illinois racing board rule requiring jockeys and other participants in horse races in Illinois to submit to random drug testing which is not founded on any individualized suspicion of wrongdoing, is constitutional.[177] In a most far-reaching decision the Court of Appeals for the District of Columbia has upheld a mandatory drug urinalysis program for all Department of Justice applicants tentatively selected for employment.[178]

In a second case involving the railroad industry, the Court has held that an employer's claim that the collective bargaining agreement gives it discretion to make changes in working conditions without prior negotiations, where the changes involved the administration of drug tests, constituted a minor dispute that is subject to the compulsory and binding arbitration provisions of the Railway Labor Act and thus made it impossible for the union to bargain initially about the matter or to bring economic pressure to bear as it would in connection with a so-called "major" dispute.[179] Conversely, however, in *Johnson-Bateman Co.*,[180] the National Labor Relations Board held that drug and alcohol testing of incumbent employees is a mandatory subject of bargaining within the meaning of the Act. The Board has declined to oblige the employer to bargain about the testing of applicants,[181] notwithstanding the fact that it must bargain with regard to antidiscrimination clauses and related conditions of employment and their relationship to applicants.[182]

In an important decision in which the drug and alcohol cases have been cited, the Board has held that an employer is mandated to bargain with a union about a no-smoking ban.[183] The Board has concluded that a ban on smoking at an employer's premises during working hours is a mandatory subject of bargaining, regardless of whether the bargaining representative seeks to obtain such a ban or to limit it or eliminate it. Once the collective bargaining agreement is negotiated, the courts of appeals are divided on the question of whether a union may obtain a preliminary injunction against the unilateral imposition of an employer's drug and alcohol testing program pending arbitration of the union's grievance.[184]

Conclusion

Pensions, health and safety, employment discrimination, drug and alcohol testing, and wrongful-discharge litigation have become the new frontier of labor law. Unlike the law relating to labor-management relations (principally the National Labor Relations Act), they directly affect the substantive terms of the employment relationship. More legislation and case law in this area promises to be with us in the future. It is possible that it will dwarf more traditional labor law before the turn of the century.

12

Conclusion

The system of American labor law and industrial relations has strengths and deficiencies. Because American society is litigious and dynamic, and because labor law will evolve and change in the coming years, the deficiencies may receive greater attention. The area of public-interest labor law will continue to grow rapidly. It may be that the legal struggle against discrimination will convince the courts and legislatures that protection against arbitrary treatment by employers for all workers is good policy and good law.[1] The difficulty thus far has been that neither labor nor business has had an adequate incentive to promote legal safeguards for unorganized workers who are not protected by union-negotiated collective bargaining agreements. The developments alluded to in Chapter 11 which provide new protections for individual employees by virtue of both common law and statutes, promised to fashion new innovations in the workplace, notwithstanding the isolated indifference of the organized sector of the economy.

More changes may result from the willingness of unions to accept seats on corporate boards, as has been done in the automobile industry. This is bound to promote reexamination of the adversary-relationship model so uncritically accepted by both labor and management in this country—the view expressed by the Supreme Court in *Insurance Agents* that collective bargaining is not some "academic search for truth."[2] The current economic climate, inextricably linked as it is to the scarcity of and uncertainty about critical resources, may focus American attention on means of achieving cooperation as an adjunct to, if not a substitute for, conflict. The success of Germany and Japan in this area may be of interest to Americans.

The search for cooperation will bring attempts to apply the experience gained in grievance arbitration to interest disputes about new contract terms. The controversy about public-sector striking has encouraged such efforts. It is quite possible that the developments in the public sector will have substantial impact on the private sector.

Finally, one must take note of an important matter that has not been discussed in this book at all: incomes policy. The decentralized nature of the American system makes any incomes policy, voluntary or otherwise, difficult to administer. It would be particularly arduous to implement such policies through national legislation, for local unions are in the cockpit in most wage negotiations. Although a number of industrial unions negotiate national pacts, decentralization places incomes policy in a totally different perspective than in the European countries, which suffer from "wage drift" (the increase of payments above nationally negotiated norms). It is difficult enough for the international unions of the United States (let alone the AFL-CIO, which has been the principal party to debates and discussions on the subject since the early 1970s) to deliver any bargain or social contract, because of their remoteness from wage negotiations. Moreover the decline of unions means that a wage explosion is not an issue as of this writing. But this is an issue that will not go away. Productivity problems, increased labor costs, inflation, and the need to be competitive internationally mean that proposals to deescalate leapfrogging wage demand—particularly in declining industries—will continue to be made.[3]

The purpose here has been to describe the labor law system briefly and clearly, with some references to the pattern of industrial relations. One hopes that this will further understanding among workers, unions, business, and government, and that this in turn will promote—in the spirit of the law—a working environment in which the standard of living will be improved and industrial peace fostered.

Notes

Preface to Third Edition

1. The Association was successful in obtaining relief against collusion engaged in by the owners toward player free agency for the 1985, 1986, and 1987 championship season. See *Major League Baseball Players Association and the Twenty-six Major League Baseball Clubs* Panel Decision No. 76 (Roberts, Chairman, September 21, 1987); *Major League Baseball Players Association and the 26 Major League Baseball Clubs,* Grievance No. 87-3 (Nicolau, Chairman, August 31, 1988); *Major League Baseball Players Association and the Twenty-Six Major League Clubs,* Grievance 88-1 (Nicolau, Chairman, July 18, 1990).

2. The football owners were found by the National Labor Relations Board to have engaged in illegal conduct during the 1987 strike. *National Football League Management Council,* 309 NLRB No. 10 (1992).

3. See Oates, "NFL's Free Agency System Rejected in Antitrust Case," *Los Angeles Times,* September 11, 1992, p. A1. Cf. *McNeil v. The National Football League,* 764 F.Supp 1351 (D. Minn. 1991); *Jackson v. National Football League,* 4-92-876 (D. Minn. 1991).

4. 309 NLRB No. 163 (1992).

Preface

1. W. Gould, "Mistaken Opposition to the N.L.R.B.," *The New York Times,* June 20, 1985, at 31, col. 2

2. This took the form of an AFL-CIO report, "The Changing Situation of Workers and Their Unions: A Report by the AFL-CIO Committee on the Evolution of Work" (February 1985). See W. Gould, "Labor Takes Look at Itself, Finds Unsettling Things," *Los Angeles Times,* March 29, 1985, pt. 11, at 7, col. 1.

Chapter 1

1. *American Can Co.,* 13 NLRB 1252 (1939).

2. Edw. 7, ch. 47.

3. Norris-LaGuardia Act, ch. 90, 47 Stat. 70 (1932), 29 USC §§101–15 (1970).

4. T. C. Johnston, *Collective Bargaining in Sweden* (1962).

5. Works Constitution Act of 1952, Bundesgesetzblatt, Teil 1, 681.

6. In 1990 the percentage of union members in the nonagricultural work force was 16 percent in the United States; 36 percent in Canada; 43 percent in Australia; 25 percent in Japan; and the most recent statistics for Great Britain in 1988 establish 46 percent for that country. See generally J. Dunlop and W. Galenson, *Labor in the Twentieth Century* (1978). The decline has been going on for some period of time. See, for instance, W. Serrin, "Union Membership Falls Sharply; Decline Expected to Be Permanent," *The New York Times,* May 31, 1983, at 1, col. 1.

7. L. Sayles and G. Strauss, *The Local Union* (1953).

8. See "After 13 Years, Auto Union Joins AFL-CIO Again," *The New York Times,* July 2, 1981, at 8.

9. S. Perlman, *A Theory of Labor Movement* (1928).

10. *Tameny v. The Atlantic Richfield Co.,* 27 Cal. 3d 167 (1980).

11. See generally "Protecting At Will Employees against Wrongful Discharge: The Duty to Terminate Only in Good Faith" (comment), 98 Harv. L. Rev. 1816 (1980); "Implied Contract Rights to Job Security" (note), 26 Stan. L. Rev. 335 (1974), C. Summers, "Individual Protection against Unjust Dismissal: Time for a Statute," 62 Va. L. Rev. 481 (1976).

12. Thirteen states have plant-closing legislation: Connecticut, Hawaii, Kansas, Maine, Maryland, Massachusetts, Michigan, Minnesota, Montana, Oregon, South Carolina, Tennessee, and Wisconsin. "Plant Closings," 9A IERM (BNA) §§507:101–119 (June 1992).

13. See generally W. Gould, *Japan's Reshaping of American Labor Law*, at 94–116 (1984).

14. See Forty-sixth Annual Report of NLRB, Fiscal Year 1979, in Labor Relations Yearbook (BNA) (1983). Figures for the years 1960–76 are collected in H.R. Rep. No. 95-637, 95th Cong., 1st Sess. 26 (1977) (chart 3). A four-year decline in the case load now appears to have reversed. See Shinoff, "The NLRB Tests Labor and Vice versa: Union Organizing and Federal Board's Case Load Both Increasing," *San Francisco Examiner*, December 12, 1985, at A-7.

Chapter 2

1. *Commonwealth v. Pullis (The Philadelphia Cordwainer's Case)*, Mayor's Court of Philadelphia (1806). See J. Commons, *Documentary History of American Society* 59 (1910).

2. 45 Mass. (4 Met.) 111 (1842).

3. *Id*. at 129.

4. A. Cox, D. Bok, and R. Gorman, *Cases and Materials on Labor Law* (85h ed., 1976). The point has been made that not only was the law repressive but that union conduct was subdued by the union leadership's view of the law. See W. Forbath, *Law and the Shaping of the American Labor Movement* (1991).

5. *Vegelahn v. Gunter*, 167 Mass. 92, 44 N.E. 1077 (1896).

6. 44 N.E. at 1080.

7. *Id*.

8. *Id*. at 1081.

9. A. Rees, *The Economics of Trade Unions* (3d ed., 1989).

10. 26 Stat. 209 (1890), as amended 15 USC §1–7 (1976).

11. 208 U.S. 274 (1908).

12. *Id*. at 301.

13. A. Mason, *Organized Labor and the Law* (1969), p. 170.

14. Clayton Antitrust Act 6, 38 Stat. 730 (1914), as amended 15 USC §15, 17, 26 (1970), 29 USC §52 (1979).

15. S. Gompers, "The Charter of Industrial Freedom-Labor Provisions of the Clayton Anti-trust Law," 21 Federationist 971 (1914).

16. 254 U.S. 443 (1921).

17. *Id.* at 469.

18. *Id.* at 470.

19. *Id.*

20. *Id.* at 471.

21. *Id.* at 477, 478.

22. *Id.* at 481 (Brandeis, J. dissenting).

23. *Id.* at 482 (Brandeis, J. dissenting).

24. *Id.* at 484 (Brandeis, J. dissenting).

25. *Id.* at 488 (Brandeis, J. dissenting).

26. *Id.* (Brandeis, J. dissenting).

27. 268 U.S. 295 (1925).

28. F. Frankfurter and N. Greene, *The Labor Injunction* (1930), p. 201.

29. Norris-LaGuardia Act, 47 Stat. 70 (1932), 29 USC §101–15 (1970).

30. Norris-LaGuardia 13(c): "The term 'labor dispute' includes any controversy concerning terms or conditions of employment, or concerning the association or representation of persons in negotiating, fixing, maintaining, changing, or seeking to arrange terms or conditions of employment, regardless of whether or not the disputants stand in the proximate relation of employer and employee."

31. 312 U.S. 219, 231 (1941).

32. *Id.* at 235.

33. *Id.* at 232.

Chapter 3

1. 29 USC §20 et seq. (1976). As in *Jones & Laughlin,* with regard to the NLRA the Court upheld the constitutionality of the FLSA in *United States v. Darby,* 312 U.S. 100 (1941). Initially, however, the Court held that the FLSA could not be applied constitutionally to state and local governments in *National League of Cities v. Usery,* 426 U.S. 833 (1976). But the Court has reversed that decision by 5–4 vote in *Garcia v. San Antonio Metropolitan Transit Authority,* 469 U.S. 528 (1985).

2. While the new law provides for a special subminimum rate for teenagers, it appears that a number of employers in industries, like fast-food restaurants, which traditionally recruit young employees, are not able to attract acceptable workers at such a rate. Uchilles, "Employers Shun Sub-minimum Range," *The New York Times,* December 31, 1990, p. 1. S. Nasar, "Forging New Insight on Minimum Wages and Jobs," *The New York Times,* June 29, 1992, p. C1, col. 3. See L. Katz and A. Krueger, "The Effect of the Minimum Wage on the Fast-Food Industry," 46 Indus. Lab. Rel. Rev. 6 (1992).

3. 40 USC §276a (1976).

4. 41 USC §35–45 (1976).

5. Only Alaska, Connecticut, Hawaii, Iowa, New Jersey, Oregon, and Rhode Island are in excess of the minimum wage for employees provided by the federal statute. California, Delaware, Idaho, Illinois, Kentucky, Maine, Maryland, Massachusetts, Minnesota, Missouri, Montana, Nebraska, Nevada, New York, North Dakota, Ohio, Oklahoma, Pennsylvania, South Dakota, Utah, Vermont, Washington, West Virginia, and Wisconsin are all at the federal rate. Below the federal rate are Arkansas, Colorado, Georgia, Indiana, Kansas, Michigan, New Hampshire, New Mexico, North Carolina, Texas, Virginia, and Wyoming. Such state laws of course have applicability to employees employed by employers that are intrastate and not interstate. Alabama, Arizona, Florida, Louisiana, Mississippi, South Carolina, and Tennessee have no minimum wage at all. Subminimum wage rates are provided for by Alaska, California, Connecticut, Illinois, Maryland, Nebraska, New Hampshire, North Carolina, North Dakota, Pennsylvania, South Dakota, Utah, Vermont, Virginia, Washington, and Wisconsin.

6. Several states have enacted legislation permitting terminated employees to collect accrued but unused vacation pay if the employment relationship is terminated; see California, Iowa, Louisiana, Michigan, New Hampshire, Ohio (for county employees), Rhode Island, and Wisconsin (for the families of deceased state employees). In addition several states protect employee entitlement to vacation in the event that they are required to perform military or jury duty; see, for example, Alabama and Arizona.

7. 44 Stat. 577 (1926), as amended 45 USC §151 et seq. (1976).

8. 48 Stat. 195 (1933).

9. *Schechter Poultry Corp. v. United States,* 295 U.S. 495 (1935).

10. 301 U.S. 1 (1937). For an excellent treatment of the early development of the NLRB, see J. Gross, *The Making of the National*

Labor Relations Board: A Study in Economics, Politics and the Law. vol. 1 (1974).

11. W. Galenson, *The CIO Challenge to the AFL* (1960).

12. L. Keyserling, "The Wagner Act: Its Origin and Current Significance," 29 Geo. Wash. L. Rev. 199 (1960).

13. *Textile Workers' Union v. Lincoln Mills*, 353 U.S. 448 (1957).

14. *United Steelworkers v. American Manufacturing Co.*, 363 U.S. 564 (1960); *United Steelworkers v. Warrior & Gulf Navigation Co.*, 363 U.S. 574 (1960); *United Steelworkers v. Enterprise Wheel & Car Corp.*, 363 U.S. 593 (1960); W. Gould, "On Labor Injunctions, Unions, and the Judges: The Boys Market Case," 1970 S.Ct. Rev. 215; B. Aaron. "Arbitration in the Federal Courts," 9 UCLA L. Rev. 360 (1962). W. Gould, "Judicial Review of Labor Arbitration Awards—Thirty Years of the Steelworkers Trilogy: The Aftermath of AT&T and Misco," 64 Notre Dame L. Rev. 464 (1989). The courts have not given the enforcement of labor contracts extraterritorial scope. *Labor Union of Pico Korea Ltd. v. Pico Products, Inc.*, 140 LRRM 2697 (2d Cir. 1992).

15. *NLRB v. United Food and Commercial Workers Union, Local 23*, 484 U.S. 112 (1987). The Court speaking through Justice Brennan referred to the General Counsel's "concededly unreviewable discretion to file a complaint . . ." and held that any General Counsel function that can be characterized as "prosecutorial" is not subject to review by any other entity under the Act. See also *NLRB v. Sears, Roebuck & Co.*, 421 U.S. 132 (1975).

16. Section 8: "The Congress shall have Power . . . To regulate Commerce with foreign Nations, and among the several States, and with the Indian Tribes. . . ."

17. The occupation-of-the-field test is vividly exemplified in *Oregon–Washington Railroad & Nav. Co. v. Washington*, 270 U.S. 87 (1926). In this case the Court struck down the Washington plant-quarantine regulation. Congress had precluded state action because a previous congressional statute on the same subject was of such immensity as to indicate that Congress intended to occupy the field. Cf. *Mintz v. Baldwin*, 289 U.S. 346 (1933), which upheld a New York statute on the grounds that congressional legislation was specific as to ground that it would not cover.

18. *San Diego Building Trades Council v. Garmon*, 359 U.S. 236, 245 (1959).

19. But there are exceptions: (1) "It is true that we have allowed the States to grant compensation for the consequences, as defined by the traditional law of torts, of conduct marked by violence and imminent threats to the public order. . ."; *International Union, United Automobile, Aircraft and Agricultural Implement Workers, etc. v. Russell*, 356 U.S. 634 (1958); (2) *United Construction Workers v. Laburnum Const. Corp.*, 347 U.S. 656 (1954); (3) We have also allowed the states to enjoin such conduct. State jurisdiction has prevailed in these situations because the compelling state interest, in the scheme of our federalism, in the maintenance of domestic peace is not overridden to the absence of clearly expressed congressional direction. We recognize the opinion in *United Construction Workers, etc. v. Laburnum Const. Corp.*, 347 U.S. 656, 74 S.Ct. 833, 835, 98 L. Ed. 1025, found support in the fact that the state remedy had no federal counterpart. But the decision was determined, as is demonstrated by the question to which review was restricted, by the "type of conduct" involved, that is, by "intimidation and threats of violence." *Id.* at 247–48.

20. For example, *Metropolitan Life Insurance Co. v. Massachusetts*, 471 U.S. 724 (1985); *Fort Halifax Packing Co., Inc. v. Coyne*, 482 U.S. 1 (1987); *New York Telephone Co. v. New York State Dept of Labor*, 440 U.S. 519 (1979); *Amalgamated Association of Street, Electric Railway & Motor Coach Employees v. Lockridge*, 403 U.S. 274 (1971); *International Association of Machinists v. Gonzales*, 356 U.S. 617 (1958); But see *Lodge 76, International Association of Machinists v. Wisconsin Employment Relations Commission*, 427 U.S. 132 (1976). In *Golden State Transit Corp. v. City of Los Angeles*, 475 U.S. 608 (1986), the Court held that the refusal to renew a corporation's taxicab franchise after the company's drivers went on strike was a policy inconsistent with the federal Act inasmuch as ". . . the bargaining process was thwarted when the city in effect imposed a positive durational limit on the exercise of economic self-help." *Id.* at 615. Indeed, because a 6–3 majority of the Court concluded that the state's action was "akin to a rule that denies either sovereign the authority to abridge a personal liberty," the city was suable for compensatory damages for its conduct. *Golden State Transit Corp. v. City of Los Angeles*, 493 U.S. 103 (1989). The theory of *Golden State* has been deemed inapplicable to the regulation of pollutants coincidental to a strike. *International Paper Co. v. Town of Jay*, 136 LRRM 2864 (1st Cir. 1991).

21. *Linn v. Plant Guard Workers*, 383 U.S. 53 (1966).

22. *Farmer v. United Brotherhood of Carpenters*, 430 U.S. 290 (1977).

23. *Sears, Roebuck & Co. v. San Diego County District Council of Carpenters*, 436 U.S. 180 (1978).

24. *Brown v. Hotel Employees, Local 54,* 468 U.S. 491 (1984). Although
the state courts are not deprived of jurisdiction where arbitration
clauses in labor contracts are at issue, the federal labor law of
contract preempts tort law based upon a violation of the collective
agreement if resolution of the claim is dependent upon the meaning of a collective bargaining agreement. *Allis-Chalmers Corp. v.
Lueck,* 471 U.S. 202 (1985). In *Lingle v. Norge Division of Magic Chef,
Inc.,* 486 U.S. 399 (1988), a unanimous Court, speaking through
Justice Stevens, held that an employee covered by a collective
bargaining agreement and a just cause clause relating to discharge
could nonetheless enforce her state law remedy for retaliatory
discharge: "In other words, even if dispute resolution pursuant to
a collective-bargaining agreement, on the one hand, and state law,
on the other, would require addressing precisely the same set of
facts, as long as the state-law claim can be resolved without interpreting the agreement itself, the claim is 'independent' of the
agreement for section 301 pre-emption purposes." A complaint
filed in state court pleading a breach of a contract of employment
guaranteeing continued employment is not necessarily preempted
by virtue of the defendant's assertion that the interpretation of the
collective bargaining agreement is required to resolve the controversy and therefore is not removable to federal court. *Caterpillar,
Inc. v. Williams,* 482 U.S. 386 (1987). Said the Court: ". . . individual
employment contracts are not inevitably superseded by any subsequent collective agreement covering an individual employee, and
claims based upon them may arise under state law." *Id.* at 396.
Other state law tort claims attempting to impose a duty of care
upon trade unions that administer collective bargaining agreements have been regarded as preempted. *International Brotherhood
of Electrical Workers, AFL-CIO v. Hechler,* 481 U.S. 851 (1987); *United
Steelworkers of America v. Rawson,* 495 U.S. 362 (1990). However, a
preemption argument entered against an employee's claim for
intentional infliction of emotional distress arising out of an employer's alleged retaliation for reporting of nuclear safety violations
is not preempted by federal whistleblowing legislation. *English v.
General Electric Co.,* 496 U.S. 72 (1990).

25. See notes 17, 19, and 20 *supra* and note 26 *infra.*

26. See *Building and Construction Trades Council v. Associated Building
and Contractors of Massachusetts/Rhode Island, Inc.,* ___U.S.___
(March 8, 1993). See also *Associated Builders v. Baca,* 769 F.Supp
1537 (N.D. Cal. 1991). In both of these cases state policies were
designed to promote a master labor agreement between the state
and a council of construction unions. In the second case a prevailing wages local ordinance was deemed to be preempted because

of its intrusiveness upon the bargaining process. Cf. *Wisconsin Department of Industry, Labor and Human Relations v. Gould, Inc.*, 475 U.S. 282 (1986). As with the controversy over union expenditures for political purposes, President Bush's attempt to exclude unionized contractors from federal projects was reversed by President Clinton. See Kelly, "President Moves in Favor of Labor," *The New York Times*, February 3, 1993, at A12, col. 1.

27. *Guss v. Utah Labor Relations Board*, 353 U.S. 1 (1957), *Polish National Alliance v. NLRB*, 322 U.S. 643 (1944). In 1983 the Court adopted a strong preemption stand when concluding that a supervisor could not sue a union for alleged interference with employment because the state court would have to decide whether the union conduct was coercive or noncoercive. *Local 926, Operating Engineers v. Jones*, 440 U.S. 669 (1983).

28. "The Board, in its discretion, may, by rule of decision or by published rules adopted pursuant to the Administrative Procedure Act, decline to assert jurisdiction over any labor dispute involving any class or category of employers, where, in the opinion of the Board, the effect of such labor dispute on commerce is not sufficiently substantial to warrant the exercise of its jurisdiction: provided, That the Board shall not decline to assert jurisdiction over any labor dispute over which it would assert jurisdiction under the standards prevailing upon August 1, 1959." NLRA 14(c)(1). 29 USC §164(c)(1) (1976). Though it has been argued by some that freezing the Board's jurisdictional yardstick is a major factor in its backlog of cases, this does not appear to be accurate. See R. Flanagan, *The Litigation Explosion*.

29. *NLRB v. Fainblatt*, 306 U.S. 601, 605–607 (1939), *NLRB v. Reliance Fuel Oil Corp.*, 371 U.S. 224 (1963).

30. *McCulloch v. Sociedad Nacional de Marineros de Honduras*, 872 U.S. 10 (1963). Accord, *Benz v. Compania Naviera Hidalgo, S.A.*, 353 U.S. 138 (1957); *Incres Steam Ship Co. v. International Maritime Workers Union*, 372 U.S. 24 (1963); *Windward Shipping (London) Limited, et al. v. American Radio Association, AFL-CIO, et al.*, 415 U.S. 104 (1974); *American Radio Association, AFL-CIO, et al. v. Mobile Steamship Association, Inc.*, 419 U.S. 215 (1974).

31. *International Longshoremen's Local 1416, AFL-CIO v. Ariadne Shipping Co. Ltd., et al.*, 397 U.S. 195 (1970).

32. The Board so held in *Allied International, Inc.*, 257 NLRB 1075 (1981). This view was confirmed by the Supreme Court in *International Longshoremen's Association v. Allied International Inc.*, 456 U.S. 212 (1982).

33. This preference contrasts with those of individual employees and minority-group organizations (e.g., the NAACP), which do not have the involvement in the appointment of Board members and the General Counsel, that labor and management organizations such as the AFL-CIO, the Chambers of Commerce, and the National Association of Manufacturers possess.

34. A minor extension of coverage occurred in 1974 to include the employees of nonprofit health-care institutions. Act of July 26, 1974, Pub. L. No. 93860, 88 Stat. 895 amended the definition of "employer" in 29 USC §152(2) (1976) to give this effect. Notwithstanding the exclusion of governmental employees, some employees funded by government are covered by the Act. See, for example, *Mayflower Contract Services v. NLRB*, 142 LRRM 2272 (8th Cir. 1993); *Long Stretch Youth Home, Inc.*, 280 NLRB 678 (1986); *Res-Care, Inc.*, 280 NLRB 670 (1986).

35. *Fort Apache Timber Co.*, 226 NLRB 503 (1976); *Southern Indiana Health Council*, 290 NLRB 436 (1988). But see *Sac and Fox Industries, Ltd.*, 307 NLRB No. 34 (1992).

36. Agricultural Labor Relations Act of 1975, Cal. Labor Code 1140 et seq. (West Supp. 1980). See H. Levy, "The Agricultural Labor Relations Act of 1975," 15 Santa Clara L. Rev. 783 (1975). There is considerable litigation about what constitutes an agricultural employee who is exempted from coverage by the National Labor Relations Act. See, for instance, *Cal-Maine Farms, Inc.*, 307 NLRB No. 66 (1992); *DeCoster Egg Farms*, 223 NLRB 884 (1976); *Camsco Produce Co.* 297 NLRB No. 157 (1990).

37. D. Bok, "Reflections on the Distinctive Character of American Labor Laws," 84 Harv. L. Rev. 1394 (1971).

38. NLRA §2 (3), 29 USC §152 (11) (1976). Independent contractors were excluded under the Taft-Hartley amendments. *NLRB v. Hearst Publications, Inc.*, 322 U.S. 111 (1944). Illegal aliens are employees within the Act's meaning; *Sure-Tan Inc. v. NLRB*, 467 U.S. 883 (1984); so are nonresident aliens who are here lawfully; *NLRB v. Actors' Equity Assn.*, 644 F.2d 939 (2d Cir. 1981). However, in *Sure-Tan*, the Court held, by a 5–4 vote, that the court of appeals had exceeded its authority by awarding a minimum amount of back pay to illegally discharged illegal aliens without regard to their availability for work. The circuits are split on the question of whether *Sure-Tan* means that relief was denied in that case to illegal aliens simply because they were not in the country and could not reenter for the purpose of taking up employment without breaking the law. See *Caamano Brothers, Inc.*, 275 NLRB 205 (1985); *Felbro,*

Inc., 274 NLRB 1268, 1269 (1985) enforcement granted in part and denied in part *sub nom., Local 512 Warehouse and Office Workers' Union v. NLRB,* 795 F.2d 705 (9th Cir. 1986); *Del Ray Tortilleria, Inc.,* 302 NLRB No. 45 (1991) enforcement denied 140 LRRM 2826 (7th Cir. 1992). Judge Cudahy in dissent at 2831 stated: "Once an alien has crossed the border, however, employment is not an additional offense (in fact, it is no crime at all)." The dissent's view is that the appropriate distinction is between having to break the law to reach the workplace and lacking a formal legal entitlement to work. Undocumented workers may maintain an action for unpaid wages and damages under the Fair Labor Standards Act. *Patel v. Quality Inn South,* 846 F.2d 700, 28 WH Cases 1105 (11th Cir. 1988), cert. denied, 489 U.S. 1011 (1989).

39. *NLRB v. The Catholic Bishop of Chicago,* 440 U.S. 490 (1979). This doctrine has been extended to commercial operations in *Faith Center-WHCT Channel 18,* 261 NLRB 106 (1982). But the appellate courts have rejected attacks on the Board's jurisdiction over nursing homes with religious connections. *NLRB v. St. Louis Christian Home,* 663 F.2d 60 (8th Cir. 1981); *Tressler Lutheran Home v. NLRB,* 677 F.2d 302 (3d Cir. 1982). The Court of Appeals for the Second Circuit has held that the New York State Labor Relations Board may constitutionally assert jurisdiction over lay teachers in church-operated schools. *Catholic High School Association v. Culvert,* 758 F.2d 1161 (2d Cir. 1985); *Christ The King Regional High School v. Culvert,* 815 F.2d 219 (2d Cir. 1987). See also *St. Elizabeth Hospital v. NLRB,* 715 F.2d 1193 (11th Cir. 1983) (religious atmosphere of hospital was secondary to promises of health-care services, involvement of NLRB in collective bargaining mediation was constitutional); *NLRB v. Kemmerer Village, Inc.,* 907 F.2d 661 (7th Cir. 1990) (a nonprofit corporation that operated a foster home that was controlled by two presbyteries within the Presbyterian Church did not fall within the "religious organization" exemption of the NLRB); *Denver Post of the National Society of Volunteers of America v. NLRB,* 732 F.2d 769 (10th Cir. 1984) (the VOA programs were not pervasively religious in character and they functioned in a secular fashion, especially since counselors were not required to have any particular religious background or training); *Volunteers of America–Minnesota Bar None Boys Ranch v. NLRB,* 752 F.2d 345 (8th Cir. 1985) (NLRB's assertion of jurisdiction does not violate the constitution where the center has as its primary purpose the care of children, not propagation of the faith); *NLRB v. Hanna Boys Center,* 940 F.2d 1295 (9th Cir. 1991) (NLRB was acting within its jurisdiction when ruling on a labor dispute involving a church-owned school's nonteaching employees); *Volunteers of America, Los Angeles v. NLRB,* 777 F.2d 1386 (9th Cir. 1985) (NLRB properly asserted jurisdiction over the

alcohol center inasmuch as the program is carried out in a secular fashion).

The Court of Appeals for the First Circuit has held that the principles of *Catholic Bishop* are inapplicable to a religious university that describes itself as a "Catholic-oriented civil institution" governed by a board of trustees, a majority of whom must be the members of the Dominican order. *Universidad Central DeBaya v. NLRB*, 793 F. 2d 383 (1st Cir. 1985).

40. *NLRB v. Bell Aerospace Co.*, 416 U.S. 267 (1974). Nonmanagerial "confidential" employees are also excluded when they are engaged in labor relations functions; *NLRB v. Hendricks County Rural Electric Membership Corp.*, 454 U.S. 170 (1982). The Board may exclude from bargaining units close relatives of owner-managers of a closely held corporation without a finding that such employees possess special job-related privileges. *NLRB v. Action Automotive, Inc.*, 469 U.S. 490 (1985). Children and the spouse of the employer are not "employees" under the Act. "In the context of corporations, the Board has limited the . . . exclusion to the children or spouses of an individual with at least a 50% ownership interest" *Id.* at 989, n.7.

41. *NLRB v. Yeshiva University*, 444 U.S. 627 (1980).

42. The Board so held in *RCA Mfg. Co.*, 2 NLRB 159 (1936). The circuit courts agreed. See, for example, *New York Handkerchief Mfg. Co. v. NLRB*, 114 F.2d 144 (7th Cir.) cert. denied, 311 U.S. 704 (1940); *NLRB v. Deutsch Co.*, 265 F.2d 478 (9th Cir. 1959), cert. denied, 361 U.S. 968, rehearing denied, 362 U.S. 945 (1960) (citing cases from Fifth and Seventh Circuits and from the Board).

43. NLRA §2(5), 29 USC §152 (5) (1970). A union may be disqualified as a labor organization if supervisors play an active and leadership role in the union. See *Sierra Vista Hospital, Inc.*, 241 NLRB 681 (1979); *Bausch & Lomb Optical Co.*, 108 NLRB 1555 (1954); *Highland Hospital v. NLRB*, 129 LRRM 2899 (2d Cir. 1988). By virtue of 9(b)(3) of the Act, unions that have—or are affiliated with labor organizations that have—guard and nonguard members may not be certified by the Board. Over the strong dissent of member Zimmerman, the Board placed more stringent limitations upon the representative functions of such "mixed" unions. See *The University of Chicago*, 272 NLRB 873 (1984); *Wells Fargo Armored Service Corporation*, 270 NLRB 787 (1984); enforcement granted sub nom. *Teamsters Local*, 807 v. NLRB, 775 F.2d 5 (2d Cir. 1985). "The evils that Congress sought to prevent include not only the domination of guard unions by non-guard unions, but also the potential of conflict of loyalty on the part of an employer's sup-

posedly most faithful and trustworthy employees when encountering demands by another union with whom they shared some relations . . . the Board has previously emphasized that a realistic potential for conflict of loyalty precludes certification of a guard union." *NLRB v. Brinks, Inc. of Florida*, 843 F.2d 448, 452 (11th Cir. 1988).

44. NLRA §9(b)(2) states in part: "The Board shall not . . . decide that any craft unit is inappropriate for such purposes on the ground that a different unit has been established by a prior Board determination . . . ." See also *American Potash & Chemical Corp.*, 107 NLRB 1418, 1422 (1954). ("It is not the province of this Board to dictate the course and pattern of labor organization in our vast industrial complex.") But see *Mallinckrodt Chemical Works*, 162 NLRB 367 (1966) (in which the Board overruled *American Potash* and reinstated history and existing patterns of collective bargaining as factors relevant to the determination of the appropriate bargaining unit) and *General Motors Corp. (Cadillac Motor Car Div.)*, 120 NLRB 1215 (1958) (in which the Board, relying on the long bargaining history of exclusive UAW representation on a multi-plant, national basis, denied severance of single-plant units as too narrow in scope and thus inappropriate).

45. See generally R. Berry and W. Gould, "A Long Deep Drive to Collective Bargaining: Of Players, Owners, Brawls, and Strikes," 31 Case W. Res. L. Rev. 685 (1981), R. Berry et al., *Labor Relations in Professional Sports* (1986); W. Gould, "Players and Owners Mix It Up," 8 *California Lawyer* 56 (August 1988).

46. Labor-Management Relations Act, Pub. L. No. 101, 80th Cong., 1st Sess. (1947) 61 Stat. 186, 29 USC §149(b)(5) et seq. (1976).

47. *NLRB v. Action Automotive, Inc.*, 469 U.S. 490 (1985).

48. *NLRB v. Metropolitan Life Ins. Co.*, 380 U.S. 438 (1965). The Board has held that an appropriate unit (there may be more than one) in multilocation industries is presumptively a single location. See *Sav-On Drugs, Inc.*, 138 NLRB 1032 (1962), *Frisch's Big Boy III–Mar, Inc.*, 147 NLRB 551 (1964) enf. denied, 356 F. 2d 895 (7th Cir. 1966); *F. W. Woolworth Co.*, 144 NLRB 807 (1968); *Dixie Belle Mills, Inc.*, 139 NLRB 629 (1962), *Metropolitan Life Ins. Co.*, 156 NLRB 1408 (1966); *Wyandotte Savings Bank*, 245 NLRB 1002 (1979); and *Bowie Hall Trucking, Inc.*, 290 NLRB 41 (1988).

49. See cases cited in note 42 *supra*. Where new employees or jobs are added, it is possible for them to be declared part of an existing unit, as an accretion to it, without a new election. See Judge Winter's discussion of this principle in *NLRB v. Stevens Ford, Inc.*,

773 F.2d 468, 472–74 (2d Cir. 1985). The policy is "restrictive" designed to apply to "new groups of employees" added subsequent to certification or recognition of the collective agreement. *United Parcel Services Inc.*, 303 NLRB No. 42 (1991); *Dennison Manufacturing Co.*, 296 NLRB No. 134 (1989); *Compact Video Services*, 284 NLRB 1108 (1987). Disputed employees must possess "little or no separate group identity" and "overwhelming community of interest" with workers in the original organized unit. *Safeway Stores*, 256 NLRB 918 (1981). The converse of the accretion issue is a spin-off where employers attempt to argue that a new facility is sufficiently dissimilar to justify nonunion status. *Rice Food Markets, Inc.*, 255 NLRB 884 (1981); *NLRB v. Coca-Cola Bottling Co.*, 936 F.2d 122 (2d Cir. 1991) said Judge Kaufman in *Coca-Cola Bottling Co.* on behalf of the Second Circuit:

For purposes of legal analysis in labor disputes over the composition of bargaining units, the most significant distinction between an accretion and a spin-off lies in allocation of the burden of proof. As the Board noted in *Rice Food Markets* . . . any party attempting to circumvent formal procedures for expansion or contraction of the bargaining unit bears a heavy burden of proving the legitimacy of such action.

If, for example, a union argues that a job site is an accretion to a pre-existing operation and, therefore, that its employees automatically should be considered party to an existing collective-bargaining agreement, the Board will require the union to establish that the new group of employees is so similar to the original that accretion into the existing bargaining unit is appropriate. This is to prevent the danger the Board foresees of such action denying workers an opportunity to ratify their representation.

Conversely, in cases such as the present one, where an employer establishes an adjunct worksite and attempts to staff it with non-union workers, though its pre-existing work force is organized, the Board will look to that employer to establish sufficient justification [dissimilarity from the remainder of the bargaining unit] for its actions. (*Id.* at 2934 note 48)

But see *Perry Broadcasting Inc.*, 300 NLRB No. 158 (1990); *Gitano Group, Inc.*, 308 NLRB No. 173 (1992).

50. *President and Fellows of Harvard College*, 269 NLRB 821 (1984).

51. *St. Francis Hospital*, 271 NLRB 948 (1984). A large unit has been fashioned for hotels. *ACL Corporation*, 273 NLRB 87 (1984).

52. *Hampton Roads Broadcasting Corp. (WCH)*, 100 NLRB 238, 239 (1952).

53. 272 NLRB 196 (1984). Member Zimmerman dissented.

54. *Id.* at 197. But see *Perry Broadcasting, Inc.,* 300 NLRB No. 158 (1990) where the Board held that *KJAZ* was "distinguishable" as a ". . . narrow exception to the long-recognized distinction for bargaining purposes between on-air and off-air employees." *Id.* at p. 6. Said the Board: "the principal factor that distinguishes this case from *KJAZ* is the much more limited role that sales employees have in producing commercials." *Id.* at p. 7.

55. *The Globe Machine and Stamping Co.,* 3 NLRB 294 (1937).

56. *American Hospital Association v. NLRB,* 111 S.Ct. 1539 (1991).

57. *Id.* at 1543.

58. The Board first required this in *Excelsior Underwear, Inc.,* 156 NLRB 1236 (1966). This decision was approved by the Supreme Court in *NLRB v. Wyman-Gordon Co.,* 394 U.S. 759 (1969). However, the Court of Appeals for the Seventh Circuit has concluded that such a rule for federal employees under the Civil Service Reform Act is an unlawful invasion of privacy. *Federal Labor Relations Authority v. United States Dept. of the Navy,* 141 LRRM 2275 (7th Cir. 1992). Accord, *Federal Labor Relations Authority v. United States Dept. of Defense,* 142 LRRM 2348 (10th Cir. 1993), which provides citations setting forth the position of all the circuits. Contra, *Federal Labor Relations Authority v. United States Dept. of Defense,* 975 F.2d 1105 (5th Cir. 1992); *Federal Labor Relations Authority v. United States Dept. of the Navy,* 966 F.2d 747 (3d Cir. 1992); *Federal Labor Relations Authority v. United States Dept. of the Navy,* 958 F.2d 1490 (9th Cir. 1992).

59. Both sides may have observers of the election, the provision for observers constituting a material term of a stipulated election agreement. But the parties may waive their right to observers, *Best Products Co.,* 269 NLRB 578 (1984). For instance, the fact that an observer arrived late was deemed to constitute a waiver of the right to an observer. *Inland Waters Pollution Control, Inc.,* 306 NLRB No. 75 (1992). Where an employer is about to relocate shortly after an election and employees have been offered jobs at the new situs, the Board can order an election at the old location prior to the move. *NLRB v. AAA Alternator Rebuilders, Inc.,* 142 LRRM 2286 (11th Cir. 1993).

60. *NLRB v. Howard Johnson Motor Lodge,* 705 F.2d 932 (7th Cir. 1983); *NLRB v. J-Wood\A Tappan Div.,* 720 F.2d 309 (3d Cir. 1983); *NLRB v. Service America Corp.,* 841 F.2d 191 (7th Cir. 1988).

61. *Todd Shipyards Corp.,* 5 NLRB 20, 25 (1988), *Edwin J. Schlacter Meat Co.,* 100 NLRB 1171 (1952).

62. *Leedom v. Kyne,* 358 U.S. 184 (1958); *Boire v. Greyhound Corp.,* 376 U.S. 473 (1964).

63. See generally *American Federation of Labor v. NLRB,* 308 U.S. 401 (1940). See also *Raley's, Inc. v. NLRB,* 725 F.2d 1204 (9th Cir. 1984), and Member Zimmerman's dissent in *A Corporation,* 273 NLRB 87 (1984).

Chapter 4

1. With respect to spies, see *NLRB v. Fansteel Metallurgical Corp.,* 306 U.S. 240, 251 (1939). The Court of Appeals for the Third Circuit has taken the position that photographing peaceful employee or union demonstrations is not per se unlawful surveillance but must be considered in light of all the circumstances. *U.S. Steel Corp. v. NLRB,* 682 F.2d 98 (3rd Cir. 1982). But see *Kallman v. NLRB,* 640 F.2d 1094 (9th Cir. 1981); *NLRB v. Colonial Haven Nursing Home,* 542 F.2d 691 (7th Cir. 1976); *Flambeau Plastics Corp.,* 167 NLRB 735 (1967) enforced 501 F.2d 128 (7th Cir. 1968); *Captain Nemo's,* 258 NLRB 57 (1981); *Cutting, Inc.,* 255 NLRB 534 (1981). The policy of the Board concerning interrogation is that, absent unusual circumstances, polling of employees is a violation unless certain specified criteria are met; *Struksnes Construction Co.,* 165 NLRB 1062, 1063 (1967). The Second Circuit has refused to enforce this policy, preferring the Board's own earlier view that the question was whether the interrogation was coercive in the totality of circumstances. *NLRB v. Lorben Corp.,* 345 F.2d 346 (2d Cir. 1965). The Court of Appeals for the Ninth Circuit has applied these rules to postrecognition disputes about majority status. Promises and threats are distinguished from objective predictions in *NLRB v. Gissel Packing Co.,* 395 U.S. 575 (1969); *Weather Tamer v. NLRB,* 676 F.2d 483 (11th Cir. 1982). Where an employer interrogates employees to verify a union's claim of majority status or to prepare a defense for an unfair labor practice trial, the employer must communicate the purpose of the interrogation, assure the worker that no reprisals will take place, and obtain the worker's participation voluntarily. Moreover the questioning must take place in a context "free from employer hostility to union activity," and the employer must not "pry into" other union activities. See *Johnnie's Poultry Co.,* 146 NLRB 770 (1964).

2. *PPG Industries, Inc.,* 251 NLRB 1146 (1980).

3. *Blue Flash Express,* 109 NLRB 591 (1954).

4. *Rossmore House,* 269 NLRB 1174 (1984) enforced sub nom. *Hotel Employees Local 2 v. NLRB,* 760 F.2d 1006 (9th Cir. 1985). The Board has held *Rossmore* applicable to "open" union sympathizers because

the employee wears a union button. *Premier Rubber Co.*, 272 NLRB 466 (1984). The circuit courts are split between the positions taken in *PPG Industries, Inc.* and *Rossmore House.* See *Midwest Stock Exchange v. NLRB*, 635 F.2d 1255 (7th Cir. 1980); *Graham Architectural Products v. NLRB*, 697 F.2d 534 (3d Cir. 1983); *TRW–United Greenfield Division v. NLRB*, 637 F.2d 410 (5th Cir. 1981); *Hotel Employees Local 2 v. NLRB, supra.*

5. *NLRB v. Curtin Matheson Scientific, Inc.*, 494 U.S. 775 (1990).

6. *Id.* at 797.

7. 296 NLRB No. 136 (1989) enf. granted 923 F.2d 398 (5th Cir. 1991). As the Board noted in this opinion which issued before *Curtin Matheson* and Chief Justice Rehnquist's concurring opinion, a number of the circuit courts of appeal have expressed disagreement with the Board's position. See *NLRB v. A.W. Thompson, Inc.*, 651 F.2d 1141 (5th Cir. 1981); *Thomas Industries v. NLRB*, 687 F.2d 863 (6th Cir. 1982); *Forbidden City Restaurant v. NLRB*, 736 F.2d 1295 (9th Cir. 1984).

8. *United States Gypsum Co.*, 157 NLRB 652 (1966).

9. The position of the circuit courts which disagree with the Board is that it is anomalous to apply the same standard to the circumstances under which an employer may withdraw recognition to a procedure, namely polling which is designed to determine whether an employer can withdraw recognition.

10. *Texas Petrochemicals v. NLRB*, 923 F.2d 398, 403 (5th Cir. 1991).

11. 375 U.S. 405 (1964). See Jackson and Heller, "Promises and Grants of Benefits under the National Labor Relations Act," 131 U. Pa. L. Rev. 1 (1982). It is an unfair labor practice for an employer to withhold wage increases or accrued benefits because of union activities and so to advise employees. On the other hand, it is not unlawful for an employer to avoid paying benefits until the election is completed and to announce this to the workers so as to avoid the appearance of election interference. But it is often difficult to distinguish between these two situations. See, for example, *Centre Engineering*, 253 NLRB 419 (1980); *Brunswick Food & Drug*, 284 NLRB 663 (1987); *Colortech Corp.*, 286 NLRB 476 (1987); *Toys-R-Us*, Inc. 300 NLRB No. 22 (1990). An employer is required to proceed with an expected wage or benefit adjustment regardless of the presence or absence of a union. *Atlantic Forest Products*, 282 NLRB 855 (1987); *Retlaw Broadcasting Co.*, 302 NLRB No. 64 (1991). Where the employer states that if the union wins the election, there will be "bargaining from ground zero" or "bargain-

ing from scratch," section 8(a)(1) is violated if the employees are left with the impression that they will lose existing benefits and that what they will receive ultimately will depend upon what the union can induce the employer to restore. On the other hand, if it is made clear that any reduction will flow from the normal give and take of negotiations with the union, the statement is lawful. *Taylor-Dunn Mfg. Co.*, 252 NLRB 799 (1980) enf'd 810 F.2d 638 (9th Cir. 1982); *Telex Communications*, 294 NLRB 1136 (1989); *Kenrich Petrochemicals*, 294 NLRB 519 (1989); *S.E. Nichols, Inc.* 284 NLRB 556 (1987); *Lear-Siegler Management Service Corp.* 306 NLRB No. 84 (1992); *Shaw's Supermarkets v. NLRB*, 132 LRRM 2364 (1st Cir. 1989). Where the employer states that wage and benefit programs would be "frozen," the Board has viewed this statement as meaning that the wage and benefit programs would not change. *Mantrose-Haeuser Co.*, 306 NLRB No. 74 (1992).

12. 375 U.S. at 409.

13. *NLRB v. Savair Mfg.*, 414 U.S. 270 (1973). The union must be careful to repudiate previous unlawful conduct in this regard when it forumlates a new policy. *K.D.I., Inc. v. NLRB*, 126 LRRM 2376 (6th Cir. 1987). However, where a waiver of initiation fees and a lower-than-usual dues structure are open to all employees, regardless of whether they support or vote for the union, the union's conduct is lawful. See, for example, *NLRB v. Whitney Museum of American Art*, 636 F.2d 19 (2d Cir. 1980). Similarly lawful is a union's insistence that employees pay initiation fees and dues before the organizational campaign commences; *Hickory Springs Mfg. Co. v. NLRB*, 645 2d 506 (5th Cir. Unit A 1980). Similarly a promise that the union will reduce initiation fees if the union wins the election is lawful because there is no improper inducement to sign authorization cards or to join the union. *Molded Acoustical Products*, 280 NLRB 1394 (1986), affirmed 815 F.2d 934 (3d Cir. 1987), cert. denied, 484 U.S. 925 (1987); *DeJana Industries, Inc.*, 305 NLRB No. 31 (1991).

14. A. Cox, *Law and the National Labor Policy* (1960). Campaigns designed to promote prejudice have been held to be unlawful by the Board. *Sewell Mfg. Co.*, 138 NLRB 66 (1962). However, where a union distributed literature—while organizing a Japanese owned company—which protrayed the Japanese business as condescending toward America, the campaign tactic was held to be lawful. *KI (USA) Corp.*, 309 NLRB No. 169 (1992).

15. 29 USC §158(a)(2) (1976) is the relevant provision. There is considerable debate about how expansively this provision should be interpreted. See *Chicago Rawhide Mfg. Co. v. NLRB*, 221 F.2d 165

(7th Cir. 1955); *NLRB v. Scott & Fetzer,* 691 F.2d 288 (6th Cir. 1982); W. Gould, *Japan's Reshaping of American Labor Law* 95–99 (1984). For another view, see Note, "Collective Bargaining as an Industrial System: An Argument against Judicial Revision of Section 8(a)(2) of the National Labor Relations Act," 96 Harv. L. Rev. 1664 (1983). On the use of company time and property by an incumbent union and the question of unlawful assistance see, for example, *Base Wyandotte Corp.,* 274 NLRB 978 (1985); *Coamo Knitting Mills,* 150 NLRB 579, 582 (1964); *Elias Mallouk Realty Corp.,* 265 NLRB 1225, 1236 (1982); *Duquesne University of the Holy Ghost,* 198 NLRB 891 (1971); *Summer Products,* 189 NLRB 826, 828 (1971); *Longchamps, Inc.,* 205 NLRB 1025, 1026 (1973). See Sockell "The Legality of Employee-Participation Programs in Unionized Firms," 37 Indus. Lab. Rel. Rev. 541 (1984).

16. 29 USC §160(c) (1976) provides in part that when it finds a person to be engaged in an unfair labor practice "the Board . . . shall issue an order requiring such person to cease and desist from such unfair labor practices, and take such affirmative action . . . as will effectuate the policies of this subchapter . . . ." See, for example, *NLRB v. Getlan Iron Works, Inc.,* 377 F.2d 894, 896 (2d Cir. 1967).

17. 309 NLRB No. 163 (1992). The Supreme Court has addressed the question of employer domination and assistance—but never in the context of genuine employee participation programs. See, for instance, *Pennsylvania Greyhound Lines,* 1 NLRB 1 (1935), enforcement denied in part 91 F.2d 178 (3d Cir. 1937) reversed. 303 U.S. 261 (1938); *NLRB v. Newport News Shipbuilding Co.,* 308 U.S. 241 (1939); *NLRB v. Cabot Carbon Co.,* 360 U.S. 203 (1959). A closely related issue is whether the employer may provide any money or any other thing of value, conduct that is prohibited by section 302(a) to union representatives in the collective bargaining process. The Act is designed to prohibit bribery and extortion schemes between employers and union officials. But at the same time union representatives often retain rights to return to the establishment and to obtain pensions when they retire. The issue arising in section 302(a) cases is whether compensation to the employee or former employee who is a union representative exists "by reason of" the services of the employee or for some other reason. See *National Fuel Gas Distribution Corporation,* 308 NLRB No. 115 (1992); *BASF Wyandotte Corp.,* 274 NLRB 978 (1985) enf'd 798 F.2d 849 (5th Cir. 1986); *Trailways Lines v. Joint Council,* 785 F.2d 101 (3d Cir. 1986); *Toth v. USX Corp.,* 883 F.2d 1297 (7th Cir. 1989).

18. *E.I. Dupont de Nemours & Co.* (Administrative Law Judge Decision, May 28, 1992).

19. Second Annual Report of the National Labor Relations Board "The statute clearly calls for the posting of notices as part of the enforcement procedures of the NLRB. The NLRB is charged with serving the public interest to enforce labor relations rights which are public, not private rights." *NLRB v. Hiney Printing Co.*, 733 F.2d 1170, 1171 (6th Cir. 1984). See generally W. Gould, *Japan's Reshaping American Labor Law* 68–69 (1984).

20. *H.J. Heinz Co. v. NLRB*, 311 U.S. 514, 522–23 (1941) (Board may order disestablishment if continued existence of a union is an obstacle to the employees' right of self-organization); *NLRB v. Pennsylvania Greyhound Lines*, 303 U.S. 261 (1938) (Board has power to require an employer to withdraw recognition from a union that it sponsors and dominates, and may sometimes order disestablishment); *NLRB v. Metropolitan Alloys Corp.*, 624 F.2d 743 (6th Cir. 1980) (disestablishment "clearly the appropriate remedy" when the union is a "company-created sham"). However, when an employer had assisted in the formation of a union but no longer dominated it "the Board did not err in failing to order disestablishment." *International Union of United Brewery Workers v. NLRB*, 298 F. 2d 297, 300 (D.C. Cir. 1961), cert. denied, sub nom. *Gulf Bottlers, Inc. v. NLRB*, 369 U.S. 843 (1962). Until the 1947 Taft-Hartley amendments the Board disestablished a company union if it was unaffiliated with a national union, but it cannot fashion a remedy on this basis now. See *Carpenter Steel Co.*, 76 NLRB 670 (1948).

21. However, the lawfulness of the exclusive hiring hall frequently establishes a de facto closed shop. *Local 357 Teamsters v. NLRB*, 365 U.S. 667 (1961). However, the Court of Appeals for the District of Columbia has compelled the Board to reexamine its definition of a valid referral system for which the union may collect a fee. *Pittsburgh Press Co. v. NLRB*, 141 LRRM 2537 (D.C. Cir. 1992).

22. Alabama, Arizona, Arkansas, Florida, Georgia, Idaho, Iowa, Kansas, Louisiana, Mississippi, Nebraska, Nevada, North Carolina, North Dakota, South Carolina, South Dakota, Tennessee, Texas, Utah, Virginia, and Wyoming. The Court of Appeals for the District of Columbia has held that a union violates federal labor law when it insists upon a contract clause assessing nonunion employees for the costs of union representation in a right-to-work state. Judge Mikva dissented. *Plumbers Local Union 141 v. NLRB*, 675 F.2d 1257 (D.C. Cir. 1982). See also *Oil, Chemical & Atomic Workers Int'l Union v. Mobil Oil Corp.*, 426 U.S. 407 (1976); *Retail Clerks v. Schermerhorn*, 373 U.S. 746 (1963). Cf. *NLRB v. Office and Professional Employees International Union, Local 2*, 134 LRRM 2213 (4th Cir. 1990) (union may not insist upon new initiation fee for a bargaining unit em-

ployee who in a right-to-work state had quit the union but who then transferred to a non-right-to-work state.

23. Pub. L. No. 96-593 (December 24, 1980). Service Employees International Union, Local 6, Case No. 19-CB-5151, Advice Memoranda of the NLRB General Counsel, 117 LRRM 1508 (September 27, 1984). In *Wilson v. NLRB*, 920 F.2d 1282 (6th Cir. 1990), the court held that this provision of the statute is facially unconstitutional in violation of the Establishment Clause of the First Amendment to the Constitution because it distinguishes between a "bona fide religion, body, or sect" that has "historically held conscientious objections to joining or financially supporting labor organizations" and other organizations.

24. *United States v. Enmons,* 410 U.S. 396 (1973).

25. *United States v. Thorodarson,* 646 F.2d 1323 (9th Cir. 1981). The Racketeer Influenced Corruption Organizations (RICO) statute was passed by Congress in 1970 as part of the Organized Crime Control Act (OCCA), Title IX, Pub. L. No. 91-452, 84 Stat. 941 (1970) (current version at 18 USC §§1961–1968 (1990). RICO was used against the International Brotherhood of Teamsters by the Department of Justice in an action widely heralded as producing more democratic procedures and elections at the national level of that union. See *United States v. International Brotherhood of Teamsters,* 708 F. Supp. 1388 (S.D.N.Y. 1989). The statute provides for both civil and criminal sanctions and in connection with the former private plaintiffs may bring actions seeking treble damages and attorneys' fees for the use of RICO vis-à-vis the various kinds of union activity; see, for instance, *Yellow Bus Lines, Inc. v. Drivers, Chauffeurs & Helpers Local Union 639,* 839 F.2d 782 (D.C. Cir.) cert. denied 488 U.S. 926 (1988), vacated, 492 U.S. 914 (1989), on remand, 883 F.2d 132 (D.C. Cir. 1989) (reissuing same decision as 839 F.2d 782), rev'd on rehearing, 913 F.2d 948 (D.C. Cir. 1990) (en banc), cert. denied, 111 S.Ct. 2839 (1991); *United States v. Local 560,* 141 LRRM 2001 (3d Cir. 1992); *Brennan v. Chestnut,* 141 LRRM 2182 (8th Cir. 1992). See generally Roukis and Charnov, "The RICO Statute: Implications for Organized Labor," 36 Lab. L. J. 281 (1985); Goldberg, "Cleaning the Labor's House: Institutional Reform Litigation in the Labor Movement," 1989 Duke L. J. 903. Unions as well as employers are now using RICO in connection with alleged racketeering in labor disputes. See generally Note, "Weeding RICO out of Garden Variety Labor Disputes," 92 Columbia L. Rev. 103 (1992).

26. Pub. L. No. 257, 86th Cong., 1st Sess. (1959). This provision has its origins in the so-called Sand Door loophole to the secon-

dary boycott provisions that, while they prohibited strikes and other concerted activity to enforce "hot cargo" agreements, permitted employers and unions to voluntarily enter into such agreements. See *Local 1976, United Brotherhood of Carpenters and Joiners of America v. NLRB*, 357 U.S. 93 (1958) [hereinafter *Sand Door*].

27. *National Woodwork Manufacturers Assoc. v. NLRB*, 386 U.S. 612 (1967); *Truck Drivers Union, Local 413 v. NLRB*, 334 F.2d, 539 (D.C. Cir. 1964), cert. denied, 379 U.S. 916 (1964).

28. 29 USC §158(e) (garment industry) and 158(f) (1976) (construction industry). However, a divided Board has held that anti-dual shop clauses prohibiting "double breasting" on the creation of a separate nonunion company in the construction industry are unlawful. *Ernest Alessio Construction Company* 310 NLRB No. 172 (1993).

29. Restrictions on payments by employers to labor organizations "shall not be applicable . . . with respect to money deducted from the wages of employees in payment of membership dues in a labor organization: Provided, that the employer has received from each employee, on whose account such deductions are made, a written assignment which shall not be irrevocable for a period of more than one year, or beyond the termination date of the applicable collective agreement, whichever occurs sooner . . . ." 29 USC §186(c) (1976).

30. *NLRB v. Plasterers' Union Local 79*, 404 U.S. 116 (1971). See generally "The Employer as a Necessary Party to Voluntary Settlement of Work Assignment Disputes under Section Lo(k) of the NLRA" (comment), 38 U. Chi. L. Rev. 889 (1971).

31. *NLRB v. Radio and Television Broadcast Engineers Union, Local 1212*, 364 U.S. 573 (1961).

32. 29 USC §160 (b) (1976).

33. This is an unfair labor practice, just as a recognition agreement according a minority union exclusive representation status is an unfair labor practice in that it coerces the majority of employees. *ILGWU v. NLRB*, 366 U.S. 781 (1961).

34. *Local Lodge No. 1424, International Association of Machinists v. NLRB*, 362 U.S. 411 (1960) [hereinafter Bryan Manufacturing].

35. *United States Postal Service Marina Mail*, 271 NLRB 397, 400 (1984). The Board, Member Zimmerman dissenting, purported to apply principles established in the area of employment discrimina-

tion and tenure denied. *Delaware State College v. Ricks*, 449 U.S. 250 (1980); *Chardon v. Fernandez*, 454 U.S. 6 (1981).

36. *A&L Underground*, 302 NLRB No. 76 (1991). Accord, *Chambersburg County Market*, 293 NLRB 654 (1989); *Chemung Contracting Corp.*, 291 NLRB 773 (1988); *Desks, Inc.*, 295 NLRB No. 1 (1989); *Teamsters Local 43 v. NLRB*, 825 F.2d 608 (1st Cir. 1987); *ACF Industries*, 234 NLRB 1063 (1978), enforced as modified 596 F.2d 1334 (8th Cir. 1979).

37. Rules and Regulation of the NLRB (Procedure) 29 CFR 101.8 (1979).

38. At one point the Board emphasized the "public interest in the vindication of statutory rights," *Clearhaven Nursing Home*, 236 NLRB 853, 854 (1978). I have held the view that this scrutiny of private settlements entered into is excessively rigid and discourages voluntary settlements and informal relationships. See W. Gould, *Japan's Reshaping of American Labor Law* 54–55 (1984). More recently the Board in *Independent Stave Co.*, 287 NLRB 740 (1987) has looked at the following factors in determining whether the Board should approve a nonboard settlement: (1) whether the parties, union, or employer, and any of the individual discriminatees have agreed to be bound by the settlement and the position taken by the Counsel regarding settlement; (2) whether the settlement is reasonable in light of the nature of the violations alleged, the risks inherent in litigation and the stage of litigation; (3) whether there has been any fraud, coercion, or duress by any of the parties in reaching the settlement; (4) whether the respondent charged with an unfair labor practice has engaged in a history of violations of the Act or has breached previous settlement agreements resolving unfair labor practice disputes. For application of these standards, see, for example, *Service Merchandise, Inc.*, 299 NLRB No. 161 (1990); *Aratex Services, Inc.*, 300 NLRB No. 18 (1990); *Amstar Sugar Corp.*, 301 NLRB No. 113 (1991) Settlements approved by the Board or non-Board settlements are not covered by this criteria and thus are less likely to give rise to disputes about the validity of releases through which a party agrees not to file unfair labor practice charges. See, for example, *Coca-Cola Bottling of Los Angeles*, 243 NLRB 501 (1979); *First National Supermarkets, Inc.*, 302 NLRB No. 113 (1991).

39. Rosenbloom, "A New Look at the General Counsel's Unreviewable Discretion Not to Issue a Complaint under the NLRA," 86 Yale L. J. 1349 (1977). The leading case which establishes this proposition in *dicta* is *NLRB v. Food and Commercial Workers, Local 23*, 484 U.S. 112 (1987). See also *NLRB v. Sears, Roebuck & Co.*, 421 U.S. 132 (1975); *United Electrical Contractors v. Ordman*, 366 F.2d 776

(2d Cir. 1966); *International Association of Machinists and Aerospace Workers, AFL-CIO v. Lubbers*, 681 F.2d 598 (9th Cir. 1982).

40. "He has the right to appear at the hearing in person or by counsel and to call, examine and cross-examine witnesses. 29 CFR: §§[sic]102.38 and 101.10 (b)(2). He is entitled to a review of an adverse Board decision by the court of appeals, 29 USCA 160(f)." *Kellwood Co. v. NLRB*, 411 F.2d 493, 499–500 (8th Cir. 1968). Charging parties who are wholly successful before the Board may intervene in review proceeding by the court of appeals; *International Union, Local 283 v. Scofield*, 382 U.S. 205 (1965). However, in injunctive proceedings under 29 USC §160(e) (1976) the charging party may appear by counsel and present any relevant testimony but may not initiate an appeal nor intervene as a party; *Solien v. Miscellaneous Drivers & Helpers U., Local No. 610*, 440 F.2d 124, 130–211 (8th Cir.), cert. denied, 403 U.S. 905, rehearing denied, 404 U.S. 960, rehearing denied, 405 U.S. 999 (1971).

41. "The Board shall have the power to petition a court of appeals of the United States . . . within any circuit . . . wherein the unfair labor practice in question occurred or wherein such person resides or transacts business, for the enforcement of such order and for the appropriate temporary relief or restraining order, and shall file in the court the record in the proceedings . . . ." NLRA Lo(e); 29 USC §160(e) (1976). While the statute vests the Board with this authority, the Board has delegated these powers to the General Counsel since at least 1955. Recently, however, the Board has begun to cut back on the General Counsel's enforcement powers, requiring that all appeals court briefs and pleadings be reviewed by the Board's solicitor one week before they are to be heard in court. See Labor Relations Yearbook (BNA) 230 (1983). There is also frequent controversy about whether an appeal should go to the Court of Appeals for the District of Columbia (the location of the Board) or one of the other circuits where the unfair labor practice occurred. See remarks by Abner J. Mikva, "Court Shoppers: And They're Off and Running," Annual Luncheon of Section of Labor and Employment Law, American Bar Association, August 12, 1981 (unpublished). In *Universal Camera Corp. v. NLRB*, 340 U.S. 474 (1951), the Court held that judicial review of Board orders should be based on the "record considered as a whole" and that the courts of appeals should defer to Board decisions unless they "cannot conscientiously find that the evidence supporting the decision is substantial."

42. See Congressional Quarterly Inc., The Supreme Court and Its Work 61–62 (1981).

Chapter 5

1. Even when an exclusive bargaining agent has been chosen, the law says that "any individual employee or a group of employees shall have the right at any time to present grievances to their employer and to have such grievances adjusted, without the intervention of the bargaining representative, as long as the adjustment is not inconsistent with the terms of a collective bargaining contract or agreement then in effect: Provided further, That the bargaining representative has been given opportunity to be present." 29 USC §159(a).

2. The Board so ruled in *Excelsior Underwear, Inc.*, 156 NLRB 1236 (1966). Seven justices approved of the rule in *NLRB v. Wyman-Gordon Co.*, 394 U.S. 759 (1969) (Fortas, J. for the court, and Black, J. concurring).

3. See *NLRB v. S&H Grossinger's, Inc.*, 372 F.2d 26, 29 (2d Cir. 1967). For some of the general problems see W. B. Gould, "Taft-Hartley Revisited: The Contrariety of the Collective Bargaining Agreement and the Plight of the Unorganized," 13 Lab. L. J. 348 (1962). Paid full-time union organizers who are hired by an employer are entitled to the same protections under the National Labor Relations Act accorded employees in the Board's view. *Oak Apparel,* 218 NLRB 701 (1975) even if they are temporary employees and excluded from the bargaining unit on that basis. *299 Lincoln Street, Inc.,* 292 NLRB 172, 180 (1988); however, the Court of Appeals for the Fourth Circuit in *H.B. Zachry Co. v. NLRB,* 886 F.2d 70 (4th Cir. 1989) has held that an employer may lawfully refuse to hire a paid union organizer because (1) to accord protection would upset the "careful balance" between labor and management struck by Congress; (2) to allow outsiders the same rights as regular employees would impinge upon self-determination of those within the bargaining unit because the union organizer would be paid by the union to cast his ballot in favor of organization; (3) the union organizer would have divided loyalties as an employee employed by employer that is a competitor. Member Oviatt concurs in the view of the Fourth Circuit, *Escada (USA), Inc.,* 304 NLRB No. 199 (1991), but the Board, while adhering to *Zachry* has generally found the decision of the Fourth Circuit's approach to be distinguishable on the ground that full-time organizers are not seeking simultaneous employment with the employer, *Fluor Daniel, Inc.,* 304 NLRB No. 100 (1991) or taking a leave of absence from the union and limiting their time devoted to organizational activity, *Willmar Electric Service, Inc.,* 303 NLRB No. 33 (1991). enf. granted 140 LRRM 2745 (D.C. Cir 1992). The Board has now squarely attacked the Fourth Circuit's position (Member Oviatt

concurring) in *Sunland Construction Co., Inc.*, 309 NLRB No. 180 (1992); *Town & Country Electric, Inc.*, 309 NLRB No. 181 (1992). Only where a union organizer-applicant files an application in the midst of a strike, may the employer discriminate against him or her.

4. *Wiese Plow Welding Co., Inc.*, 123 NLRB 616 (1959); *Allied Lettercraft Co., Inc.*, 272 NLRB 612 (1984). But there appears to be increasing reluctance on the part of some Board Members to accept the small plant doctrine. Member Raudabaugh announced his refusal to rely upon it in *Almet, Inc.*, 305 NLRB No. 77 slip op. (1991). In that same decision, Chairman Stephens concluded that "the small size of a plant alone would [not] be sufficient to give rise to an inference that an employer knew of any union activities occurring there." However, Chairman Stephens expressed his willingness to consider this as one of a number of factors. *Id.* at 1 n.5; *Food Cart Market*, 286 NLRB 1016, 1018 (1987).

5. 321 U.S. 322 (1944).

6. *Id.* at 336.

7. *Id.* at 337–39.

8. *Edward G. Budd Mfg. Co. v. NLRB*, 138 F.2d 86, 90 (3d Cir. 1943).

9. For example, *NLRB v. Jacob E. Decker & Sons*, 636 F.2d 129 (5th Cir., Unit A, 1981); *NLRB v. Big Three Welding Equipment Company*, 359 F.2d 77 (5th Cir. 1966).

10. *Precise Window Manufacturing, Inc. v. NLRB*, 140 LRRM 2321 (8th Cir. 1992); *NLRB v. Collier*, 553 F.2d 425 (5th Cir. 1977); *Bin-Dicator Co.*, 356 F.2d 210 (6th Cir. 1966); *Family Nursing Home & Rehabilitation Ctr., Inc.*, 295 NLRB No. 95 (1989).

11. *Mt. Healthy City School District Board of Education v. Doyle*, 429 U.S. 274 (1977).

12. *Givhan v. Western Line Consolidated School District*, 439 U.S. 410 (1979).

13. W. Gould, "The Supreme Court and Labor Law: The October 1978 Term," 21 Ariz. L. Rev. 621, 622–625 (1979).

14. 251 NLRB No. 150 (1980); *NLRB v. Great Dane Trailers, Inc.*, 388 U.S. 26 (1967).

15. 251 NLRB 1083 (1980).

16. 462 U.S. 393 (1983).

17. *Id.* at 403.

18. *Id.* at 401 n.6.

19. *NLRB v. Great Dane Trailers, Inc,* 388 U.S. 26 (1967), *American Ship Building Co. v. NLRB,* 380 U.S. 300 (1965), *Radio Officers' Union v. NLRB,* 347 U.S. 17 (1954); *Local 357, Teamsters v. NLRB,* 65 U.S. 667 (1961). One of a wide variety of issues relating to discrimination is whether the award of superseniority to union stewards is lawful. See, for example, *NLRB v. Milk Drivers & Dairy Employees, Local 338,* 531 F.2d 1162 (2d Cir. 1976); *United Electrical Radio & Machine Workers of America, Local 623 (Limpco),* 230 NLRB 406 (1977) enforced sub nom. *D'Amico v. NLRB,* 582 F.2d 820 (3d Cir. 1978); *Gulton Electro-Voice, Inc.,* 266 NLRB 406, enforced sub nom. *Local 900, International Union of Electrical, Radio & Machine Workers v. NLRB,* 727 F.2d 1184 (D.C. Cir. 1984); *NLRB v. Niagara Machine & Tool Workers,* 746 F.2d 143 (2d Cir. 1984); *(2d Cir. 1984); Local 1384, UAW v. NLRB,* 756 F.2d 482 (7th Cir. 1985); *NLRB v. Harvey Hubble, Inc.,* 767 F.2d 1100 (4th Cir. 1985); *NLRB v. Wayne Corp.,* 776 F.2d 745 (7th Cir. 1985); *WPIX, Inc. v. NLRB,* 870 F.2d 858 (2d Cir. 1989); *NLRB v. Joy Technologies, Inc.* 142 LRRM 2865 (3d Cir. 1993).

20. *NLRB v. Burnup and Sims, Inc.,* 379 U.S. 21 (1964). In this decision the Supreme Court held that an employer's good-faith discharge of employees engaged in protected activities whom he mistakenly believed in good faith to have engaged in misconduct was a violation of the Act. Even if the employee is not engaged in protected activities the discharge may still be unlawful where the employer is ". . . aware that a union organizing campaign is underway . . . [because] the employer's action has the same potential deterrent effect on other employees . . . ." *Ideal Dyeing & Finishing Co., Inc.* 300 NLRB 303 (1990); accord, *Teledyne Industries, Inc.,* 295 NLRB 161 (1989).

21. 324 U.S. 793 (1945); W. B. Gould, "The Question of Union Activity on Company Property," 18 Vand. L. Rev. 73 (1964); W. B. Gould, "Union Organizational Rights and the Concept of Quasi-public Property," 49 Minn. L. Rev. 505 (1965).

22. *Id.* at 802–803 and 802 n.8.

23. *Id.* at 803 n.10.

24. *T.R.W. Bearings,* 257 NLRB 442 (1981).

25. *Our Way, Inc.,* 268 NLRB 394 (1984). Noting that the Fair Labor Standards Act requires employers to count breaks of less than twenty minutes duration as hours worked for minimum and over-

time purposes and that employees are generally paid for this time, the Board has taken the view that employees will understand that such breaks are not encompassed by the term "work time" in a no-solicitation or distribution rule of the employer. *Jay Metals, Inc.,* 308 NLRB No. 40 (1992).

26. *Id.* at 395. The Board, Member Zimmerman's dissent notwithstanding, was of the view that, until *T.R.W. Bearings,* "working time" rules were presumptively lawful. The Board relied upon *Essex International,* 211 NLRB 749 (1974).

27. *Hammary Manufacturing Corp.,* 265 NLRB 57 (1982); *Saint Vincent's Hospital,* 265 NLRB 38 (1982).

28. *Id.* at 58, n.4; *Serv-Air, Inc. v. NLRB,* 395 F.2d 557 (10th Cir. 1968).

29. *Emerson Electric Co., U.S. Electrical Motor Division,* 187 NLRB 294 (1970).

30. *NLRB v. Babcock and Wilcox Co.,* 351 U.S. 105, 112 (1956). The rule relating to nonemployee access under the California Agricultural Labor Relations Act appears to be more liberal. See *Agricultural Labor Relations Board v. Superior Court,* 16 Cal. 3d 392 (1976), appeal dismissed, 429 U.S. 802 (1976).

31. *NLRB v. Babcock & Wilcox Co.,* 351 U.S. 105, 107, n.1 (1956). The Court of Appeals for the Eleventh Circuit has held in *Southern Services, Inc. v. NLRB,* 139 LRRM 2601 (11th Cir. 1992) that where an employer and its subcontractor prohibit employee distribution of literature during nonworking time, the rules of *Republic Aviation Corp.* and not *Babcock & Wilcox* apply. Said the court:

. . . the modern practice of subcontracting for services does not automatically curtail section 7 rights. Nor does the conduct of distributing union literature transform the status of a subcontract employee such as Copeland [the employee in question] from that of a business invitee to that of a mere trespasser . . . When the relationship situates the subcontract employee's workplace continuously and exclusively upon the contracting employer's premises, the contracting employer's rules purporting to restrict that subcontract employee's right to distribute union literature among other employees of the subcontractor must satisfy the test of *Republic Aviation.* Our holding is narrow. We do not intend [as the employer's] . . . apparently fear, to extend distribution rights to casual visitors on [the subcontractor's] . . . property or to the host of other business invitees who enter there, such as firemen, policemen, auditors, and utility workers. The rule we announce applies to subcontract employees whose continuous and exclusive workplace is on [the subcontractor's] . . . premises, and affects only their right to distribute union literature to their fellow subcontract employees in non-working areas during non-working time. (*Id.* at 2604)

32. *Id.* at 112–13.

33. *NLRB v. Magnavox Co.,* 415 U.S. 322, 325 (1974).

34. *Eastex, Inc. v. NLRB,* 437 U.S. 556 (1978).

35. See *Local 174, International Union, UAW v. NLRB,* 645 F.2d 1151 (D.C. Cir. 1981), in which distributing literature on company property was held unprotected when "the principal thrust of the leaflet was to induce employees to vote for specific candidates, not to educate them on political issues relevant to their employment conditions." *Id.* at 2563. Compare *Fun Striders, Inc. v. NLRB,* 686 F.2d 659 (9th Cir. 1981). See *Motorola, Inc.,* 305 NLRB No. 69 (1991) where the Board held that the distribution to employees of literature prepared by the Citizens Advocating the Protection of Privacy as an appeal to legislators to protect the employees interests was protected under *Eastex.* This was part of an effort to pass a city ordinance banning mandatory drug testing in the workplace and concerned the employees' working conditions because they faced the implementation of mandatory drug testing and the possibility of discharge or discipline for refusing to be tested. Running for union office has been regarded as unprotected conduct. *Office and Professional Employees International Union, AFL-CIO v. NLRB,* 142 LRRM 2064 (2d Cir. 1992).

36. 406 U.S. 535 (1972).

37. *Id.* at 545.

38. *Id.* at 544–45.

39. *Id.* at 547.

40. 424 U.S. 507 (1976).

41. *Id.* at 521–22, footnote omitted.

42. *Scott Hudgens,* 230 NLRB 414 (1977).

43. *Amalgamated Food Employees Union v. Logan Valley Plaza,* 391 U.S. 308 (1968), overruled in *Hudgens,* 424 U.S. 507, 518 (1976).

44. *Pruneyard Shopping Center v. Robins,* 447 U.S. 74 (1980).

45. *Seattle First National Bank,* 243 NLRB 898 (1979), modified, 651 F.2d 1272 (9th Cir. 1980); see also *Grant Food Store Markets v. NLRB,* 241 NLRB 727 (1979), rev'd., 633 F.2d 18 (6th Cir. 1980). Subsequent to these initial decisions under the authority of *Jean Coun-*

try, 291 NLRB 11 (1988), discussed *infra,* the Board over the emphatic dissent of Member Johansen, held picketing unprotected since the audience could be reached effectively outside the building. *40–41 Realty Associates,* 288 NLRB 200 (1988), affirmed mem. sub nom. *Amalgamated Dental Union Local 32-A v. NLRB,* 867 F.2d 1423 (2d Cir. 1988). See, however, where the employees and customers have been more difficult to reach because of the absence of a single entrance to the building the picket activity has been viewed by the Board as protected. *Little & Co.,* 296 NLRB No. 89 (1989); see also *Polly Drummond Thriftway,* 292 NLRB 331 (1989), enforced. 882 F.2d 512 (3d Cir. 1989).

46. *Hutzler Bros. v. NLRB,* 630 F.2d 1012 (4th Cir. 1980).

47. *Fairmont Hotel,* 282 NLRB 139 (1986).

48. 291 NLRB 11 (1988).

49. *Id.* at 13.

50. *Id.*

51. *Id.* at 16.

52. *Id.*

53. *Lechmere, Inc. v. NLRB,* 112 S.Ct. 841 (1992).

54. *Id.* at 2227.

55. *Id.* at 2230.

56. *Id.* at 2231. Distribution of literature by off-duty employees on company property is protected under Section 7. *Tri-County Medical Center,* 222 NLRB 1089 (1976); *E.R. Carpenter,* 284 NLRB 273 (1987); *Orange Memorial Hospital,* 285 NLRB 1099 (1987); *St. Luke's Hospital,* 300 NLRB No. 108 (1990); *NLRB v. Pizza Crust Co.,* 862 F.2d 49 (3d Cir. 1988); *NLRB v. Ohio Masonic Home,* 892 F.2d 449 (6th Cir. 1989); *Sahara Tahoe Corp.,* 292 NLRB 812 (1989).

57. *Sentry Markets, Inc.,* 296 NLRB No. 5 (1989), enforced. 135 914 F.2d 113 (7th Cir. 1990). See also, *The Red Stores, Inc.,* 296 NLRB 450 (1989). Area wage standard activity, a form of consumer publicity, while viewed as protected activity because of the union's legitimate interest in protecting the wage standards of its members who are employed by competitors of the employer that is picketed or handbilled, ". . . falls [nonetheless] at a relatively weak point along the continuum of possible activities protected by Section 7." (*The Red Stores, Inc., supra* at p. 453) Chairman Stephens has expressed the view in a concurring opinion that "Section 7 does not

extend to the protection of appeals against ownership of companies by persons of foreign nationalities, at least where there is no claim that workers are being discriminated against or otherwise mistreated or that jobs are being exported." (*The Red Food Stores, Inc., supra* at p. 545) But the Board has not subscribed to Chairman Stephen's view. When a union engages in union organizational activities, access has been granted to an offshore oil platform. See *McDermott Marine Construction*, 305 NLRB No. 62 (1991). Acord, *Laborer's Local Union No. 24 v. NLRB*, 904 F.2d 715 (D.C. Cir. 1990).

58. *Sparks Nugget, Inc., v. NLRB*, 140 LRRM 2747 (9th Cir. 1992).

59. *International Society for Krishna Consciousness, Inc. v. Lee*, 60 USLW 4749 (1992). While the *Krishna* decision does not apply to labor, First Amendment rights were first held applicable to union activity in *Thomas v. Collins*, 323 U.S. 516 (1945). See *National Treasury Employees Union v. King*, 140 LRRM 2929 (D.C.D.C. 1992).

60. *Sparks Nugget v. NLRB, supra* at 2753.

61. *Davis Supermarkets, Inc.*, 306 NLRB No. 86 (1992); *New Jersey Bell Telephone Co.*, 308 NLRB No. 32 (1992); *Susquehanna United Super, Inc.*, 308 NLRB No. 43 (1992); *Great Scot, Inc.*, 309 NLRB No. 84 (1992). The Court of Appeals for the Sixth Circuit has denied nonemployee union organizers access to retail establishments in which an imbalance in communication flows was previously presumed to exist. *Oakwood Hospital v. NLRB*, 983 F.2d 698 (6th Cir. 1993).

62. *San Diego Building Trades Council v. Garmon*, 359 U.S. 236 (1959).

63. *Sears, Roebuck & Co. v. San Diego County District Council of Carpenters*, 436 U.S. 180, 198–207 (1978).

64. In *Bill Johnson's Restaurants v. NLRB*, 461 U.S. 731 (1983), the Court held that an unfair labor practice may not be found on a basis of the employer's initiation of a state court proceeding on which it has a reasonable basis for filing. But the Court held that its holding was inapplicable to preemption cases in which the states lack jurisdiction. In *ILA v. Davis*, 476 U.S. 380 (1986), the Court held that preemption could not be presumed on the basis of a mere filing of a charge without putting forth "enough evidence to enable the court to find that the Board reasonably could uphold a claim based upon such an interpretation." *Id.* at 395. Prior to the issuance of a complaint, the filing of a lawsuit can only be the basis of an unfair labor practice violation where independent evidence of a retaliatory or unlawful purpose is proved.

65. *Makro, Inc.,* 305 NLRB No. 81 (1991) There is an affirmative obligation to terminate the lawsuit which is designed to enjoin the picketing. *Oakwood Hospital,* 305 NLRB No. 82 (1991) The *Makro* decision applies to criminal charges as well. *Johnson & Hardin Co.,* 305 NLRB No. 83 (1991).

66. *New Jersey Bell Telephone Co., supra* at slip op. p.5.

67. *Marshall Field & Co.,* 98 NLRB 88 (1952), enforced as modified, *Marshall Field & Co. v. NLRB,* 200 F.2d 375 (7th Cir. 1953); *May Department Stores Co.,* 59 NLRB 976 (1944), enforced as modified, 154 F.2d 533 (8th Cir. 1946); *Goldblatt Bros., Inc.,* 77 NLRB 1262 (1948); *Montgomery Ward & Co., Inc. v. NLRB,* 692 F.2d 1115 (7th Cir. 1982), cert. denied, 461 U.S. 914 (1983); *Montgomery Ward & Co. v. NLRB,* 782 F.2d 389 (6th Cir. 1984); *Ameron Automotive Center, a Division of the Kelly-Springfield Tire Co.,* 265 NLRB 511 (1982); *F.W. Woolworth Company d/b/a Woolco Division,* 265 NLRB No. 58 (1982); *Hughes Properties, Inc. d/b/a Harolds Club,* 267 NLRB 1167 (1985), enforced 758 F.2d 1320 (9th Cir. 1985).

68. *Marriott Corp.,* 223 NLRB 978 (1976); *Bankers Club, Inc.,* 218 NLRB 22 (1975); *McDonald's Corp.,* 205 NLRB 404 (1973); see generally *Beth Israel Hospital v. NLRB,* 437 U.S. 483 (1978); *Times Publishing Co. v. NLRB,* 605 F.2d 847 (5th Cir. 1979).

69. See *supra* note 1, chapter 3.

70. *St. John's Hospital and School of Nursing, Inc.,* 222 NLRB 1150 (1976).

71. *Beth Israel Hospital v. NLRB,* 437 U.S. 483, 495 (1978). In *Manchester Health Center v. NLRB,* 861 F.2d 50 (2d. Cir. 1988), the court held that a rule which was part of a strike settlement subsequent to a "bitter and divisive strike" could properly limit discussion of union affairs to nonpatient areas bearing nonwork done because (1) there was not a competing labor organization for which there could be made a claim that the antisolicitation rule was designed to suppress its activities; (2) the rules were not discriminatory, applied evenhandedly to strikers and nonstrikers; (3) the rule applied to other forms of discussion about controversial matters in the presence of patients.

72. *NLRB v. Baptist Hospital, Inc.,* 442 U.S. 773 (1979). The wearing of union insignia or a button as a statutory section 7 right has frequently conflicted with dress codes. *Holladay Park Hospital and Oregon Nurses Association, Inc.,* 262 NLRB 26 (1982); *Pay'n Save Corp. v. NLRB,* 641 F.2d 697 (9th Cir. 1981); *NLRB v. Harrah's Club,* 337

F.2d 177 (9th Cir. 1964); *Davison-Paxor Co. v. NLRB*, 462 F.2d 364 (5th Cir. 1972); *Midstate Telephone Corp. v. NLRB*, 706 F.2d 401 (2d Cir. 1983); *Southern California Edison Company*, 274 NLRB 1121 (1985).

73. *Cashway Lumber, Inc.*, 202 NLRB 380 (1973).

74. *Vincent's Steak House*, 216 NLRB 647 (1975); *Helton v. NLRB*, 658 F.2d 583 (D.C. Cir. 1981); *Container Corporation of America*, 244 NLRB 318 (1979), enforced in part sub nom. *NLRB v. Container Corporation of America*, 649 F.2d 1213 (6th Cir. 1981); *NLRB v. Honeywell Inc.*, 722 F.2d 405 (8th Cir. 1983); *ITT McDonnel and Miller*, 267 NLRB 1093 (1983); *Roadway Express, Inc. v. NLRB*, 831 F.2d 1285 (6th Cir. 1987) Apparently literature that might not be tolerated as a union insignia can be protected when it is displayed on a bulletin board. *Southern Bell Telephone Company*, 276 NLRB 1053 (1985).

75. *May Department Store*, 136 NLRB 797 (1962), enforcement denied, 316 F.2d 797 (6th Cir. 1962). But the Sixth Circuit did find an imbalance where there were also unfair labor practices in *Montgomery Ward and Co. v. NLRB*, 339 F.2d 889 (6th Cir. 1965).

76. *NLRB v. Drivers, Chauffeurs, Helpers, Local Union No. 639*, 362 U.S. 274 (1960).

77. *Id.* at 284.

78. *Id.*

79. 29 USC §158(b)(7) (1976) provides that it shall be an unfair labor practice for a labor organization or its agents to picket or cause to be picketed, or threaten to picket or cause to be picketed, any employer where an object thereof is forcing or requiring an employer to recognize or bargain with a labor organization as the representative of his or her employees, or forcing or requiring the employees of an employer to accept or select such labor organization as their collective bargaining representative, unless such labor organization is currently certified as the representative of such employees:

a. where the employer has lawfully recognized in accordance with this subchapter any other organization and a question concerning representation may not appropriately be raised under section 159(c) of this title,

b. where within the preceding twelve months a valid election under section 159(c) has been conducted, or

c. where such picketing has been conducted without a petition under section 159(c) of this title being filed within a reasonable period of time not to exceed thirty days from the commencement of such pick-eting: Provided, That when such a petition has been filed the Board shall forthwith, without regard to the provisions of section 159(c) (1) of this title or the absence of a showing of substantial interest on the part of the labor organization, direct an election in such a unit as the Board finds to be appropriate and shall certify the results thereof: Provided further, That nothing in this subparagraph (c) shall be con-strued to prohibit picketing or other publicity for the purpose of truthfully advising the public (including consumers) that an employer does not employ members of, or have a contract with, a labor organi-zation, unless an effect of such picketing is to induce any individual employed by any other person in the course of his employment, not to pick up, deliver, or transport any goods or not to perform any services. Nothing in this paragraph (7) shall be construed to permit any act which would otherwise be an unfair labor practice under this subsection.

80. For example, *Giant Food Markets, Inc.*, 241 NLRB 727, enforce-ment denied, 633 F.2d 18 (6th Cir. 1980); see also *International Hod Carriers, Local No. 41 (Calumet Contractors Association)*, 133 NLRB 512 (1961) and *Houston Building and Construction Trades Council ("Claude Everett Construction")*, 136 NLRB 321 (1962). The Supreme Court has had to address difficult problems involving an uncer-tified union's picket line in the construction industry prior to its establishment of majority status. See *NLRB v. Local 103, Iron Work-ers*, 434 U.S. 335 (1978).

81. *Thornhill v. Alabama*, 310 U.S. 88 (1940).

82. *International Brotherhood of Teamsters, Local 695 v. Vogt, Inc.*, 354 U.S. 284 (1957). The Court there discussed earlier cases, including *Building Service Employees v. Gazzam*, 339 U.S. 532 (1950), *Interna-tional Brotherhood of Teamsters v. Hanke*, 339 U.S. 470 (1950) and *Giboney v. Empire Storage & Ice Co.*, 336 U.S. 490 (1949). The distinction is discussed in A. Cox, "Strikes, Picketing, and the Constitution," 4 Vand. L. Rev. 574, 591–602 (1950–51). Picketing in furtherance of an unlawful objective is not protected by the First Amendment. See, most recently, *NLRB v. Retail Store Employees' Union*, 447 U.S. 607, 616 (1980); *Carvel Corporation*, 273 NLRB No. 81 (1984). But see *Miller v. United Food and Commercial Workers Union, Local 498*, 708 F.2d 467 (9th Cir. 1983); *Johansen v. San Diego County Council of Carpenters*, 745 F.2d 1289 (9th Cir. 1984).

83. *Burlington Northern Railroad Co. v. Brotherhood of Maintenance of Way Employes*, 481 U.S. 429 (1987). In *Burlington*, Justice Brennan, speaking for a unanimous Court, said:

The historical background of the Norris-LaGuardia Act thus reveals that Congress intended to preclude courts from enjoining secondary as well as primary activity, and that the railroads were to be treated no differently from other industries in this regard. (*Id.* at 439)

84. *Connell Construction Co. v. Plumbers Local 100*, 421 U.S. 616 (1975); Cf. *United Mine Workers v. Pennington*, 381 U.S. 657 (1965).

85. As Judge Reinhardt's opinion in *NLRB v. Ironworkers Local 433*, 128 LRRM 2873, 2877 (9th Cir. 1988) notes, there are no magic incantations of phrases or words that constitute sufficient evidence to establish the threat of economic pressure.

86. *NLRB v. International Rice Milling Co.*, 341 U.S. 665 (1951). Cf. *NLRB v. Local 825, Operating Engineers*, 400 U.S. 297 (1971).

87. *NLRB v. Business Machines and Office Appliance Mechanics Conference Board, Local 459 IUE ("Royal Typewriter")*, 228 F.2d 553 (2d Cir. 1955), cert. denied, 351 U.S. 962 (1956); *Douds v. Metropolitan Federation of Architects*, 75 F. Supp. 672 (S.D.N.Y. 1948). Sometimes the ally doctrine issues involve the question of whether two companies are in fact one employer given common ownership and interrelationship of operations. See, for example, *Boich Mining Co.*, 301 NLRB No. 123 (1991).

88. See *supra* note 21, chapter 4.

89. The Court has held that a valid work-preservation objective may exist even where technological innovation makes it impossible for the union to pursue the identical work performed in the past by bargaining-unit members. See *NLRB v. International Longshoremen's Union, AFL-CIO*, 447 U.S. 490 (1980) [hereinafter ILAI]; *NLRB v. International Longshoremen's Association, AFL-CIO*, 473 U.S. 61 (1985) [hereinafter ILAII]. Similar problems arise under the Taft-Hartley Amendments as well where, for instance, unions picket to reinstate an employer-employee relationship, where the employer now deals with independent contractors, notwithstanding the fact that independent contractors are not covered by the Act. *Chipman Freight Services, Inc. v. NLRB*, 843 F.2d 1224 (9th Cir. 1988); *Production Workers, Local 707 v. NLRB*, 793 F.2d 323 (D.C. Cir. 1986); *Military Traffic Management Command*, 288 NLRB 1224 (1988). However, secondary pressure cannot be aimed at self-employed individuals or independent contractors for the purpose of imposing compulsory membership upon them even if the object is to have them remain union members. *Local 812, International Brotherhood of Teamsters v. NLRB*, 138 LRRM 2697 (2d Cir. 1991).

90. 341 U.S. 675 (1951).

91. *Id.* at 690.

92. *Local 761, International Union of Electrical, Radio and Machine Workers, AFL-CIO v. NLRB*, 366 U.S. 667 (1961). A reserved gate may be improperly "tainted" if used by employees of the primary employer in more than a *de minimis* fashion. See *Mautz & Oren, Inc. v. Teamsters, Shelvers & Helpers Union, Local 279*, 882 F.2d 1117 (7th Cir. 1989).

93. The bill (H.R. 4250) was approved by the House Education and Labor Committee; 94 Labor Relations Reporter No. 23, p. 1 (March 21, 1977). The full House defeated the bill on March 23 by a vote of 217–205; *Id.* no. 25, p. 1 (March 28, 1977). See also *J.F. Hoff Electric Co. v. NLRB*, 642 F.2d 1266 (D.C. Cir. 1980). See especially the standards for common situs picketing set forth in *Moore Dry Dock*, 92 NLRB 547 (1950).

94. The veto occurred on January 5, 1976 (Bureau of National Affairs, Labor Relations Yearbook 8, 1976).

95. *Connell Constr. Co. v. Plumbers Local 100*, 421 U.S. 616 (1975). The obverse of the *Connell* question—namely whether unions can complain under the antitrust law against employer conspiracies to boycott unionized contractors—was answered negatively in an 8–1 decision of the Court. *Associated General Contractors of California, Inc. v. California State Council of Carpenters*, 459 U.S. 519 (1983).

96. 456 U.S. 645 (1982).

97. *Id.* at 660. The Court stated that the top-down effect was "limited" in a number of ways by other provisions of the NLRA: (1) prohibitions against recognitional picketing, (2) the right of employees to challenge a construction union's representative status despite a valid pre-hire agreement, (3) prohibitions against discrimination against nonunion members in the hiring hall, (4) the Denver Building Trades protection of employees employed by nonunion contractors.

98. *Id.* at 663–64.

99. *NLRB v. Fruit and Vegetable Packers, Local 760 ("Tree Fruits")*, 377 U.S. 58 (1964).

100. *Id.* at 61 n.3. See *NLRB v. Servette, Inc.*, 377 U.S. 46 (1964); 129 U. Pa. L. Rev. 221 (1981).

101. *Id.* at 72. See also *Carey v. Brown*, 447 U.S. 455 (1980).

102. *NLRB v. Retail Store Emp. Union Local 1001*, 447 U.S. 607 (1980).

103. *Id.* at 616. The Court acted upon the earliest NLRA secondary boycott case in which First Amendment arguments had been rejected. *Electrical Workers v. NLRB,* 341 U.S. 694, 705 (1951).

104. 447 U.S. at 619 (Stevens J. concurring).

105. *International Longshoremen's Ass'n v. Allied International,* 456 U.S. 212, 226–27 n.26 (1982).

106. *NAACP v. Claiborne Hardware,* 458 U.S. 886 (1982). See generally Harper, "The Consumer's Emerging Right to Boycott: NAACP v. Claiborne Hardware and Its Implications for American Labor Law," 93 Yale L. J. 409 (1984).

107. *Edward J. DeBartolo Corp. v. Florida Gulf Coast Bldg. and Trades Council,* 485 U.S. 568 (1988).

108. *Id.* at 575. Earlier the constitutional issues were avoided in *Edward J. DeBartolo v. NLRB,* 463 U.S. 147 (1983). On remand, the Board has applied the "struck product" analysis utilized by the Supreme Court in secondary consumer picketing cases. *The Edward J. DeBartolo Corp.,* 273 NLRB 1431 (1985); see generally *Service Employees, Local 399 v. NLRB,* 723 F.2d 746 (9th Cir. 1984); Goldman, "The First Amendment and Nonpicketing Labor Publicity under Section 8(b)(4)(ii)(B) of the National Labor Relations Act," 36 Vand. L. Rev. 1469 (1983).

109. *Id.* at 576. (Emphasis supplied.)

110. 395 U.S. 575 (1969).

111. *Id.* at 602. The Fourth Circuit had found the cards to be inherently unreliable. See *Id.* at 585. Employees are presumed to have designated the union as their bargaining agent where the authorization card so states unless oral misrepresentations clearly cancel the language on the card. A single purpose authorization card remains valid for bargaining order purposes even if the solicitor orally represents that the purpose is to obtain an election. The Board has taken the position that ambiguous cards, which state that the union will represent the signer in "collective bargaining" and that the "purpose" of the card is to obtain an election, will not establish a basis for a *Gissel* bargaining order. *Nissan Research and Development, Inc.,* 296 NLRB No. 80 (1989), Member Craycraft dissenting at slip op. p.9. But some of the circuits have accepted dual purpose cards in support of a bargaining order. See *NLRB v. Fosdal Electric,* 367 F.2d 784 (7th Cir. 1966); *Auto Workers v. NLRB,* 366 F.2d 702 (D.C. Cir. 1966); *NLRB v. C.J. Glasgow Co.,* 356 F.2d 476 (7th Cir. 1966); *Sahara Datsun v. NLR,* 811 F.2d 317

(9th Cir. 1987), cert. denied 454 U.S. 835 (1987); *NLRB v. Anchorage Times Publishing Co.*, 637 F.2d 1359 (9th Cir. 1981). The Board, over Member Dennis's dissent, will not use or rely upon English-language cards for Spanish speakers. *Superior Container, Inc.*, 276 NLRB 521 (1985). But see *NLRB v. American Art Industries*, 415 F.2d 1223 (5th Cir. 1969).

112. *Id.* at 602. Rather, determination of whether a *Gissel* order is necessary rests on consideration of both the nature and pervasiveness of the employer's misconduct as well as the amount of turnover. Where the Board finds that a practice is particularly pervasive or enduring, it need make only minimal findings that the effects have not been dissipated by subsequent employee turnover. Conversely, where the practices at issue are not especially pervasive or permanent in nature, the Board needs to make careful determinations respecting the effect of subsequent employee turnover. *Amazing Stores, Inc. v NLRB*, 887 F.2d 328 (D.C. Cir. 1989) The same circuit has held that the Board must explain why traditional remedies and a rerun election will not effectuate the purposes of the Act and provide specific findings. *Avecor, Inc., v. NLRB*, 931 F.2d 924 (D.C. Cir. 1991), cert. denied 112 S.Ct. 912 (1992); *Somerset Welding & Steel, Inc. v. NLRB*, 142 LRRM 2356 (D.C. Cir. 1993). Mere turnover is not a basis for elimination of the duty to bargain. *NLRB v. Creative Food Design*, 852 F.2d 1295 (D.C. Cir. 1988). But the Seventh Circuit has taken the position that considerable turnover with substantial passage of time and changed circumstances at the plant can be a basis for a representation election and not a *Gissel* bargaining order. *Impact Industries, Inc. v. NLRB*, 847 F.2d 379 (7th Cir. 1988); Accord, *Montgomery Ward & Co., Inc. v. NLRB*, 904 F.2d 1156 (7th Cir. 1990); *NLRB v. Koenig Iron Works, Inc.*, 856 F.2d 1 (2d Cir. 1988). Cf. *Georgetown Hotel v. NLRB*, 835 F.2d 1467 (D.C. Cir. 1987). But delay and turnover will not work against the *Gissel* order where ordering another election would ". . . merely by sending the parties back to the Board's glacial processes with no assurance that years from now a certification based upon a second election will not be challenged on exactly the same grounds . . . [we strive to] marginally reduce the incentives of employers to take advantage of the Board's inexcusably slow processes." *NLRB v. Star Color Plate Service*, 843 F.2d 1507 (2d Cir. 1988). Where an employer grants recognition and a petition based upon support prior to the grant of recognition is filed on behalf of a rival union simultaneous or within a reasonable period of time of the recognition of the other union an election will be ordered. *Bruckner Nursing Home*, 262 NLRB 955 (1982); *Rollins Transportation Systems, Inc.*, 296 NLRB No. 108 (1989); *Human Development Association v. NLRB*, 937 F.2d 657 (D.C. Cir. 1991).

113. 29 USC §159 (c)(1)(B) (1976). See *Gissel*, 395 U.S. at 594–95. Where an employer voluntarily recognizes a union, it waives its right to insist upon an election. *NLRB v. Creative Food Design Ltd.*, 852 F.2d 1295 (D.C. Cir. 1988).

114. *Linden Lumber Division, Summer & Co. v. NLRB*, 419 U.S. 301 (1974).

115. *United Dairy Farmers Cooperative Assn. v. NLRB*, 633 F.2d 1054 (3d Cir. 1980). *J.P. Stevens & Co., Gulutan Div. v. NLRB*, 441 F.2d 514 (5th Cir. 1971). Where two unions are competing, the Board has regarded the cards as unreliable; *Midwest Piping & Supply Co.*, 63 NLRB 1060 (1945). However, the Board has modified *Midwest Piping* so that an employer is obliged to bargain with an incumbent union despite the filing of a rival union representation petition, *RCA Del Caribe, Inc.*, 262 NLRB 963 (1982). Moreover unlawful company assistance will not be equated with company recognition of a rival union in an initial organizational context before a valid election petition has been filed and where the recognized union's majority is uncoerced and unassisted.

116. 242 NLRB 1026 (1979). See also "United Dairy Farmers Cooperative Association: NLRB Bargaining Orders in the Absence of a Clear Showing of a Pro-union Majority" (comment), 80 Colum. L. Rev. 840 (1980). The discussion of this case is taken from W. Gould, "Recent Developments under the National Labor Act: The Board and the Circuit Courts," 14 U.C. Davis L. Rev. 497 (1981).

117. *Id.*

118. *Id.*

119. *United Dairy Farmers Cooperative Assn. v. NLRB, supra* at 1066.

120. The Third Circuit has also had occasion to deal with the *Gissel* bargaining order problem in a case where the union did not hold a minority of authorization cards: *NLRB v. K&K Gourmet Meats, Inc.*, 640 F.2d 460 (3d Cir. 1981). See also *NLRB v. Unit Train Sales*, 636 F.2d 1121 (6th Cir. 1980).

121. 633 F.2d at 1066.

122. *Id.* at 1067.

123. *Id.* at 1068.

124. *Id.* at 1069.

125. *Id.* at 1069, n.16. On remand, Chairman Fanning and Member Jenkins adhered to their original view that the Board possesses the

requisite authority to fashion a bargaining order. Member Zimmerman, without expressing a view, acceded to the Third Circuit view; *United Dairy Farmers*, 257 NLRB 772 (1981).

126. *Conair Corp.*, 261 NLRB 1189 (1982)

127. *Conair Corp. v. NLRB*, 721 F.2d 1355 (D.C. Cir. 1983).

128. 270 NLRB 587 (1984).

129. *Id.* at 10.

130. Section (8)(f) states that it is not an unfair labor practice to conclude an agreement in the building and construction industry with a labor organization because (1) majority status ". . . has not been established under the provisions of section 8 of this Act prior to the making of such an agreement or (2) such agreement requires, as a condition of employment, membership in such labor organization after the seventh day following the beginning of such employment or the effective date of the agreement, whichever is later . . . ."

131. 282 NLRB 1375 (1987) enforcement granted 843 F.2d 770 (3d Cir. 1988). Cf. *Comtel Systems Technology, Inc.*, 305 NLRB No. 30 (1991).

132. 282 NLRB at 1385 (footnotes omitted). A recently expired construction industry agreement will serve as an adequate showing of interest or surrogate for the normal 30 percent requirement. *Stockton Roofing Co.*, 305 NLRB No. 88 (1991). An employer may not file a representation petition when confronted with a union demand that it sign a section 8(f) agreement because such an agreement provides for no presumption of majority status subsequent to its expiration. *PSM Steel Construction, Inc.*, 309 NLRB No. 185 (1992); *Albuquerque Insulation Contractor*, 256 NLRB 61 (1981).

133. The presumption of majority status during the one year certification period is irrebuttable. *Brooks v. NLRB*, 348 U.S. 96 (1954).

134. Indeed the Board has recently held that four weeks of bargaining and less than three months of recognition was a reasonable period of time after which majority status could be questioned. *Tajon, Inc.*, 269 NLRB 327 (1984). See also *Brennan's Cadillac, Inc.*, 231 NLRB 225 (1977) (3 months adequate; two members dissenting). Cf. *Vantran Elec. Corp.*, 231 NLRB 1014 (1977) (4½ months inadequate; one member dissenting), enforcement denied, 580 F.2d 921 (7th Cir. 1978). After a reasonable period of time has

elapsed, a good-faith doubt about the incumbent union's majority status may be manifested through either a good-faith doubt that the union possesses majority status or actual evidence of lack of majority status. *Sofro, Inc.*, 268 NLRB 159 (1983); *Celanese Corporation of America*, 95 NLRB 664 (1951); *Terrell Machine Company*, 173 NLRB 1480 (1969) enforced, 427 F.2d 1008 (4th Cir. 1970); *Dalewood Rehabilitation Hospital Inc., d/b/a Golden State Habilitation Convalescent Center v. NLRB*, 566 F.2d 77 (9th Cir. 1977); *National Cash Register Co. v. NLRB*, 494 F.2d 189 (8th Cir. 1974); *Laystrom Manufacturing Co.*, 151 NLRB 1482 (1965), enforcement denied, 359 F.2d 799 (7th Cir. 1966).

135. AFL-CIO No-Raiding Pact. There are problems in bringing together all parties in one proceeding. See *Transportation-Communication Employees Union v. Union Pacific Railroad*, 385 U.S. 157 (1966); *Columbia Broadcasting System v. American Recording v. Broadcasting Association*, 414 F.2d 1326 (2d Cir. 1969).

135. *Appalachian Shale Products Co.*, 121 NLRB 1160 (1958).

137. *Id.*

138. *Id.*

139. *Hershey Chocolate Corp.*, 121 NLRB 90 (1958); *General Extrusion Co.*, 121 NLRB 1165 (1958).

140. *General Cable Corp.*, 189 NLRB 1123 (1962), set the maximum time at three years. *American Seating Corp.*, 106 NLRB 250 (1950) had set the bar at the lesser period of the agreement and a permitted maximum period (then two years).

Chapter 6

1. *NLRB v. Insurance Agents' International Union*, 361 U.S. 477 (1960).

2. *Id.* at 488–89.

3. Two of the leading cases taking opposite sides are *Anchortank, Inc. v. NLRB*, 618 F.2d 1158 (5th Cir. 1980) and *Ontario Knife v. NLRB*, 687 F.2d 840 (2d Cir. 1980). These and other decisions are discussed in W. Gould, "Recent Developments under the National Labor Relations Act: The Board and the Circuit Courts," 14 U.C. Davis L. Rev. 497 (1981). See generally A. Cox, "The Right to Engage in Concerted Activities," 26 Ind. L. J. 819 (1951).

4. The Board's rule is set forth in *Alleluia Cushion Company*, 221 NLRB 999 (1975). The Sixth Circuit approved the rule in *NLRB*

v. Lloyd A. Fry Co., 651 F.2d 442 (6th Cir. 1981). But see *Krispy Kreme Doughnut Corp. v. NLRB*, 685 F.2d 804 (4th Cir. 1980).

5. *Meyers Industries, Inc.*, 268 NLRB 493 (1984), at 497 remanded sub nom. *Price v. NLRB*, 755 F.2d 941 (D.C. Cir. 1985). The Second Circuit has been less patient with the Board. *Ewing v. NLRB*, 732 F.2d 1117 (2d Cir. 1985). See also *JMC Transport, Inc. v. NLRB*, 272 NLRB 545 (6th Cir. 1985). Application of the *Meyers Industries* rule is set forth in *Access Control Systems*, 270 NLRB 823 (1984); *Mannington Mills, Inc.*, 272 NLRB 176 (1984); *Bearden and Company d/b/a, D.A. Collins Refractories*, 272 NLRB 1215 (1984).

6. 465 U.S. 822 (1984).

7. *Id.* at 840.

8. *ABF Freight Systems, Inc.*, 271 NLRB 35 (1984).

9. *NLRB v. J. Weingarten, Inc.*, 420 U.S. 251 (1975). However, a minority union representative does not have the right to represent employees even in the railway industry. *Landers v. National Railroad Passenger Corp.*, 485 U.S. 652, (1988).

10. *New Jersey Bell Telephone Co.*, 308 NLRB No. 32 (1992).

11. *Taracorp Industries, A Division of Taracorp, Inc.*, 278 NLRB 376 (1984).

12. *Materials Research Corp.*, 262 NLRB 1010 (1982).

13. *E.I. du Pont de Nemours v. NLRB*, 707 F.2d 1076 (9th Cir. 1983); *ITT Corporation v. NLRB*, 719 F.2d 851 (6th Cir. 1983); *E.I. du Pont de Nemours v. NLRB*, 724 F.2d 1061 (3d Cir. 1988).

14. *Sears, Roebuck & Co.*, 274 NLRB 230 (1985). Cf *Taracorp Industries, supra* note 11. The Court of Appeals for the Third Circuit followed the Board's reversal in *Slaughter v. NLRB*, 876 F.2d 11 (3d Cir. 1989). The Court of Appeals for the Fifth Circuit has reached this result in connection with the Railway Labor Act. *Johnson v. Express One International*, 944 F.2d 247 (5th Cir. 1991).

15. *New York Times v. Sullivan*, 376 U.S. 254 (1964), *Letter Carriers v. Austin*, 448 U.S. 264 (1974); *NLRB v. Greyhound Lines, Inc.*, 660 F.2d 854 (8th Cir. 1981). To some extent, public sector employees enjoy First Amendment protection against employer retaliation for free speech. *Pickering v. Board of Education*, 391 U.S. 563 (1968); *Perry v. Sindermann*, 408 U.S. 593 (1972); *Mt. Healthy City Board of Education v. Doyle*, 429 U.S. 274 (1977). A 5–4 majority of the Court has held protected against discharge an employee who was dis-

missed for stating the following when an attempt was made upon the life of President Reagan in 1981: "If they go for him again, I hope they get him." *Rankin v. McPherson*, 483 U.S. 378 (1987). Said Justice Marshall for the majority: "The burden of caution employees bear with respect to the words they speak will vary with the extent of authority and public accountability the employee's role entails. Where, as here, an employee serves no confidential, policymaking, or public contact role, the danger to the agency's successful function from that employee's private speech is minimal." *Id.* at 390. But see also *Connick v. Myers*, 461 U.S. 188 (1988).

16. *Jeannette Corporation v. NLRB*, 582 F.2d 916 (3d Cir. 1976).

17. For example, *NLRB v. Red Top, Inc.*, 455 F.2d 721 (8th Cir. 1972); *Bettcher Mfg. Corp.*, 76 NLRB 526 (1948).

18. *Linn v. Plant Guard Workers*, 883 U.S. 58, 58 (1966). However, an employer may institute a well-founded libel and business interference action that has a reasonable basis in state court regardless of retaliatory motive under the First Amendment and the Board may not enjoin the action. *Bill Johnson's Restaurant v. NLRB*, 461 U.S. 731 (1983). Summary dismissal of a state court action will provide the basis for a finding of unlawful retaliatory conduct. *Phoenix Newspapers*, 294 NLRB No. 3 (1989); *H.W. Barss Co., Inc.*, 296 NLRB No. 151 (1989). A union's good-faith filing of criminal charges against a company president can constitute protected union activity undertaken to vindicate section 7 rights to be free from physical coercion and intimidation. *Spartan Equipment Co., Inc.*, 297 NLRB No. 3 (1989). Contrarily, a divided Court has concluded that unions are not liable under Reconstruction statutes to deprive nonunion workers of First Amendment rights through violent behavior. *Carpenters Local 610 v. Scott*, 463 U.S. 825, (1983). The Court of Appeals for the Fifth Circuit has held that the Board's exclusive jurisdiction preempts the Civil Rights Act of 1871 actions aimed at obtaining free elections. *Hobbs v. Hawkins*, 141 LRRM 2026 (5th Cir. 1992).

19. *Great Lakes Steel*, 236 NLRB 1033 (1978). Accord, *Samsonite Corporation*, 206 NLRB 848 (1978).

20. "Animal exuberance," referred to in *NLRB v. Illinois Tool Work*, 153 F.2d 811, 815–16 (7th Cir. 1946), it is taken from the Supreme Court's language in *Milk Wagon Drivers v. Meadowmoor Dairies, Inc.*, 812 U.S. 287, 293 (1941). In *NLRB v. Thor Power Tool Company*, 351 F.2d 584, 587 (7th Cir. 1965), the court stated that employees are permitted "some way for impulsive behavior which must be balanced against the employer's right to maintain order and respect."

21. *Tyler Business Services, Inc.*, 256 NLRB 567 (1981), enforcement denied, 680 F.2d 838 (4th Cir. 1982). Where employee concerted activity consists of joining together to protest the malicious workplace rumors concerning the extramarital sexual conduct of two female employees with a male coemployee, their conduct is protected. *Gatliff Coal Co. v. NLRB*, 953 F.2d 247 (6th Cir. 1992).

22. 846 U.S. 464 (1958).

23. *The Patterson-Sargent Company*, 115 NLRB 1627 (1956). Employee complaints to a newspaper's advertisers constitutes protected activity rather than a product of disparagement in *Sierra Publishing Co. v. NLRB*, 889 F.2d 210 (9th Cir. 1989). Said Judge Fletcher: ". . . the law does favor a robust exchange of viewpoints. The mere fact that economic pressure may be brought to bear on one side or the other is not determinative, even if some economic harm actually is suffered. The proper focus must be the manner by which that harm is brought about." *Id.* at 2967. Of course, in order for disloyalty to come into play, something more than an appeal to employees is required. See *Emporium Capwell Co. v. Western Additional Community Organization*, 420 U.S. 50 (1975); *United Cable Television Corp.*, 299 NLRB No. 20 (1990); *Kinder-Care Learning Centers, Inc.*, 299 NLRB No. 164 (1990); *Golden Day Schools*, 236 NLRB 1292 (1978), enfd. 644 F.2d 834 (9th Cir. 1981); But see *Brownsville Garment Co., Inc.*, 298 NLRB No. 66 (1990); *El San Juan Hotel*, 289 NLRB 1453 (1988); *Cincinnati Suburban Press*, 289 NLRB 966 (1988); *Sacramento Union*, 291 NLRB 966 (1988), enfd. 899 F.2d 210 (9th Cir. 1989).

24. *George A. Hormel & Co. v. NLRB*, 962 F.2d 1061 (D.C. Cir. 1992).

25. *Coors Container Co. v. NLRB*, 628 F.2d 1283, 1288 (Loth Cir. 1980). The Board has also held that a union sticker on an employee's crane is protected. *Malta Construction Company*, 276 NLRB 1464 (1985). Chairman Dotson dissented.

26. *Sullair P.T.O., Inc., v. NW*, 641 F.2d 500, 508 (7th Cir. 1981). See also *Timpte, Inc. v. NLRB*, 590 F.2d 871 (10th Cir. 1979; *Maryland Drydock Co. v. NLRB*, 188 F.2d 588 (4th Cir. 1950); *NLRB v. Garner Tool & Die Manufacturing, Inc.*, 498 F.2d 263 (8th Cir. 1974); *Coors Container Co. v. NLRB, supra*, note 25. A satiric letter which is not ". . . a medium intended to resolve or call attention to conditions of employment" is unprotected. *New River Industries v. NLRB*, 945 F.2d 1290 (4th Cir. 1991).

27. *NLRB v. Prescott Industrial Products Company*, 500 F.2d 6, 11 (8th Cir. 1974).

28. *Southwestern Bell Telephone Company*, 200 NLRB 667 (1972). The language was more obviously obscene and similarly unprotected in *Caterpillar Tractor Company*, 276 NLRB 1323 (1985).

29. 142 LRRM 2265 (5th Cir. 1993). Similar language with a similar result are found in *Meco Corporation v. NLRB*, 142 LRRM 2734 (D.C. Cir. 1993).

30. *Inland Steel Company*, 257 NLRB 125 (1981). See also *Borman's Inc. v. NLRB*, 676 F.2d 1188 (6th Cir. 1982); *Southern California Edison Company*, 274 NLRB 1121 (1985).

31. *NLRB v. Nevis Industries*, 647 F.2d 905 (9th Cir. 1981).

32. *Kenrich Petrochemicals, Inc. v. NLRB*, 907 F.2d 400 (3d. Cir. 1990).

33. *NLRB v. Sheraton Puerto Rico Corp.*, 651 F.2d 49 (1st Cir. 1981).

34. 262 NLRB 402 (1982) aff'd sub nom. *Automobile Salesman's Union Local 1095 v. NLRB*, 711 F.2d 888 (D.C. Cir. 1988).

35. *Id.* at 404.

36. *NLRB v. Washington Aluminum Co.*, 370 U.S. 9 (1962). Even if the employees' refusal to work is based upon their view that they are "wet and uncomfortable [and seek] . . . to protest their supervisor's lack of concern," their conduct is protected activity. *Quality C.A.T.V., Inc.*, 278 NLRB 1282 (1986).

37. *NLRB v. Sands Mfg. Co.*, 306 U.S. 332 (1939). There are exceptions to this rule in the case of "serious" unfair labor practices: see *Arlan's Department Store*, 188 NLRB 802, 807 (1961); *Mastro Plastics v. NLRB*, 350 U.S. 270 (1956); *NLRB v. Northeast Oklahoma City Mfg. Co.*, 681 F.2d 6691 (10th Cir. 1980); *Dow Chemical Co. v. NLRB*, 686 F.2d 1852 (3d Cir. 1980); *Caterpillar Tractor Co. v. NLRB*, 658 F.2d 1242 (7th Cir. 1981). The Board has held that sympathy strikes are unprotected activity when there is a broad no-strike clause in the collective bargaining agreement. *Indianapolis Power & Light Company v. NLRB*, 898 F.2d 524 (7th Cir. 1990) enforcement granted. Employer retaliation against union officials for instigating or involving themselves with unprotected strike activity may only be justified by an explicit waiver in the collective agreement. *Metropolitan Edison Company v. NLRB*, 460 U.S. 693 (1983). Where union officials are faced with dismissal for involvement in such activities, the Board has held that relinquishment of the union office for the term of the contract is lawful. Moreover the strike is not deemed unprotected even if engaged in in the teeth of a no-strike clause where objective evidence indicates that it was engaged in because

"abnormally dangerous" working conditions prompted it. *Gateway Coal Co. v. Mine Workers*, 414 U.S. 368 (1974); *Anaconda Aluminum Co.*, 197 NLRB 336 (1972); *TNS, Inc.*, 309 NLRB No. 190 (1992). Meanwhile a cooling-off period imposed prior to the contract's expiration by section 8(d) of the Act obliges the parties not to engage in strikes or lockouts, *NLRB v. Lion Oil Co*, 352 U.S. 282 (1957), and where unions violate the obligation workers lose their status as "employees" under the Act, *Fort Smith Chair Co.*, 143 NLRB 514, enforced 886 F.2d 788 (D.C. Cir. 1968), cert. denied, 879 U.S. 888 (1964). The Board has held that the burden of filing statutory notification with mediation agencies rests exclusively with the initiating party (proposing contract modification) and that the initiating party's failure to file such a notice cannot serve to preclude the noninitiating party from undertaking otherwise lawful economic action. *United Artists Communications, Inc.*, 274 NLRB 75 (1985) overruling *Hooker Chemical Corp.*, 224 NLRB 1535 (1976) enforcement denied 573 F.2d 965 (7th Cir. 1978). Where the employer encourages the union to engage in a strike during the sixty-day period, the employer may not avail itself of the protection that would otherwise be afforded by section 8(d). *ABC Automotive Products Corp.*, 307 NLRB No. 36 (1992).

38. *Hydrogics, Inc.*, 293 NLRB No. 129 (1989). The Board in *Spedrack, Inc.*, 293 NLRB No. 128 (1989) has stated that full-fledged bargaining should occur in connection with reopeners, and that to do otherwise would impose conditions that ". . . would turn reopener bargaining into little more than a charade that would barely differentiate from the kinds of discussion that may lawfully occur even in the absence of a reopener." *Id.* at slip op. at p. 4. Accord, *Century Wine and Spirits*, 304 NLRB No. 69 (1991).

39. *Elk Lumber Co.*, 91 NLRB 333 (1950); *NLRB v. Montgomery Ward & Co. Inc.*, 157 F.2d 486, 496 (8th Cir. 1946). See generally W. Gould, "The Status of Unauthorized and (Wildcat) Strikes under the National Labor Relations Act," 52 Cornell L. Q. 672 (1967).

40. *Mike Yurosek & Son, Inc.*, 306 NLRB No. 210 (1992); *Mike Yurosek & Son, Inc.*, 310 NLRB No. 139 (1993).

41. *NLRB v. Fansteel Metallurgical Corp.*, 306 U.S. 240 (1939), *Johns-Manville Products Corp. v. NLRB*, 557 F.2d 1126 (5th Cir. 1977); *NLRB v. Pepsi-Cola Bottling Company*, 449 F.2d 824 (5th Cir. 1971). *Roseville Dodge v. NLRB*, 882 F.2d 1335 (8th Cir. 1989); *Molon Motor and Coil Corp. v. NLRB*, 965 F.2d 532 (7th Cir. 1992). See Member Dennis's dissent in *Waco, Inc.*, 273 NLRB 746 (1985). See Gould, op. cit. The Board has taken the position that words as well as

physical conduct can constitute strike misconduct which justifies the employer's refusal to reinstate the striker. *Clear Pine Mouldings, Inc.*, 268 NLRB 1044 (1984). In this decision the Board repudiated the *Thayer* doctrine, which balanced the severity of the employer's unfair labor practice against the gravity of the striker's misconduct. Moreover it is unlawful for employers to engage in disparate treatment of strikers and nonstrikers who are equally culpable of misconduct. *Garrett Railroad Car v. NLRB*, 683 F.2d 731 (3d Cir. 1982); Member Johansen's dissent in *Bingham-Williamette Co.*, 279 NLRB 270 (1986).

42. *The Emporium Capwell Co. v. Western Addition Community Organization*, 420 U.S. 50 (1975); *NLRB v. Draper Corp.*, 145 F.2d 199 (4th Cir. 1944), Gould, op. cit. The refusal to cross a picket line as well as the strike is protected. *NLRB v. Rockaway News Supply Co., Inc.*, 345 U.S. 871 (1953), *NLRB v. Southern Greyhound Lines*, 426 F.2d 1299 (5th Cir. 1970); *NLRB v. L.G. Everist, Inc.*, 334 F.2d 312 (8th Cir. 1964); *ABS Co.*, 269 NLRB No. 138 (1984); *Business Services by Manpower, Inc.*, 272 NLRB 827 (1984); *Dave Castellino & Sons*, 277 NLRB 453 (1985).

43. *NLRB v. R. C. Can Co.*, 328 F.2d 974 (5th Cir. 1964); Gould, op. cit., pp. 678–80, 682–90. However, the court of appeals subsequently warned that *R.C. Can* must be applied with "great care," *NLRB v. Shop Rite Foods*, 430 F.2d 786, 790 (5th Cir. 1970), and the Board appears to concur in this view, *Energy Coal Income Partnership 1981-1*, 269 NLRB 770 (1984); *AAL, Inc.*, 275 NLRB 84 (1985).

44. 29 USC §§176 et seq. (1976). See, for example, *United Steelworkers v. United States*, 361 U.S. 39 (1959); *Youngstown Sheet and Tube Co. v. Sawyer*, 343 U.S. 579 (1952) (the steel seizure case).

45. NLRA §§206–210.

46. Sen. Rep. No. 105 on S.B. 11 1126. Cong. Rec. 3951 Sen. (April 23, 1947) (remarks of Senator Taft).

47. *Dorchy v. Kansas*, 272 U.S. 306 (1926), *UAW v. Wisconsin Employment Relations Board*, 336 U.S. 245 (1949); *United Federation of Postal Clerks v. Blount*, 325 F. Supp. 879 (D.C.D.C.), aff'd, 404 U.S. 802 (1971). By virtue of the doctrine of preemption, however, states have been unable to restrict emergency strikes in the private sector. *International Union UAW v. O'Brien*, 339 U.S. 454 (1950); *Street Employees Division 1287 v. Missouri*, 374 U.S. 74 (1963).

48. 304 U.S. 333 (1938).

49. *NLRB v. Curtin Matheson Scientific, Inc.*, 494 U.S. 775, (1990). However, a union's ability to effectively represent such workers has

been diminished by a decision of the Court of Appeals for the Seventh Circuit to the effect that the union is not entitled to the names of strike replacements even where a "clear and present danger" that disclosure will result in harassment of such employees is not in evidence. *Chicago Tribune Co. v. NLRB*, 962 F.2d 712 (7th Cir. 1992).

50. 29 USC §159 (c)(3) (1976). The right to vote exists whether replacement has been accomplished by an outside permanent replacement or bargaining unit personnel. *St. Joe Minerals Corp.*, 295 NLRB No. 59 (1989). Where the job is eliminated for economic reasons unrelated to the strike itself, the right to vote is terminated. *Kable Printing Co.*, 238 NLRB 1092 (1978); *K&W Trucking Co.*, 267 NLRB 68 (1983); *Lamb-Grays Harbor Co.*, 295 NLRB 355 (1989).

51. *NLRB v. International Van Lines*, 409 U.S. 48 (1972); *Climate Control Corporation*, 251 NLRB 751 (1980). ". . . an employer's unfair labor practices during an economic strike do not *ipso facto* convert it into an unfair labor practice strike. Rather the General Counsel must prove that the unlawful conduct was a factor (not necessarily the sole or predominant one) that caused a prolongation of the work stoppage. In determining this causal nexus, the General Counsel may rely upon both subjective and objective factors." *Chicago Beef Co.*, 298 NLRB No. 156, p. 2 (1990) enf'd. 944 F.2d 905 (6th Cir. 1991); *C-Line Express*, 292 NLRB 638 (1989) enforcement denied on other grounds, 873 F.2d 1150 (8th Cir. 1989) ". . . unlawful discharges by their nature have a reasonable tendency to prolong the strike and therefore afford a sufficient basis for finding a conversion to an unfair labor practice strike." A causal connection between unfair labor practices and the strike must be demonstrated in order to establish that employees are unfair labor practice strikers. *L.A. Water Treatment, Division of Chromalloy American Corp.*, 286 NLRB 868 (1987); *Typoservice Corp.*, 203 NLRB 1180 (1973). *Gloversville Embossing Corp.*, 297 NLRB No. 21 (1989). Unlawful conduct that is incompletely cured at the time of the strike does not make a strike an unfair labor practice strike unless the conduct is a contributing cause to it. *General Industrial Employees Union, Local 42, Distillery Workers International Union v. NLRB*, 951 F.2d 1308 (D.C. Cir. 1991). Strikers who are discharged are entitled to back pay from the date of discharge without a request for reinstatement. *Abilities & Goodwill, Inc.*, 241 NLRB 27 (1979); *NLRB v. Lyon & Ryan Ford, Inc.*, 647 F.2d 745 (7th Cir. 1981).

52. *NLRB v. Erie Resistor Corp.*, 373 U.S. 221 (1963).

53. *Brotherhood of Railroad Trainmen v. Jacksonville Terminal Co.*, 394 U.S. 369 (1969).

54. Indeed, prior to *Erie Resistor,* a lower court held that *Mackay* permits employers to award superseniority. United also refused to hire trainees who did not cross the picket line. "United Strike: It's a Matter of Principle Now," *Business Week,* June 10, 1985, p. 48, col. 1. While this conduct would be unlawful under the NLRA, *Phelps Dodge v. NLRB,* 313 U.S. 177 (1941), the answer has yet to be provided by the Supreme Court under the NRLA. See note 54 *infra.*

55. United's practices were held unlawful by the Seventh Circuit in *Airline Pilots Association v. United Airlines, Inc.,* 802 F.2d 886 (7th Cir. 1986) and the Eleventh Circuit has come to a similar conclusion in *Eastern Airlines v. Airline Pilots Association,* 920 F.2d 722 (11th Cir. 1990). Cf. *International Association of Machinists and Airspace Workers, AFL-CIO v. Alaska Airlines, Inc.,* 813 F.2d 1038 (9th Cir. 1987); *Nelson v. Piedmont Airlines,* 750 F.2d 1284 (4th Cir. 1984); *Brotherhood of Locomotive Firemen and Engineermen v. National Mediation Board,* 410 F.2d 1025 (D.C. Cir. 1969); *Airline Pilots Association v. Alaska Airlines,* 785 F.2d 328 (9th Cir. 1984).

56. 489 U.S. 426 (1989)

57. *NLRB v. Fleetwood Trailer Co.,* 389 U.S. 375 (1967). Of course the question of whether permanent replacements have been hired is also an important one. Where replacements have not yet completed their postinterview test at the conclusion of the strike, they may not be discharged as temporary employees. *Solar Turbines Inc.,* 302 NLRB No. 3 (1991). Similarly the Board has held that permanent replacements cannot oust strikers where the departments into which they were hired remained closed during the strike. *Waterbury Hospital v. NLRB,* 950 F.2d 849 (2d Cir. 1991). The failure to consider unconditional offers to return to work more than six months after the conclusion of the strike may violate the Act. *Teledyne Industries, Inc.,* 298 NLRB No. 148 (1990).

58. *Id.* at 878. The burden of showing that the striker has obtained regular and substantially equivalent employment rests with the employer. *Arlington Hotel Co.,* 273 NLRB 210 (1984); *Salinas Valley Ford Sales, Inc.,* 279 NLRB 679 (1986); *Oregon Steel Mills, Inc.,* 300 NLRB No. 105 (1990). Striker qualifications for the job as well as the question of whether the job is substantially equivalent are interwoven, but mere fact that strikers are qualified to fill the jobs is not dispositive of the question of whether they are substantially equivalent to their former jobs. *Rose Printing Co.,* 304 NLRB No.

132 (1991); *California Distribution Centers, Inc.*, 308 NLRB No. 11 (1992). A refusal to accept an offer of reinstatement to a job which is not the same or substantially equivalent does not "extinguish entitlement to full reinstatement to the former or substantially equivalent job." Accordingly the employer has no obligation to provide such an offer. *Id.* The employer's transfer of strikers to another plant does not necessarily preclude a finding that the jobs are substantially equivalent. *NLRB v. American Olean Tile Co.*, 826 F.2d 1496 (6th Cir. 1987).

59. *Laidlaw v. NLRB*, 414 F.2d 99 (7th Cir. 1969), cert. denied, 897 U.S. 920 (1970); *American Machine Corp. v. NLRB*, 424 F.2d 1821 (5th Cir. 1970). For some of the problems in determining whether replacements are laid off or discharged by virtue of strikers section 7 rights, see *Harrison Ready Mix Concrete, Inc.*, 272 NLRB 331 (1984). Inevitably complexity relating to this issue has spawned litigation about what an employer may say during an organizational campaign about the right to strikers. See, for instance, *Eagle Comtronics, Inc.*, 263 NLRB 515 (1982); *Tri-Cast, Inc.*, 274 NLRB 377 (1985); *John W. Galbreath & Co.*, 288 NLRB No. 95 (1988).

60. *Brook Research and Manufacturing*, 202 NLRB 684 (1978). But the Court of Appeals for the Seventh Circuit has recognized business justification defenses. See *Giddings & Lewis, Inc. v. NLRB*, 710 F.2d 1280 (7th Cir. 1983).

61. *Giddings & Lewis v. NLRB*, 675 F.2d 926 (7th Cir. 1982). The Board's view is that the question is whether permanent replacements have had a "reasonable expectancy of recall": ". . . the objective factors relevant to the replacements' reasonable expectancy of recall would include, *inter alia*, evidence concerning the employer's past business experience, the employer's future plans, the length of the layoff, the circumstances of the layoff and what the employee was told regarding the likelihood of recall . . . ." *Aqua-Chem, Inc.*, 288 NLRB 1108 (1988) enf'd 910 F.2d 1487 (7th Cir. 1991), petition for rehearing denied 922 F.2d 403 (Judge Posner dissenting with Judge Coffey, Easterbrook and Manion); *Lone Star Industries, Inc.*, 279 NLRB 550 (1986); *Mike Yurosek & Son, Inc.*, 295 NLRB 304 (1989); *Delta-Macon Brick & Tile, Inc.*, 297 NLRB No. 178 (1990) enforcement denied 943 F.2d 567 (5th Cir. 1991); *NLRB v. Bingham-Willamette*, 857 F.2d 661 (9th Cir. 1988).

62. 463 U.S. 491 (1983). Cf. *Deeds v. Decker Coal Co.*, 246 Mont. 220, 135 LRRM 3049 (S.C. Mont, 1990).

63. Justice Blackmun wrote a separate concurring opinion.

64. *Machinists v. Wisconsin Employment Relations Commission*, 427 U.S. 132, 140 (1976); *NLRB v. Nash-Finch*, 404 U.S. 188, 144 (1971). Compare the New Jersey Supreme Court's treatment of state law prohibiting some strikebreaking. *U.S. Chamber of Commerce v. New Jersey*, 110 LRRM 2828 (N.J. 1982). See also, *Greater Boston Chamber of Commerce v. City of Boston*, 778 F.Supp. 95 (D.C. Mass. 1991) The Court's invalidation of a municipal ordinance conditioning a renewal of a taxi cab company's operating franchise on settlement of a labor dispute by a certain date under the preemption doctrine presages difficulties for state or local regulation of strikebreaking. *Golden State Transit Corp. v. City of Los Angeles*, 475 U.S. 608 (1986); *Golden State Transit Corp. v. City of Los Angeles*, 493 U.S. 103 (1989). Cf. *Wisconsin Department of Industry, Labor and Human Relations v. Gould*, Inc., 475 U.S. 282 (1986).

65. See *Belknap, Inc. v. Hale*, *supra* note 61, at 498–99. ("The Court's change in the law of permanency weakens the rights of strikers and undermines the protection afforded those rights by the Act. Such adjustments in the balance of power between labor and management are for Congress, not this Court.")

66. 380 U.S. 300 (1965).

67. In *American Ship Building*, 380 U.S. at 307, the Court lists some lockouts previously found exempt by the Board. These include the response to a "whipsaw" strike in *NLRB v. Truck Drivers Local 449* (*"Buffalo Linen"*), 353 U.S. 87 (1957).

68. *American Ship Building*, 380 U.S. at 305.

69. *NLRB v. Truck Drivers Local 449* (*"Buffalo Linen"*), 353 U.S. 87 (1957). But employer withdrawal from multiemployer bargaining is carefully circumscribed; *Charles D. Bonanno Linen Service, Inc. v. NLRB*, 454 U.S. 404 (1982). "Lockouts are generally permissible in anticipation of a strike or in support of an employer's legitimate position." *Riverside Cement Co.*, 296 NLRB No. 104 (1989), p. 6.

70. *NLRB v. Brown*, 380 U.S. 278 (1965).

71. See, for example, *Inland Trucking Co. v. NLRB*, 440 F.2d 562 (7th Cir. 1971) (use of temporary replacements and a lockout when no strike per se a violation). But cf. *Inter-collegiate Press, Graphic Arts Div.*, 486 F.2d 837 (8th Cir. 1973), cert. denied, 416 U.S. 938 (1974) (interests must be balanced case by case).

72. *Harter Equipment, Inc.*, 280 NLRB 597 (1986) enforcement granted 829 F.2d 458 (3d Cir. 1987). Accord, *International Brotherhood of Boilermakers v. NLRB*, 858 F.2d 756 (D.C. Cir. 1988). But

workers cannot be replaced unless there is a timely announcement to strikers that the employer is locking them out in support of its bargaining position. *Eads Transfer, Inc.,* 304 NLRB No. 90 (1991).

In a more controversial portion of the *Harter* opinion, the Board said:

Initially, we find that the use of temporary employees reasonably serves precisely the same purpose served by the lockout, i.e., bringing economic pressure to bear in support of a legitimate bargaining position. After *American Shipbuilding*, the validity of such a business purpose is unassailable. We do not perceive any persuasive reason why coupling this purpose with a desire to remain in operation with temporary employees would impermissibly color an employer's otherwise legitimate interest. There can be no more fundamental employer interest in the continuation of business operations. *Exercising the right to a lockout in a bargaining dispute does not necessitate forgoing the option to secure business earnings any more than exercising the right to strike requires employees to forgo attempts to secure income by temporary alternative employment, strike benefits, or unemployment compensation (where permitted by state law).* In sum, the use of temporary employees to remain in operation after a lawful lockout is "a measure reasonably adapted to the achievement of a legitimate end." (*Id.* at 599; emphasis supplied)

73. See also Case Comment, 85 Harv. L. Rev. 680 (1972).

74. *Insurance Agents,* 361 U.S. at 484. Indeed in the 1990s questions still abound as to what is a reasonable location for bargaining and what party is bargaining in bad faith because of its position on the situs for negotiation. *I. Appel Corp.,* 308 NLRB No. 67 (1992).

75. *NLRB v. Reed & Prince Mfg. Co.,* 205 F.2d 131 (1st Cir.), cert. denied, 346 U.S. 887 (1953); *Pittsburgh-Des Moines Corp. v. NLRB,* 663 F.2d 956 (9th Cir. 1981); *Pease Company v. NLRB,* 666 F.2d 1044 (6th Cir. 1981); *NLRB v. A-1 King Size Sandwiches,* 732 F.2d 872 (11th Cir. 1984).

76. 343 U.S. 395 (1952). While this case supports a laissez-faire approach, the Board ". . . in some instances [determines that] specific proposals might become relevant to determining whether a party has bargained in bad faith . . . relying on the Board's cumulative institutional experience in administering the Act, we shall continue to examine proposals when appropriate and consider whether, on the basis of objective factors, a demand is clearly designed to frustrate agreement on a collective-bargaining contract." *Reichhold Chemicals, Inc.,* 288 NLRB 69 (1988) enforcement granted and modified, 906 F.2d 719 (D.C. Cir. 1990); *Litton Microwave Cooking Products,* 300 NLRB No. 37 (1990); *Concrete Pipe and*

Products Corp., 305 NLRB No. 21 (1991), enforcement granted sub. nom. *United Steelworkers of America Local 14534 v. NLRB*, 142 LRRM 2177 (D.C. Cir. 1993); *Hydrotherm*, 302 NLRB No. 153 (1991); *Radisson Plaza Minneapolis*, 307 NLRB No. 10 (1992); *Bethea Baptist Home*, 310 NLRB No. 28 (1993). The Board regulates method of collective bargaining and thus indirectly agreements as well. For instance, one party may not insist on the exchange of written proposals in advance of face to face negotiations. *Holiday Inn Dowtown-New Haven*, 300 NLRB No. 98 (1990); *Fountain Lodge, Inc.*, 269 NLRB 674 (1984); *Chemung Contracting Corp.*, 291 NLRB 773 (1988).

77. *Id.* at 404.

78. 29 USC §158(d).

79. *NLRB v. Bildisco and Bildisco*, 465 U.S. 513 (1984).

80. 11 USC §1113, congressional statute modifying *NLRB v. Bildisco and Bildisco*, 465 U.S. 513 (1984). This statute requires an employer filing for bankruptcy to "bargain" with the union over necessary modifications of the collective bargaining agreement before filing an application seeking rejection of the collective bargaining agreement. The court can only approve rejecting the collective bargaining agreement if the union refuses to accept the employer's proposal without good cause and "the balance of the equities" favors rejection. If the court does not rule on the employer's application within thirty days, the employer can terminate or alter the collective bargaining agreement. See generally *Truck Drivers Local 807, International Brotherhood of Teamsters v. Carey Transportation, Inc.*, 816 F.2d 82 (2d Cir. 1987); *Wheeling Pittsburgh Steel Corp. v. United Steelworkers of America*, 791 F.2d 1074 (3d Cir. 1986); *International Brotherhood of Teamsters v. IML Freight, Inc.*, 789 F.2d 1460 (10th Cir. 1986); *In re Century Brass Products, Inc. v. International Union, UAW*, 793 F.2d 265 (2d Cir. 1986); *In re Mile Hi Metal Systems, Inc. v. Mile Hi Metal Systems, Inc.*, 899 F.2d 877 (10th Cir. 1990); *In re Continental Airlines Corp. v. Airline Pilots Association, International*, 907 F.2d 1500 (5th Cir. 1990). "A Debtor may sell the assets of the business unencumbered by a collective bargaining agreement if that agreement has been rejected pursuant [to the statute] . . . this statute requires unions to face those changed circumstances that occur when a company becomes insolvent, and it requires all affected parties to compromise in the face of financial hardship. At the same time, [the statute] . . . also imposes requirements on the debtor to prevent it from using bankruptcy as a judicial hammer to break the union." *In re Maxwell Newspapers*, 142 LRRM 2049, 2051 (2d cir. 1992).

81. *NLRB v. Wooster Division of Borg-Warner Corp.*, 356 U.S. 342 (1958).

82. *Alamo Cement Co.*, 281 NLRB 737, 738 (1986); *Rangaire Acquisition Corp.*, 309 NLRB No. 167 (1992); *Litton Systems*, 300 NLRB 324 (1990), enforced. 949 F.2d 249 (8th Cir. 1991).

83. *NLRB v. Katz*, 369 U.S. 736 (1962); In *The Daily News of Los Angeles*, 304 NLRB No. 63 (1991) enforcement denied 142 LRRM 2001 (D.C. Cir. 1992) Court of Appeals for the District of Columbia distinguished *Katz* and held that where an increase in pay is fixed as to timing but discretionary as to amount the employer may discontinue it. Contrarily, *Katz* mandates the employer to bargain before continuing the practice. Subsequent to impasse, an employer may institute its conditions unless a party avoids the other side's earnest efforts to engage in bargaining so as to avoid or delay the process or where economic exigencies compel prompt action. *M&M Contractors*, 262 NLRB 1472 (1982); *Master Window Cleaning, Inc.*, 302 NLRB No. 63 (1991). But the implementation of something more substantial than what was offered is bad-faith bargaining. *NLRB v. Crompton-Highland Mills*, 337 U.S. 217 (1949); *Central Mettalic Casket Co.*, 91 NLRB 572 (1950). Cf. *NLRB v. Exchange Parts Co.*, 375 U.S. 405 (1964). However, the Second Circuit Court has held that an employer did not violate the Act when it hired replacements at a rate of pay higher than that offered to strikers. *Auto Worker Local 259 v. NLRB*, 776 F.2d 23 (2d Cir. 1985). But ". . . [t]he crucial point . . . is that after impasse is reached an employer may unilaterally implement new terms of employment only if reasonably comprehended in a pre-impasse offer." *Cuyamaca Meats, Inc. v. San Diego Pension Trust Fund*, 827 F.2d 491 (9th Cir. 1987); *Lapham-Hickey Steel Corp. v. NLRB*, 904 F.2d 1180 (7th Cir. 1990); *Emhart Indus. v. NLRB*, 907 F.2d 372 (2d Cir. 1990); *Southwest Forest Indus., Inc. v. NLRB*, 841 F.2d 270 (9th Cir. 1988).

84. See, for example, *NLRB v. Tomco Communication Inc.*, 567 F.2d 871, 881 (9th Cir. 1978). The leading case defining impasse is *Taft Broadcasting Co.*, 163, NLRB 475, 478 (1967) enforced, 395 F.2d 622 (D.C. Cir. 1968). Unlawful unilateral action that impedes bargaining makes it less likely that impasse will be found. *Intermountain Rural Electric Association*, 305 NLRB No. 107 (1991). Accord, *La Porte Transit Co., Inc. v. NLRB*, 888 F.2d 1182 (7th Cir. 1989). The Board has found an impasse where there was only three meetings between labor and management. *Lou Stecher's Super Markets*, 275 NLRB 475 (1985); See also, *Bell Transit Company*, 271 NLRB 1272 (1984); *NLRB v. Powell Electrical Manufacturing Co.*, 906 F.2d 1007 (5th Cir. 1990). In establishing that an unfair refusal to bargain

exists because of insistence upon a nonmandatory subject to the point of impasse, it needs to be proven that the nonmandatory subject is the sole cause of impasse. *Phillip Carey v. NLRB,* 331 F.2d 720 (6th Cir. 1964) cert. denied, 379 U.S. 888. If one party impedes bargaining through insistence upon permissive subject matter, the employer may act unilaterally though it may not deal with employees directly. *Inland Tugs v. NLRB,* 918 F.2d 1299 (7th Cir. 1990).

85. *Teamsters Local Union No. 639 v. NLRB,* 136 LRRM 2329, 2332 (D.C. Cir. 1991).

86. The contrast is stated in *NLRB v. International Van Lines,* 409 U.S. 48, 50–51 (1972). The decision rested on other grounds.

87. *NLRB v. Salvation Army Day Care Centers,* 763 F.2d 1, 7 (1st Cir. 1985), quoting *NLRB v. Massachusetts Nurses Assn.,* 557 F.2d 894, 898 (1st Cir. 1977).

88. *Mental Health Services, Northwest, Inc.,* 300 NLRB No. 123 (1990).

89. *Lapeer Foundry & Machine,* 289 NLRB 952 (1988); *Georgia Pacific Corp.,* 275 NLRB 67 (1985); *Tuskegee Area Transportation System,* 308 NLRB No. 47 (1992).

90. *NLRB v. Columbus Printing Pressmen Local 252,* 543, F.2d 1161 (5th Cir. 1976); *La Crosse Electrical Contractor., Association,* 271 NLRB 250 (1984); *Sheet Metal Workers Local 59,* 227 NLRB 520 (1976). A union may lawfully submit disputed issues to interest arbitration and seek to compel arbitration through a suit in federal court on attempt to enforce an aware in court, provided that the employer is at least arguably bound by the interest arbitration clause and that the union, prior to invoking interest arbitration negotiated in good faith. *Collier Electric Co.,* 296 NLRB No. 144 (1989); *West Coast Sheet Metal, Inc. v. NLRB,* 938 F.2d 1356 (D.C. Cir. 1991); *Local Union No. 54 Sheet Metal Workers' International Association, AFL-CIO,* 297 NLRB No. 104 (1990).

91. The case law is hostile to attempts to deal directly with employees. *Medo Photo Supply Corp. v. NLRB,* 321 U.S. 678 (1944); *Inland Tugs, supra; Toledo Typographical Union No. 63 v. NLRB,* 907 F.2d 1220 (D.C. Cir. 1990) denied enforcement in *The Toledo Blade Co.,* 295 NLRB No. 68 (1989) (author of employer insistence upon a proposal authorized "buyouts" without involvement in union). Similar problems arise in connection with employer insistence that individuals execute grievances filed by unions, again a practice generally discouraged. *Latrobe Steel Co.,* 244 NLRB 528 (1979) enforced as modified 630 F.2d 171 (3d Cir. 1980) cert. denied 454 U.S. 821 (1981); *Athey Products Corp.,* 303 NLRB No. 8 (1991).

Where management insists upon broad contract clauses that provide broad discretion, the same issues relating to bargaining with individuals arises. *NLRB v. American National Insurance Co.*, 343 U.S. 395 (1952); *Colorado-Ute Electric Association v. NLRB*, 939 F.2d 1392 (10th Cir. 1991); *Cincinnati Newspaper Guild, Local 9 v. NLRB*, 938 F.2d 284 (D.C. Cir. 1991). Cf. *McClatchy Newspapers*, 299 NLRB No. 156 (1990) enforcement denied 140 LRRM 2249 (D.C. Cir. 1992). As noted in the text, *Borg-Warner* held that an employer's proposal to modify the certified unit is unlawful if insisted upon to the point of impasse as a permissive subject. *Boise Cascade Corp. v. NLRB*, 129 LRRM 2744 (D.C. Cir. 1988). On the other hand, the employer's proposals that are designed to remove a union's exclusive jurisdiction over works assignments are mandatory and lawful even if insisted upon to the point of impasse. *Local 666 IATSE v. NLRB*, 134 LRRM 2388 (D.C. Cir. 1990).

92. *Borg-Warner*, 356 U.S. at 350.

93. *Id.*

94. See W. Gould, *Japan's Reshaping of American Labor Law* 124–128 (1984).

95. See *Fitzsimmons Manufacturing Company*, 251 NLRB 375, (1980), enforced, 670 F.2d 663, (6th Cir. 1982); *KDEN Broadcasting Co.*, 225 NLRB 25 (1976); *Cascade Corporation*, 192 NLRB 533 (1971).

96. *NLRB v. Financial Institution Employees of America, Local 1182*, 475 U.S. 192 (1986)

97. *Id.* at 209.

98. *General Electric Co. v. NLRB*, 415 F.2d 512 (2d Cir. 1969) ("coalition bargaining"). For an excellent discussion of this subject, see S. Goldberg, "Coordinated Bargaining Tactics of Unions," 54 Cornell L. Rev. 897 (1969). Cf. *NLRB v. St. Joseph's Hospital*, 755 F.2d 260 (2d Cir. 1985).

99. *NLRB v. Bartlett-Collins Co.*, 639 F.2d 652 (10th Cir. 1981); *Latrobe Steel Co. v. NLRB*, 630 F.2d 171 (3d Cir. 1980); *Hutchinson Fruit Company, Inc.*, 277 NLRB No. 54 (1985); *NLRB v. Pennsylvania Telephone Guild*, 799 F.2d 84 (3d Cir. 1986). See "AMC Objects to the Taping of Contract Talks," *Wall Street Journal*, June 19, 1985, at 39.

100. *Fibreboard Paper Products Corp. v. NLRB*, 379 U.S. 203 (1964). But similar contracting out disputes in the public sector arising out of the Civil Service Reform Act of 1978 are not negotiable under

that statute. *Department of the Treasury v. Federal Labor Relations Authority,* 133 LRRM 3066 (1990). Under the authority of this line of cases, a majority of the Board has held that an employer may not unilaterally disarm guards in a mental health clinic. *Northside Center for Child Development, Inc.,* 310 NLRB No. 20 (1993).

101. *Id.* at 225.

102. *First National Maintenance Corp. v. NLRB,* 452 U.S. 666, 677–78 (1981).

103. *Textile Workers Union v. Darlington Manufacturing Co.,* 380 U.S. 263 (1965). The Court has held that the employer's right to close its business under *Darlington* exists under the Railway Labor Act. *Pittsburgh & Lake Erie Railroad Co. v. Railway Labor Executives Association,* 491 U.S. 490 (1989). Cf. *Mid-South Bottling Co. v. NLRB,* 876 F.2d 458 (5th Cir. 1989).

104. *NLRB v. Adams Dairy, Inc.,* 350 F.2d 108, 113 (8th Cir. 1965), cert. denied, 382 U.S. 1011 (1966), *Royal Typewriter Co. v. NLRB,* 533 F.2d 1030, 1039 (8th Cir. 1976) *(dicta); NLRB v. Thompson Transport Co.,* 406 F.2d 698, 703 (10th Cir. 1969); *NLRB v. Transmarine Navigation Corp.,* 380 F.2d 933, 939 (9th Cir. 1967); *NLRB v. Royal Plating and Polishing Co.,* 350 F.2d 191, 196 (3d Cir. 1965).

105. *NLRB v. First National Maintenance Corp.,* 627 F.2d 596 (2d Cir. 1980); *Broadway Motor Trucks v. NLRB,* 582 F.2d 720 (3d Cir. 1978).

106. *NLRB v. First National Maintenance Corp.,* 627 F.2d at 601–02 (footnote omitted).

107. *First National Maintenance Corp. v. NLRB, supra* note 103, at 686–87. Justice Brennan dissented in an opinion joined in by Justice Marshall. See W. Gould, "The Supreme Court's Labor and Employment Docket in the October 1980 Term: Justice Brennan's Term," 53 U. Colo. L. Rev. 116–18 (1981).

108. ". . . barring particularly unusual or emergency circumstances, the union's right to discuss with the employer how the impact of the sale on the employees can be ameliorated must be reckoned with (as must compliance with other governmental requirements) sufficiently before its actual implementation so that the union is not confronted at the bargaining table with a sale that is a fait accompli. Thus, the Union [is] . . . entitled as much notice of the closing and determination of employees as was needed for meaningful bargaining at a meaningful time." *Williamette Tug and Barge Co.,* 300 NLRB No. 32 (1990); *Metropolitan Teletronics,* 279 NLRB 957 (1986) enforcement granted 819 F.2d 1130 (2d Cir. 1987); *Los Angeles Soap Co.,* 300 NLRB No. 33 (1990).

109. *Bob's Big Boy Family Restaurant,* 264 NLRB 1369 (1982).

110. *The Liberal Market, Inc.,* 264 NLRB 807 (1982), *Otis Elevator Company,* 269 NLRB 891 (1984), *Bostrom Discussion, VOP, Inc.,* 272 NLRB 999 (1984); *Fraser Shipyards, Inc.,* 272 NLRB 496 (1984), *The Kroger Company,* 273 NLRB 462 (1984), *Garwood-Detroit Truck Equipment, Inc.,* 274 NLRB 113 (1985). *Storer Cable TV of Texas, Inc.,* 295 NLRB 295 (1989). See *Olivetti Office U.S.A., Inc. v. NLRB,* 926 F.2d 181 (2d Cir. 1991); *BPS Guard Service, Inc.,* 300 NLRB No. 160 (1990) (frequently disputes arise as to whether an employer's decision involves a partial closing and is therefore enveloped by *First National Maintenance* or simply involves hours, *United States Postal Service,* 306 NLRB No. 120 (1992); or layoffs *Lapeer Foundry and Machine, Inc.,* 289 NLRB 952 (1988). Where the change is a basic alteration of the enterprise, there is no bargaining obligation. *Noblit Brothers, Inc.,* 305 NLRB No. 37 (1991). See *Newspaper Guild Greater Philadelphia, Local 100 v. NLRB,* 636 F.2d 550 (D.C. Cir. 1980) on remand *Peerless Publications,* 283 NLRB 334 (1987), holding that rules designed to prevent employees from engaging in activities that might compromise editorials and journalism are central to ultimate products and therefore not subject to mandatory bargaining; for a decision or holding that the core purpose of the enterprise is not involved in a code of ethics where the primary function of the employer is the generation and transmission of electricity, see *American Electric Power Co.,* 302 NLRB No. 161 (1991).

111. 303 NLRB No. 66 (1991) remanded in *Food & Commercial Workers Local 150-A v. NLRB,* 880 F.2d 1422 (D.C. Cir. 1989).

112. *Id.* at 17–18.

113. *Id.* at 18. *Contra, Arrow Automotive Industries, Inc. v. NLRB,* 853 F.2d 223 (4th Cir. 1988).

114. *Mid-State Ready Mix,* 307 NLRB No. 129 (1992).

115. *Holmes & Narver/Morrison-Knudsen,* 309 NLRB No. 12 (1992). In some situations, where the employer did not bargain to the point of impasse, a per se refusal to bargain will be found.

116. *Milwaukee Spring Division of Illinois Coil Spring Company,* 265 NLRB 206 (1982).

117. *Milwaukee Spring Division,* 268 NLRB No. 87 (1984) enforcement granted sub nom. *International Union, UAW v. NLRB,* 765 F.2d 175 (D.C. Cir. 1985).

118. *Industry City Associates,* 307 NLRB No. 211 (1992).

119. *Robertshaw Controls Co. v. NLRB,* 386 F.2d 377 (4th Cir. 1967).

120. *Metropolitan Edison Co. v. NLRB,* 460 U.S. 693, 708 (1983); *Gannett Rochester Newspapers,* 305 NLRB No. 134 (1991).

121. *Michigan Bell Telephone Co.,* 306 NLRB No. 54 (1992), slip op. p. 2. See also *Murphy Oil U.S.A.,* 286 NLRB 1039 (1987); *Jones Dairy Farm,* 295 NLRB No. 20 (1989); *GTE Automatic Electric,* 261 NLRB 1491 (1982); *Outboard Marine Corp.,* 307 NLRB No. 204 (1992).

122. 29 USC §§2101, 2101 notes, 2102–2109.

123. Thirteen states have plant closing legislation of their own: Connecticut, Hawaii, Kansas, Maine, Maryland, Massachusetts, Michigan, Minnesota, Montana, Oregon, South Carolina, Tennessee, and Wisconsin.

124. *NLRB v. General Electric Co.,* 418 F.2d 786 (2d Cir. 1969), cert. denied, 897 U.S. 965 (1970).

125. *Reichhold Chemicals (Reichhold 2),* 288 NLRB 69 (1988) aff'd in relevant sub nom. *Teamsters Local 515 v. NLRB,* 906 F.2d 719 (D.C. Cir. 1990).

126. *Hydrotherm,* 302 NLRB No. 153, slip op. p. 12 (1991). Cf. *American Meat Packing Co.,* 301 NLRB No. 119 (1991); *Industrial Electric Reels, Inc.,* 310 NLRB No. 169 (1993).

127. *NLRB v. Truitt Manufacturing Co.,* 351 U.S. 149 (1956). Cf. *Advertisers Manufacturing Company,* 275 NLRB 100 (1985). See also *NLRB v. Acme Industrial Co.,* 385 U.S. 432 (1967). See generally Bartosic and Hartley, "The Employer's Duty to Supply Information to the Union," 58 Cornell L. Rev. 28 (1972).
Similarly the Court has limited information about employee test scores, which are characterized as confidential. *NLRB v. Detroit Edison Co.,* 440 U.S. 301 (1979). There are frequent disputes about employee personnel records. Compare *Washington Gas Light Company,* 278 NLRB 220 (1984) with *New Jersey Bell Telephone Co. v. NLRB,* 720 F.2d 789 (3d Cir. 1983). There are disputes about access to witness statements as well. *NLRB v. New Jersey Bell Telephone Co.,* 936 F.2d 144 (3d Cir. 1991); *Diversy Wyandotte Corp., Dekalb,* 302 NLRB No. 158 (1991); *Union Telephone and Telegraph Co.,* 309 NLRB No. 85 (1993). Unions are entitled to information concerning names of union officials who have applied to supervisory positions. *NLRB v. U.S. Postal Service,* 841 F.2d 141 (6th Cir. 1988). Unions have had difficulty in obtaining access to information regarding nonunit work, *Bohemia, Inc.,* 272 NLRB 1128 (1984); *United States*

Postal Service, 261 NLRB 505 (1982). But see *E. I. Dupont de Nemours v. NLRB,* 744 F.2d 536 (6th Cir. 1984). Employers have, however, been obliged to disclose relevant information on some bargaining issues. *Minnesota Mining and Mfg. Co.,* 261 NLRB 27 (1982) enfd. 711 F.2d 348 (D.C. Cir. 1988); *NLRB v. American National Can Co.,* 924 F.2d 518 (4th Cir. 1991).

128. *Neilsen Lithographing Co. v. NLRB,* 854 F.2d 1063, 1065 (7th Cir. 1988).

129. *Neilsen Lithographing Co.,* 305 NLRB No. 90 (1991). Accord, *Burruss Transfer, Inc.,* 307 NLRB No. 31 (1992); *Concrete Pipe & Products Corps.,* 305 NLRB No. 21 (1991); *Armored Transport of California, Inc.,* 288 NLRB No. 70 (1988); *A.M.F. Bowling Co., Inc.,* 303 NLRB No. 23 (1991); *Parsons Electric Company,* 304 NLRB No. 115 (1991); *United Paperworkers International Union v. NLRB,* 141 LRRM 2985 (6th Cir. 1992).

130. *United Steelworkers Local 571 v. NLRB,* 401 F.2d 434 (D.C. Cir. 1968) cert. denied 395 U.S. 946 (1969); *NLRB v. Western Wirebound Box Co.,* 356 F.2d 88 (9th Cir. 1966).

131. *United Steelworkers of America, Local Union 14534 v. NLRB,* 142 LRRM 2177 (D.C. Cir. 1993).

Chapter 7

1. Proposed Amendments to the National Labor Relations Act: Hearings on H.R. 8410 Before the Subcommittee on Labor-Management Relations of the House Committee on Education and Labor, 95th Cong., 1st Sess. 389 (statement of John H. Fanning). This proved to be a slight exaggeration. See chapter 1, note 14.

2. H.R. Rep. No. 95-687, 95th Cong., 1st Sess. 21 (1977). See Weiler, "Promises to Keep: Securing Workers' Rights & Self-organization under the NLRA", 96 Harv. L. Rev. 1769 (1983).

3. *Local 60, United Brotherhood of Carpenters v. NLRB,* 365 U.S. 651, 655 (1961); *NLRB v. Seven-Up Bottling,* 344 U.S. 344, 346 (1953). See also, for example, *NLRB v. J. S. Alberici Construction Co.,* 591 F.2d 463, 470 n.8 (8th Cir. 1979); *Packing House and Industrial Services v. NLRB,* 590 F.2d 688, 697 (8th Cir. 1978).

4. The circuit courts have gone farther, holding that the proper test is what the employees would have earned but for the wrongful dismissal and that this may be less than the result of multiplying the actual wage before dismissal by the time since dismissal if the employer would have discharged the employee anyway for legitimate reasons; *NLRB v. Fort Vancouver Plywood Co.,* 604 F.2d 596 (9th

Cir. 1979); *J.S. Alberici Construction Co.; Florsheim Shoe Store Co. v. NLRB,* 565 F.2d 1240 (2d Cir. 1977); *Sunderstrand Heat Transfer, Inc. v. NLRB,* 538 F.2d 1257 (7th Cir. 1976); *NLRB v. Local No. 2 of United Association of Plumbing and Pipefitting Industry,* 360 F.2d 428, 434 (2d Cir. 1966). Support for the "but for" test was found in *Golden State Bottling Co. v. NLRB,* 414 U.S. 168, 189–90 (1974). But see *Packing House and Industrial Services v. NLRB,* 590 F.2d at 697–98 (antiunion animus justifies order reinstating entire work force of predecessor company), following *NLRB v. International Van Lines,* 409 U.S. 48, 53 (1972).

5. *NLRB v. Gullett Gin Co.,* 340 U.S. 361 (1951). Cf. *NLRB v. State of Illinois Department of Employment Security,* 138 LRRM 2764 (N.D. Ill. 1991).

6. "The reasonableness of a worker's effort to secure substantially equivalent employment is determined by, *inter alia,* the economic climate in which the worker finds himself, the worker's skill and qualifications, and the worker's age and personal limitations." *Lundy Packing Co. v. NLRB,* 856 F.2d 627 (4th Cir. 1988). There is an obligation to seek new employment which is substantially equivalent to the position lost. *Kawasaki Motors v. NLRB,* 850 F.2d 524 (9th Cir. 1988). If a worker is required to lower his sights, the obligation exists only after a reasonable period of time. *Rainbow Coaches,* 280 NLRB No. 17 (1986); *Arlington Hotel Co., Inc.,* 287 NLRB No. 87 (1987). Conversely, there is no duty to search for a more lucrative interim employment once the discriminatee has embarked on a "legitimate course of interim employment." *F.E. Hazard, Ltd.,* 303 NLRB No. 130 (1991); *Fugazy Continental Corp.,* 276 NLRB 1334 (1985) enforcement granted 817 F.2d 979 (2d Cir. 1987). Employee misconduct forfeits both reinstatement and backpay. *Precision Window Manufacturing, Inc.,* 303 NLRB No. 141 (1991) enforcement denied 963 F.2d 1105 (8th Cir. 1992). Interim earnings that would not have been obtained from the employer in any event are not deductible. *Seattle Seahawks,* 304 NLRB No. 78 (1991) enforcement granted 142 LRRM 455 (D.C. Cir. 1993); *E.D.P. Medical Computer Systems,* 293 NLRB 857 (1989).

7. S. Rep. No. 95–628, 95th Cong. 2d Sess. 11 (1978).

8. W. Gould, "Prospects for Labor Law Reform: The Unions and Carter," *The Nation,* April 16, 1977, at 466–67.

9. in response to J.P. Stevens's many unfair labor practices, the Board has devised extraordinary remedies. For example, 380 F.2d 292 (2d Cir. 1967) requires that the employer post the Board notice of its violation in the plant where the unfair labor practice

occurred, and also in all of the company's forty-three plants, and that the notice be mailed to all employees in all plants; 441 F.2d 514 (5th Cir. 1971) and 461 F.2d 490 (4th Cir. 1972) require that the employer give the union, upon request, reasonable access to plant bulletin boards for a period of one year and that the Board order to be read to employees during working time; 406 F.2d 1017 (4th Cir. 1968) and 417 F.2d 533 (5th Cir. 1969) require the employer to give a list of names and addresses of all employees in all plants to the union; and 464 F.2d 1326 (2d Cir. 1972), cert. denied, 410 U.S. 926 (1973) provides for the payment to the NLRB of costs and expenses, counsel fees, and salaries in a civil contempt proceeding. Traditional remedies were regarded as insufficient for *J.P. Stevens* in 475 F.2d 973 (D.C. Cir. 1973) and compliance fines were imposed in 563 F.2d (2d Cir. 1977) but denied in 434 U.S. 1064 (1978). The history has been recounted in the context of more violations in *J.P. Stevens v. NLRB*, 638 F.2d 676 (4th Cir. 1980). The employer was also required to read the order in *Domsey Trading Corporation* 310 NLRB No. 127 (1993). Another egregious illustration of recidivist behavior warranted a corporatewide remedy in *Beverly California Corp.* 310 NLRB No. 37 (1993).

10. "Oversight Hearings on the National Labor Relations Board: Hearings before the Sub-committee on Labor-Management Relations of the House Committee on Education and Labor", 94th Cong., 1st Sess. 295–489.

11. *54th Annual Report of the National Labor Relations Board* (1989) at p. 249.

12. See *supra* note 35, chapter 4.

13. *54th Annual Report of the National Labor Relations Board* (1989) at p. 14.

14. There is no duty to bargain after an election and before certification where there are unresolved objections not claimed to be frivolous *Sunderstrand Heat Transfers, Inc. v. NLRB*, 538 F.2d 1257, 1259 (7th Cir. 1976), overruling the Board citing *General Electric Co.*, 163 NLRB 198 (1967), *Trinity St Co.*, 103 NLRB 1470 (1953); *Harbor Chevrolet Co.*, 93 NLRB 1326 (1951). If the Board certifies a union, the employer may refuse to bargain and not be guilty of an unfair labor practice if the employer carries the heavy burden of showing that the certification was incorrect [*NLRB v. Allis-Chalmers Corp.*, 601 F.2d 870, 871–72 (5th Cir. 1979); *NLRB v. Newton-New Haven Co.*, 506 F.2d 1035 (2d Cir. 1974); *NLRB v. Clarytona Manor, Inc.*, 479 F.2d 976 (7th Cir. 1973)].

15. *Ex-Cell-O Corp.,* 185 NLRB 107 (1970), rev'd and remanded to the Board, sub nom., *International Union, UAW v. NLRB,* 449 F.2d 1046, 1050 (D.C. Cir. 1971). The Board later reaffirmed its position in a case where the violation was "clear and flagrant" [*Tiidee Products, Inc.,* 194 NLRB 1234 (1972), enforced, 502 F.2d 349 (D.C. Cir. 1974), cert. denied, 421 U.S. 991 (1975)]. An additional problem for the formulation of expansive remedies is the Supreme Court's decision in *H.K. Porter Company v. NLRB,* 397 U.S. 99 (1970), which precludes the imposition of contract terms upon the parties as a remedy for unfair labor practice violations. But see *United States Postal Service,* 309 NLRB No. 3 (1992).

16. *Tiidee Products, Inc., supra.* But the court of appeals eliminated the award of litigation expenses. In a later case the Board refused litigation expenses, the court of appeals awarded them, but the Supreme Court reversed, saying this determination was for the Board [*NLRB v. Food Store Employees Local 347 (Hecks Inc.),* 417 U.S. 1 (1974)]. On remand, the Board stood by the rule of *Tiidee Products* but distinguished *Hecks, Inc.* on the ground that here the employer's position was debatable [*Hecks, Inc.,* 215 NLRB 765, 767 (1974)].

17. 29 USC §160 (j) (1976).

18. 29 USC §160 (1) (1976).

19. These are those practices that violate 8(b)(4)(A)–(C) or 8(b)(7) or 8(c), namely 29 USC §§158 (b)(4)(A)–(C), 158 (b)(7), 158(c)(1976). Included are the rules against secondary boycotts and recognitional picketing. See chapter 3.

20. W. Gould, *Black Workers in White Unions* (1977), pp. 281–315.

21. "Oversight Hearings on the National Labor Relations Board: Hearings before the Subcommittee on Labor-Management Relations of the House Committee on Education and Labor," 94th Cong., 1st Sess. 348 (statement of Jack Crowley).

22. "AFL-CIO Chief Calls Labor Laws a Dead Letter," *Wall Street Journal,* August 16, 1984, at 8; "Kirkland's Call to Void Labor Laws Ignites a Growing National Debate," *Wall Street Journal,* November 6, 1984, at 29, col. 3; W. Gould, "Mistaken Opposition to the NLRB," *The New York Times,* June 20, 1985, at 31, col. 2.

Chapter 8

1. See generally "Proceedings of the Twenty-Sixth Annual Meeting, National Academy of Arbitrators: Arbitration of Interest Disputes" (1974).

2. Noble, "Postal Contract Includes a Raise and Concession," *The New York Times,* December 25, 1984. 39 USC §101 et seq. (1984 Supp.).

3. Connecticut, Connecticut Gen. Stat. §22a–2.85g (1990); Delaware, 19 Del. C. §1615 (1991); Hawaii Rev. Stat. ch. 89, §89-1 et seq. as last amended eff. 7-1-84 (mandatory, package, firefighters only); Code of Iowa, ch. 20, §20-1 et seq. (1991); Maine, 13 M.R.S. §1958-B (1991); Massachusetts, A.L.M. ch. 150E, §9 (1992) (for police and firefighters but with different subject matter scope for each); Minnesota, Minn. Stat. §179A.16 (1991); Montana, title 39, ch. 31, Parts 1–4, MCA (1973) as last amended eff. 7/1/83 (at request of either party, package for firefighters in municipalities); Nebraska, R.R.S. Neb. §81-1382 (1991); Nevada, N.R.S. §288.101 et seq. (1991) (mandatory for firefighters and used under some conditions for other local government employees); New Jersey, §34:13A-16 (1991); North Dakota, N.D. Cent. Code §15-29-08 (1991) (Salaries and other monetary and fringe benefits for teachers); Ohio, Ohio Rev. Code Title 41, §4117.14 (1991); Vermont, 21 VSA §1733 (1991); Washington, RCW 47.64, 2701 (1991); Wisconsin, W.S.A. ch. 111, §111.70 et seq. as last amended eff. 3-20-84 (agreement of parties on order of Wisconsin Employment Relations Commission leads to either final offer or conventional arbitration for police and firefighters).

4. The twenty-four jurisdictions that currently have interest arbitration statutes are Alaska, Connecticut, Delaware, District of Columbia, Hawaii, Illinois, Indiana, Iowa, Maine, Massachusetts, Michigan, Minnesota, Montana, Nevada, New Jersey, New York, Ohio, Oregon, Pennsylvania, Rhode Island, Vermont, Washington, Wisconsin, and Wyoming. CCH, Labor Law Reporter, "State Laws."

5. For example, S.560, 92d Cong., 1st Sess. (1971).

6. Proceedings of the Twenty-Sixth Annual Meeting, National Academy of Arbitrators, Arbitration of Interest Disputes 79–80 (1976).

7. *NLRB v. Weingarten, Inc.,* 420 U.S. 251 (1975).

8. *Baton Rouge Waterworks Co.,* 246 NLRB 995 (1979).

9. The Supreme Court has rejected the proposition that failure to adhere to two arbitration awards and not to give them any "effect would impair the effectiveness of the dispute resolution process for which the parties bargained." *Metropolitan Edison Co. v. NLRB,* 460 U.S. 693 (1983). See also *Oil, Chemical and Atomic Workers, Local*

4-16000 v. Ethyl Corp., 644 F.2d 1044 (5th Cir. 1981); *Boston Shipping Association, Inc. v. International Longshoremen's Association (AFL-CIO)*, 659 F.2d 1 (1st Cir. 1981).

10. 29 USC §158(a)(5)(1976).

11. W. Usery, "Why Strikes Occur during the Term of Contract Agreements," 1976 Labor Relations Yearbook 181, 182 (Bureau of National Affairs); Southeastern Conference on Bargaining Trends (remarks of John Canestraight), 1976 Labor Relations Yearbook 175 (Bureau of National Affairs).

12. W. Gould, *Black Workers in White Unions* 211–42 (1977), W. Gould, "Labor Arbitration of Grievances Involving Racial Discrimination," 118 U. Pa. L. Rev. 40 (1969).

13. 42 USC §2000 (1976).

14. W. Gould, "Labor Arbitration of Grievances Involving Racial Discrimination," 118 Pa. L. Rev. 40, 46 (1969).

15. For example, *Acuff v. United Paperwork*, 404 F.2d 169 (5th Cir. 1968), cert. denied, 894 U.S. 987 (1969).

16. 353 U.S. 448 (1957).

17. *United Steelworkers v. American Manufacturing Co.*, 363 U.S. 564 (1960); *United Steelworkers v. Warrior and Gulf Navigation Co.*, 363 U.S. 574 (1960); *United Steelworkers v. Enterprise Wheel and Car Corp.*, 363 U.S. 593 (1960).

18. In *Pennoyer v. Neff*, 95 U.S. 714 (1878), the Supreme Court found that due process demanded the traditional rule of the common law: that jurisdiction over an individual could be achieved only by his voluntary appearance or by personal service of process within the state. This position was gradually liberalized in two ways. First, the need for presence within the state was given up (at first for particular sorts of cases, and then generally) when the court decided that it was enough for the person to have certain minimum contacts with the state sufficient to satisfy traditional notions of fair play and substantial justice [*International Shoe Co. v. Washington*, 826 U.S. 810 (1945)]. The various states are free to take as much of this constitutionally permitted jurisdiction as they desire. Second, the permissible means of service have been liberalized. The means must be reasonably calculated to apprise the out-of-state person of the suit *(International Shoe Co.)*. Once again, within those limits, the states are free to specify the permissible means of service.

19. The Court decided that the statute authorized federal courts to fashion a body of federal common law, and that the statute, as thus interpreted, was constitutional.

20. 353 U.S. at 458. The Court extended the reach of section 801, and the authority of the courts to establish a federal common law to union constitutions and suits by local unions against internationals to enforce them, in *Plumbers and Pipefitters v. Local 334*, 452 U.S. 615 (1981).

21. *Groves v. Ring Screw Works*, 111 S.Ct. 498 (1990).

22. "Final adjustment by a method agreed upon by the parties is declared to be the desirable method for the settlement of grievance disputes arising over the application or interpretation of an existing collective bargaining agreement." 1129 USC §173(d)(1976).

23. *International Association of Machinists v. Cutler-Hammer, Inc.*, 271 App. Div. 917, 67 N.Y.S.2d 317 (1947), affirmed 297 N.Y. 519, 74 N.E.2d 464 (1948).

24. *Warrior and Gulf Navigation Co.*, 363 U.S. 574 (1960).

25. *Id.* at 581–82. On the other hand, the Court of Appeals for the District of Columbia Circuit has held that where the parties expressly provide through a no-oral-modification clause, federal labor policy promotes its enforcement in order to enable those who value certainty to have it even if at the price of relinquishing greater flexibility. *Martinsville Nylon Employees Council Corp. v. NLRB*, 140 LRRM 2873 (D.C. Cir. 1992).

26. *Id.* at 578.

27. *Id.* at 580.

28. *Groves v. Ring Screw Works*, 111 S.Ct. 498 (1990). Cf. *Local 705 v. Schneider, 705 International Brotherhood of Teamsters v. Schneider Tank Lines*, 958 F.2d 171 (7th Cir. 1992).

29. *AT&T Technologies, Inc. v. Communications Workers of America*, 475 U.S. 643 (1986). In a second opinion of a similar nature, Justice Kennedy, speaking for a 6–3 majority in *Litton Financial Printing Division v. NLRB*, 501 U.S. 111 S.Ct. 2215 (1991), held that the presumption in favor of arbitrability does not apply to disputes about the arbitrability of postexpiration grievances. Cf. *Nolde Bros., Inc. v. Bakery Workers*, 430 U.S. 243 (1977).

30. *W.R. Grace & Company v. Local Union 759, International Union of the United Rubber, Cork, Linoleum and Plastic Workers of America*, 461

U.S. 757 (1983). Subsequent to *W.R. Grace,* courts have identified "well-defined and dominant" public policies, see, for example, *Amalgamated Meat Cutters and Butcher Workmen of North America v. Great Western Food Company,* 712 F.2d 122 (5th Cir. 1988) (arbitration award reinstating driver caught drinking on duty violated public policy against professional drivers drinking and driving); *U.S. Postal Service v. American Postal Workers Union, AFL-CIO,* 786 F.2d 822 (1st Cir. 1984) (arbitration award reinstating postal employee convicted of embezzling postal funds violated public policy of trust and efficiency for the postal service); *Northrop Corporation v. Triad Financial Establishment,* 598 F.Supp. 928 (C.D. CA. 1984) (portion of arbitration award vacated because public policy involving Department of Defense regulations and a Saudi Arabian decree prevented performance of certain phases of a marketing agreement); *Stead Motors of Walnut Creek v. Automotive Machinists Lodge No. 1173,* 132 LRRM 2689 (9th Cir. 1989) (en banc) (California's general interest in safe motor vehicles does not form an explicit and well-defined dominant public policy that would bar reinstatement of a mechanic who committed reckless acts in the course of his or her employment.) The principle that arbitrators must be faithful to the contract and not "manifest an infidelity to this obligation" can be found in *United Steelworkers of America v. Enterprise Wheel and Car Corp.,* 363 U.S. 598, 597 (1960).

31. *United Paperworkers International Union v. Misco,* 484 U.S. 29 (1987).

32. *Id.* at 43. See generally Gould, "Judicial Review of Labor Arbitration Awards—Thirty Years of the Steelworkers Trilogy: The Aftermath of AT&T and Misco," 64 Notre Dame L. Rev. 464 (1989).

33. 398 U.S. 235 (1970).

34. *Id.* at 244.

35. *Id.* at 245. See *Dowd Box Co. v. Courtney,* 368 U.S. 502 (1962).

36. *Id.* at 248 (footnote omitted).

37. *Id.* at 251.

38. *Id.* at 250.

39. *Buffalo Forge Co. v. United Steelworkers,* 428 U.S. 397 (1976); W. Gould, "On Labor Injunctions Pending Arbitration: Recasting Buffalo Forge," 80 Stan. L. Rev. 588 (1978); see also W. Gould, "On Labor Injunctions, Unions and the Judges: The Boys Market Case," 1970 S.Ct. Rev. 215. The Supreme Court later relied on both *Boys Markets* and *Buffalo Forge* in ruling that an injunction could not be

issued against the International Longshoremen's Association for refusing to handle cargo bound to or coming from the Soviet Union in protest of the invasion of Afghanistan. *Jacksonville Bulk Terminals, Inc. v. International Longshoremen's Assoc.,* 457 U.S. 702 (1982). The Court found that the underlying dispute, "whether viewed as an expression of the Union's 'moral outrage' at Soviet military policy or as an expression of sympathy for the people of Afghanistan, is plainly not arbitrable under the collective bargaining agreement." *Id.* at 711.

40. *Teamsters, Local 174 v. Lucas Flour Co.,* 369 U.S. 95 (1962).

41. *Drake Bakeries v. Bakery Workers,* 370 U.S. 254 (1962).

42. *Carbon Fuel v. United Mine Workers,* 444 U.S. 212 (1979). This decision does not deal with local union liability. The question is often an academic one, since locals often do not have much money in their treasuries.

43. *Atkinson v. Sinclair Roofing Co.,* 370 U.S. 238 (1962).

44. *Complete Auto Transit, Inc. v. Reis,* 451 U.S. 401 (1981).

45. See note 39. Local union liability was established on one or another of these theories in *Easzor Express, Inc. v. International Brotherhood of Teamsters,* 520 F.2d 951 (3d Cir. 1975), cert. Denied, 424 U.S. 935 (1976); *United Steelworkers of America v. Lorain,* 616 F.2d 919 (6th Cir. 1980); *Keebler v. Bakery Workers, Local 492-A,* 104 LRRM 2625 (ED. Pa., 1980). See generally M. Whitman, "Wildcat Strikes: The Union's Narrowing Path to Rectitude," 50 Ind. L. J. 472 (1975) W. Gould, "Taft-Hartley Comes to Great Britain," 81 Yale L. J. 1421 (1972).

46. *Metropolitan Edison Co. v. NLRB,* 460 U.S. 693 (1983). The Court also concluded that statutory immunization may be waived in the collective bargaining agreement.

47. *Id.* at 1472.

48. The leading case in which the deferral doctrine was developed is *Spielberg Manufacturing Co.,* 112 NLRB 1080 (1955). See also International Harvester Co., 13 NLRB 928 (1962), enforced sub nom. *Ramsey v. NLRB,* 327 F.2d 784 (7th Cir.), cert. denied, 377 U.S. 1003 (1964). The problems involved in applying *Spielberg* are still considerable. See, for example, *NLRB v. Ancus Bros. Inc.-Maxwell,* 620 F.2d 867 (3d Cir. 1980); *NLRB v. Max Factor & Co.,* 640 F.2d 197 (9th Cir. 1980); cert. denied, 451 U.S. 983 (1981); "Judicial Review and the Trend toward More Stringent NLRB Standards on Arbitral Deferrals" (Comment), 129 U. Pa. L. Rev. 788 (1981).

49. *Olin Corporation,* 268 NLRB 573 (1984).

50. *Id.*

51. *Collyer Insulated Wire,* 192 NLRB 837 (1971). The Board has extended the deferral obligation to a grievance procedure that does not provide for arbitration. *August A. Busch & Co., of Massachusetts, Inc.,* 309 NLRB No. 111 (1992). See *William E. Arnold Co. v. Carpenters District Council,* 417 U.S. 12, 16–17 (1974); *Carey v. Westinghouse Electric Corp.,* 375 U.S. 261, 270–72 (1964).

52. For example, *General American Transport Corp.,* 228 NLRB No. 102 (1977) (the Board refused to extend *Collyer* to 8(a)(3) cases); *Machinists Lodges 700, 743, 1746 v. NLRB,* 525 F.2d 237 (2d Cir. 1975); *IBEW Local 2188 v. NLRB,* 494 F.2d 1087 (D.C. Cir. 1974), cert. denied, 419 U.S. 834 (1974); *Kansas Meat Packers,* 198 NLRB 543 (1972), *Anaconda Wire and Cable Co.,* 201 NLRB 839 (1973).

53. *United Technologies Corporation,* 268 NLRB 557 (1984).

54. 376 U.S. 543 (1964).

55. 482 U.S. 27, 43 (1987).

56. *Id.* at 41.

57. *Capitol Steel and Iron Co.,* 299 NLRB No. 91 (1990).

58. *NLRB v. Burns International Security Services,* 406 U.S. 272 (1972). Under the Court's holding, the successor may establish its own terms and conditions of employment unless it declares its intention to hire the predecessors employees. Under such circumstances the successor would be bound by the predecessor's terms and conditions of employment unless it made it clear that it was offering employment on different terms. *Spruce Up Corp.,* 209 NLRB 194 (1974); *Worcester Manufacturing, Inc.,* 306 NLRB No. 39 (1992). Where the successor has unlawfully discriminated against the employees of the predecessor, the terms and conditions of the previous employment relationship will be imposed pending good faith negotiations between the parties. *U.S. Marine Corp. v. NLRB,* 944 F.2d 1305 (7th Cir. 1971).

59. *H. K. Porter v. NLRB,* 397 U.S. 99 (1970).

60. *Howard Johnson Co. v. Detroit Local Joint Executive Board, Hotel Employees International Union,* 417 U.S. 249 (1974). Cf. *United States Can Co. v. NLRB,* 142 LRRM 2313 (7th Cir. 1993). Judicial determination of the successorship issue does not preclude the Board's authority. *Local 32B-32J Service Employees International Union v. NLRB,* 142 LRRM 2238 (2d Cir. 1993).

61. *Republic Steel Corp. v. Maddox*, 379 U.S. 650 (1965). The decision authorizing individual actions is *Smith v. Evening News Association*, 371 U.S. 195 (1962).

62. 386 U.S. 171 (1967).

63. 459 U.S. 212, (1983).

64. *Id.* at 602–603 (White, J. dissenting). The employee who seeks back-pay relief in a duty of fair representation case has a constitutional right to a jury trial under the Seventh Amendment.

65. 415 U.S. 36 (1974).

66. 415 U.S. 36, 60 (1974).

67. *Id.* at n. 21.

68. *Basic Vegetable Products, Inc.*, 64 Labor Arbitration Reports 620 (1975); Settlement Agreement between Weyerhauser Co. and International Woodworkers of America, May 1979 (in the author's files).

69. *Barrentine v. Arkansas-Best Freight System*, 450 U.S. 728 (1981). Chief Justice Burger dissented, in an opinion joined in by Justice Rehnquist.

70. *McDonald v. City of West Branch*, 466 U.S. 284, 286 (1984).

71. 111 S.Ct. 1647 (1991).

72. 81 Stat. 602, as amended, 29 USC §621. The Court had previously held that arbitration agreements could be enforceable pursuant to the FAA. See *Mitsubishi Motors Corp. v. Soler Chrysler-Plymouth, Inc.*, 473 U.S. 614 (1985); *Shearson/American Express, Inc. v. McMahon*, 482 U.S. 220 (1987); *Rodriguez de Quijas v. Shearson/American Express, Inc.*, 490 U.S. 477 (1989).

73. Justice Stevens filed a dissenting opinion that was joined in by Justice Marshall.

74. *Gilmer, supra* at note 71.

75. *Id.* at 27.

76. *Service Employees International Union v. County of Napa*, 99 Cal. App. 3d 946, 160 Cal. Rptr. 810 (1979); J. Toole, "Judicial Activism in Public Sector Grievance Arbitration: A Study of Recent Developments," 33 Arbitration J. 6 (1978). In the matter of the Arbitration between *The City of Plattsburgh v. Local 788 and New York Council 66, AFSCME, AFL-CIO*, 485 N.Y.S.2d 618, 619 (A.D. 3d 1985) ("the

policy of favoring arbitration in private sector labor relations does not apply equally in the field of public employment . . . Absent a clear, unequivocal agreemnt to the contrary, it must be taken for granted that the public body did not intend to refer a particular matter to arbitration"). But see *The City and County of Denver v. Denver Firefighters, Local 858 AFL-CIO,* 663 P.2d 1032, 1041 (Colo. 1983) (firefighters filed complaint against the city claiming city breached collective bargaining agreement in refusing to submit a grievance to binding arbitration. Court found that "on its face . . . claim is arbitrable because it requires interpretation and application of standards of employer conduct agreed to by the City"); *In the Matter of Arbitration: Nicolet High School District v. Nicolet Education Association,* 348 N.W.2d 175, 178 118 W.2d 707 (Wis. 1984) ("This court has developed several well-settled rules governing review of arbitrator's decisions. An arbitrator's award is presumptively valid, and it will be disturbed only when its invalidity is demonstrated by clear and convincing evidence"), *Board of Control of Ferris State College v. Michigan AFSCME, Council 25, Local 1609,* 361 N.W.2d 342, 343 Mich. App. 1984) (Court follows the standard of limited review from the *Steelworkers Trilogy,* "drawing its essence from the collective bargaining agreement," a position that has also been adopted by the Michigan Supreme Court).

77. T. Kochan, "Dynamics of Dispute Resolution in the Public Sector," in Public Sector Bargaining (Industrial Relations Research Association Series, 1979), pp. 150, 154.

78. *Id.* at 175.

Chapter 9

1. *Steele v. Louisville and Nashville Railroad,* 323 U.S. 192 (1944) (a duty of fair representation under the Railway Labor Act, 45 USC §§151 et seq.). The Supreme Court found a duty of fair representation under the NLRA in *Syres v. Oil Workers Local 23,* 350 U.S. 892 (1955) *(per curiam),* reversing 223 F.2d 739 (5th Cir. 1955). The Board first found a breach of the duty of fair representation to violate §8(b) in *Miranda Fuel Co.,* 140 NLRB 181 (1962), enforcement denied 326 F.2d 172 (2d Cir. 1963).

2. *Air Line Pilots Association, International v. O'Neill,* 111 S.Ct. 1127 (1991). The Civil Service Reform Act of 1978 creates no implied private cause of action on behalf of federal employees for a union's breach of a statutory duty of fair representation because, under that statutory scheme, claims are to be adjudicated administratively by the Federal Labor Relations Authority. *Karahalios v. National Federation of Federal Employees, Local 1263,* 489 U.S. 527 (1989).

3. *Vaca v. Sipes*, 386 U.S. at 190.

4. The decision that seems to have gone furthest in establishing the duty of fair representation obligation for negligent union behavior is *Dutrisac v. Caterpillar Tractor Co.*, 749 F.2d 1270 (9th Cir. 1983); see also *De Anyo v. Sindicato ec Trabajadores Packing, AFL-CIO*, 425 F.2d 281, (1st Cir. 1970) (union's total failure to investigate and process grievances is deemed arbitrary and thus a breach of its duty of fair representation); *Ruzicka v. General Motors Corp.*, 523 F.2d 306, affirmed on rehearing, 528 F.2d 912 (6th Cir. 1975) (union's negligent failure to file for arbitration of employee's grievance within prescribed time limits held to constitute a breach of its duty of fair representation); *Malone v. U.S. Postal Service*, 526 F.2d 1099 (6th Cir. 1975) (union's negligent failure to take any action in processing employee's grievance held to be a breach of its duty of fair representation), *Robesky v. Quantas Empire Airways*, 573 F.2d 1082 (9th Cir. 1978) (duty of fair representation violated by union's nondisclosure of information critical to employee's determination of whether to accept employer's settlement offer); *Thomas v. United Parcel, Inc.*, 132 LRRM 3052 (7th Cir. 1989) (strict standard of competency for union officials processing grievances not imposed, but general definition of standard not articulated). Cf. *Price v. Southern Pacific Transp. Co.*, 586 F.2d 750 (9th Cir. 1978) (union's failure to file a grievance had to be neither egregious nor arbitrary). See generally A. Cox, "Rights under a Labor Agreement," 69 Harv. L. Rev. 601 (1956); K. Hanslowe, "Individual Rights in Collective Labor Relations," 45 Cornell L. Q. 25 (1959); C. Summers, "The Individual Employee's Rights under the Collective Bargaining Agreement: What Constitutes Fair Representation?" 126 U. Pa. L. Rev. 251 (1977). Punitive damages are not available when the duty is violated. *IBEW v. Faust*, 442 U.S. 42 (1979).

5. *Conley v. Gibson*, 355 U.S. 41 (1957); *Ford Motor Co. v. Huffman*, 345 U.S. 330 (1953). The Court has held that the union's duty of fair representation is applicable to its administration of a hiring hall. *Breininger v. Sheet Metal Workers*, 493 U.S. 67 (1989).

6. *Air Line Pilots International Association v. O'Neill, supra* note 2. Said the Court: ". . . Congress did not intend judicial review of a union's performance to permit the court to substitute its own view of the proper bargain for that reached by the union. Rather, Congress envisioned the relationship between the courts and labor unions as similar to that between the courts and the legislature." *Id.* at 25.

7. *Clayton v. International Union, UAW*, 451 U.S. 679 (1981). The employee has the obligation to exhaust the procedures set forth

in the collective bargaining agreement. [*Republic Steel Corp. v. Maddox*, 379 U.S. 650 (1965).]

8. *Acuff v. United Papermakers*, 404 F.2d 169 (5th Cir. 1968), cert. denied, 394 U.S. 987 (1969).

9. *Smith v. Hussmann Refrigerator Co.*, 619 F.2d 1229 (8th Cir. 1980). See also *Clark v. Hein-Werner Corp.*, 8 Wis.2d 264, 99 N.W.2d 132 (1962).

10. *Hines v. Anchor Motor Frieght*, 424 U.S. 554 (1976).

11. *Id.* at 571. Punitive damages may not be obtained in a duty of fair representation case. *Electrical Workers v. Foust*, 442 U.S. 42 (1979). A jury trial may be obtained where money damages are sought. *Teamsters, Local 391 v. Terry*, 494 U.S. 558 (1990).

12. *United Parcel Service, Inc. v. Mitchell*, 451 U.S. 56 (1981). The result in *United Parcel* was to reduce the period from six years (contract actions) to ninety days (arbitration awards). Only Justice Stevens dissented. The statute of limitations for breach of collective-bargaining agreements is state law [*Auto Workers v. Hoosier Cardinal Corp.*, 383 U.S. 696 (1965)].

13. *Del Costello v. International Brotherhood of Teamsters*, 462 U.S. 151, 66 (1983). The majority of the circuit courts of appeal have chosen to apply *Del Costello* retroactively; see *Graves v. Smith's Transfer Corporation*, 736 F.2d 819 (1st Cir. 1984); *Assad v. Mt. Sinai Hospital*, 725 F.2d 837 (2d Cir. 1984), *Perez v. Dana Corporation, Parish Frame Division*, 718 F.2d 581 (3d Cir. 1983); *Murray v. Branch Motor Express Company*, 723 F.2d 1146 (4th Cir. 1983); *Edwards v. Sea-Land Service, Inc.*, 720 F.2d 857 (5th Cir. 1983); *Lincoln v. Machinists and Aerospace Workers*, 723 F.2d 627 (8th Cir. 1983); *Rogers v. Lockheed Georgia Company*, 720 F.2d 1247 (11th Cir. 1983). The Ninth Circuit has not applied *Del Costello* retroactively. See *Edwards v. Teamsters Local Union No. 36, Building Material and Dump Truck Drivers*, 719 F.2d 1036 (9th Cir. 1983).

14. 373 U.S. 734 (1963).

15. 388 U.S. 175 (1967).

16. W. Gould, "Solidarity Forever—Or Hardly Ever," 66 Cornell L. Rev. 77 (1980).

17. *Pattern Makers' League of North America v. NLRB*, 473 U.S. 95 (1985). Under a maintenance of membership provision in the collective bargaining agreement that gives workers a period of time in which to opt in or opt out of the union, there is a right to resign

even when there is no hiatus between the contracts that require membership. *Asarco, Inc.,* 309 NLRB No. 166 (1992). Written notice of an intent to resign from the union can be required. *Michigan Model Manufacturers Association, Inc.,* 310 NLRB No. 153 (1993). The Court has also held that unions may discipline supervisor members so long as the discipline is not imposed in connection with collective bargaining or grievance administration responsibilities exercised by such supervisor members. *NLRB v. International Brotherhood of Electrical Workers, Local 340,* 481 U.S. 573 (1987). Recognitional picketing that does not require the employer to accept contract terms relating to the selection of grievance representatives is not violative of the Act. In *Land Lakes Management, Inc. v. NLRB,* 142 LRRM 2774 (D.C. Cir. 1993). Cf. *Local 60, United Association of Journeyman & Apprentices of the Plumbing and Pipefitting Industry v. NLRB,* 941 F.2d 1326 (5th Cir. 1991).

18. *Id.* at 110–14. The principles of *Pattern Makers* have been applied to the right of the individual to repudiate an authorization to have his or her dues checked off for a period of a year under a collective bargaining agreement. The right to refrain means, in the Board's view, that it is

. . . reasonable for us to conclude that an employee who has promised only to pay union "membership" dues by checkoff for 1 year has not necessarily thereby obliged himself to continue paying such dues throughout that period—i.e., to continue assisting the union—*even* where he is no longer a union member. We will require clear and unmistakable language waiving the right to refrain from assisting a union, just as we require such evidence of waiver with regard to other statutory rights . . .

The policy [set forth in *Pattern Makers*] warrants the application of a test that will assure that the extraction of moneys from an employee's wages to assist a union, if not authorized by a lawful union—security clause, is in accord with the employee's voluntary agreement. If the employee did not agree, when he signed the authorization, to have "regular membership dues" deducted even when he is no longer a union member, then the employee's continued financial support of the union is not "voluntary" after he has resigned . . .

Explicit language within the checkoff authorization clearly setting forth an obligation to pay dues even in the absence of union membership will be required to establish that the employee has bound himself or herself to pay the dues even after resignation of membership. If an authorization contains such language, dues may properly continue to be deducted from the employee's earnings and turned over to the union during the entire agreed-upon period of irrevocability, even if the employee states he or she has had a change of heart and wants to revoke the authorization.

Lockheed Space Operations Co., Inc., 302 NLRB No. 49 (1991), pp. 19–20, 21, and 22. See also *United States Postal Service,* 302 NLRB

No. 50 (1991); *National Oil Well, Inc.*, 302 NLRB No. 59 (1991); *Stone Container Corp.*, 302 NLRB No. 139 (1991).

19. *NLRB v. Boeing Co.*, 412 U.S. 67 (1973).

20. *Abood v. Detroit Board of Education*, 431 U.S. 209 (1977).

21. Pub. L. 86-257, Sept. 14, 1959, 73 Stat. 519, 29 U.S.C. §§401 et seq. (1976). This statute has spawned litigation about the union's fiduciary duty to members; see, for instance, *Morrisey v. Curran*, 650 F.2d 1267 (2d Cir. 1981). The Court has held in *Reed v. United Transportation Union*, 488 U.S. 319 (1989) that the appropriate statute of limitations for free speech and assembly cases is borrowed from state personal injury actions.

22. *United Steelworkers of America, AFL-CIO-CLC v. Sadlowski*, 457 U.S. 102, 109 (1982).

23. *Id.* at 124. But see *Reed v. United Transportation Union, supra*, where Justice Brennan, speaking for the Court, stated that Landrum-Griffin's protection of free speech and assembly ". . . was patterned after the First Amendment." *Id.* at 326. The "some evidence" standard that applies to a union decision relating to procedural deficiency in due process disputes, does not apply to the free speech guarantees of the statute. *Black v. Ryder/P.I.E. Nationwide*, 140 LRRM 2904 (6th Cir. 1992).

24. *Id.* at 124.

25. *Id.*

26. *Finnegan v. Leu*, 456 U.S. 431 (1982).

27. *Id.* at 437.

28. *Id.* at 441 n. 11. See *Cotter v. Owens*, 753 F.2d 223 (2d Cir. 1985).

29. *Sheet Metal Workers' International Association v. Lynn*, 488 U.S. 347 (1989).

30. *Id.* at 355. The establishment of a rival union with dual unionism is not speech protected by Landrum-Griffin. *Ferguson v. International Association of Iron Workers*, 854 F.2d 1169 (9th Cir. 1988).

31. *Alvey v. General Electric Co.*, 622 F.2d 1279 (7th Cir. 1980). See generally A. Cox, "Internal Affairs of Labor Unions under the Labor Reform Act of 1959," 58 Mich. L. Rev. 819 (1960).

32. *Williams v. International Typographical Union*, 423 F.2d 1295 (10th Cir.), cert. denied, 400 U.S. 824 (1970).

33. 665 F.2d 1096 (D.C. Cir. 1981).

34. *Bauman v. Presser,* (D.C. DC. 1984)

35. *Id.* at 2396.

36. *Ackley v. Western Conference of Teamsters,* 958 F.2d 1463 (9th Cir. 1992). Cf. *Acri v. International Association of Machinists,* 781 F.2d 1393 (9th Cir.), cert. denied, 479 U.S. 816 (1986).

37. The court said that in order to maintain an action predicated upon misrepresentation and nondisclosure, there must be a causal relationship between the alleged misrepresentation and the injury and a showing that the outcome of the ratificaiton vote would have been different, *and* that had it been different, the company would have acceded to the union's demands. This is an extremely rigid test, initially established in *Acri,* and one which the court in *Ackley* characterized as "rightly . . . difficult to satisfy. . . ." *Id.* at 1473.

38. *Ackley, supra* at note 36.

39. The court stated further:

Time is of the essence during contract negotiation and ratification; a few days may mean the difference between an amicable resolution of labor-management differences and a bitter and extended strike. Similarly, when a strike is in progress, if it cannot be ended by a quick ratification vote conducted immediately after a tentative agreement is reached, both sides may suffer serious and even irreparable economic injury—economic injury that both would desperately wish to avoid. Unlike other elections, a contract ratification vote cannot be scheduled in advance, or set for some pre-established date. No one knows until an agreement is reached whether or when negotiators will arrive at a contract. Because there may be an urgent need for speedy ratification, there may not be an opportunity for full argument on each of the provisions of the contract. In addition, ratification procedures must be tailored to the unique characteristics and needs of each union. Some unions span large geographic areas, while others are purely local in nature. The members of some unions work at fixed locations; in other unions, members spend a considerable amount of their working time on the road or in the air. As a result of these and other differences, some groups of union members may prefer that the union hold ratification meetings, while others may opt for mail balloting procedure. Neither of these procedures is ideal. Mail balloting may impede full debate on important issues, while an open meeting procedure may preclude the type of review of the entire contract that might otherwise be desirable. The individual unions are better suited than the courts to the task of determining what is best for their members—when and under what circumstances ratification votes are appropriate and what procedures are best suited to their members' needs and work schedules. (*Id.* at 38)

40. *Merk v. Jewel Food Stores,* 945 F.2d 889 (7th Cir. 1991) cert. denied 111 S.Ct. 1951 (1992).

41. *Id.* at 905. The court distinguished *Chrysler Worker's Association v. Chrysler Corp.,* 834 F.2d 573 (6th Cir. 1987) on the ground that transfer rights were involved in the former case whereas in *Merk* a reduction of a wage level in the bargaining unit across the board was involved here. Cf. *Gatliff Coal Co. v. Cox,* 152 F.2d 52 (6th Cir. 1945).

42. *Id.* at 905.

43. 29 USC §461.

44. 29 USC §§481 et seq.

45. 29 USC §481 (e)(1976). See generally *Hodgson v. Local 6799, United Steelworkers,* 403 U.S. 333 (1971), *Wirtz v. Hotel, Motel and Club Employees Union, Local 6,* 391 U.S. 492 (1968); *Calhoon v. Harvey,* 379 U.S. 134 (1964).

46. 404 U.S. 528 (1972).

47. *Local No. 82, Furniture and Piano Moving v. Crowley,* 467 U.S. 526 (1984).

48. 111 S.Ct. 880 (1991).

49. *Id.* at 887–88.

50. *Theodus v. McLaughlin,* 852 F.2d 1380 (D.C. Cir. 1988).

51. 18 USC §1961–68 (1970). See chapter 4, footnote 22.

52. Cf. *United States v. Congress of Industrial Organizations,* 335 U.S. 106 (1948).

53. *International Association of Machinists v. Street,* 367 U.S. 740 (1961). Cf. *Railway Clerks v. Allen,* 373 U.S. 113 (1963). The seminal case is *Railway Employees v. Hanson,* 351 U.S. 225 (1956). See also *Pipefitters Local 562 v. United States,* 407 U.S. 385 (1972). Although the Supreme Court has not confronted the issue, the weight of authority is that union members may not object to dues spent for purposes that are not germane to collective bargaining. *Kidwell v. TCIU,* 946 F.2d 283 (4th Cir. 1991) *cert. denied.*

54. 487 U.S. 735 (1988).

55. *Abood v. Detroit Board of Education,* 431 U.S. 209 (1977).

56. Executive Order requiring federal contractors to notify workers of rights under *Beck v. Communications Workers,* signed by President

Bush April 13, 1992, 72 DLR D-1, 1992. For a thorough analyses of *Beck*, see Dau-Schmidt, "Union Security Agreements under the National Labor Relations Act: The Statute, the Constitution, and the Court Opinion in *Beck*," 27 Harv. J. on Legis. 51 (1990); "Topol, Union Shops, State Action and the National Labor Relations Act," 101 Yale L. J. 1135 (1992).

57. Kelly, "President Moves in Favor of Labor," *The New York Times*, February 3, 1993, at A12, col. 1.

58. *Ellis v. Brotherhood of Railway, Airline and Steamship Clerks*, 466 U.S. 435 (1984).

59. *Id.* at 1890. Accord, in the public sector arena, *Chicago Teachers, Union Local No. 1 v. Hudson*, 475 U.S. 292 (1986).

60. *Chicago Teachers Union Local No. 1 v. Hudson, supra.*

61. *Id.* at 295.

62. *Ellis v. Railway Clerks, supra* note 57.

63. *Lehnert v. Ferris Faculty Association*, 111 S.Ct. 1950 (1991).

64. *International Association of Machinists v. Street, supra* note 53.

Chapter 10

1. The following states have public-employee legislation: Alabama, Alaska, California, Connecticut, Delaware, Florida, Georgia, Hawaii, Idaho, Illinois, Indiana, Iowa, Kansas, Louisiana, Maine, Maryland, Massachusetts, Michigan, Minnesota, Missouri, Montana, Nebraska, Nevada, New Hampshire, New Jersey, New Mexico, New York, North Dakota, Ohio, Oklahoma, Oregon, Pennsylvania, Rhode Island, South Dakota, Tennessee, Texas, Vermont, Washington, Wisconsin, Wyoming, and Washington, D.C. The Indiana Public Employees Collective Bargaining Act was repealed effective September 1, 1982. However, teachers in Indiana still have a statutory right to bargain collectively. Five states—Virginia, North Carolina, Louisiana, West Virginia, and South Carolina—although they do not have any public employee bargaining laws, have recognized grievance procedures for some public employees.

2. H. Edwards, "The Emerging Duty to Bargain in the Public Sector," 71 Mich. L. Rev. 885, 896 (1973).

3. 5 USC §1101 et seq. Pub. L. No. 95-454, 92 Stat. 1111. The Supreme Court has addressed the authority of the Federal Labor Relations Authority, which has jurisdiction over unfair labor practice matters under the Civil Service Reform Act, in a variety of

areas. See, for instance, *Federal Labor Relations Authority v. Aberdeen Proving Ground*, 485 U.S. 409 (1988); *Department of the Treasury, Internal Revenue Service v. Federal Labor Relations Authority*, 494 U.S. 922 (1990); *Fort Stewart Schools v. Federal Labor Relations Authority*, 495 U.S. 641 (1990).

4. 39 USC §1206.

5. *American Federation of State, County and Municipal Employees, AFL-CIO v. Woodward*, 406 F.2d 137 (8th Cir. 1969).

6. *United States Civil Service Commission v. National Association of Letter Carriers*, 413 U.S. 548, 564 (1973); *Pickering v. Board of Education*, 391 U.S. 563, 568 (1968).

7. *Shelton v. Tucker*, 364 U.S. 479 (1960).

8. There is authority on policemen: *Lutine v. Van Cleave*, 483 F.2d 966, 967 (10th Cir. 1978); *Vorbeek v. McNeal*, 407 F. Supp. 733 (E.D. Mo. 1976) (three-judge court), affirmed, 426 U.S. 948, rehearing denied, 429 U.S. 874.

9. It is permissible to prevent fire-department officers from joining the same union as rank-and-file employees. *Firefighters' Local 2498 v. York County*, 589 F.2d 775 (4th Cir. 1978); *Elk Grove Firefighters' Local No. 2340 v. Williss*, 400 F. Supp. 1097 (N.D. Ill. 1975), affirmed, 539 F.2d 714 (7th Cir. 1976); *Firefighters v. City of Tupelo*, 489 F.Supp. 1224 (N.D. Miss. 1977). A regulation prohibiting police officers from joining "any labor organization whose membership is not exclusively limited to full-time law enforcement officers" impermissibly limits police officers' rights of association under the First Amendment; *Mescall v. Rochford*, 101 LRRM 8186 (N.D. Ill. 1979), aff'd 655 F.2d 111 (7th Cir. 1981).

10. *United Federation of Postal Clerks v. Blount*, 825 F. Supp. 879 (D.C.D.C. 1971) (three-judge court), affirmed, 404 U.S. 802; *Vorbeek v. McNeil, supra* note 8; *Loutine v. Van Cleave, supra* note 8.

11. *County Sanitation District No. 2 of Los Angeles v. County Employees Association SEIU*, 88 Cal.3d 564 (1985).

12. *Smith v. Arkansas State Highway Employees*, 441 U.S. 468 (1979).

13. *City of Madison, Joint School District No. 8 v. Wisconsin Employment Relations Commission*, 429 U.S. 167 (1976).

14. *Perry Education Association v. Perry Local Educators' Association*, 460 U.S. 37 (1983).

15. *NLRB v. Magnavox Co.,* 415 U.S. 322 (1974); Helton v. NLRB, 656 F.2d 888 (D.C. Cir. 1981).

16. *Ysleta Federation of Teachers v. Ysleta Independent School District,* 720 F.2d 1429 (5th Cir. 1988).

17. *Minnesota State Board for Community Colleges v. Knight,* 465 U.S. 271 (1984).

18. *Board of Regents v. Roth,* 408 U.S. 564 (1972); *Perry v. Sindermann,* 408 U.S. 598 (1972); *Arnett v. Kennedy,* 416 U.S. 134 (1974); *Goss v. Lopez,* 419 U.S. 565 (1975); *Bishop v. Wood,* 426 U.S. 841 (1976); *Davis v. Scherer,* 468 U.S. 183, (1984), *Cleveland Board of Education v. Loudermill,* 470 U.S. 532 (1985).

19. *Cleveland Board of Education,* 470 U.S. 532, 37 (1985).

20. *Elrod Burns,* 427 U.S. 347 (1976); *Branti v. Finkel,* 445 U.S. 507 (1980).

21. *Rutan v. Republican Party of Illinois,* 497 U.S. 62 (1990).

22. Governor's Commission on Public Employment Relations, Final Report (State of New York, 1966).

23. Wellington, *Unions and the Cities* (1972); H. Wellington and R. Winter, "The Limits of Collective Bargaining in Public Employment," 78 Yale L. J. 1107 (1969).

24. J. Burton and C. Krider, "The Role and Consequences of Strikes by Public Employees," 79 Yale L. J. 419 (1969).

25. R. Smith, H. Edwards, and R. T. Clark, *Labor Relations Law in the Public Sector* 259–73 (1974).

26. *Detroit Police Officers Association v. Detroit,* 391 Mich. 44, 214 N.W.2d 803 (1974).

27. *San Jose Police Officers Association v. San Jose,* 78 Cal. App.3d 935, 144 Cal. Rptr. 638 (1978).

28. *Bureau of Alcohol, Tobacco and Firearms v. Federal Labor Relations Authority,* 464 U.S. 89, 107 (1983).

29. There were eight such states: the five in the text plus Montana, Oregon, and Wisconsin [T. Kochan, "Dynamics of Dispute Resolution in the Public Sector," in Public-Sector Bargaining (Industrial Relations Research Association Series, 1979), pp. 150, 154–55]. In 1980 only Idaho could be added to the list. California has required public employers to exhaust administrative remedies before the state labor-relations agency before seeking injunctions against

strikes [*San Diego Teachers Association v. Superior Court*, 24 Cal.3d 1, 154 Cal. Rptr. 893 (1979)]. Cf. *Holland School District v. Holland Education Association*, 380 Mich. 314, 157 N.W.2d 206 (1968). But the Seventh Circuit Court of Appeals has held that the California approach does not apply under the federal statutory scheme [*United States v. PATCO*, 653 F.2d 1134 (7th Cir. 1981), cert. denied, 454 U.S. 1083 (1981)].

30. *County Sanitation of Los Angeles v. SEIU*, 38 Cal.3d 564, 586 (1985).

31. W. Gould, "Managing Emergency Strikes," New Leader, March 14, 1966; K. Hanslowe, The Emerging Law of Labor Relations in Public Employment (1967).

32. The Civil Service Reform Act of 1978, Pub. L. 95-454, Oct. 13, 1978, 92 Stat. 111. 5 USC §7119(c)(s)(A)(ii) (1979 Supp.).

33. Kochan, op. cit. at 156; W. Gould, "Public Employment: Mediation, Fact Finding and Arbitration." 55 ABA J. 835, 838 (1969).

Chapter 11

1. Labor and management must be represented equally on the board of trustees [29 USC §186(c)(5)]. Cf. *NLRB v. Amax Coal Co.*, 453 U.S. 322 (1981), in which the Court held, 8–1, that under both the NLRA and ERISA trustees administer the trusts in the interest of employees and their families rather than that of the appointing party.

2. 29 USC §1001(b) (1976).

3. Pub. L. 96-364, 94 Stat. 1209–1210. The remedy for violations of the 1980 amendment does not extend to the employer's breach of a statutory duty under the National Labor Relations Act as opposed to its contractual duty under the collective bargaining agreement. *Laborers Health and Welfare Trust Fund for Northern California v. Advanced Lightweight Concrete Co.*, 484 U.S. 539 (1988).

4. 446 U.S. 359 (1980).

5. *Alessi v. Raybestos-Manhattan, Inc.*, 451 U.S. 504 (1981).

6. *Greater Washington Board of Trade v. District of Columbia*, 948 F.2d 1317 (D.C. Cir. 1991, reh'g denied, 1992). Cf. *Donnelley & Sons Co. v. Prevost*, 915 F.2d 787 (2d Cir. 1990).

7. 111 S.Ct. 478 (1990). ERISA provides the exclusive remedy in connection with such actions even though the action is not instituted to obtain the pension benefits lost but rather other damages.

8. *Industrial Union Department, AFL-CIO v. American Petroleum Institute,* 448 U.S. 607, 611 (1980). See "The Significant Risk Requirement in OSHA Regulation of Carcinogens" (Comment), 33 Stan. L. Rev. 551 (1981).

9. *Id.* at 615 quoting 29 USC §652(d).

10. *Id.* at 642.

11. The Court did not reach this issue in *American Petroleum.*

12. *AFL-CIO v. Marshall,* 617 F.2d 636, 643 (D.C. Cir. 1979).

13. *Industrial Union Department, AFL-CIO v. Hodgson,* 499 F.2d 467, 478 (D.C. Cir. 1974).

14. *American Textile Manufacturers Institute, Inc. v. Donovan,* 452 U.S. 490 (1981). Chief Justice Burger, Justice Rehnquist, and Justice Stewart were the dissenters.

15. *Id.* at 495. A Court of Appeals has held that OSHA cannot issue broad standards for hundreds of chemical substances in the workplace without evaluation of each one. *AFL-CIO v. OSHA,* 965 F.2d 962 (11th Cir. 1992). Swoboda, "At Labor, One Falls through the Cracks," *The Washington Post Weekly Edition,* March 29–April 4, 1993, at 32.

16. *American Petroleum,* 448 U.S. at 652; *Whirlpool Corp. v. Marshall,* 445 U.S., 20–21 (1980).

17. *Marshall v. Barlow's Inc.,* 436 U.S. 307 (1978). However, the Court has held that the same constitutional requirements do not apply in the case of the Federal Mine Safety and Health Act of 1977, 30 USC §301. See *Donovan v. Dewey,* 452 U.S. 594 (1981).

18. *Taylor v. Brighton Corp.,* 616 F.2d 256 (6th Cir. 1980).

19. *Bethlehem Steel Corp. v. Occupational Safety and Health Review Commission,* 540 F.2d 157 (3d Cir. 1976). ("Repeated" implies at least two previous instances, and application of the statute requires willfulness.) However, see *Todd Shipyards Corp. v. Secretary of Labor,* 589 F.2d 688 (9th Cir. 1978) (one previous instance suffices and the statute requires repeated infractions or willfulness); *George Hyman Construction Co. v. Occupational Safety and Health Review Commission,* 582 F.2d 834 (4th Cir. 1978); *Todd Shipyards Corp. v. Secretary of Labor,* 566 F.2d 1327 (9th Cir. 1977).

20. *NLRB v. Washington Aluminum Co.,* 370 U.S. 9 (1962).

21. *Gateway Coal Co. v. UMW,* 414 U.S. 368, 385 (1974); *NLRB v. Knight Morky Co.,* 251 F.2d 753 (6th Cir. 1957), cert. denied, 357 U.S. 927 (1958). See Atleson, "Threats to Health and Safety: Employees Self Help under the NLRA," 59 Minn. L. Rev. 647 (1975).

22. *Whirlpool Corp. v. Marshall,* 445 U.S. 1 (1980).

23. *Id.* at 20–21.

24. 112 S.Ct. 2374 (1992). Cf. *Martin v. OSHRC,* 499 U.S. 111 S.Ct. 1171. (1991).

25. *Id.* at 2388. Justice Kennedy filed a separate concurring opinion. Justice Souter, joined by Justices Blackmun, Stevens, and Thomas dissented.

26. 42 USC §706(f), as amended, 86 Stat. 103 (1972).

27. 42 USC §§703–04 (1976).

28. *Equal Employment Opportunity Commission v. Arabian American Oil Co.,* 111 S.C. 1227 (1991). See generally Bellace, "The International Dimension of Title VII," 24 Cornell Int'l L. J. 1 (1991). On another issue relating to foreign employers and government, the Supreme Court has held that American subsidiaries of Japanese companies are not protected by the treaty between the United States and Japan that allows companies of each nation to employ executives of their own choice in the other nation. *Sumitomo Shoji America, Inc. v. Avagliamo,* 457 U.S. 176 (1982). The Court of Appeals for the Seventh Circuit, in an opinon authored by Judge Posner, held that discrimination on the basis of Japanese citizenship as authorized by the treaty is not actionable under the statute as discrimination on the basis of national origin. *Fortino v. Quasar Co.,* 950 F.2d 389 (7th Cir. 1991). Earlier the Supreme Court has distinguished between discrimination on the basis of national origin, which is prohibited, and discrimination on the basis of citizenship, which is not. *Espinoza v. Farah Mfg. Co.,* 414 U.S. 86 (1973).

29. The Civil Rights of 1991, Pub. L. 102–166, November 21, 1991, 105 Stat. 1071.

30. W. Gould, "The Supreme Court and Employment Discrimination Law in 1989: Judicial Retreat and Congressional Response," 64 Tul. L. Rev. 1485 (1990).

31. Civil Rights Act of 1991, Pub. L. 102–166, November 21, 1991, 105 Stat. 1071.

32. *Davis et al. v. City and County of San Francisco,* U.S. App. Lexis 24836 (9th Cir. 1991) wherein the Ninth Circuit endorsed retroac-

tivity essentially because Congress did not generally prohibit retro-active application. For a contrary result see *Gersman v. Gha*, 59 FEP Cases 1277 (D.C. Cir. 1992); *Holt v. Michigan Department of Corrections*, 59 FEP Cases 1261 (6th Cir. 1992); *Vogel v. City of Cincinnati*, 959 F.2d 594 (6th Cir. 1992); *Luddington v. Indiana Bell Telephone Co.*, No. 91-2320 (7th Cir. June 15, 1992); *Mozee v. American Commercial Marine Serv. Co.*, 963 F.2d 929 (7th Cir. 1992); *Fray v. Omaha World Herald Co.*, 960 F.2d 1370 (8th Cir. 1992); *Johnson v. Uncle Ben's*, 965 F.2d 929 (7th Cir. 1992); *Luddington v. Indiana Bell*, 966 F.2d 225 (7th Cir. 1992).

33. *International Brotherhood of Teamsters v. United States*, 431 U.S. 324 (1977). See also *Hazelwood School District v. United States*, 433 U.S. 299 (1977) (further defining the appropriate use of statistics).

34. Statistics were first used in class-action cases such as International Brotherhood of Teamsters. See *Davis v. Califano*, 613 F.2d 957 (D.C. Cir. 1978). Earlier decisions, for instance, *EEOC v. New York Times Broadcasting Service*, 542 F.2d 356 (6th Cir. 1976); *King v. Yellow Freight System, Inc.*, 523 F.2d 879 (8th Cir. 1975) had held only that the statistical evidence in such cases was relevant.

35. 401 U.S. 424 (1971).

36. Even when the practice that excludes disproportionately is eliminated, an individual denied employment because of a non-job-related procedure can be a victim of discrimination. *Connecticut v. Teal*, 457 U.S. 440 (1982); Cf. *Costa v. Marhey*, 706 F.2d 1 (1st Cir. 1982), cert. denied, 464 U.S. 1017 (1984).

37. The theory was applied under §1981 to New York City school teachers in *Chance v. Board of Examiners*, 458 F.2d 1167 (2d Cir. 1972), later appeal, 561 F.2d 1079 (1977). In 1976 the Supreme Court ruled that the theory could not be applied to cases brought on constitutional grounds *Washington v. Davis*, 426 U.S. 299 (1976). Title VII now applies to governmental bodies, Pub. L. 92-261, §2(1), 86 Stat. 103 amending 42 U.S.C. §2000e(a) See *New York City Transit Authority v. Beazer*, 440 U.S. 568 (1979).

38. *General Building Contractors Association v. Pennsylvania*, 458 U.S. 375 (1982). Indeed, where employers have required college degrees for positions with responsibility and risk, *Griggs* has not been followed. *Davis v. City of Dallas*, 777 F.2d 205 (5th Cir. 1985). See especially *Spurlock v. United Airlines, Inc.*, 475 F.2d 216 (10th Cir. 1972).

39. *Dothard v. Rawlinson*, 433 U.S. 321 (1977).

40. 442 F.2d 385 (5th Cir.), cert. denied 404 U.S. 950 (1971). See also *Weeks v. Southern Bell Tel. & Tel. Co.*, 408 F.2d 228 (5th Cir. 1969).

41. *Diaz v. Pan American World Airlines, supra* at 388.

42. *Backus v. Baptist Medical Center,* 510 F.Supp. 1191 (E.D.Ark. 1981), vacated because of mootness, 671 F.2d 1100 (8th Cir. 1982).

43. *Id.* at 1195.

44. *Forts v. Ward,* 621 F.2d 1210 (2d Cir. 1980).

45. *Torres v. Wisconsin Dept. of Health and Social Services,* 48 FEP Cases 270 (7th Cir. 1988).

46. *Western Air Lines, Inc. v. Criswell,* 472 U.S. 400, 412 (1985). See also *Johnson v. Mayor of Baltimore,* 472 U.S. 353 (1985); *Trans World Airlines v. Thurston,* 469 U.S. 111 (1985).

47. 490 U.S. 642 (1989).

48. *Id.* at 659.

49. *Id.* at 660.

50. *Id.* at 657.

51. Civil Rights Act of 1991, Pub. L. 105(B)(i).

52. *Id.*

53. *McDonnel Douglas Corp. v. Green,* 411 U.S. 792 (1973); *Furnco Construction Co. v. Waters,* 438 U.S. 567 (1978).

54. *Texas Dept. of Community Affairs v. Burdine,* 450 U.S. 248 (1981). See also *United States Postal Service Board of Governors v. Aikens,* 460 U.S. 711 (1983); *Anderson v. City of Bessemer City,* 470 U.S. 564 (1985).

55. *Bell v. Birmingham Linen Service,* 715 F.2d 1552 (11th Cir. 1983), cert. denied, 467 U.S. 1204 (1984).

56. *Conner v. Fort Gordon Bus Company,* 761 F.2d 1495 (11th Cir. 1985); *Miles v. M.N.C. Corporation,* 750 F.2d 867 (11th Cir. 1985).

57. 490 U.S. 228 (1989). Illustrative of the mixed motive cases are those in which the employer acquires after the fact information about a classification of an application or other kinds of job misconduct. The test may be whether the employer would have acted in the same manner if it had the relevant information. See, for

example, *Washington v. Lake County, Illinois,* 59 FEP Cases 989 (7th Cir. 1992).

58. Justice Brennan announced the opinion of the Court in which he was joined by Justice Marshall, Justice Blackmun, and Justice Stevens. Justice O'Connor filed a separate concurring opinion, and Justice Kennedy, along with Chief Justice Rehnquist and Justice Scalia, dissented.

59. Civil Rights Act of 1991, Pub. L. 107(B)(i)(ii).

60. *International Brotherhood of Teamsters v. U.S.,* 431 U.S. 324 (1977). See also *American Tobacco Co. v. Patterson,* 456 U.S. 63 (1982) (not an unlawful employment practice to apply different standards pursuant to a bona fide seniority plan as long as differences are not a result of intentional discrimination and are not limited to seniority systems adopted before effective date of Civil Rights Act); *Pullman-Standard v. Swint,* 456 U.S. 273 (1982) (a showing of disparate impact is insufficient to invalidate a seniority system, even though the result may be to perpetuate pre-Act discrimination).

61. For example, *id.* at 337 (of 6,742 employees, 314 were black and 257 Spanish surnamed).

62. *Lorance v. AT&T Technologies,* 490 U.S. 900 (1989).

63. *Id.* The Court relied upon previous decisions such as *Delaware State College v. Ricks,* 449 U.S. 250 (1980) and *United Airlines, Inc. v. Evans,* 431 U.S. 553 (1977).

64. Civil Rights Act of 1991, Pub. L. 112, November 21, 1991.

65. It was included in an amendment by Representative Howard Smith of Virginia, an attempt to prevent passage of the bill. See 88 Cong. Rec. 2576-584 and 2804.

66. 29 USC §206(d) (1976).

67. State courts, like federal courts, possess jurisdiction over title VII claims. *Yellow Freight Systems v. Donnelly,* 494 U.S. 820 (1990). Moreover, where a state statute provides greater benefits, namely unpaid leave and reinstatement to employees disabled by pregnancy, the statute does not mandate inconsistency with federal law and is not preempted by title VII. *California Federal Savings & Loan Association v. Guerra,* 479 U.S. 272 (1987).

68. 3 C.F.R. 169 (1974).

69. April 9, 1866, Ch. 31, 14 Stat. 27. These provisions are currently embodied in 42 USC §§1981, 1983. Sometimes it is difficult to

define race for the purpose of this Reconstruction legislation. For instance, since Jews were considered to be members of a distinct race at the time of the statute's enactment, Jews may sue under this statute for violations motivated by racial prejudice. *Shaare Tefila Congregation v. Cobb,* 481 U.S. 615 (1987). As with the Constitution itself, *Griggs* standards do not apply. *St. Francis College v. Al-Khazraji,* 479 U.S. 812 (1987).

70. *Patterson v. McLean Credit Union,* 491 U.S. 164 (1989) which effectively made the statute applicable only to racial discrimination in connection with hiring but not "post-contract formation racial harassment in employment." Congress appears to have reversed this decision through section 101(2)(b) which states that ". . . the term 'make and enforce contracts' include the making, performance, modification, and termination of contracts, and the enjoyment of all benefits, privileges, terms, and conditions of the contractual relationship."

71. Civil Rights Act of 1991, Pub. L. 102–166, November 21, 1991, 105 Stat. 1071.

72. 42 USC §2000e-5(e) (1976).

73. *General Electric Co. v. Gilbert,* 429 U.S. 125 (1976).

74. 42 USC §2000e(k) (1979 Supp.) Some states have passed legislation explicitly providing for pregnancy leave and the validity of such legislation has withstood challenge. See *California Federal Savings & Loan Ass'n v. Guerra, supra* not 67.

75. *Newport News Shipbuilding and Dry Dock Co. v. EEOC,* 462 U.S. 669 (1983).

76. See Report of Families and Work Institute (May 1991); "Bush Vetoes Bill Making Employees Give Family Leave," *The New York Times,* September 23, 1992, p. 1A., col. 6. Cf. "In Family-Leave Debate, A Profound Ambivalence," *The New York Times,* October 7, 1992, p. 1A, col. 6.

77. Clinton Signs Family Leave Bill into Law, 142 LRR 175 (1993).

78. Of those 27 states that have comprehensive family leave legislation, 18 cover the public sector employees only. The 9 states with family leave provisions covering both private and public sectors are California, Connecticut, District of Columbia, Hawaii, Maine, New Jersey, Oregon, Vermont and Wisconsin. Those states legislating family leave in the public sector only are: Alabama, Alaska, Colorado, Florida, Georgia, Illinois, Iowa, Kansas, Kentucky, Maryland, Nebraska, North Carolina, North Dakota, Oklahoma, South Caro-

lina, South Dakota, Utah, and West Virginia. Only 10 states—Arkansas, Idaho, Indiana, Michigan, Mississippi, New Mexico, Ohio, Texas, Virginia, and Wyoming—have no family leave, maternity leave, or paternity leave legislation on the books.

79. *City of Los Angeles Dept. of Water & Power v. Manhart,* 435 U.S. 702 (1978).

80. *Arizona Governing Committee for Tax Deferred Annuity v. Norris,* 463 U.S. 1073 (1983).

81. *Florida v. Long,* 487 U.S. 223 (1988).

82. *Phillips v. Martin Marietta Corp.,* 400 U.S. 542 (1971).

83. For example, *Willingham v. Macon Telegraph Publishing Co.,* 507 F.2d 1084 (5th Cir. 1975) (en banc), *Gerdom v. Continental Airlines, Inc.,* 692 F.2d 602 (9th Cir. 1982), cert. denied, 460 U.S. 1074 (1983) (policy requiring an exclusively female category of flight attendants to adhere to weight restrictions constitutes discriminatory treatment on basis of sex), *Ulane v. Eastern Airlines,* 742 F.2d 1081 (7th Cir. 1984) (title VII is not so expansive in scope as to prohibit discrimination against transsexuals).

84. *Garcia v. Gloor,* 609 F.2d 156 (5th Cir. 1980). Where an important aspect of a position involves oral communication skills, a "heavy Filipino accent" can constitute a basis for excluding an otherwise qualified applicant. *Fragante v. City and County of Honolulu,* 888 F.2d 591 (9th Cir. 1989). Cf. *Megia v. New York Sheraton Hotel,* 459 F.Supp. 375 (S.D.N.Y. 1978); *Carino v. University of Oklahoma Board of Regents,* 750 F.2d 815 (10th Cir. 1984); *Berke v. Ohio Dept. of Public Welfare,* 628 F.2d 980 (6th Cir. 1980).

85. *Meritor Savings Bank v. Vinson,* 477 U.S. 57 (1986). See generally Estrich, "Sex at Work," 43 Stan. L. Rev. 813 (1992). Where a sexual relationship is a substantial factor in the denial of a job to the plaintiff employee, one court has held that title VII is violated. *King v. Palmer,* 778 F.2d 878 (D.C. Cir. 1985). But for a contrary conclusion see: *DeCinto v. Westchester County Medical Center,* 807 F.2d 304 (2d Cir. 1986) cert. denied, 484 U.S. 825 (1987); *Miller v. Alcoa,* 45 FEP Cases 1775 (W.D. Pa. 1988).

86. *Id.* at 70.

87. *Id.* at 68. Plaintiff's posing for nude pictures does not constitute a defense to a claim. *Burns v. McGregor Electronic Industries,* 61 FEP Cases 592 (8th Cir. 1993).

88. *Id.* at 72. Agency principles cannot be disregarded. Justice Marshall with whom Justices Brennan, Blackmun, and Stevens joined, filed a special concurring opinion in which he concluded that his authority is an abuse of the authority vested in him or her by the employer that enables him or her to:

commit the wrong: it is precisely because the supervisor is understood to be clothed with the employer's authority that he is able to impose unwelcome sexual conduct on subordinates. There is therefore no justification for a special rule, to be applied *only* in "hostile environment" cases, that sexual harassment does not create employer liability until the employee suffering the discrimination notifies other supervisors. No such requirement appears in the statute, and no such requirement can coherently be drawn from the law of agency. (*Id.* at 77)

The supervisor's conduct must take place within the scope of employment, although the question of whether the employer knew or should have known will apply in connection with harassment by a coworker. *Kauffman v. Allied Signal,* 59 FEP Cases 606 (6th Cir. 1992).

89. *Ellison v. Brady,* 924 F.2d 872, 879 (9th Cir. 1991). See Estrich, *supra* note 85. However, the opinion of the Ninth Circuit as to what standard of conduct must be demonstrated is not entirely agreed upon. Indeed there appears to be a split in the circuits, with some adopting the Ninth Circuit's "reasonable woman" standard while other courts of appeals require an analysis of whether the employee claiming sexual harassment personally suffered psychological harm as a result of the abusive working environment. For examples of the former, see *Andrews v. City of Philadelphia,* 895 F.2d 1469 (3d Cir. 1990), or *Burns v. McGregor Electronics Industries,* 955 F.2d 559 (8th Cir. 1992). For examples of the latter standard, see *King v. Board of Regents of the University of Wisconsin et al.,* 898 F.2d 533 (7th Cir. 1990), or *Brooms v. Regal Tube Co.,* 881 F.2d 412 (7th Cir. 1989). The Supreme Court has recently consented to hear a case involving this issue that will likely resolve the split in the lower courts; *Harris v. Forklift Systems, Inc.,* 976 F.2d 733 (6th Cir. 1992) cert. granted 61 U.S.L.W. 3600. 1993 U.S. Lexis 1937 (1993).

90. *Intlekofer v. Turnage,* 59 FEP Cases 929 (9th Cir. 1992). Sometimes an arbitration award will prevent an employer from carrying out its duty to eliminate sexual harassment in the work place. *Newsday, Inc. v. Long Island Typographical Union,* 135 LRRM 2659 (2d Cir. 1990).

91. W. Gould "Letter to the Editor," *The New York Times,* October 20, 1991, p. 14, col. 5.

92. Pub. L. §1977A(3)(b)(3)(A-B) provides that the cap is $50,000 for an employer with between 14 and 101 employees; $100,000 for 100–201; $200,000 for 200–501; and $300,000 for an employer with more than 500 employees. Cases involving racial discrimination, which are instituted under Reconstruction legislation, provide for punitive and compensatory damages that are not capped.

93. *County of Washington v. Gunther,* 452 U.S. 161 (1981). See also *IUE v. Westinghouse Electric Corp.,* 631 F.2d 1094 (3d Cir. 1980); *Spaulding v. Univ. of Washington,* 740 F.2d 686 (9th Cir. 1984).

94. *Id.* at 166–67. See also *American Federation of State, County and Municipal Employees v. State of Washington,* 770 F.2d 1401 (W.D.W.A. 1983), *American Federation of State, County and Municipal Employees v. State of Washington,* 578 F.Supp. 846 (W.D.W.A. 1983), reversed, 38 FEP Cases 1353 (9th Cir. 1985). Federal District Judge Tanner ordered $800 million in back pay to 15,000 women who earned less then men on the state payroll for jobs deemed to be of comparable worth. "U.S. Drops a Fight on Comparable Worth," *The New York Times,* September 15, 1984 at 6. *Spaulding v. University of Washington,* 740 F.2d 686 (9th Cir. 1984), cert. denied 469 U.S. 1036 (1985).

95. 111 S.Ct. 1196 (1991).

96. *Id.* at 17.

97. In this connection the Court cited *Muller v. Oregon,* 208 U.S. 412 (1908), which held that social and economic legislation which would otherwise be unconstitutional was constitutional where it applied to women alone because of their special situation in society.

98. *United Auto Workers v. Johnson Controls, Inc., supra* at 47.

99. J. Gross, "In Reversal, California Governor Signs a Bill Extending Gay Rights," *The New York Times,* September 26, 1992, Col. 4; G. Webb, "Gay Rights Bill is Signed," *The San Jose Mercury News,* September 26, 1992, p. 1, col. 4; G. Lucas, "Wilson Signs Bills Bolstering Civil Rights Laws," *San Francisco Chronicle,* September 25, 1992, p.A21, col. 1.

100. 24 Cal.3d 458 (1979). A more detailed discussion of this issue is contained in Simon and Daley, "Sexual Orientation and Workplace Rights: A Potential Land Mine for Employers?" 18 Employee Relations L. J. 29 (1992).

101. *Soroka v. Dayton-Hudson Corp.,* 235 Cal.App.3d 654 (1991) review granted 1992 W.L. 20751 (Cal.) January 31, 1992.

102. *Collins v. Shell Oil Co.,* 56 FEP Cases 440 (Alameda Co. S.Ct. 1991)

103. *Dubbs v. Central Intelligence Agency,* 866 F.2d 1114 (9th Cir. 1987); *Watkins v. United States Army,* 847 F.2d 1329 (9th Cir. 1988). But see *Ben-Shalom v. Marsh,* 881 F.2d 454 (7th Cir. 1989).

104. *Meinhold v. U.S. Department of Defense,* 1993 U.S. Dist. Lexis 726; 61 FEP Cases 1361 (C.D. Calif. 1993).

105. *Corporation of the Presiding Bishop of the Church of Jesus Christ of Latter-Day Saints v. Amos,* 483 U.S. 327 (1987).

106. *Trans World Airlines, Inc. v. Hardison,* 432 U.S. 63 (1977). Cf. *Ansonia Board of Education v. Philbrook,* 479 U.S. 60 (1986).

107. *Goldman v. Weinberger,* 475 U.S. 503 (1986).

108. 494 U.S. 872 (1990)

109. Justice O'Connor wrote a separate concurring opinion, which was joined by Justices Brennan, Marshall, and Blackmun in part, but the last three judges filed a separate dissenting opinion.

110. *Id.* at 885.

111. *Hobbie v. Unemployment Appeals Commission of Florida,* 480 U.S. 136 (1987).

112. *Frazee v. Illinois Department of Employment Security,* 489 U.S. 829 (1989).

113. *Thomas v. Review Board,* 450 U.S. 707 (1981).

114. 29 USC §§31–41c, 42-1 to 426, 701–09, 720–24, 730–32, 740, 741, 750, 760–64, 770–76, 780–87, 790–94 (1976) and 41 C.F.R. §60-741.1 et seq.

115. Pub. L. 101–336.

116. *School Board of Nassau County, Florida v. Arline,* 480 U.S. 273 (1987).

117. 29 U.S.C. §621 et seq. (1988).

118. Willfull violations trigger an award of liquidated damages. *Hazen Paper Company v. Biggins,* U.S., 61 USLW 4323 (April 20, 1993).

119. *Id.* at 29.

120. 29 USC §631(c)(i) (1988).

121. *Gregory v. Ashcroft*, 111 S.Ct. 2395 (1991).

122. Aaron Bernstein, "Putting Mandatory Retirement out to Pasture," *Business Week*, June 10, 1985 at 104, 105.

123. *Public Employees Retirement System of Ohio v. Betts*, 492 U.S. 158 (1989).

124. 29 USC §623(f) (1992 Supp.). Although this legislation has broad impact, several types of early retirement programs—such as those that provide fixed bonuses, service-based benefits, and salary percentage incentives—will remain lawful provided that they are truly voluntary. The issue of what constitutes "voluntariness" is uncertain and will likely lead to future litigation. Moreover, although the legislation arguably prohibits plans that reduce or eliminate early retirement incentives that decrease as employees age, commentators have suggested that such a conclusion is far from entirely clear. See, for example, R. S. Smith and W. A. Kohlburn, "Early Retirement Incentive Plans after the Passage of the Older Workers Benefit Protection Act," 11 St. Louis Univ. Pub. L. Rev. 263, 270 (1992).

125. 422 U.S. 405 (1975).

126. *Id.* at 419–22. The Court, by a 6–3 vote, has held that an employer's unconditional offer of a previously denied job to a job applicant who charged the employer with hiring discrimination generally tolls back-pay liability even if the employer does not offer retroactive seniority. *Ford Motor Co. v. EEOC*, 458 U.S. 219 (1982).

127. *Great American Savings and Loan Association v. Novotny*, 442 U.S. 366, 374–75 (1979) ("the majority of federal courts have held that the Act does not allow a court to award general or punitive damages"). See *De Grace v. Rumsfeld*, 614 F.2d 796, 808 (1st Cir. 1980) (agreeing with "all the 808 circuits which have addressed the matter"); *Harrington v. Vandalia-Butler Board of Education*, 585 F.2d 192 (6th Cir. 1978), cert. denied, 441 U.S. 932 (1979); *Richerson v. Jones*, 551 F.2d 918, 926–28 (3d Cir. 1977); *EEOC v. Detroit Edison Co.*, 515 F.2d 301, 308–510 (6th Cir. 1975), vacated on other grounds and remanded sub nom., *Detroit Edison Co. v. EEOC*, 431 U.S. 951 (1977). But see *Clairborne v. Illinois Central Railroad*, 588 F.2d 148, 154 (5th Cir. 1978), cert. denied, 442 U.S. 984 (1979) (dicta).

128. *Johnson v. Railway Express*, 421 U.S. 454, 459–60 (1975).

129. For example, *Scott v. University of Delaware*, 601 F.2d 76, 81 n. 8 (8th Cir. 1979), cert. denied, 444 U.S. 981; *Claiborne v. Illinois Central Railroad*, 588 F.2d at 158–54 (punitive damages under 42

USC §1981 even if action brought under both that and title VII); *Allen v. Amalgamated Transit Union*, 554 F.2d 876, 888 (8th Cir. 1977), cert. denied. 484 U.S. 891; *Gill v. Manuel*, 488 F.2d 799, 801 (9th Cir. 1973); *Caperci v. Huntoon*, 397 F.2d 799 (1st Cir. 1968), cert. denied, 898 U.S. 940; *Mansell v. Saunders*, 872 F.2d 578 (5th Cir. 1967).

130. *Dyna-Med, Inc. v. Fair Employment and Housing Commission*, 43 Cal.3d 1379, 241 Cal.Rptr. 67, 743 P.2d 1323 (1987).

131. Chapter 1991, A.B. No. 311, approved by the governor, September 24, 1992.

132. Unions are liable, for instance for refusing to file grievances alleging racial discrimination that charge the employer with violating the collective bargaining agreement's prohibition against racial discrimination. *Goodman v. Lukens Steel Co.*, 482 U.S. 656 (1987).

133. For example, *United States v. Trucking Employers, Inc.*, 561 F.2d 818, 818 (D.C. Cir. 1977).

134. See, for example, *Associated Contractors of Massachusetts, Inc. v. Altshuler*, 490 F.2d 9 (1st Cir. 1973), cert. denied, 416 U.S. 957 (1974); *Contractors Association of Eastern Pennsylvania v. Secretary of Labor*, 442 F.2d 159 (3d Cir. 1971), cert. denied, 404 U.S. 854; *Weiner v. Cuyahoga Community College District*, 19 Ohio St. 2d 35, 249 N.E.2d 907 (1969), cert. denied, 396 U.S. 1004 (1970). See also *Regents of the University of California v. Bakke*, 438 U.S. 265, 801–02 (1978).

135. *Regents of the University of California v. Bakke*, 438 U.S. 265 (1978).

136. *United Steelworkers of America v. Weber*, 448 U.S. 193, (1979). See also *Detroit Police Officers' Association v. Young*, 808 F.2d 671 (6th Cir. 1979).

137. 476 U.S. 267 (1986). Justice Marshall, speaking for both Justices Brennan and Blackmun, dissented in part on the ground that societal discrimination could serve as a basis for the provisions of the collective bargaining agreement.

138. *Local 28 of the Sheet Metal Workers' International Association v. EEOC*, 478 U.S. 421 (1986)

139. *Local No. 98, International Association of Firefighters v. City of Cleveland*, 478 U.S. 501 (1986).

140. *United States v. Paradise*, 480 U.S. 149 (1987).

141. 480 U.S. 616 (1987).

142. *Id.* at 633.

143. *City of Richmond v. Croson,* 488 U.S. 469 (1989).

144. *Metro Broadcasting, Inc. v. Federal Communications Commission,* 497 U.S. 547 (1990).

145. *Lamprecht v. Federal Communications Commission,* 958 F.2d 382 (D.C. Cir. 1992).

146. *Id.* at 391.

147. See 58 Am. Jur. 2d Master & Servant 27 (1970).

148. *Woolley v. Hoffmann-La Roche, Inc.,* 491 A.2d 1257, 1266 (N.J. 1985). But see the same court's ruling that employees on annual salary are at will. *Bernard v. IMI Systems, Inc.,* 8 IER Cases 326 (N.J. 1993).

149. *Novosel v. Nationwide Insurance Co.,* 721 F.2d 894 (3d Cir. 1988). But see *Korb v. Raytheon Corp.,* 410 Mass. 581 (1991); *Smith Pfeiffer v. The Superintendent of the Walter E. Frenold State School,* 404 Mass. 145 (1989); *Smith v. Calgon Carbon Corp.,* 917 F.2d 1338 (3d Cir. 1990). On the relationship between antidiscrimination law and the wrongful dicharge public policy exception, see generally *Rojo v. Kliger,* 52 Cal.3d 65 (1990); *Gantt v. Sentry Insurance,* 1 Cal.4th 1083 (1992).

150. *Woolley,* 491 A.2d 1257; *Weiner v. McGraw-Hill, Inc.,* 57 N.Y.2d 458, 457 N.Y.S.2d 193 (1982); *Wieder v. Skala,* 8 IER Cases 132 (New York Court of Appeals 1992); *Touissant v. Blue Cross Blue Shield of Michigan,* 408 Mich. 579, 292 N.W.2d 880 (1980). This holding seems to have been limited somewhat in recent years. *Rowe v. Montgomery Ward & Co.,* 437 Mich. 627 (1991); *Dumas v. Auto Club Insurance Association,* 437 Mich. 521 (1991). Cf. *Elsey v. Burger King Corp.,* 5 IER Cases 1458 (6th Cir. 1990). *Fogel v. Trustees of Iowa College,* 446 N.W.2d 451 (1989); *McDonald v. Mobil Coal Producing, Inc.,* 789 P.2d 866 (1990).

151. *Crenshaw v. Bozeman Deaconess Hospital,* 693 P.2d 487 (Mont. 1984)

152. Alabama, Alaska, Arizona, Arkansas, California, Colorado, Connecticut, District of Columbia, Hawaii, Idaho, Illinois, Indiana, Iowa, Kansas, Kentucky, Maryland, Massachusetts, Michigan, Minnesota, Missouri, Montana, Nebraska, Nevada, New Hampshire, New Jersey, New Mexico, North Carolina, North Dakota, Ohio, Oklahoma, Oregon, Pennsylvania, South Carolina, South Dakota,

Tennessee, Texas, Utah, Vermont, Virginia, Washington, West Virginia, Wisconsin, and Wyoming.

153. Alabama, Alaska, Arizona, Arkansas, California, Colorado, Connecticut, District of Columbia, Georgia, Hawaii, Idaho, Illinois, Kansas, Maine, Maryland, Michigan, Minnesota, Montana, New Hampshire, New Jersey, New Mexico, New York, Ohio, Oklahoma, Oregon, South Dakota, Texas, Utah, Vermont, Washington, West Virginia, Wisconsin, and Wyoming.

154. Alabama, Alaska, Arizona, California, Colorado, Connecticut, Delaware, Idaho, Iowa, Massachusetts, Montana, Nevada, and New Hampshire.

155. *Tameny v. Atlantic Richfield Co.*, 27 Cal. 3d 167 (1980).

156. *Pugh v. See's Candy, Inc.*, 116 Cal. App. 3d 311, 171 Cal. Rptr. 917 (1981). But see *Arledge v. Stratmar Systems, Inc.*, 948 F.2d 845 (2d Cir. 1991).

157. 47 Cal.3d 654 (1988).

158. The Court of Appeals for the Seventh Circuit appears to have adopted a contrary view in *Belline v. K-Mart Corp.*, 940 F.2d 184 (7th Cir. 1991).

159. *Shoemaker v. Myers*, 52 Cal.3d 1 (1990); *Livitsamos v. The Superior Court of Los Angeles County*, 7 IER Cases 745 (Cal. S.Ct. 1992).

160. But see *Shapiro v. Wells Fargo Realty Advisors*, 152 Cal.App.3d 467, 199 Cal.Rptr. 613 (1984). In *Courtney v. Canyon Television & Appliance, Inc.*, 899 F.2d 845 (9th Cir. 1990), the court held a disclaimer to the effect that an employee handbook was not a contract valid where ". . . the handbook did not reflect contractual terms of employment, and that, at any time, management could make unilateral changes in or exceptions to the policies. In addition, Courtney has failed to present any evidence to suggest that Canyon's actions were not consistent with the disclaimer." But see *Seubert v. McKesson Corp.*, 223 Cal.App.3d 1514 (1990). See also *Slivinsky v. Watkins-Johnson Co.*, 221 Cal.App.3d 799 (1990); *McLain v. Great American Insurance Companies*, 208 Cal.App.3d 1476 (1979), two cases seemingly in conflict discussed with *Seubert*.

161. *McDonald v. Mobil Coal Producing, Inc.*, 789 P.2d 866 (1990).

162. *Gilmer v. Interstate/Johnson Lane Corp.*, 111 S.Ct. 1647 (1991).

163. *Allis-Chalmers Corp. v. Lueck*, 471 U.S. 202 (1985); *Electrical Workers v. Hechler*, 481 U.S. 851 (1987); *United Steelworkers of America v. Rawson*, 482 U.S. 901 (1990).

164. *Lingle v. Norge Division of Magic Chef, Inc.* 486 U.S. 399, 409 (1988). A suit involving an individual contract of employment theory regarding employees to whom a collective bargaining agreement is applicable may not be "completely preempted." *Caterpillar, Inc. v. Williams,* 482 U.S. 386 (1987). See also *English v. General Electric,* 496 U.S. 72 (1990) where the Court held that a nuclear plant employee's state law claim for intentional infliction of emotional distress arising out of the employer's alleged retaliation for reporting of nuclear safety violations did not fall within the field of nuclear safety so as to be implicitly preempted by federal regulation. But preemption under the Employee Retirement Income Security Act remains a formidable problem, particularly inasmuch as so many wrongful discharge claims assert that the employer is attempting to avoid the payment of benefits or a pension. *Ingersoll-Rand Co. v. McClendon, supra* note 7.

165. Connecticut, Delaware, Illinois, Iowa, Kansas, Louisiana, Maine, Maryland, Michigan, New York, Oklahoma, Oregon, Texas, Washington, and Wisconsin. Address by W. Gould, American Arbitration Association, 7th Annual Arbitration Day Conference in Los Angeles, California (November 15, 1984).

166. "To Strike A New Balance: A Report of the Ad hoc Committee on Termination at Will and Wrongful Discharge," Labor and Employment Law News, State Bar of California (February 8, 1984); Uniform Law Commissioners' Model Employment Termination Act drafted by the National Conference of Commissioners on Uniform State Laws (1991). See generally W. Gould, "The Idea of the Job as Property in Contemporary America: The Legal and Collective Bargaining Framework," 1986 *Brigham Young University Law Review* 885; W. B. Gould, "Stemming the Wrongful Discharge Tide: A Case for Arbitration," 13 *Employee Relations Law Journal* 404 (Winter 1987/88).

167. *Luedtke v. Nabors Alaska Drilling, Inc.,* 768 P.2d 1123 (1989).

168. *Semore v. Pool,* 217 Cal.App.3d 1087 (4th District, Division 2 1990).

169. *Hennessey v. Coastal Eagle Point Oil Co.,* 7 IER Cases 1057 (New Jersey Supreme Court, 1992). See also *Luck v. Southern Pacific Transportation Co.,* 267 Cal.Rptr. 618 (Court of Appeal), cert. denied 498 U.S. 939, 111 S.Ct. 344 (1990). See also *Harrington v. Almy,* 8 IER Cases 449 (1st Cir. 1992).

170. *O'Connor v. Ortega,* 480 U.S. 709 (1987).

171. *Skinner v. Railway Labor Executives' Association,* 489 U.S. 602 (1989).

172. *Id.* at 631. A dissenting opinion was filed by Justice Marshall, with whom Justice Brennan joined.

173. 489 U.S. 656 (1989). In this 5–4 decision, Justice Scalia filed a dissenting opinion in which Justice Stevens joined, with Justice Marshall writing a short separate dissenting opinion in which Justice Brennan joined.

174. *American Federation of Government Employees, AFL-CIO v. Skinner,* 885 F.2d 884, 891 (D.C. Cir. 1989).

175. *Bluestein v. Skinner,* 908 F.2d 451 (9th Cir. 1990).

176. *International Brotherhood of Teamsters v. Department of Transportation,* 932 F.2d 1293 (9th Cir. 1991). Accord, *National Federation of Federal Employees v. Cheney,* 884 F.2d (D.C. Cir. 1989); *National Treasury Employees v. Yeutter,* 918 F.2d 968 (D.C. Cir. 1990); *Rushton v. Nebraska Public Power District,* 844 F.2d 562 (8th Cir. 1988); *Hartness v. Bush,* 919 F.2d 170 (D.C. Cir. 1990); *Caruso v. Ward,* 72 N.Y.2d 432 (1988).

177. *Dimeo v. Griffin,* 943 F.2d 679 (7th Cir. 1991). This was a rehearing that reversed the opinion at 924 F.2d 664.

178. *William v. Thornburg,* 928 F.2d 1185 (D.C. Cir. 1991).

179. *Consolidated Rail Corp. v. Railway Labor Executives Association,* 491 U.S. 299 (1989).

180. 295 NLRB No. 26 (1989). Accord, *Kysor/Cadillac,* 307 NLRB No. 98 (1992). Cf. *Chicago Tribune Co.,* 304 NLRB No. 62 (1991) addressing the applicability of the collective bargaining process to this issue and the question of whether the union waived its right to bargain. In this case the Board held that it had not. Earlier the Board had come to a similar conclusion with regards to polygraph testing. *Medicenter, Mid-South Hospital,* 221 NLRB 1337 (1975). Congress has carefully regulated polygraph testing through the Employee Polygraph Act of 1988, Pub. L. 100–347, 102 Stat. 646.

Frequently there is controversy about the ability of the union to have access to names of individuals who inform upon employees accused of drug use. The Board said:

. . . the Respondent is required to supply the Union with a summary of the informant's statements. This summary should be drafted to include the information on which the respondent relied to meet the threshold "suspicion" standard for peforming the drug tests . . . we have found that the Respondent's interest in protecting the identity of informants is overwhelming, [and therefore] this summary need not, however, contain any information from which the identity of the informants can be ascertained, and any doubt whether the information can be used to identify the informants should be resolved in favor of nondisclosure.

Pennsylvania Power and Light Co., 301 NLRB No. 138 (1991), pp. 11–12.

181. *Star Tribune,* 295 NLRB No. 63 (1989).

182. *Westinghouse Electric Corp.,* 239 NLRB 106 (1978) *enforced as modified sub nom. Electrical Workers IUE,* 648 F.2d 18 (D.C. Cir. 1980); *East Dayton Tool & Die Co.,* 239 NLRB 141 (1978). In addition to federal law there are numerous state drug-testing laws—nineteen jurisdictions as of late 1992—that regulate this subject matter. See generally Berlin, "More State Laws Now Regulate Drug Testing in the Work Place," *The National Law Journal,* July 8, 1991, p. 19.

183. *W/I Forest Products Co.,* 304 NLRB No. 83 (1991). Seventeen states regulate smoking in public workplaces only: Alaska, Arizona, Arkansas, Connecticut, Florida, Hawaii, Idaho, Iowa, Kansas, Michigan, Nevada, New Mexico, North Dakota, Ohio, Oklahoma, Oregon, and Wisconsin. Fifteen states plus the District of Columbia also restrict smoking in private workplaces: California, Colorado, Indiana, Maine, Minnesota, Montana, Nebraska, New Hampshire, New Jersey, New York, Pennsylvania, Rhode Island, Utah, Vermont, and Washington. Three states regulate smoking as a result of executive order only Colorado, Maryland, and Massachusetts.

184. Compare *Local Union No. 733, IBEW v. Ingalls Shipbuilding Division, Litton Systems, Inc.,* 906 F.2d 149 (5th Cir. 1990) with *Local 2-286 v. Amoco Oil Co.,* 885 F.2d 697 (10th Cir. 1989).

Chapter 12

1. "Protecting at Will Employees against Wrongful Discharge: The Duty to Terminate Only in Good Faith," 93 Harv. L. Rev. 1816 (1980); C. Summers, "Individual, Protection against Unjust Dismissal: Time for a Statute," 62 Va. L. Rev. 481 (1976), C. Peck, "Unjust Discharges from Employment: A Necessary Change in the Law," 40 Ohio St. L. J. 1 (1979).

2. *NLRB v. Insurance Agents' International Union,* 361 U.S. 477, 488 (1960).

3. For example, L. Thurow, *The Zero-Sum Society* (1980). For a perceptive discussion of recent and unsuccessful efforts, see R. Flanagan, "The National Accord As a Social Contract," 84 Indus. Lab. Rel. Rev. 35 (1981).

Index